Lecture Notes
in Business Information Processing 129

Hakikur Rahman
Anabela Mesquita
Isabel Ramos
Barbara Pernici (Eds.)

Knowledge and Technologies in Innovative Information Systems

7th Mediterranean Conference
on Information Systems, MCIS 2012
Guimaraes, Portugal, September 8-10, 2012
Proceedings

 Springer

Volume Editors

Hakikur Rahman
Universidade do Minho
Dep. Sistemas de Informação
Guimaraes, Portugal
E-mail: hakik@dsi.uminho.pt

Anabela Mesquita
Instituto Politecnico do Porto
S. Mamede Infesta, Portugal
E-mail: sarmento@iscap.ipp.pt

Isabel Ramos
Universidade do Minho
Dep. Sistemas de Informação
Guimaraes, Portugal
E-mail: iramos@dsi.uminho.pt

Barbara Pernici
Politecnico di Milano
Dipt. di Elettronica e Informazione
Milano, Italy
E-mail: barbara.pernici@polimi.it

ISSN 1865-1348   e-ISSN 1865-1356
ISBN 978-3-642-33243-2   e-ISBN 978-3-642-33244-9
DOI 10.1007/978-3-642-33244-9
Springer Heidelberg Dordrecht London New York

Library of Congress Control Number: 2012945934

ACM Computing Classification (1998): J.1, J.3, H.3.5, H.4

Typesetting: Camera-ready by author, data conversion by Scientific Publishing Services, Chennai, India

Printed on acid-free paper

Springer is part of Springer Science+Business Media (www.springer.com)

MCIS 2012
Preface

The 7th Mediterranean Conference on Information Systems (MCIS2012), with the theme "Adopting Emergent Knowledge and Technologies to Develop Innovative Information Systems (CloudWisdom)" aimed to inspire innovative and informative information systems (IS) researches in order to promote smart, sustainable and inclusive growth in the Mediterranean region. In this aspect, to raise the visibility of IS researches and incorporate learning policy and practice, MCIS 2012 was a distinctive platform of information interchange and knowledge acquisition.

With the evolution of technologies, innovative IS are capable of supporting a vast clientele, thus customers, suppliers, or other agencies through the creation of new solutions and innovations. These systems can also provide day-to-day customer transaction processing with appropriate reporting. Furthermore, incorporating new information architecture, along with evolving strategies on the free flow of IS, can generate reports based on real-time data. Apart from this, innovative IS allows for faster and accurate strategic decisions, enables improved portfolio performance analysis, and also facilitates customer retention analysis. However, given the number of various technologies in the system architecture, configuring an innovative IS remains a major challenge for researchers and practitioners.

With this in mind, the MCIS 2012 topics comprised theories, research, and practices based on knowledge management and innovation in organizations and society, innovative business models, collaboration and adequate negotiations within IS, evaluating risk and risk management, and utilizing intelligent tools to process huge amounts of information through the involvement of crowd wisdom and crowd creation, proposed as CloudWisdom.

Papers in this volume have been divided into five sections, with the following themes:

Theme 1: Emerging and Innovative Information Systems
Theme 2: Enterprise Systems and Enterprise Engineering
Theme 3: Web 2.0 Enabled Business Models
Theme 4: Information Quality Management and Data Accuracy
        in Innovative IS
Theme 5: ICT Applications: The Healthcare Sector

We expect that the topics presented will assist to foster ground-breaking IS research to improve the quality of life in the Mediterranean region through endorsing the distributed intelligence of the Mediterranean population at large and promoting the value of knowledge they produce and preserve.

Hakikur Rahman
Anabela Mesquita
Isabel Ramos
Barbara Pernici

Conference Organization

Conference Chairs

António Dias   Figueiredo, Portugal
Isabel Ramos   Universidade do Minho, Portugal
Eileen Trauth   Penn State University, USA

Program Chairs

Barbara Pernici   Politecnico di Milano, Italy
José Esteves   IE Business School, Spain
José Tribolet   Instituto Superior Técnico, Portugal
Angelika Kokkinaki   University of Nicosia, Cyprus

Doctoral and Junior Faculty Professional Development Consortium Chairs

João Álvaro Carvalho   Universidade do Minho, Portugal
Raul Vidal   Faculdade de Engenharia da Universidade do Porto, Portugal

Publicity Co-chairs

Abd-El-Kader Sahraoui   Laboratoire d'Analyse et d'Architecture des Systèmes, France

Nancy Pouloudi   Athens University of Economics and Business, Greece

Organization Chairs

Rui Dinis   Universidade do Minho, Portugal
Filipe Sá Soares   Universidade do Minho, Portugal
Anouck Adrot   George State University, USA

Panel Chairs

Marô Saccol   UNISINOS, Brazil
Cristiane Pedron   Instituto Superior de Economia e Gestão, Portugal

Workshop Chairs

José Luís Mota Pereira   Universidade do Minho, Portugal

Publications Chairs

Anabela Sarmento   ISCAP, Portugal
Hakikur Rahman   Universidade do Minho, Portugal

Submissions Chairs

Pedro Pimenta   Universidade do Minho, Portugal
Jorge Sá   Universidade do Minho, Portugal

Sponsors

Universidade do Minho

Guimaraes capital Europeia da Cultura

Lecture Notes in Business Information Processing (LNBIP)

Association for Information Systems (AIS)

Table of Contents

Theme 4: Information Quality Management and Data Accuracy in Innovative IS

Theme 5: ICT Applications: The Healthcare Sector

Students' Misconceptions of Java Exceptions

Rami Rashkovits and Ilana Lavy

The Academic College of Emek Yezreel, ISRAEL
{ramir,ilanal}@yvc.ac.il

Abstract. This study examines how Information Systems Engineering School students understand the mechanism of exception handling. The main contributions of this paper are as follows: we provide an analysis tool to measure the level of understanding of exception handling mechanism in Java, based on the SOLO taxonomy; we present and analyse strategies to handle exceptions; we present and analyse solutions provided by novice programmers; the students' responses to the questionnaire were classified and analysed in order to determine their level of understanding of the mechanism. The results obtained reveal that only few participants provided a solution that was classified to one of the two highest understanding levels, while many provided solutions that demonstrate only basic understanding. The participants had difficulties in utilising the advanced exception handling mechanisms, and in exhibiting a high level of abstraction with regard to the proper design of a hierarchy of exceptions.

Keywords: Exception handling, class hierarchy, novice programmers.

1 Introduction

A substantial amount of research has been performed in order to develop tools and techniques to support programmers in incorporating exception handling into their programs [16,18]. Nevertheless, recent studies indicate that many computer applications demonstrate poor quality in designing error handling [5,10]. Madden and Chambers [12] argued that novice programmers had difficulties in designing and implementing error-handling constructs in their programs. Moreover, it was found that programmers in the software industry tend to avoid error handling issues and consider it to be tangential to the programming of the main functionality [19].

Large software systems are usually very complex. In such systems, the code devoted to exception handling is extensive and complex. In reality, up to two-thirds of a program is dedicated to exception handling [10]. Therefore, using the exception mechanism provided by the software language may contribute significantly to the modularity, readability and maintainability of the code [8,9].

Object-oriented programming languages provide an exception-handling mechanism enabling the separation of handling an error from its detection. The exception-handling mechanism permits a method (i.e., a function) to notify on problems by throwing

H. Rahman et al. (Eds.): MCIS 2012, LNBIP 129, pp. 1–21, 2012.

exceptions and pass on information regarding the errors which have been detected to other parts of the program. The thrown exception may be caught by other functions along the calling chain, allowing the handling of the detected error. The information regarding the error which is passed on, from the method that throws the exception to the method that catches it, may include all the information needed to handle the error. Specifically, it may include a meaningful name, textual description of the error, the location in the code where the error occurred and other related values. The use of this mechanism allows programmers to provide a context-based reaction to errors, thus enhancing reuse of software modules, therefore improving the overall quality of the program. Moreover, the exception-handling mechanism enables the establishment of proper management of exceptions according to their nature. Specifically, it enables programmers to treat related exceptions jointly or separately. For instance, if a withdrawal transaction is performed in a banking system, and exception may be raised either when the current balance does not allow taking away the sum requested or when the account is blocked for security reasons. The programmer may design exceptions in such a way that both cases could be handled together (i.e., displaying a general message that the transaction is rejected) or separately (i.e., allowing the account holder to withdraw smaller amount in the case of balance problem, and taking away the ATM card in the case of the security problem). Even though the exception-handling mechanism suggests simple and elegant way to handle errors, programmers still exhibit poor use of it, and as a result the software they develop is less qualitative.

In a previous study [15], we examined the scope of implementation of the Java exception mechanism among third year Management Information Systems (MIS) students after they had studied and applied this issue. The results obtained revealed that the majority of students have difficulties in designing and implementing an appropriate exception handling mechanism. More specifically, the students had difficulties in exhibiting high levels of assimilation concerning a proper design for a hierarchy of exceptions.

We assume that the tendency of industry programmers to avoid using exceptions properly originates in their professional education. In the present study, we explore the MIS students' understanding of the Java exception mechanism. Since we believe that a profound understanding of the exception-handling mechanism is essential to its proper implementation, we explore various aspects of the Java syntax concerning throwing and catching of Java exceptions.

The main contributions of this paper are as follows: we provide an analysis tool to measure the level of assimilation of exception handling mechanism; we present and analyse strategies to handle exceptions; we present and analyse solutions provided by novice programmers.

This paper is organized as follows. Section 2 describes the theoretical background including the Java exception-handling mechanism, difficulties in understanding the exceptions' mechanism, and the mapping of levels of understanding to the SOLO taxonomy. Section 3 introduces the study environment and the methods including the questionnaire used to evaluate the levels of understanding. Sections 4 describe the results obtained and discuss the findings. Finally, Section 5 presents our conclusions.

2   Theoretical Background

In this section, we present a brief literature review regarding exception-handling mechanisms in Java and the difficulties in understanding the exception-handling mechanism. As the analysis of the research findings is based on the students' levels of understanding, we present the Structure of the Observed Learning Outcome (SOLO) taxonomy as a theoretical basis.

2.1   Exceptions-Handling Mechanism in Java

The Java programming language comprises a mechanism with which to handle exceptions. When an exception occurs during the execution of a method, the programmer can identify the erroneous situation and raise an appropriate exception. The programmer also has to catch and handle the exceptions raised whenever it is possible to create a solution to the exception which has been detected (if such a thing is available). Figure 1 presents the Java exceptions' class hierarchy, in which exceptions are objects whose classes descend from the Throwable class.

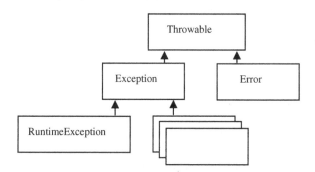

Fig. 1. Java Exceptions' class hierarchy

Throwable serves as a base class for the Error and Exception classes. Error is used as a base class for serious problems, such as the OutOfMemoryError error, which are not usually recoverable. Exception is used as a base class for logical problems that can often be handled and resolved. Errors are usually thrown by the Java library packages or the Java virtual machine (JVM: the Java runtime engine) itself. Exceptions are intended to be extended and thrown by programmers to represent abnormal conditions in the program which require special handling. Programmers can use predefined exceptions defined in the Java language (e.g. FileNotFoundException) or define their own exceptions by extending the Java Exception class or one of its descendants. The Exception class has a message attribute that can be used to describe the exception in text. It also includes methods that allow an inquiry to be conducted into the exception (i.e., type, place, cause, stack trace, etc.). When the programmer defines a new type of exception, he or she may add attributes and methods to indicate the abnormal situation it represents, if this is useful.

In Java, an exception thrown from a method must be declared in its signature (checked exception), unless it extends RuntimeException (unchecked exception). Both checked and unchecked exceptions can be caught and handled in the same manner. Unchecked exceptions are exceptions which are usually ones that the program cannot recover from, such as NullPointerException. Since such exceptions could occur anywhere in the program due to careless programming, Java do not force the programmer to declare RuntimeException and its descendants in the signature of every method. Checked exceptions are ones that the program may recover from, and hence Java forces the programmer to declare them explicitly, so that other methods could catch and handle them.

When an exception is thrown, the JVM stops the execution of the running method and looks for the adjacent try-catch clause that catches the exception which has been thrown. If the appropriate try-catch clause is not found in the running method, JVM uses the program stack in order to find the caller method and to continue this process until an appropriate handler is found. The program control is then transferred to the beginning of the appropriate catch handler (similar to the goto statement). When one method calls another one which declares on a potential exception throw, it must either surround the method call with a try-catch clause, or instead declare on the caller's signature that it may throw the specified exception. The programmer usually handles exceptions when he or she can do something about it. Otherwise, he or she defers exception handling to the caller, who also may handle the exception or defer it further. In order to further increase readability, the programmer can surround several methods by the try-catch clause block, thus allowing better separation of the normal flow of the code from the code segments dealing with exception handling. Inside the catch clause, the programmer can execute corrective commands, log the exception, notify the user and ask for his or her reaction, and so forth. She or he may also re-throw the exception (or another exception) to be handled elsewhere (by the caller's caller), or ignore it and do nothing. The try statement may also include a finally clause which is always executed whether or not a catch clause is executed. The finally clause is usually used to clean up resources, e.g., through file closure. The programmer may construct a hierarchy of exceptions, in which various subclasses may inherit an exception. The advantages of such a hierarchy are revealed when the programmer catches these exceptions and handles them. The programmer can catch and handle each exception separately or jointly. When an exception is raised by the methods called inside the try-catch block, the JVM looks for the appropriate handler. It starts with the first clause, and continues until one is found. The JVM considers either a handler who refers directly to the caught exception or one who refer to one of its ancestors. Once the JVM find an appropriate handler it calls off the search.

To summarise, the exception-handling mechanism in general uses meaningful names for exceptions, separates the normal flow of the program from the exceptional flow and implements the errors via objects that may carry additional information regarding the context of the exception. In addition, it allows the programmer to handle exceptions wherever he or she considers it to be appropriate (either close to or far from the exception detection site), and enables the programmer either to deal with each exception separately or to manage some of them together. For all of these reasons, the use of this exception-handling mechanism results in more easily understandable and maintainable programs.

2.2   Difficulties in Understanding the Exception-Handling Mechanism

Exception handling is perceived as being a relatively difficult task by novice programmers [16]. Robillard and Murphy [17] stated that a lack of knowledge regarding the design and implementation of exceptions can lead to complex and spaghetti-like exception-handling codes. They also claimed that the global flow of exceptions and the emergence of unanticipated exceptions are the main causes of difficulties in designing exception constructs. When a range of exceptions share a common context, a class hierarchy of these exceptions is desirable. In such cases, there are situations in which the same reaction is needed when either one of the related exceptions occurs, while in other situations, an individualised reaction needs to be applied. The construction of a proper hierarchy of exceptions necessitates a high level of abstraction ability, which is not possessed by all novice or even experienced programmers. In a previous study [15], the students were asked to design and implement an exception mechanism in a given problem. We found that IS students have difficulties in coping with the exception-handling mechanism. In the present research, we explore the IS students' understanding rather than their application of that mechanism.

2.3   Mapping Levels of Understanding – The SOLO Taxonomy

In the research literature, there are several taxonomies by which learning processes and levels of understanding are classified [3]. Biggs and Collis [1] developed a system for classifying the quality of students' work, known as the SOLO taxonomy. The main advantage of the SOLO taxonomy, in relation to other educational hierarchies, is its generality: it is not content-dependent, making it usable across a number of subject areas. The SOLO taxonomy has five levels of understanding that can be encountered in learners' responses to academic tasks [2]:

1. *Prestructural* — the task is not accessed appropriately, and/or the student has not understood the task;
2. *Unistructural* — one or several aspects of the task are picked up and used (level of understanding is nominal);
3. *Multistructural* — several aspects of the task are learned but are treated separately. The student still lacks the "full picture" (understanding is equivalent to knowing about);
4. *Relational* — the task's components are integrated into a coherent whole, with each part contributing to the overall meaning (understanding in the form of appreciating relationships);
5. *Extended abstract* — the integrated whole at the relational level is reconceptualised at a higher level of abstraction, which enables it to be generalised to a new topic or area. The integrated whole derived at the previous level is conceptualised at a more abstract level so that it can be used in different settings (understanding in the form of transferring concepts and involving metacognition).

3   The Study

In this section we present the data concerning the study participants and the context of the study and methods of the data analysis.

3.1   Environment and Population

The data were collected during the 2011 academic year. The study subjects were fourth (and final) year students on a B.Sc. degree course in Information Systems Engineering School in an academic college in Israel. Forty students participated in the research, who had all graduated from the following programming courses: "Introduction to programming with C", "Object-oriented programming with Java", and "Data structures and algorithms with Java". All these courses include references to exception handling, and the students were provided with problems which necessitated the implementation of Java's exception-handling mechanism. The participants were provided with a questionnaire which included various questions concerning the understanding of throwing and catching exceptions. During the engagement with the questionnaire, the students were not allowed to use any supplementary material, and had to rely on their previous knowledge.

3.2   Methods of Analysis

For the analysis process, we chose our interpretation of the SOLO taxonomy [2] in order to evaluate the students' understanding of the exception-handling mechanism in Java. Based on the SOLO taxonomy, we defined five categories relating to the level of understanding of the exception-handling mechanism comprised throwing and catching exceptions:

1. First level of understanding - The student exhibits no understanding of the exception-handling mechanism. This category fits into the pre-structural level in the SOLO taxonomy.
2. Second level of understanding – The student understands that a method that throws an exception must add to its signature a 'throws' declaration with the specified type of exception. She also understands that the thrown exception can be caught and handled inside the calling method in a catch-clause referring to this exception. This category fits into the unistructural level in the SOLO taxonomy.
3. Third level of understanding – In addition to the understanding stated in the second level, the student understands that the non-hierarchically-related thrown exceptions can be caught and handled inside the calling method in separate catch-clauses referring to these exceptions. She also understands that a try-catch block can contain one or more commands, and when an exception is thrown the fluent execution stops and the control is passed to the appropriate catch-clause and continues from there. In addition, she understands that the thrown exceptions can be caught and handled along the calling chain in such a way that some exceptions may be handled in one location while others in a different one. This category fits into the multistructural level in the SOLO taxonomy.

4. Fourth level of understanding - In addition to the understanding stated in the third level, the student understands that a method that throws hierarchically-related types of exceptions should add to its signature a 'throws' declaration that refers only to the exception that is located higher in the hierarchy, omitting the derived one. Furthermore, she understands that hierarchically-related exceptions can be caught either in a common catch-clause referring to the exception that is located higher in the hierarchy if the reaction is the same, or in separate catch clauses if the reactions are different. This category fits into the relational-structural level of the SOLO taxonomy.

5. Fifth level of understanding - In addition to the understanding stated in the fourth level, the student understands that a method that throws hierarchically-related types of exceptions that cover their super-class should add to its signature a 'throws' declaration that refers only to their super-class. She also understands that the thrown exceptions can be caught and handled along the calling chain either in a common catch-clause referring to their super-class exception if the reaction is the same for all of them, or in separate catch clauses if the reaction is different. In addition, she understands that an exception can be caught and re-thrown further in the calling chain, and that in the case of an overridden method, the override method can throw only those exceptions that are identical or derived from the exceptions that are declared in the 'throws' declaration of the overridden method. This category fits into the *extended-abstract* level in the SOLO taxonomy.

3.3   Questionnaire

The questionnaire (Appendix A) consists of 12 questions in which the students' understanding of the exception mechanism is addressed. The students were instructed to avoid code duplication in their solutions. Questions 1-2 address the second level of understanding. Questions 3-4 address the third level of understanding. Questions 5-8 address the forth level of understanding and Questions 9-12 address the fifth level of understanding. The expected solutions to these questions are presented in Appendix B.

4   Results and Discussion

In what follows we present an analysis of the students' responses to the questionnaire according to the understanding levels stated earlier.

Analysis of the students' solutions provided to the questionnaire is summarized in Figure 2. As shown, we added intermediate levels between the 5 levels declared. We classified students to one of the fifth levels of understanding given that he answered correctly all the questions up to that level. However, if such a student provided partially correct answers to the next level, we classified her at an intermediate level between the previous level and the next one. For example, if a student provided fully correct answers to all questions up to level 3 questions, she was classified at the third level of understanding. If that student provided correct answers to some (and most) of the questions of the next question, she will also be classified at the 4- level.

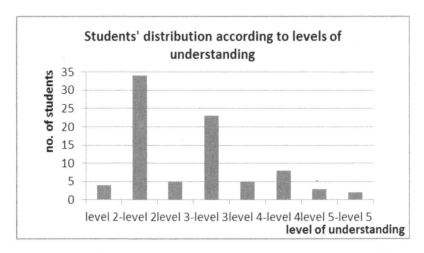

Fig. 2. Students' distribution according to understanding levels

4.1   Level 2 of Understanding

Analysis of the data received from the questionnaire reveals the following: 34 out of 40 (85%) provided fully correct answers to the first two questions and hence were classified as being in the second level of understanding. As for the other 6 students, 2 of them provided incorrect answers while the other 4 provided a variation of the following solution:

```
void fat() throws Boom {...}
void bar() {
     try{
           fat();
     } catch (Exception e) {System.out.println ('*'); }
}
```

Although the above solution is syntactically correct, it demonstrates the students' tendency to provide a simplified and effortless solution in which all exceptions are caught and handled using the general Java exception; hence we classified such a solution as level 2- of understanding. The simplified solution above emanates from the students' tendency to invest minimal efforts in providing a solution that works. This observation is consistent with Clancy [7], who claimed that many students see program maintenance, modification and extension as academic exercises. They are concerned about minimizing typing and about facilitating superficial changes to program syntax.

4.2   Level 3 of Understanding

Twenty-three students out of 40 (57.5%) provided fully correct answers to the next two questions (questions 3 and 4) and hence were classified at the third level of understanding. As for the other 17 students, 5 provided one correct answer and hence were classified as level 3-. The remaining 12 did not provide any correct answers and hence were not categorized at the third level of understanding at all. One typical faulty answer was as follows:

```
void bar() {
    try{
            fat();
    } catch (Exception e) {System.out.println ('*'); }

    try{
            fly();
    } catch (Exception e) {System.out.println ('#'); }
```

Although this solution is syntactically correct and may run properly, it demonstrates the students' lack of understanding that each type of exception may be caught in its own catch-clause and that not all exceptions have to be handled in a catch-clause referring to the general Exception class of Java. This finding is in line with Cabral and Marques [5], who asserted that programmers tend to catch all kinds of exceptions in the general exception catch-clause.

In addition, many students fail to understand the difference between the invocation of *fly()* when it is depending or not on the proper termination of *fat()*, and hence they provided similar solutions to questions 3 and 4. This may indicate that many students had not internalized that when an exception is thrown from a command within a try-catch block the block execution stops and the control is passed to the appropriate catch-clause, and continues from there.

4.3   Level 4 of Understanding

Eight students out of 40 (20%) provided fully correct answers to the next four questions (5, 6, 7 and 8) and hence were classified at the fourth level of understanding. As for the other 32 students, 5 provided three correct answers and hence were classified as level 4-. The remaining 23 provided fewer than three correct answers and hence were not categorized at the fourth level of understanding at all.

Among the four questions of level 4, several typical faulty answers were provided by the students. Obviously, since they were asked to transfer the catching and handling of the thrown exceptions from *bar()* to *zip()*, they should have changed the signature of *bar()* to:

```
void bar() throws Boom,Baz
```

Another faulty answer was the omission of either *Boom* or *Baz* in the throws-clause of the *bar()* method as follows:

```
void bar() throws Boom          or      void bar() throws Baz
```

These omissions can be attributed to the students' habit of relying on the automatic correction of the development environment and hence they do not pay enough attention to these syntax details. As for the handling of exceptions along the calling chain, many students fail to transfer correctly the handling from *bar()* to *zip()*. Some of them caught all exceptions in *bar()*, while others omitted the throws-clause of the transferred exception from the signature of *bar()*. This may indicate a lack of understanding that when an exception is thrown, Java seeks an appropriate catch-clause up the calling chain until it is found. Hence, the catch-clause can be located anywhere between main() and the method in which the exception was thrown, according to the programmer's decision regarding the optimal location. This finding is in line with Cabral and Marques [5], who found that the majority of programmers tend to catch exceptions one level up from where they are thrown. The faulty answer to question 7 was the redundant addition of *BazPlus* to the throws-clause of *bar()* as follows:

```
void bar() throws Baz, BazPlus
```

Although this solution can be compiled and run properly, it may indicate the students' lack of understanding of the exception hierarchy concerning the throws declaration, namely, the students' specification of *BazPlus* in the throws clause, although it is derived from *Baz* which is already partly defined there. This finding is in line with our previous study [15], who found that students have difficulties in designing and implementing hierarchies of related exceptions.

Another faulty answer to question 7 was the reversed order of the catch-clauses in *zip()* as follows:

```
void zip() {
    try{
            bar();
    } catch (Baz e) {System.out.println ('#'); }
      catch (BazPlus e) {System.out.println ('@');}
}
```

This faulty answer may point to a lack of understanding of exception hierarchy concerning the catching location of hierarchically-related exceptions. Namely, when the order is reversed, the *BazPlus* exception is caught by the catch-clause referring to *Baz* since *BazPlus* is derived from *Baz*.

The faulty answer (to question 8) was the redundant addition of the catch-clause referring to the *BazPlus* exception as follows:

```
void zip() {
    try{
            bar();
    } catch (BazPlus e) {System.out.println ('$');}
      catch (Baz e) {System.out.println ('$');}
}
```

This faulty answer may point again to a lack of understanding of exception hierarchy concerning the catching location of hierarchically-related exceptions. Namely, when a common reaction is required to hierarchically-related exceptions, one catch-clause referring to the class located higher in the hierarchy is sufficient. This kind of error may originate in the students' tendency to act in a 'safe' way. Namely, they address explicitly all the exceptions specified in the question without investing any additional effort to reach a more elegant solution.

4.4   Level 5 of Understanding

Only two students out of 40 (5%) provided fully correct answers to the next four questions (9, 10, 11, and 12) and hence were classified at the fifth level of understanding. As for the other 38 students, 3 provided three correct answers and hence were classified as level 5-. The remaining 35 provided fewer than three correct answers and hence were not categorized at the fifth level of understanding at all.

Among the four questions of level 5, several typical faulty answers were provided by the students. The faulty answer to question 9 was either the omission of the throws-clause in the signature of *bar()*, or surplus specifications of *BazPlus*, as follows:

```
void bar()   or   void bar()   throws Baz, BazPlus
```

As for question 10, one of the students provided a variation of the correct solution as follows:

```
void bar() throws BazPlus {
    try{
            foo() ;
            fat();
            fly();
    } catch (Boom e) {System.out.println ('*'); }
      catch (Baz e) {
            if (e instanceof BazPlus)
                    throw e;
            else
                    System.out.println ('#');
    }
}

void zip() {
    try{
            bar();
    } catch (BazPlus e) {System.out.println ('@'); }
}
```

Although this kind of solution is correct, it is less elegant than the expected solution since it is more complex. However, it indicates a profound understanding of the exception mechanism and hence was considered as a fully correct solution.

Many students fail to catch and re-throw the *BazPlus* exception within *bar()*, and provided a variation of the following solution:

```
void bar() throws BazPlus {
    try{
            foo() ;
            fat();
            fly();
    } catch (Boom e) {System.out.println ('*'); }
      catch (Baz e) {System.out.println ('#'); }
}

void zip() {
    try{
            bar();
    } catch (BazPlus e) {System.out.println ('@'); }
}
```

This solution demonstrates again that the students had not internalized that an exception is caught whenever an appropriate catch-clause is found, even though it refers to an ancestor class of the thrown exception. Namely, the students did not understand that the *BazPlus* exception is caught by the catch-clause referring to *Baz* and therefore will not reach the catch-clause in *zip()* unless it is re-thrown.

One of the faulty answers to question 11 was the specification of the exceptions within the throws-clause of *bar()* instead of specifying their super-class - the abstract *Problem* exception, as follows:

```
void bar() throws Baz,BazPlus,Boom
```

Another faulty answer to question 11was the specification of separate catch-clauses in *zip()* for each exception instead of one catch-clause referring to *Problem* exception, as follows:

```
void zip() {
    try{
            bar() ;
    } catch (Boom e) {System.out.println ('$'); }
      catch (BazPlus e) {System.out.println ('$'); }
      catch (Baz e) {System.out.println ('$'); }
}
```

In these faulty answers it can be observed that the concept of exception hierarchy is not quite clear to the students. This is demonstrated by their inability to provide a common reaction to related exceptions. In addition, when the students had to transfer the catching and handling of the exceptions further in the calling chain, they tended to specify a list of related hierarchy instead of using their super-class.

Almost all the students failed to provide a fully correct solution to question 12. Some marked all the presented exceptions, while others specified only *Baz* and *Bug* that appeared in the question. The first solution indicates a lack of understanding that overriding a method must conform to its signature including its throws-clause. Namely, the students marked exceptions which were not specified in the original signature of *bar()* or their derived classes. The second solution indicates a lack of understanding that the override method is allowed to throw exceptions derived from those classes declared in the original throws-clause of the overridden method.

To summarize, most students demonstrated a basic understanding of the exception-handling mechanism. This understanding is demonstrated by their ability to provide correct solutions when one exception is thrown and they are required to catch and handle it one level up in the calling chain. However, most students demonstrated a lack of understanding concerning the following: use of multiple exceptions in one place; catching and handling exceptions further up in the calling chain; working with hierarchies of exceptions when joint or separated handling is required; and overriding methods that throw exceptions. This lack of understanding results in the students' poor qualities in using, designing and implementing exceptions [5,19].

5   Concluding Remarks

In this paper, we have presented and analysed college students' understanding concerning exception handling. The results which have been obtained reveal that the majority of students have difficulties in understanding various constituents of the exception-handling mechanism in Java. Although the students had been taught and had used exception-handling mechanisms, they did not properly understand the advanced exception-handling mechanisms offered by Java programming language. The students had difficulties in exhibiting high levels of understanding concerning the proper use of related and unrelated exceptions given to them. These results are consistent with previous research regarding the object-oriented design capabilities of novice programmers [11,14,20].

There is no doubt that the exception mechanism offers a significant improvement to the traditional error handling. Nevertheless, the time portion devoted to it in the curriculum of IS students is minor, and as a consequence the students do not understand it and its benefits profoundly. Usually, this topic is studied towards the end of the semester, since it relies on the understanding of the following issues: flow of control, method design, class hierarchy, polymorphism, and method override. Difficulties in understanding these issues results in difficulties in understanding the exception mechanism. Moreover, in many cases the students are not asked to implement it in other contexts, and hence tend to estimate it as unimportant, and they do not exercise it sufficiently.

Most of the study participants are unfamiliar with all the possibilities encompassed by the exception mechanism and hence are unable to use them properly. They demonstrate basic knowledge of this mechanism and are able to throw and catch an exception within the calling method. However, more complex constructs such as defining a class hierarchy of exceptions and handling them either commonly or separately is beyond the average ability demonstrated by them.

The classification of the levels of understanding according to our SOLO-based five levels of understanding may seem rigid; however, it provided a coherent view of the understanding spectrum observed. Students who failed to provide a fully correct solution to a certain level were not able to provide correct solutions to upper levels. Finally, we believe that further research with a large number of participants should be conducted in order to confirm our results. In the future we intend to explore the understanding of Java exceptions in more complex software systems such as multi-threaded and distributed systems.

References

1. Biggs, J.B., Collis, K.F.: Evaluating the quality of learning: The SOLO taxonomy. Structure of the Observed Learning Outcome. Academic Press, New York (1982)
2. Biggs, J.B.: Enhancing teaching through constructive alignment. Higher Education 32(3), 347–364 (1996)
3. Bloom, B.S.: Taxonomy of Educational Objectives, the classification of educational goals – Handbook I: Cognitive Domain. McKay, New York (1956)
4. Cabral, B., Marques, P.: Making exception handling work. In: Proceedings of the 2nd Conference on Hot Topics in System Dependability, Seattle, WA, p. 9 (2006)
5. Cabral, B., Marques, P.: Exception Handling: A Field Study in Java and .NET. In: Bateni, M. (ed.) ECOOP 2007. LNCS, vol. 4609, pp. 151–175. Springer, Heidelberg (2007)
6. Chick, H.: Cognition in the formal modes: Research mathematics and the SOLO taxonomy. Mathematics Education Research Journal 10(2), 4–26 (1998)
7. Clancy, M.: Misconceptions and attitudes that interfere with learning to program. In: Fincher, S., Petre, M. (eds.) Computer Science Education Research, pp. 85–100. Taylor & Francis, Lisse (2004)
8. Filho, F.C., Cacho, N., Figueiredo, E., Maranhao, R., Garcia, A., Rubira, C.M.F.: Exceptions and aspects: The devil is in the details. In: Proceedings of the 14th ACM SIGSOFT International Symposium Foundations of Software Engineering, Portland, OR, USA, pp. 152–162 (2006)
9. Filho, F.C., Garcia, A., Rubira, C.M.F.: Exception handling as an aspect. In: Proceedings of the 2nd Workshop Best Practices in Applying Aspect-Oriented Software Development, Vancouver, BC, Canada, pp. 1–6 (2007)
10. Garcia, A.F., Rubira, C.M.F., Romanovsky, A., Xu, J.: A comparative study of exception handling mechanisms for building dependable object-oriented software. The Journal of Systems and Software 59, 197–222 (2001)
11. Lavy, I., Rashkovits, R., Kouris, R.: Coping with abstraction in object orientation with special focus on interface class. The Journal of Computer Science Education 19(3), 155–177 (2009)

12. Madden, M., Chambers, D.: Evaluation of student attitudes to learning the Java language. In: Proceedings of the Inaugural Conference on the Principles and Practice of Programming, Dublin, Ireland, pp. 125–130 (2002)
13. Manila, L.: Progress reports and novices' understanding of program code. In: Proceedings of the 6th Koli Calling Baltic Sea Conference on Computing Education Research, Uppsala, Sweden, Koli Calling, pp. 27–31 (2006)
14. Or-Bach, R., Lavy, I.: Cognitive activities of abstraction in object-orientation: An empirical study. The SIGCSE Bulletin 36(2), 82–85 (2004)
15. Rashkovits, R., Lavy, I.: Students' strategies for exception handling. The Journal of Information Technology Education (JITE) 10, 183–207 (2011)
16. Robillard, M.P., Murphy, G.C.: Analyzing Exception Flow in Java^{TM} Programs. In: Nierstrasz, O., Lemoine, M. (eds.) ESEC/FSE 1999. LNCS, vol. 1687, pp. 322–337. Springer, Heidelberg (1999)
17. Robillard, M.P., Murphy, G.C.: Designing robust JAVA programs with exceptions. In: Proceedings of the 8th ACM SIGSOFT International Symposium on Foundations of Software Engineering, vol. 25(6), pp. 2–10. ACM Press, New York (2000)
18. Robillard, M.P., Murphy, G.C.: Static analysis to support the evolution of exception structure in object-oriented systems. ACM Transactions on Software Engineering and Methodology 12(2), 191–221 (2003)
19. Shah, H., Görg, C., Harrold, M.J.: Understanding Exception Handling: Viewpoints of Novices and Experts. IEEE Transactions on Software Engineering 99, 150–161 (2010)
20. Sim, E.R., Wright, G.: The difficulties of learning object-oriented analysis and design: An exploratory study. Journal of Computer Information Systems 42(4), 95–100 (2001)
21. Topi, H., Valacich, J.S., Kaiser, K., Nunamaker, J.F., Sipior, J.C., de Vreede, G.J., Wright, R.T.: Curriculum guidelines for undergraduate degree programs in information systems. ACM/AIS task force (2010),
http://blogsandwikis.bentley.edu/iscurriculum/index.php/IS_2010_for_public_review (retrieved)

Appendix A: Questionnaire

Hereby, the following hierarchy of exceptions:

```
abstract class Problem extends Exception{}
class Bug extends Exception {}
class Baz extends Problem {}
class Boom extends Problem {}
class BazPlus extends Baz {}
```

When addressing the following questions please provide solutions that avoid code duplication.

1. Given the following class, how should the signatures of *foo()*, *fat()* and *fly()* method be modified?

```
class class1 {
    void foo(){
        if (Math.random() < 0.5)
            throw new BazPlus();
    }

    void fat(){
        if (Math.random() < 0.5)
            throw new Boom();

    }

    void fly(){
        if (Math.random() < 0.5)
            throw new Baz();

    }
}
```

2. The method *bar()* was added to *Class1* as follows. Modify *bar()* in such a way that it will catch the exception that might be thrown from *fat()* and react by printing *.

```
void bar(){
    fat();
}
```

3. The method *bar()* was modified as follows. Modify *bar()* in such a way that it will catch the exception that might be thrown from *fat()* or *fly()* and react by printing * when *Boom* is caught and # when *Baz* is caught. Note that each of the called methods should be invoked independently, regardless of the proper or erroneous termination of the other method.

```
void bar(){
        fat();
        fly();
}
```

4. Repeat the previous question, with the following guidelines: *fly()* should be called only if *fat()* was terminated properly. If *Boom* is caught * is printed , and # when *Baz* is caught.

```
void bar(){
        fat();
        fly();
}
```

5. The method *zip()* was added to *class1* as follows. Modify *bar()* and *zip()* in such a way that the exception that might be thrown from *fat()* or *fly()* will not be caught by *bar()*, but by *zip()* which will react by printing * in case of *Boom*, and # in case of *Baz*.

```
void zip(){
        bar();
}
```

6. Modify *bar()* and *zip()* from the previous question in such a way that *Boom* is caught by *bar()* that reacts by printing * and *Baz* is caught by *zip()* which reacts by printing #.

7. The method *bar()* was modified as follows. Modify *bar()* and *zip()* in such a way that *zip()* will catch the exceptions that might be thrown from *foo()* or *fly()* and react by printing @ when *BazPlus* is caught, and # when *Baz* is caught.

```
void bar(){
        foo();
        fly();
}
```

8. Repeat the previous question with the following guidelines: when either *BazPlus* or *Baz* is thrown, *zip()* catches it and reacts by printing the $ sign.

9. The method *bar()* was modified as follows. Modify *bar()* and *zip()* in such a way that *bar()* will catch the exception that might be thrown from *fat()* and react by printing * when *Boom* is caught. The *Baz* and *BazPlus* exceptions should be caught by *zip()* which reacts by printing # in case of *Baz*, and @ in case of *BazPlus*.

```
void bar(){
        foo();
        fat();
        fly();
}
```

10. Repeat the previous question with the following guidelines: when either *Baz* or *Boom* is thrown, *bar()* catches it and reacts by printing * in case of *Boom* and # in case of *Baz*. However, if *BazPlus* is thrown, *zip()* should catch it and react by printing @.

11. Repeat the previous question with the following guidelines: when either *Baz*, *BazPlus* or *Boom* is thrown, *bar()* ignores it, and it should be caught by *zip()* which reacts by printing $.

12. Assuming that *bar()* signature in class **class1** is as follows:

> void *bar()* throws *Baz,Bug*

Then, given the following class, which of the following types of exceptions might be thrown from the overridden *bar()* in class2?

```
class class2 extends class1{
        void bar()throws _____ {} //override
}
```

☐   *Problem*
☐   *Bug*
☐   *Baz*
☐   *Boom*
☐   *BazPlus*

Appendix B: Solutions

Question 1:
```
void foo() throws BazPlus
void fat() throws Boom
void fly() throws Baz
```

Question 2:
```
void bar() {
 try{
    fat() ;
 } catch (Boom e) {System.out.println ('*'); }
}
```

Question 3:
```
void bar() {
 try{
    fat() ;
 } catch (Boom e) {System.out.println ('*'); }

 try{
    fly();
 } catch (Baz e) {System.out.println ('#'); }
}
```

Question 4:
```
void bar() {
 try{
    fat() ;
    fly();
 } catch (Boom e) {System.out.println ('*'); }
         catch (Baz e) {System.out.println ('#'); }
}
```

Question 5:
```
void bar() throws Boom, Baz {
 fat() ;
 fly();
}

void zip() {
 try{
    bar() ;
 } catch (Boom e) {System.out.println ('*'); }
   catch (Baz e) {System.out.println ('#'); }
}
```

Question 6:

```
void bar() throws Baz {
 try{
    fat() ;
    fly();
 } catch (Boom e) {System.out.println ('*'); }
}

void zip() {
 try{
    bar()
 } catch (Baz e) {System.out.println ('#'); }
}
```

Question 7:

```
void bar() throws Baz {
    foo() ;
    fly();
 }

void zip() {
 try{
    bar() ;
 } catch (BazPlus e) {System.out.println ('@'); }
   catch (Baz e) {System.out.println ('#'); }
}
```

Question 8:

```
void zip() {
 try{
    bar() ;
 } catch (Baz e) {System.out.println ('$'); }
}
```

Question 9:

```
void bar() throws Baz {
 try{
    foo() ;
    fat();
    fly();
 } catch (Boom e) {System.out.println ('*'); }
}

void zip() {
 try{
    bar();
 } catch (BazPlus e) {System.out.println ('@'); }
   catch (Baz e) {System.out.println ('#'); }
}
```

Question 10:

```
void bar() throws BazPlus {
  try{
      foo() ;
      fat();
      fly();
  } catch (Boom e) {System.out.println ('*');
      catch (BazPlus e) { throw e; }
      catch (Baz e) {System.out.println ('#');
  }
  void zip() {
  try{
      bar();
  } catch (BazPlus e) {System.out.println ('@'); }
  }
```

Question 11:

```
void bar() throws Problem {
  foo();
  fat();
  fly();
  }

  void zip() {
  try{
      bar() ;
  } catch (Problem e) {System.out.println ('$'); }
  }
```

Question 12:

- ☐ *Problem*
- ✓ *Baz*
- ✓ *Bug*
- ☐ *Boom*
- ✓ *BazPlus*

The Domain of a First-Person Perspective Systems Analysis

Takeshi Kosaka

Tokyo University of Science,
kosaka@ms.kuki.tus.ac.jp

Abstract. Information systems as well as work systems are no longer emerging but emergent. An idea of emerging systems with final forms is replaced by that of emergent systems with continuous changes (Truex et al, 1999). Along this change, business professionals are inevitably expected to take the initiatives in IS development. The existing systems analysis has been for IT specialists. Therefore a different systems analysis is required for business professionals. It is a first-person perspective systems analysis (1ppSA). The need for the 1ppSA has been economically and sociologically justified. However, the research of the 1ppSA has drawn little attention from researchers. We consider it is because the domain of 1ppSA is not yet articulated. In order to identify and locate the domain, we build a map of SA, a topology of SA, and then use philosophy and its history to examine the validity of the topology of SA. Philosophy is used for examination because it provides us with epistemology and has been considered a fundamental discipline for sciences. Through the examination it is made clear that the domain is independent from that of the others. It is also noted that its foundational method is considered a phenomenological one.

Keywords: Systems analysis, first-person perspective, philosophy, phenomenology.

1 Introduction

There is a variety of systems analysis (SA) when SA is considered a process that results in the determination of information systems (IS) needs. The aim of our research is to identify and locate the domain of a first-person perspective systems analysis (1ppSA) among them. The 1ppSA has drawn little concern from researchers. We consider it is because the domain of 1ppSA is not well articulated and thereby the method is not well recognized among researchers.

We can see the needs for the 1ppSA as follows. According to Truex et al. (1999), information systems (IS) as well as business or work systems are no longer emerging systems but emergent ones that continue to evolve, therefore business professionals are inevitably expected to take the initiatives in IS development. Because of no more expectation for stable IS, an idea of emerging systems with final forms are replaced by that of emergent systems with continuous changes (Truex et al, 1999). This change also drives up a diversification of SA. Here, we see SA by business professionals, ie, a 1ppSA, with the support of IT professionals.

H. Rahman et al. (Eds.): MCIS 2012, LNBIP 129, pp. 22–35, 2012.
© Springer-Verlag Berlin Heidelberg 2012

Advancement of information technology (IT) has brought about this move to the emergent from the emerging. The move is economically required as well, politically unavoidable, and also sociologically desirable.

Economically it is likely for the move to be inevitable. Knowledge workers have gained more power while companies have lost it against them. In the decreasing transaction cost brought by IT, Hagel et al (2010), in their book, describe some of the inevitable changes impacting businesses, a shift from push to pull. They explain how the world is currently moving from valuing stocks of knowledge to flows of knowledge. The value of the stock in US firms has constantly decreased from about 4 % to only 1% on ROA over the 40 years (Deloitte, 2011), suggesting that many companies will disappear in a decade unless substantial actions are made. They argue that companies cannot help but make a big shift from scalable efficiency (economy of scale) to scalable collaboration among knowledge workers and customers. Their book is about scalable pull, embracing hundreds of thousands of participants in pull platforms. Companies cannot keep potent knowledge workers only by pushing ideas from management. Companies need to make possible collaboration among knowledge workers in pull platforms more than ever.

The move becomes politically unavoidable. An organization is not always a rational entity that is presupposed in the conventional SA. This implies "a shift from a view that an organization is something 'out there' and reified as is common within organizational theory, to a view that an organization is internal to each of us ... " (Goldspink and Kay, 2003). A new business practice emerges from several practices co-existing in an organization. As mentioned by Feenberg (1991, p.14), technology is not a destiny but a scene of struggle. It is a social battlefield, or perhaps a better metaphor would be 'a parliament of things' on which civilizational alternatives are debated and decided. Truex et al. (1999) say "the dialectics of the process center politics, conflicts and struggles between social forces in the organization." In these scenes, main actors are not SA specialists but business professionals themselves.

The move is also sociologically desirable. Giddens (1993, p.28) says, "The more we know the conditions of our own actions and the overall development of our society, the more we are able to gain influences over various affairs of our lives." Bourdieu (1991, p.90) also said, "Ambition of sociologists is to become free from the principles which govern the present by highlighting them." One role of sociologists should be to give weapon rather than to preach down to people (Bourdieu, 1991, p.121). Therefore it is desirable for workers to have weapon that enables them to practice SA by themselves in order to innovate themselves.

SA is a core of IS development (ISD), therefore, the need for the 1ppSA coincides with the move. However, the research of the 1ppSA is inactive or low-key among researchers only with a few researches related to the 1ppSA. Researches such as Alter (2002), Checkland (1999) and Whitaker (2007) could be considered of the 1ppSA. Alter (2004) advocates systems analysis by business professionals by saying, "An effective systems analysis method for business professionals could help them analyze systems for themselves and could help them communicate with peers and IT professionals." His idea is similar to the ideas of sociologists as mentioned above.

There could be a few possible reasons for the 1ppSA being low-key among researchers.   One may be that the domain of 1ppSA is not well articulated. Another may be that the 1ppSA is considered a derivative of the existing SA. Still another is that the basic method of the 1ppSA is not shared among researchers.

There are few researches on the domain of the 1ppSA except Checkland (1999), however he mainly discusses the process of SA from the perspective of systems thinking, not the domain of SA. Therefore, we have to identify and locate the domain of the 1ppSA among a variety of SA. We do it by making a map of SA, a topology of SA, thereby locating the existing approaches on the map and finding a separate, untouched domain for the 1ppSA.

We construct the topology of SA by reviewing the prior literature and examine its validity through philosophy. We use philosophy and its history or development instead of empirical data to examine the topology of SA. Philosophy and its history are used here because it has been considered the most basic discipline for sciences (Rorty, 1979, p.132; Husserl, 1999, p.43). Through the examination, the theoretical existence of the 1ppSA is expected to be made clear.

It is necessary to mention the scope of SA. Although there has never been its universally accepted definition, SA is usually used as a term that collectively describes the early phase of systems development (Whitten et al, 2004, p.186). It is generally considered that SA consists of requirements determination, requirements structuring, alternative generation, and selection (Hoffer et al., 2002, p.200). Our research focuses on an approach toward the requirements structuring. It means that we are concerned with the early part of SA.

In the sections below, firstly we review prior literature. Next we build a hypothetical model for a topology of SA. We then transform the hypothetical model into a working model expressed in philosophical terms for examination. Next we examine the working model with major philosophies each of which is considered different from one another. Finally, we present some brief discussion and conclusions.

2   Review of Prior Literature

Firstly we review prior literature by classifying them into two types. One is related to SA in particular. The other is to IS development (ISD) in general.

There are few previous researches concerning the topology of SA. We have to go back to Wood-Harper and Fitzgerald (1982). They classified SA approaches used then by a classification scheme using general systems and science. The research was considered useful then, but it is a practical classification of the existing SA approaches of those days.   Therefore, it is not exhaustive so that it does not include the 1ppSA.

Since there is no relevant literature directly related to our research concern, there is a need to expand the scope of prior literature. SA is a phase of ISD. Therefore, literature concerning classification of ISD is then reviewed as follows. Reviews of ISD literature is expected to bring ideas for constructing the topology of SA where the 1ppSA is to be located.

In the area of ISD classification, a framework by Hirschheim and Klein (1989) is considered influential. They developed four possible stories of ISD by referring to the four paradigms by Burrell and Morgan (1979), and then verified the validity of each story also by using the Burrell and Morgan's paradigms. Their framework is based on the epistemology of subjective and objective and the ontology of order and conflict that Burrell and Morgan proposed. Their framework is very useful to help IT practitioners and researchers comprehend the diversity of ISD practices. Although their framework does not include the 1ppSA, their efforts in applying the paradigms of Burrel and Morgan is insightful also for our research because they paved an avenue to use a term 'subjective' in the field of IS research. The 1ppSA is closely related to the subjective perspective of business professionals. Therefore, one of dimensions of the topology we construct is considered this distinction between subjective and objective.

Iivari, Hirschheim and Klein have been making efforts in establishing IS discipline by building a framework for a body of knowledge (BoK) of ISD. Iivari and Hirschheim (1996) evaluated the existing eight ISD approaches from the perspective of organizational roles and informational requirements. Their classification is insightful but too general as far as SA is concerned. Iivari, Hirschheim and Klein (2004) see as a problem that the subject matter of IS research has become rich and diverse and that this diversity has led some to question whether IS research has any real accumulative tradition. In order to overcome the problem, they promote the idea of a BoK by proposing a four-level hierarchical coding scheme. Their interest is related to a framework for an action-oriented BoK of ISD in general while our interest is to the domain of SA in particular. However, their efforts is insightful because the classification and coding scheme based on the framework are thought to help establish IS discipline. Therefore, following their idea that the classification and coding scheme help establish a discipline, we also build a map for the classification of SA, a topology of SA, to establish the domain of the 1ppSA.

In democratic societies and companies, participatory design has been practiced. Although the 1ppSA does not always mean only participation, a sort of a first-person perspective has been a concern in participatory design particularly in Scandinavian countries. An influential paper in the area of participatory design is considered Kensing and Munk-Madsen (1993) who created a model of the communication between users and IT professionals. The model is based on two distinctions. One is related to three domains of discourse: users' present work, new system and technological options, and the other is to two levels of knowledge: abstract knowledge and concrete experience. Also using ethnographic techniques and intervention, Kensing, Simonsen and Bødker (1996) proposed the MUST method for participatory design based on the model developed by Kensing and Munk-Madsen (1993). For our purpose, it is important that they clarified six knowledge domains concerning IS design. It is thought to be helpful for IT designers and users to have successful communication paths. Although, the six domains are not related to the domain of SA, their concern to users' present work and concrete experience is insightful for our research. Participation and user's concrete experience at the present work means the importance of working knowledge at the workplace in ISD. Here we use a term 'working knowledge' as implicit and explicit knowledge working at the workplace. It is the working knowledge that it is often difficult to capture by observation and interview. We take the working knowledge into consideration in building the topology of SA.

Based on the findings mentioned above, we build the topology of SA in order to identify and locate the domain of the 1ppSA.

3   A hypothetical Model for a Topology of SA

The aim of our research is to identify and locate the theoretical domain of the 1ppSA. The task is similar to making a map that is made of two dimensions of latitude and longitude. Our trial to build a topology of SA, a sort of map, is the first one in this area. Therefore we keep our trial as simple as possible. We firstly build a hypothetical model for the topology of SA in two dimensions.

For latitude as the first dimension, we introduce a distinction between the external entity and the internal entity. The idea of this distinction is brought from the distinction between objective and subjective in Burrell and Morgan (1979). Therefore, this distinction finally results in objective knowledge and subjective knowledge, as well as the types of knowledge acquisition process appropriated in SA practices, that is, the objective stance and the subjective stance.

For longitude as the second dimension, we introduce the distinction related to the existence of a concern toward working knowledge and work systems at the workplaces. This distinction is thought of from the importance of working knowledge in participatory design mentioned before. It is therefore a distinction between a direct concern and an indirect concern to working knowledge and work systems at the workplace, that is, use and non-use of working knowledge

Table 1. A topology of SA

	Direct concern to working knowledge	Indirect concern to working knowledge
Objective (external)	3ppSA (Third–Person Perspective SA) SA Specialists practice SA	exoSA (Exogenous SA) Dependency on external information
Subjective (internal)	1ppSA (First-Person Perspective SA) Business Professionals practice SA	endoSA (Endogenous SA) Dependency on ideas of the strong

The combination of the two dimensions results in four quadrants shown in Table 1. Briefly speaking, the first dimension, latitude, is related to who are concerned with the creation or acquisition of knowledge in SA. The second dimension, longitude, is related to what are used in SA. And, each quadrant is related to how knowledge is created or acquired. The more detail reasons why we take these dimensions are also found in the following explanation of each quadrant.

In making a map, it is expected that we can identify and locate an unknown area, ie, the domain of the 1ppSA, through the mapping of known areas on the map. Before going to the hypotheses testing which locates the unknown area, we make a brief mapping between the existing types of SA and the quadrants in the topology of SA.

In the left side of Table 1, there are two quadrants we name as a third-person perspective SA (3ppSA) and a first-person perspective SA (1ppSA). We can find the conventional approach of SA at the intersection of the external and the direct concern.

A specialist as an external agent observes, surveys and analyzes the working knowledge and work systems. His or her observation and analysis are of a third person perspective because he or she tries to perform objective analysis on the assumption of rational organizations in favour of realism. Here we label this quadrant as a logical type of a 3ppSA. JAD and RAD are regarded as derivatives in this quadrant as applications of the 3ppSA with enhanced user participation.

We find a logical type of a new SA at the intersection of the internal and the direct concern. In this quadrant business professionals practice SA by themselves with the some occasional helps of SA specialists. SA in general includes several phases with a logical design at the final phase. Business professionals are supposed to practice primarily the early phases of SA. Here we label the SA in this quadrant as a logical type of a first-person perspective SA (1ppSA).

In the right side of Table 1, there are two quadrants we name as the exogenous SA and the endogenous SA. Both of them have indirect concern to working knowledge and works systems. They show their concern to the pre-existing knowledge rather than to working knowledge.

We find a kind of SA, that depends the external knowledge, at the intersection of the external entity and the indirect concern. In short of talented systems analysts, it is IT practitioners who search for external knowledge from the beginning, instead of practicing the 3ppSA. There is so much external knowledge readily available at present that IT practitioners tend to seek external knowledge that fits in with their thinking and behaviour. There is the belief that a better solution could be obtained from external software vendors (Lyytinen, et al, 1999). Therefore, organizations are keen to learn from external sources and are generally eager to accommodate new technologies (Lyytinen, et al, 1999). The fact that there are a wide variety of software packages embodying best practices tends to promote their dependency on external knowledge. The importance of external knowledge is becoming greater in ISD contexts in recent years. Among the benefits of external knowledge are keeping pace with technological changes and managing the downside risks of systems development (Lyytinen et al., 1999). As a result, it is not uncommon that many IT practitioners tend to produce IS requirements in reference with external software packages as a template for requirement structuring. We label the SA in this quadrant as a logical type of exogenous SA (exoSA).

We find another kind of SA, that focuses on a will of the power, at the intersection of the internal entity and the indirect concern. There are IT professionals or SA specialists who pay their concern mainly to the voices of top management or big figures in the organization prior to paying attention to business professionals or workers at the workplace. Often in authoritative or traditional organizations top management themselves innovate or change their organizations with thier own plans or ideas often coming from external consultants. They often do not think that they have to listen to the voices at the workplace, and also sometimes think that they have to enforce changes at the workplace. In these circumstances they tend to use a silver bullet theory that IT itself has the power to create organizational changes. Since the silver bullet is expected to change the behaviour of workers who use IT by enabling new work practices and preventing old ones, users are the intended target of change (Markus and Benjamin, 1997). This view of ISD is not new. In fact, under the name of "technological determinism", it has been the subject of much academic debate (Markus et al., 1997). Therefore, this type of SA goes along with technological determinism often favoured by the logic of the strong or the power. Here IT professionals or SA specialists have a role to describe what the strong intends to do, and to inscribe the interests of the strong into IS (Latour, 1995). We label the SA in this quadrant as a logical type of endogenous SA (endoSA).

With the above discussion we have created the topology of SA which consists of four logical types of SA, located the existing SA in it, and found a possible domain of the 1ppSA.

4   A Working Model for a Topology of SA

In positive studies, theoretical hypotheses are transformed into working ones for test. Following this procedure we transform the hypothetical model for a topology of SA to a working model in order to examine it. In our research we examine it with philosophy instead of empirical data. Here we transform the hypothetical model into a working one with use of philosophical terms.

We use philosophy and its history or development in order to examine the topology of SA for two reasons. Firstly, modern philosophy is a study of cognition or consciousness, ie, understanding in particular. Philosophy has been considered the most fundament discipline for sciences after Kant's epistemology-oriented philosophy was widely accepted (Rorty, 1979, p.132). According to Dewey (2008, p.22), philosophy can proffer nothing but hypotheses, but these hypotheses are of value only as they render men's minds more sensitive to life about them. With the help of philosophy we are expected to be more sensitive to the topology of SA, the 1ppSA in particular.

Second, for the necessity of history, activity theorist, Engestrom   (1999, p.244) says:

"A host of different classifications and typologies have been offered, but each one of them seems to be equally arbitrary. The reason is that the classifications and typologies have no historical basis. As long as the historical steps of the societal production of models remain obscure, psychologists are bound to keep inventing their private favorite typologies."

Following the development of philosophy, we create four simplified structures between   subject (a person) and object in order to find relations between the hypothetical model and a variety of philosophies

Modern philosophy has been concerned with the elucidation of the problem of cognition. It has been the criticism against the theory of knowledge of 'the agreement of subject and object' which positivism presupposes. Philosopher, Takeda (2004, pp.54-70), mentions that we could have correct cognition, that is, truth if there were the agreement of subject and object. Understanding the impossibility of this agreement of subject-object created problems of belief conflict, such as a conflict between Catholicism and Protestantism that is difficult to be overcome.

Based on his research, it is thought that there are historically several types of belief conflict. We identified and illustrated them in Figure 1. The first one is that a person, ie, a subject, can have a right understanding of an object that is out there (Type 1 in Figure 1). This is usually called as the naive model. The second one is that every thought is incorrect (Type 2), the correct one being somewhere else. He calls this as Cantian model. The third one is that there are no correct weltanschauungs but a strong one (Type 3). He calls this as Nietzschean model. His translation of

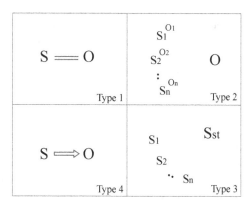

Fig. 1. Simplified relations between subject and object

the truth problem into these belief conflicts reflects the historical development of philosophy. We use this translation for the testing of the working model.

In addition to the historical development of philosophy on the plane of epistemology, we also use phenomenology of Husserl as the latest philosophy. Husserl no longer addresses the long-standing problem of the agreement of subject-object. It is well pointed out by Merleau-Ponty (2002, xviii), who describes, "We must not, therefore, wonder whether we really perceive a world, we must instead say: the world is what we perceived." (Type 4)   Husserl (1970, p.177) mentions: "As their interest is not aimed at the ready-made world, phenomenologists go back to the ways in which subjectivity has brought about and continue to shape the world through its concealed internal method." Husserl changed the problem of agreement of subject-object to the constitution of conviction. This shift is endorsed by his sentence: "It can always happen that the further course of experience will compel us to abandon what has already been set down ..." (Husserl, 2002, p.144)

The development of philosophy can be summarized as follows. The problem of the agreement of subject-object was replaced with the problem of belief conflict, and further replaced with the constitution of conviction. The development of philosophy is considered useful for the examination of our model, because each philosophy continues to be worthwhile over a long period by weathering the hardships.

In the following, to operationalize the hypothetical model into a working model, we use subjective and objective, and subject and object as philosophical terms. As mentioned earlier, there has been a longstanding issue, the subject-object problem in the history of philosophy. The problem arose from the premise that the universe or world consists of objects or entities perceived by subjects or observers. This resulted in several standpoints about the issue of the relationship between subject and object. In the following, we paraphrase each logical type of SA as a relationship between subject and object, and further replace the external and the internal with objective and subjective respectively.

Firstly, we discuss the 3ppSA, where SA specialists assume a view of rational organization, and apply it to all things and events. Therefore a SA specialist is considered an external agent who takes an assumption of God's eye view.

An organization is regarded as an objective existence 'out there' that is separated from and can be observed by a SA specialist as an external agent.

The 1ppSA has a different relation between subject and object from the relation seen in the 3ppSA that the subject stands outside of the object as an objective observer. In the 1ppSA, the subjects reside within or around the object. There are multiple views floating in an organization. Success of innovation depends on accommodation or consensus among peers on the work systems prior to building IS. It is not an easy task to achieve accommodation or consensus at the surface level of knowledge captured by a SA specialist. Business professionals need to understand why and how their own specific views and attitudes toward their work systems have been constituted from a first-person perspective. In other words, to become free from the principles which govern the present, business professionals need to be aware of knowledge about the conditions and structures in between the subject and the object that govern their thinking.

The exoSA is a type of SA in which SA specialist or IT practitioners might face multiple conflicting views about the work sytems and IS within the organization. In case of no criteria that determine which is appropriate among alternatives, or in case of no appropriate alternatives, IT practitioners tend to seek for an outside best practice instead of negotiation or own creation. This is the case that there are several views as subjective images among stakeholders. No single view dominates the situation. People do not think every view has the ring of truth, so that they seek for something best outside as an objective existence.

The endoSA is a type of SA in which SA specialists or IT practitioners might face multiple views about the work systems and IS within the organization. However, they think that they have a criterion that determines the best or the most valuable among alternatives in contrast to the situation of the exoSA. They do not mind what the objective reality is, and are simply agents who describe, as a subjective image, what the strong power tell about the work sytems and IS. They believe that the best man wins, that is, truth resides within the strong discourse.

5   Verification of the Working Model

Since four logical types of SA are ready for test, we verify them from the philosophical standpoint. We examine whether each logical type of SA can be related to one of major philosophical standpoints. If it comes true, then we can regard a logical type of SA as an independent one that should not be confused with other types of SA. It means that a type of SA is not an application or extension of another type of SA. Each is worth attention and research, the research of the 1ppSA in particular.

We take into consideration major philosophical standpoints in a historical order, because philosophy developed and created a new standpoint by referring to the knowledge of the preceding philosophies.

5.1   Naïve Ontology and the 3ppSA

Kant established epistemology in philosophy with his Copernican turn that inverted the traditional relation between subject and object. Kant (1998, p.110) says, "Up to now it has been assumed that all our cognition must conform to the objects; but all attempts to find out something about them a priori through concepts that would extend our cognition have, on this presupposition, come to nothing."

Until Kant's proposition, philosophers as well as the lay public had no doubt that the object 'out there' determines the cognition of the subject. Although epistemology entered into philosophy after this, most of the lay public still thinks that the object determines the cognition of the subject. This traditional thinking is usually called as naïve ontology, where objective cognition is made possible by the unconscious assumption of God's eye view. It is the 3ppSA that is based on this relation between subject and object.

5.2   Kant Philosophy and the exoSA

Kant (1998, p.110) continues, "Hence let us once try whether we do not get farther with the problems of metaphysics by assuming that the object must conform to our cognition..." His point is that the subject determines the object in some way. Knowledge is then found in the structure of the subject itself, instead of in an objective reality. This thinking belongs to idealism, and he made an extensive study about cognition of cognition, meta-cognition, i.e., the transcendental. His philosophy is, thereafter, called transcendental idealism.

In his philosophy, a human constitutes knowledge through inner intellectual mechanisms called as category, an original pure concept of synthesis, i.e. categories of quantity, quality, relation and modality. Kant (1998, p.213) says "by these concepts alone can it [understanding] understand something in the manifold of intuition, i.e., think an object for it." Here, it is not warranted that all humans constitute the same knowledge through the categories although the categories are shared among them. It is the categories that only ensure human to be able to think.

There is a key idea 'thing in itself' as the object in his philosophy. Kant (1998, p.115) says, "we can have cognition of no object as a thing in itself, but ... as an appearance; ... mere objects of experience." Kant (1998, p.115) says, "even if we cannot cognize these same objects as things in themselves, we at least must be able to think them as things in themselves." Therefore, humans want to believe in the existence of an object, however cannot cognize it as thing in itself directly. As a result there is a possibility of multiple versions of cognition, often conflicting, about the same object as thing in itself.

In the exoSA, all internal cognitions are equally considered inappropriate or incorrect, thereby an external knowledge being introduced instead as an appropriate or correct knowledge. Therefore, it is the exoSA that fits this philosophy, because the distinction of multiple incorrect internal cognitions and a correct external knowledge is equivalent to the distinction between multiple cognitions among people and the same 'thing in itself' in Kant philosophy.

5.3   Nietzscheanism and the endoSA

About a hundred years after, Nietzsche appeared with a significantly different philosophy from Kant. Between Kant and Nietzsche there was an influential philosopher, Hegel. He inherited Kant philosophy, finished up the German idealism and published an influential book called as 'Phenomenology of Spirit' in which he described an evolution of consciousness through dialectics. Although it is very important in philosophy in general, we skip 'Phenomenology of Spirit' because it is considered a completed version of German idealism stemming from Kant philosophy.

It is Nietzsche who made a sweeping criticism over the modern belief that there should be one and only one truth and that human can reach it through reason. Since modern philosophy was completed by Nietzsche, Nietzscheanism deserves a discussion here. His idea of 'will to power' is a breakthrough to cognition. It transformed the traditional way of thinking in philosophy.

'Will to power' of a subject became a key to truth in his philosophy. "The valuation, 'I believe that this and that is so,' is the essence of 'truth'" (Nietzsche, 2010, p.197). "Thus it is necessary that something should be assumed to be true, not that it is true" (p.197). "The hypothesis which gives the intellect the greatest feeling of power and security, is preferred, valued, and marked as true" (p.207). "The intellect sets its freest and strongest faculty and ability as the criterion of what is most valuable, consequently of what is true..." (p.207). Thus, he abandoned a traditional question about a relation between subject and object, and instead introduced power to truth with a concept of existentialism.

The endoSA goes basically with the idea of the strong person. IT professionals have 'indirect concern' to working knowledge and work sytems, instead they firstly pay their attention to the ideas and plans of the strongest person in the organization. IT professionals work as an agent of the power at the moment or the would-be power in the future. This style of thinking and behaviour corresponds to human attitudes toward truth in Nietzscheanism. IT professionals believe that the idea of the power finally dominate the organization as often practiced with the silver bullet theory. It is, therefore, that they practice the idea of Nietzscheanism in organizations.

5.4   Phenomenology and the 1ppSA

Next, we take phenomenology but have to mention why we do so. Widely known philosopher in the 20th century is Heidegger, whose work is fundamentally based on phenomenology of Husserl as well as the ideas of Kierkegaard and Nietzsche. Social constructionism has also its roots in phenomenology as Berger and Luckmann (1966, p.20) put, "the method we consider best suited to clarify the foundations of knowledge in everyday life is that of phenomenological analysis." Thus it is worth taking phenomenology here.

Husserl was the principal founder of phenomenology. He sought to study the structure of consciousness as experienced in a first-person perspective. Merleau-Ponty (1964, p.178) gives a consummate expression of a phenomenological world: "The world is all around me, not in front of me." Husserl (1999, p.17) says "In all of its manifestations, knowledge is a mental experience: knowledge belongs to a knowing subject."

Phenomenology is not concerned with an objective view like God's eye view, but with constituting. "The phenomenological world is not the bringing to explicit expression of a pre-existing being, but the laying down of being. Philosophy is not the reflection of a pre-existing truth, but, like art, the act of bringing truth into being."

(Merleau-Ponty, 2002, xxii-xxiii) Laying down of being is made by phenomenological methods of epoche and transcendental reduction. "Things are in them not as they might be in a case or container, rather, things constitute themselves in these experiences even though they are not to be found in them in the real sense." (Husserl, 1999, p.68) It means that constituting takes place in between the subject and the object.

Husserl admits that there are multiple views about the world and that they need to be accommodated.

"Prescientifically, in everyday sense-experience, the world is given in a subjectively relative way. ... In dealing with one another, we have long since become aware of this discrepancy between our various ontic validities. But we do not think that, because of this, there are many worlds. Necessarily, we believe in the world, whose things only appear to us differently but are the same." (Husserl, 1970, p.23)

Because of multiple different views and of needs for accommodation, people have to understand their own conditions and structures by which their constituting or laying down of being is made. For this purpose, "[we go back] to the ways in which this subjectivity has, 'has brought about,' and continues to shape the world through its concealed internal 'method'" (Husserl, 1970, p.177). Merleau-Ponty (1964, p.48) says it in simple words: "By a truly radical reflection, which reveals the prejudices established in us by the external environment, he attempts to transform this automatic conditioning into a conscious conditioning." This radical reflection is made possible with phenomenological methods.

The 1ppSA is of a first-person perspective. It admits multiple views that need to be accommodated. It is the 1ppSA in which people attempt to transform automatic conditioning into a conscious conditioning in order to understand why and how their own specific views and attitudes toward their work systems have been constituted. Although its methods are not readily available, the idea of the 1ppSA is considered within that of phenomenology. Kosaka (2010) also shows that phenomenology can be considered a basic theory for the 1ppSA in terms of problem of knowledge, mode of knowledge, and methods. Therefore it is reasonable to consider the 1ppSA as an instance of phenomenology, not that of other philosophies discussed above.

Based on the above discussion, we can see the theoretical existence of the 1ppSA where business professionals practice SA by themselves.

6   Discussion and Conclusion

In order to examine the existence of the domain of the 1ppSA, we constructed a topology of SA, ie, a map of two dimensions, one dimension being subjective or objective, and the other is concern or non-concern to working knowledge and work systems at the workplace. Since SA is regarded as a process that results in IS requirements, there appeared four independent types of SA on the map, each being supported by a different philosophy. The domain of the 1ppSA was identified and located as a separate, independent area on the map. Furthermore, practices often seen in real situations were also identified as independent areas. SA based on external best practices was justified by Kant philosophy, and the existence of SA using manager's ideas often related to silver bullet is supported by Nietzscheanism. As expected, the conventional SA, the 3ppSA, conformed to the naïve philosophy. The domain of the 1ppSA was theoretically supported, but also the foundational method of the 1ppSA was made clear as phenomenology. The practical usefulness of our research findings is that researchers can proceed to develop a method of the 1ppSA in less uncertainty and that they can develop the method based on phenomenology without searching from scratch.

Our research has some limitation. Use of philosophy is considered a very powerful test because philosophy is the most basic discipline for sciences. However, we did not have an exhaustive survey for possible alternatives. Therefore, this is not meant to rule out the need to explore other alternatives. Our examination of the domain is theoretical, so that each logical type of SA in the topology of SA is considered independent from each other. But this does not exclude a practical mixture of different types of SA in real situations. Therefore there remains a work to bridge a gap between our theoretical thinking and practices in real situations.

References

Alter, S.: The Work System Method for Understanding Information Systems and Information System Research. In: Proceedings of Eighth Americas Conference on Information Systems, pp. 2372–2380 (2002)

Alter, S.: Desperately Seeking Systems Thinking in the Information Systems Discipline. In: Proceedings of International Conference on Information Systems, pp. 757–769 (2004)

Berger, P.L., Luckmann, T.: The Social Construction of Reality: A Treatise in the Sociology of Knowledge. Doubleday (1966)

Bourdieu, P.: Sociology of sociology. Fujiwarashoten (1991) (in Japanese translation)

Burrell, G., Morgan, G.: Sociological Paradigms and Organizational Analysis. Heinemann, London (1979)

Checkland, P.: Systems Thinking, Systems Practice. Wiley (1999)

Deloitte (2011), http://www.johnseelybrown.com/SI_IndustryPerspectives_112009.pdf (accessed February 21, 2012)

Dewey, J.: Reconstruction in Philosophy. Cosimo Classics (2008)

Engeström, Y.: Learning by Expanding: An Activity-Theoretic Approach to Developmental Research. Shinyousha (1999) (in Japanese translation)

Feenberg, A.: Critical Theory of Technology. Oxford University Press (1991)

Giddens, A.: Sociology. Jiritsushuppan (1993) (in Japanese translation)

Goldspink, C., Kay, R.: Organizations as Self-organizing and Sustaining Systems. International Journal of General Systems 32(5), 459–474 (2003)

Hagel III, J., Brown, J.S., Davison, L.: The Power of Pull. Basic Books (2010)

Hirschheim, R., Klein, H.: Four Paradigms of Information Systems Development. Communications of the ACM 32(10), 1199–1216 (1989)

Hoffer, J.A., George, J.F., Valacich, J.S.: Systems Analysis and Design. Prentice-Hall (2002)

Husserl, E.: Crisis of European Sciences and Transcendental Phenomenology. Northwestern University Press (1970)

Husserl, E.: The Idea of Phenomenology. Kluwer Academic Publishers (1999)

Husserl, E.: Ideas: General Introduction to Pure Phenomenology, Reprint edn. Routlege (2002)

Iivari, J., Hirschheim, R.: Analyzing Information Systems Development: A Comparison and Analysis of Eight IS Development Approaches. Information Systems 21, 551–575 (1996)

Iivari, J., Hirschheim, R.A., Klein, H.K.: Towards a distinctive body of knowledge for information systems experts: Coding ISD process knowledge in two IS journals. Information Systems Journal 14, 313–342 (2004)

Kant, I.: Critique of Pure Reason. Cambridge University Press (1998)

Kensing, F., Munk-Madsen, A.: PD: Structure in the Toolbox. Communications of the ACM 36(4), 78–83 (1993)

Kensing, F., Simonsen, J., Bødker, K.: Must – a Method for Participatory Design. In: Proceedings of the Fourth Biennial Conference on Participatory Design (1996)

Kosaka, T.: Phenomenology as a Base of Systems Analysis. In: Proceedings of the Mediterranean Conference on Information Systems (2010)

Latour, B.: Social Theory and The Study of Computerized Work Sites. In: Orlikowski, W.J., Walsham, G., Jones, M.R., DeGross, J.I. (eds.) Information Technology and Changes in Organizational Work, pp. 295–307 (1995)

Lyytinen, K., Robey, D.: Learning failure in Information Systems Development. Information Systems Journal 9, 85–101 (1999)

Markus, L.M., Benjamin, R.I.: The Magic Bullet Theory in IT-Enabled Transformation. Sloan Management Review, 55–68 (Winter 1997)

Merleau-Ponty, M.: The Primacy of Perception. Northwestern University Press (1964)

Merleau-Ponty, M.: Phenomenology of Perception, 2nd edn. Routledge (2002)

Nietzsche, F.: The Will to Power, vol. I and II. Digireads.com (2010)

Rorty, R.: Philosophy and the Mirror of Nature: Thirtieth-Anniversary Edition. Princeton University Press (1979)

Takeda, S.: Genshougaku wa shikou no genri de aru (Phenomenology as a principle of thought). Chikumashobou (2004) (in Japanese)

Truex, D.P., Baskerville, R., Klein, H.: Growing Systems in Emergent Organizations. Communications of the ACM 42(8), 117–123 (1999)

Whitaker, R.: Applying Phenomenology and Hermeneutics in IS Design. Informing Science Journal 10, 63–96 (2007)

Whitten, J.L., Bentley, L.D., Dittman, K.C.: Systems Analysis and Design Methods. Irwin (2004)

Wood-Harper, A.T., Fitzgerald, G.: A Taxonomy of Current Approaches to Systems Analysis. The Computer Journal 25(1), 12–16 (1982)

Information Seeking Strategies in Organizational Information Architecture

Andrea Herbst and Jan vom Brocke

University of Liechtenstein, Fürst-Franz-Josef-Strasse, 9490 Vaduz, Liechtenstein
{andrea.herbst,jan.vom.brocke}@uni.li

Abstract. Organizational users daily manage a tremendous amount of information. Their management can be challenging for many users. Especially retrieving unstructured information from the organizational file server involves often major difficulties. Causes are, for instance, an intransparent filing structure as well as limited search and retrieving functions. Failure of information retrieval can result in major organizational inefficiencies such as recreating already existing information or wrong decision making due to an incomplete information base. Locating needed information requires the user's engagement in an information search process in the organizational information infrastructure. This search process shows usually different information seeking behaviors. The paper at hand reports on an empirical study on information seeking strategies of users in the organizational information architecture and in particular at the organizational file server. Investigating such information seeking strategies can help to identify information seeking patterns of organizational users as well as determining information seeking problems, which influence the users' decision on the search strategy. The results of the study indicate that users apply many different strategies when searching information on the file server. The strategies which are applied depend on the user's personal preferences, information seeking constraints as well as problems encountered during the information search process. A further important aspect on the selection of the search strategy is the level of contextual information about the needed item a user might possess. It is hoped that the identification of the search patterns can inform information system designers for developing innovative systems and interfaces which facilitate a more effective and efficient information search process.

Keywords: Information-seeking strategies, information-seeking constraints, document management, organizational file server.

1 Introduction

Organizational users daily manage a tremendous amount of information [1]. Dozens of emails and hundreds of documents on the file server are just few examples of the information users have to keep track of [2]. Managing this variety of information in the diverse systems can be challenging and time-consuming for many users [3].

H. Rahman et al. (Eds.): MCIS 2012, LNBIP 129, pp. 36–50, 2012.

Especially retrieving unstructured information, which is typically stored on the organizational file server and which usually does not follow any predefined filing structure involves often major difficulties. Causes are, for example, limited technical capabilities of file server solutions for searching and retrieving information. Hence, when engaging in the search for unstructured information on the file server users experience usability problems, such as weak search interfaces, poor navigation and inappropriate visualization of information.

Timely retrieval of accurate information is a critical success factor for many organizations [4]. However, problems user experience when seeking information can reach from missing or outdated information items to too much information, making it difficult to identify the relevant ones [5]. Studies show that worker waste between 15% and 35% of their working time with locating needed information in the organizational information architecture [6]. In some cases they even fail to obtain needed information. Such information retrieval failure can result in organizational inefficiencies such as recreating already existing information or wrong decision making due to an incomplete information base [6].

Locating and retrieving needed information requires the user's engagement in an information search process in the organizational information infrastructure. When engaging in such search processes users often show different information seeking behaviors [7]. One worker might just use the hierarchical tree structure of the file server to locate the desired folder where the information is anticipated and then scan the content of this folder, whereas others conduct a full text search in order to search through the content of the entire file server. The initiation of an information search process results usually from a perceived information need of a user [8]. By making use of formal or informal information sources or services a user intends to meet this perceived need [8]. Following Belkin et al. [7] we term the different behaviors to retrieve information 'information seeking strategies'.

This paper reports on an empirical study on information seeking strategies of users in the organizational information architecture and in particular on the organizational file server. Investigating information seeking strategies can help to identify information seeking patterns of organizational users as well as determining information seeking problems, which influence the users' decision on the search strategy. The research in particular addresses the following two research questions:

What are information seeking strategies in organizational information architecture?
What barriers do organizational users perceive during their search for information?

Studies of information seeking behavior across a diversity of specialized fields already exist [7, 9-11]. However, what has not been sufficiently taken into account so far is the identification of search patterns in information systems as well as search problems which can inform information system designers to develop systems and interfaces that facilitate a more effective and efficient information search process in the organizational information architecture.

The paper proceeds as follows. Section 2 gives a brief overview of three information seeking models. Section 3 provides an overview of the study conducted and section 4 reports on the results of the study. Section 5 discusses the results obtained from the study and the paper finally concludes with outlining implications for research and practice as well as limitations.

2   Related Work

Information seeking strategies and patterns of people in their daily business have been of high interest to information science scholars and have evolved as an extensively developed research area for decades [12]. As a result, various models concerning individual information seeking strategies have emerged. This chapter gives a brief overview of three selected models.

Ellis [10] model, which was derived from a grounded theory approach originally consisted of six characteristics of information seeking patterns of social scientists. This model was later extended by two more characteristics and also further applied to engineers and research scientists of an industrial environment [11]. The eight following categories describe their identified information seeking patterns: (1) Surveying concerns the initial search for information either by informal personal contact or by using a computerized search in order to gain an overview on existing information. (2) Chaining refers to following chains of items through citation. (3) Monitoring is characterized by activities which are carried out in order to maintain awareness of new developments or technologies through following particular sources. (4) Browsing concerns the scanning of material and can also be understood as an important part in monitoring. (5) Distinguishing involves the ranking of identified information sources based on the users perception. (6) Filtering refers to the use of criteria in order to search for information in such a way that the results are as relevant and precise as possible. (7) Extracting aims at locating material of interest by working through sources. Finally, (8) ending means the finish of the information search process [11].

The information search process from a user perspective is described by Kuhlthau [9]. In the context of her research she understands the information search process as the "constructive activity of finding meaning from information". (p. 361) Her model incorporates three perspectives: affective (feelings), cognitive (thoughts) and physical (actions). The research at hand did not focus on user feelings in context of searching for information. Therefore, only the perspectives of thoughts and actions are of greater relevance. Kuhlthau [9] identified in total six information search process stages, which are summarized below. (1) Initiation describes the point where a person becomes first aware of an information need. Thoughts in this stage mainly involve the understanding of the task at hand and relating it to prior experiences. Discussing potential themes and strategies are common actions in this stage. (2) Selection involves the identification and choice of the overall topic of interest or the intended approach. Thoughts in this stage concern the assessment of the topic against the personal interest, requirements of the assignment and resources available. (3) Exploration seeks to increase the personal understanding of the topic of interest by investigating information. Thoughts are becoming more focused and actions imply locating information, reading them and connecting the new information with prior knowledge. (4) Formulation aims at focusing on a more specific area of the information topic and thoughts involved in this stage usually concerns the identification and selection of ideas from the information. (5) Collection contains the gathering of information which is relevant to the area of focus. In this stage the information systems and the user cooperate most efficient and effective. Thoughts concern the definition, extension and support of the area of focus and actions contain the selection of relevant information. The final stage is (6) presentation which marks the end of the search process and involves preparation for using or presenting the gathered information. Synthesizing the topic with the gathered information concerns most often the thoughts and actions taken in this stage are a final summary search, where usually results show a decreasing relevance and a raising redundancy [9].

Belkin et al. [7] argues that when users are searching in information systems such as databases they show different behavior, which he terms information seeking strategies. He identifies the following four dimensions of such strategies. (1) Method of interaction, which refers to either a well-defined search (searching) or rather looking around for something interesting (scanning). (2) The goal of interaction can either be learning-oriented (learning) that is inspecting content or browsing among items or the main task can be the identification of useful items (selection). (3) Mode of retrieval can either refer to looking around in a group of items (recognition) or conducting a specific search for items on identified topics (specification). (4) Resource considered concerns either the usage of information descriptors (meta-information) or the information itself (information items) [7]. Considering Belkin et al. [7] items as a dichotomy allows the identification of 16 different information search strategies. Within these 16 strategies a user might move from one strategy to another while conducting a single information search [7].

In the contrast to Belkin et al. [7], the models of Ellis [10, 11] and Kuhlthau [9] address the information seeking behavior over a longer period of time. Additionally they focus on the search process as the refinement of the problem area whereas Belkin et al. [7] model can be rather understood as an action model, focusing on the actions carried out while searching for information [8].

3   Study Overview

The study at hand investigates information search strategies in an organizational setting and in particular addresses the search for information at the file server. For this purpose the case study methodology was chosen. Case study research aims at investigating phenomena within its natural context by applying various methods of data collection [13, 14]. It is "particularly suited to research questions, which require detailed understanding of social or organizational processes because of the rich data collected in context" [14]. Investigating information seeking patterns in the organizational infrastructure is of high practical relevance and cannot be separated from its context in which the information search takes place. Hence, a close connection to the data is desired and the phenomenon of interest should be studied in its natural context. Case studies can consist of multiple or single cases and various levels of analysis [15, 16]. For the research at hand a single case study approach was chosen due to the high exploratory nature of the research [13]. The studied organization is one of the internationally leading manufacturers for intelligent heating, cooling and ventilation systems. 1.300 employees in 15 subsidiaries worldwide aim at generating innovative and superior climate solutions which are exported in more than 50 countries. Data sources included a workshop, presentations and interviews with employees from different organizational units and departments. A total of twelve persons were interviewed with an average interview length of around 30 minutes. The interviewees were selected by the organization due to their affiliation to different business units. Their hierarchical level reached from operational to managerial positions (measured on a scale from 1 (operational) to 3 (managerial) to 5 (executive)) as shown in Table 1.

Table 1. Position of interviewees

Position	Frequency	Percentage	Accumulated
1 (operational)	4	33%	33%
2	4	33%	67%
3 (managerial)	3	25%	92%
4	1	8%	100%
5 (executive)	0	0%	100%

Data collection took place in February 2012 and all interviews were audio-taped. The interviews then were summarized on 5 to 8 pages for each interview. The interviews were semi-structured and focused on the following areas: (1) information seeking approach, (2) desired file server architecture for an enhanced information retrieval and (3) information collaboration. The software tool NVivo 9 was used in order to analyze and code the data.

4   Case Results

4.1   Case Overview

The organization is in the process of replacing their current file server with a new intranet solution based on the SharePoint technology. The goal of this project is to create a self-administrating collaboration platform which also contains functions for storing and retrieving documents and information. Within this new solution employees can access information by using a search tool, similar to the search in web search engines. The user can enter one or more search terms in a search field and after initiating the search the system conducts a full-text search. Results can additionally be narrowed down by applying filters using assigned tags, such as company, language, year of creation among others. The results are arranged in a list where each item is displayed with its full title, the path were the information or document is stored, the size of the document and the date when the document was added to the system. Only information and documents where the user has access privileges are shown in the result list.

The organization was concerned that not all employees would get along with the new search-tool. The idea emerged to provide a second view on the documents and information similar to the hierarchical tree structure of the windows explorer. Therefore, one of the goals of this project was to investigate information seeking patterns of employees in order to enhance the development of a design for such a structured view on documents and information. The next chapter summarizes the results of the case study.

4.2 Results

The interviews covered questions concerning information seeking in general and the applied information seeking strategies in daily business. Further we asked the interviewees how a file server should be structured in order to enhance information seeking. Finally, we were interested in their behavior concerning information and document sharing in organizational collaboration.

Information seeking of individual users in organizations plays an important role. As mentioned earlier users spend a considerable amount of their business time with the search for information [6]. In the current study we asked the interviewees how often they search for documents and information in their daily business. Nearly half of the interview partners stated that searching for information is part of their daily business. Four interviewees stated that they do not search for information very often, two probands stated that due to being new at the position they could not tell and one did not provide any answer.

We further asked the interview partners of how much time they spent with searching for information and documents. The received answers ranged from a percentage to a search time in minutes or hours per week or even per month. For comparability reasons we converted all answers into minutes spent for search per week. We further analyzed the search time in context to the position of the interviewees. The results indicate that searching for information consumes a considerable amount of an employees working time. Answers' reached from 15 to 240 minutes per week. Four interview partners did not specify any search time. Putting the search time in context to the position of the interviewees further indicates that the search time rises with the level of the position of the interview partner. Calculating the average search time for each position of the eight valid responses show that the average search time for an employee on the operational level (1) is 45 minutes, for an employee on a level between operational and managerial (2) is 125 minutes and for an employee on the managerial level (3) 180 minutes as illustrated in Fig. 1.

This result is not surprising as employees on the organizational level usually have a constant work routine, handling the same type of information and documents every day. Employees on a higher level of hierarchy, on the other hand, have often more responsibility and, therefore, require information for decision purposes which they do not need on a regular basis.

We further asked the users of how they engage in the search for information. It became apparent that due to the existing system landscape users are not always aware of where required information can be found. As such users often have to engage in

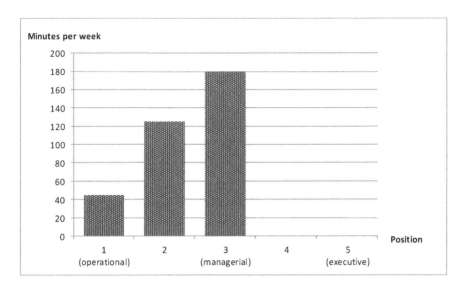

Fig. 1. Average search time per position

information seeking approaches in various systems in order to successfully locate needed information and documents. In all cases users mentioned the file server as a possible source for information as well as diverse databases and the personal email account. When searching for information and documents at the file server users deploy different strategies. The chosen strategy depends on the personal user preferences, existing software on the personal computer (PC) but also certain constraints such as time or creator constraints, which are further outlined below. Table 2 shows a summary of the identified search strategies.

The search strategies are not static but rather get adapted in several cycles depending on the success of the search. In strategy 2, for example, a user selects a specific folder in which he anticipates the information (1), then runs a full text search via the windows-explorer search assistant (2) and finally sorts the results (3) to ease selection of the needed item. If the user can't find the information he goes back and changes the location to a folder one level above and repeats the search until the information can be found. All probands stated that they would search for information by themselves first. However, 50% of the interviewees mentioned that if the information search is not successful they rather contact a fellow employee for requesting the information than engaging in a time-consuming search.

Viewing the search strategies from a higher level, they can be divided into two groups: One group uses more a search function such as the windows-explorer search assistant (search function) and the other group rather uses the tree structure of the fileserver to navigate to the required document (tree structure). It can be assumed that the search strategy is influenced by the hierarchical position of an employee. However, our results indicate that the position of an employee has no impact on the overall search preference as illustrated in Fig. 2.

Table 2. Identified information search strategies

| | Search Strategies | | | | | | | | |
	S1	S2	S3	S4	S5	S6	S7	S8	S9
selecting specific folder	1	1	1						
scanning through items	2							2	3
running windows-explorer search assistant		2	2	1			1		
conducting full text search			3	2	2	2	3		
running windows desktop search (indexed)					1	1			
applying sort function		3							
using preview function					3				
deploying search criteria for specific data types							2		
determining the topic area									1
digging through tree structure								1	2
Frequency	1	1	2	3	1	1	1	1	1

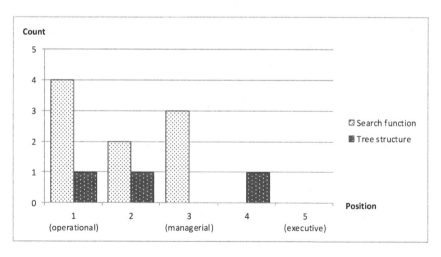

Fig. 2. Search strategies per position (n=12)

As mentioned above, several constraints influencing the user selection of the information seeking strategy could be identified, namely time, creator and access constrains, which are explained below.

1. **Time constraints** refer to information and documents which were handled by the user some time ago and where the user does not recall the location of the information anymore. This makes it difficult for the user to successfully retrieve information. The following quote supports this time matter (quotes were translated from German to English):

   For example, if I have nothing to do with a certain topic for about 6 months, then it gets difficult to find the information again, not to mention the difficulties for a colleague.

2. **Creator constraints** concern the fact that the creator of information has the power to file and share documents and information. Therefore, information might not be accessible through the file server at all because it was never stored there. But even if information and documents are stored on the fileserver the information search might be difficult due to an intransparent filing structure. An interviewee stated that as followed:

   Another important aspect is that we have an enormous know how but I think that not much of this knowledge gets distributed outside the own departmental structure. In other words one has to know who possesses the knowledge in order to contact that person and retrieve the information needed quickly.

3. **Access constraints** are characterized by missing access privileges to certain information or documents. As in most other organizations the file server of the investigated organization is structured by departments and usually only their members have access to the departmental files. In the current study missing access privileges were mentioned in two contexts: (a) the information seeker cannot access needed information and (b) other employees cannot access folders on the file server but need the access for collaboration purposes. Of the interviewees 67% mentioned access privileges in at least one of these perspectives as hindering for the information seeking process. Further, access restrictions was one of the mentioned reasons for contacting a fellow colleague in order to request the information as stated by this proband:

   First I select the topic. When I know that the topic concerns a certain department I directly jump to their folders and start digging within their tree structure. If I don't have the privileges for the files I just call them.

Experiencing these constrains within the search process can initiate a change in the information seeking strategy. Such changes contain for example the change from a formal to an informal search for example by asking a fellow colleague for support but also the usage of a full text search instead of scanning through the existing files in the tree structure.

However, interviewees also stated problems which impede the information seeking on the file server. The problems mentioned can be divided into three clusters. One cluster concerns problems with the filing structure on the file server, the second cluster comprises problems with information quality and the third cluster contains all remaining problems which are not related to one of the first two clusters.

Table 3. Information seeking problems

Filling structure	Information quality	Others
• Individual filing logic • Non-transparency of the file server • Deep and highly branched filing structure • Obsolete folders	• Timeliness of information • Information none-traceable and creator unknown • Quantity of the hits • Relevance of the information	• Laborious search • High access time • Scanned documents

The individual filing logic refers to the individual decision of each employee how and where he or she files information on the shared file server. This can create difficulties in searching information in a filing structure created by another person as confirmed by the following quote.

> The filing of our information within the projects is rather informal. We have our main folder, then projects and within the project folder the filing of information is very individual. [...] This is not structured and it is very difficult to structure it.

Such an individual filing can result in an intransparent structure making it difficult to search for information by recognition. An interviewee states that as followed:

> The retrieval of information from other individuals usually requires more search effort.

A deep and highly branched filing structure also often hinders employees in effectively searching for information as supported by the following:

> The structure is highly branched and often one has to dig very deep. Such a structure can consist of 20 folders with 20 subfolders and it can happen that one searches through 40 folders for nothing and then has to continue the search in even further folders.

What further complicate the search are obsolete folders which are not needed anymore but still remain on the file server as suggested by an interviewee:

> In the past, the folder structure of the file server was open and new folders could be added or existing ones changed. Today this is rather restrictive, new folders have to be added by the IT department. However, on the file server still exist a lot of old folders, which nobody needs anymore but still remain there. As longer the folder list gets as more unclear the structure becomes.

But also problems concerning the information quality can affect the information seeking process. For example information can be non-traceable and its creator can be unknown, making it difficult to retrieve information by applying other search strategies. A proband states that as followed:

> A problem for example is that documents cannot be found and it is unknown who has created them and where they can be found.

Even if information can be found the question concerning the timeliness of information remains as stated by the following quote:

> *And then remains the question, if the information which one has retrieved is up to date. Or is it just an outdated version or only a copy of the original? This one never really knows.*

Finally, the amount of the results and the relevance of the resulting information were mentioned as hindering successful information seeking. The following quote supports this problem.

> *Filtering the relevant and important information [is a problem when searching for information] also when searching in the email account. It is difficult to always find the adequate objects when using the keyword search. We produce a huge amount of data and often the proper keywords in the documents are missing.*

The final cluster contains three further problems. One problem mentioned is the high effort for searching information not just at the file server but across all important sources. An interviewee explained that as followed:

> *The search process is actually too laborious. There is no central entry point for the search. Using the desktop search for emails and the indexed drives is more or less working. However, this search does not include the search in [other sources]. These other sources have to be searched additionally.*

However, even when conducting a full text search on the file server, there is the risk that not all documents are included in this search. For example, documents, which were formerly scanned and where no text recognition was applied, are not included in a full text search.

> *[A problem is that] documents, which I'm looking for, are scanned. Then the full text search is not working and, therefore, the keyword search does not discover all relevant documents.*

Finally, it was mentioned that when information are requested from other people due to access restrictions, the duration until the information are received depends on the availability of the needed person.

> *When one knows where the information is stored then the information can be retrieved quickly. In the case that this is not known, it might be necessary to request the information from other people. The duration until the information is retrieved then depends on how quickly one catches the responsible person.*

This list of information seeking problems is not intended to be exhaustive. Further problems can occur when searching for information on the file server. However, the identified information seeking problems have certainly an influence on the strategy a user applies when searching for information. Therefore, such problems need to be considered when designing innovative systems and interfaces which are intended to facilitate an effective and efficient information storage and search.

Finally, we asked the interviewees how the structure of a file server should be designed in order to facilitate the overall information search process. The results show that the identified preferences are highly divers. From twelve interviews we could identify nine different preferences for potential file server structures, which are presented in Table 4. These preferences include also mixed solutions, where two different structures are combined. Preference 7, for example, suggests using departments as the main structure and then subdividing each department due to their projects.

Table 4. Preferences for a file server structure

oriented by ...	P1	P2	P3	P4	P5	P6	P7	P8	P9
Processes	1			1					2
Departments		1					1		1
Business units			1					1	
Products				2	1				
Projects				.			2		
Document type								1	
Subjects						1			
Corporate- and brand environment					2				
Frequency	1	2	2	1	1	1	2	1	1

The high diversity of the preferences clearly demonstrates that designing an organization-wide valid file structure on the file server to facilitate the information search process could be difficult. Therefore, new technological solutions are required that reduce or even eliminate the information seeking problems and improve the information seeking process of organizational users.

In summary it can be said that the interview results show that user engage in very different ways in the existing infrastructure to search for information. The search behavior of the users is influenced by various aspects. This include for example personal search preferences and existing software on the PC. The search behavior is further influenced by problems arising during the search such as limitations in the filing structure and it is also affected by information seeking constraints such as time, access and creator constrains. When experiencing information seeking problems or constraints users often change their information seeking strategy in order to obtain access to needed information. The next chapter will further discuss the results from the case study by applying existing information seeking strategy models.

5   Discussion

Summarizing the case study results, it can be observed that in all cases of the information seeking strategies users have a clear idea on what kind of information they are looking for. Applying the Belkin et al. model [7] it can be said that information seeking on the file server follows usually a well-defined search with the goal of selecting useful items. However, what is quite different between the various users is the mode of retrieval. Some users rather dig through the tree structure in the windows explorer and expect to find the information by recognition while others specify their search with key terms. Although Belkins' et al. [7] model explains different information seeking strategies, it does not give explanation why user chose diverse search strategies.

Ellis [10, 11] information-seeking behavior model engage with the behavioral patterns in the actual search activity [8]. The model also shows the course of narrowing down the search process. Concerning the information search at the organizational file server some of the categories of the Ellis model could not be confirmed in this study. For example, the two categories chaining and monitoring information was not mentioned by the interviewees. The other six categories surveying, as the start of the search, browsing as the scanning of material, distinguishing as the ranking of the information material, filtering as applying filter functions for reducing the resulting amount to the most relevant ones, extracting as going through the sources to identify relevant material and ending as the end of the search process could be observed in this study. However, applying Ellis [10, 11] categories does not allow the identification of the different interaction patterns with the information systems when engaging in the information search process. A similar result can be noticed when applying the model of Kuhlthau [9]. Her model represents rather stages of the search process in which the behavioral patterns may occur [8]. In the research at hand the information seeking stages could be observed, but also Kuhlthaus' [9] model does not explain why user interact with the information system in different ways.

All three models do not specify if a certain level of contextual information about the needed documents or information items is assumed or required. However, several of the identified search strategies in this research, such as selecting specific folders, scanning through items, or digging through the existing tree structure, require a certain level of such contextual information. The need for such contextual information in the search process was also confirmed by Alvarado et al. [1]. A user probably would have difficulties in finding information, for example, by digging through the tree structure if he or she has no knowledge about where the information is stored. As higher the level of contextual information is as more specific a user can select the information-seeking strategy. For example, selecting a specific folder and running a full text search by using a certain data type requires at least partial knowledge about the location of the information and its data type. This is very similar with requesting information from a fellow employee. A user has to know whom to ask in order to request the needed information informally. Therefore, it can be said that the level of contextual information has a significant influence on the applied information search strategy. In existing information-seeking models the level of contextual information has not been sufficiently considered so far.

One further goal of the case study was to identify preferences for an organizational file server structure in order to identify similarities. It was hoped that these findings could inform organizations concerning the design of a common, organization-wide structure of a file server in order to facilitate the overall information search process. However, the results show a high diversity in the preferences. Therefore, achieving a universal, organization-wide structure of a file server could be difficult. As a consequence, new technological solutions are required that are independent of a hierarchical filing structure and that support users in their information seeking process. One possible solution could be the storage of information without any filing structure. A virtual filing structure view could be created by applying meta-information to the information. The advantage of this solution is that the virtual structure could be adjusted to each individual user, allowing them to create his preferred view, for example, by departments, processes, products etc. Such a solution would also have the advantage that none or only a low level of contextual information is required in order to engage in the information-seeking process.

6   Conclusion

The paper at hand reported on an empirical study of users' information seeking strategies in the organizational information architecture and in particular on the organizational file server. The results of the study show that user engage in a variety of different information seeking strategies. Some user conduct a full text search whereas others locate needed information only by using the hierarchical tree structure of the file server and some apply hybrid forms. It could also be observed that these information seeking strategies are not static but rather are adjusted in various cycles until the search is successful. The decision of what strategy is applied depends on personal preferences, existing software on the PC and is further influenced on information-seeking problems and information-seeking constraints, such as time, creator and access constrains. Experiencing such constraints and problems might cause the user to adjust the information-seeking process in order to successfully retrieve needed information. Finally, it could be observed that the level of contextual information about the needed item has an influence on the strategy a user chooses for seeking information. The result of the research suggests that new technological solutions are required which goes beyond a hierarchical filing structure of documents and information in order to facilitate an effective and efficient information seeking.

For practitioners the results of this study imply to think in new ways of how to manage and store unstructured information and documents in organizations and to provide new systems and interfaces in order to facilitate the information-seeking in organizations. For research the identification of information-seeking strategies can give interesting insights in how users engage with search interfaces and how the contextual information of users influences the search strategy.

However, also some limitations of the research have to be considered. First of all the study only consisted of a single case study and only a small number of people have been interviewed for this purpose. Secondly, the investigated information-seeking strategies only concern the information seeking behavior on the organizational file server and do not include an overall search or the search in other systems. Although suggested by other researchers the interviews did not cover question concerning the feeling user experienced while seeking information on the file server, leaving out cognitive aspects. Some of these shortcomings will be addressed in further research.

References

1. Alvarado, C., Teevan, J., Ackerman, M.S., Karger, D.: Surviving the Information Explosion: How People Find Their Electronic Information (2003),
   `http://dspace.mit.edu/handle/1721.1/6713`
2. Boardman, R., Sasse, M.A.: Stuff goes into the computer and doesn't come out: a cross-tool study of personal information management. In: Proceedings of the SIGCHI Conference on Human Factors in Computing Systems (CHI 2004), pp. 583–590 (2004)
3. Kolekta, R., Baboo, J., Machaka, P., Chandran, G.: Databases–Personal Information Management (2012), `http://people.cs.uct.ac.za/~gchandran/`
   `PIM%20-%20DB%20Final%20version%207%20%28greg%20robert%`
   `20Pheeha%29.pdf`
4. Puzicha, J.: Finding information: intelligent retrieval & categorization (2011),
   `http://www.aiim.org/pdfdocuments/36879.pdf`
5. Farhoomand, A.F., Drury, D.H.: Managerial information overload. Communications of the ACM 45, 127–131 (2002)
6. Feldman, S.: The high cost of not finding information. KM World 13, 8–10 (2004)
7. Belkin, N.J., Marchetti, P.G., Cool, C.: BRAQUE: Design of an interface to support user interaction in information retrieval. Information Processing & Management 29, 325–344 (1993)
8. Wilson, T.D.: Models in information behaviour research. Journal of Documentation 55, 249–270 (1999)
9. Kuhlthau, C.C.: Inside the search process: Information seeking from the user's perspective. Journal of the American Society for Information Science 42, 361–371 (1991)
10. Ellis, D.: A behavioural approach to information retrieval system design. Journal of Documentation 45, 171–212 (1989)
11. Ellis, D., Haugan, M.: Modelling the information seeking patterns of engineers and research scientists in an industrial environment. Journal of Documentation 53, 384–403 (1997)
12. Leckie, G.J., Pettigrew, K.E., Sylvain, C.: Modeling the information seeking of professionals: a general model derived from research on engineers, health care professionals, and lawyers. The Library Quarterly 66, 161–193 (1996)
13. Benbasat, I., Goldstein, D.K., Mead, M.: The case research strategy in studies of information systems. MIS Quarterly 11, 369–386 (1987)
14. Hartley, J.: Case study research. In: Cassell, C., Symon, G. (eds.) Essential Guide to Qualitative Methods in Organizational Research, pp. 323–333. Sage Publications, Thousand Oaks (2004)
15. Eisenhardt, K.M.: Building theories from case study research. Academy of Management Review 14, 532–550 (1989)
16. Yin, R.K.: Case Study Research: Design and Methods. Sage Publications, Thousand Oaks (2003)

Trust in e-Voting Systems: A Case Study

João Palas Nogueira and Filipe de Sá-Soares

Universidade do Minho, Centro Algoritmi, Campus de Azurém, 4800-058 Guimarães, Portugal
palasnogueira@gmail.com, fss@dsi.uminho.pt

Abstract. The act of voting is one of the most representative of Democracy, being widely recognized as a fundamental right of citizens. The method of voting has been the subject of many studies and improvements over time. The introduction of electronic voting or e-voting demands the fulfillment of several requirements in order to maintain the security levels of the paper ballot method and the degree of trust people place in the voting process. The ability to meet those requirements has been called into question by several authors. This exploratory research aims to identify what factors influence voters' confidence in e-voting systems. A case study was conducted in an organization where such a system has been used in several elections. A total of 51 e-voters were interviewed. The factors that were found are presented and discussed, and proposals for future work are suggested.

Keywords: e-voting, trust, electronic voting systems, e-voting requirements.

1 Introduction

The act of voting is a key part in democracy and one of its cardinal rights. The evolution that occurred in the voting process over times enables present day free elections to be framed in a well defined set of stages and requirements, which when properly implemented and enforced confer the fundamental characteristics of credibility and trust to all involved in the election – promoters, developers, electoral commissions, auditors, and most importantly, candidates and voters.

The method of voting has undergone changes in the various stages that make up its life cycle in order to improve its speed, security, flexibility, availability, and cost, especially during the authentication of the voter, the casting of the vote, and the tabulation stages.

As illustrations of the improvements implemented over time, there is the use of paper ballots, the development of specific legislation to streamline the voting process, and the introduction of mechanical means that made the process faster. In the recent past, we have witnessed the introduction of information technologies (IT) in the voting process, not without ups and downs along the way, seeking the transformation of the traditional voting system (paper ballot) in an electronic voting system.

However, the introduction of these technological elements in the elections has not been easy or consensual, especially with regard to the suspicions that they raise, their ability to meet the requirements that made paper ballot method trustworthy, and to a

H. Rahman et al. (Eds.): MCIS 2012, LNBIP 129, pp. 51–66, 2012.

set of new questions concerning basic values like the anonymity of the vote and the accuracy of the system.

IT systems are currently used in many sensitive areas of society, such as for processing personal data, clinical data, or financial transactions. However, it seems these areas gather a greater consensus and apparently greater confidence on the use of IT by those involved than the introduction of these same technologies in the voting process.

In fact, electronic voting systems (EVS) are not yet widely used in elections of greater relevance and we observe countries moving forward and backward in implementing EVS for national elections: while some countries are already using EVS for several years, others banned its use. Between these extremes, there are cases of success and failure in the use of EVS [1], [2], [3], [4], [5], [6].

Among the various aspects that may facilitate or inhibit the success of EVS, trust has been recognized as a key factor [7], [8]. Along the quest for a completely trustworthy e-voting system – one that does not lose, add, alter, disregard, or disclose ballots – there is also the need to ensure that voting stakeholders also trust the system really has those properties [9].

The ability to demonstrate that EVS are trustworthy has a direct impact in the legitimacy and acceptance of the voting results, and it may be considered a prerequisite for shifting from the traditional voting systems to the voting systems on the Internet. Indeed, the integral acceptance of EVS must encompass all of society, including all voters and not just those who are predisposed to use them. If there is a large number of voters skeptical about this method of voting, trust in democracy may be compromised [6], [10].

The relevance of trust in e-voting may also be appreciated if one considers the potential goals of a deliberate attack launched against EVS, namely to produce an incorrect tabulation of votes, to prevent electors to cast their votes, to raise doubts about the legitimacy of the results of the election, to delay the promulgation of the results, and to violate the anonymity of the vote [11]. The possibility of any of these goals being achieved or the actual verification of their satisfaction casts a shadow of doubt among the electorate, severely affecting their confidence in those systems.

The belief that trust plays a major role in the adoption and acceptance of EVS as innovative technological systems with social impact motivated the execution of this work. Knowing what instills confidence into electors regarding the use of EVS will help to understand voters' attitude towards e-voting and to devise better ways to design and deploy these systems.

Therefore, the aim of this study is to identify what factors influence voters' trust in EVS.

2   Literature Review

2.1   Voting Systems

The voting systems are the means used by people who have the right to vote (the voters) to freely choose between different options.

Until the mid-nineteenth century, the elections were conducted without much control and privacy [12]. Everybody swore before a judge to be entitled to vote and having not already done, and the act of voting was exercised verbally, which means that a trust relationship was established between the voters and those who led the election (the judges). It was by then that were laid the foundations of the now widely accepted voting system.

Worldwide, the most used and accepted voting system is the paper ballot voting system (PBVS). Briefly, the voter attends in person (with some exceptions referred to in the legislation) and makes a mark in his or her choice of vote on paper and puts it in a ballot. At the end of the period stipulated for the voting process, the votes cast in the ballot are manually counted.

This voting system is mature and has been used innumerous times, which gives it a high degree of confidence for all to see. However, it still has certain limitations, both in terms of assuring the satisfaction of certain requirements (e.g., ensure that only those registered may vote or that the content of the vote is not eliminated during or after the voting period) and when compared to other voting systems (e.g., the delay and potential errors in the manual counting of the votes or the mandatory presence of voters in pre-established places in order to vote). Therefore, it is not surprising that other alternatives to the traditional system of voting have emerged, such as EVS.

Electronic voting or e-voting is a voting system that uses in any of its phases electronic means to assist the voting process. In the context of e-voting we may consider two main voting systems: poll-site electronic voting systems (PEVS) and remote electronic voting systems (REVS). The former, as in PBVS, implies the presence of the elector to vote in a pre-defined and controlled place by the electoral commission. The latter does not imply the presence of the voter in a previously defined place: the vote can be cast anywhere using the Internet as a medium of communication between the system and the voter. This study focuses on this type of electronic voting systems.

Regardless of the voting system used, in order to have quality and to transmit the necessary confidence to those involved in the voting process, the voting system will have to satisfy a set of requirements.

2.2 Requirements of Voting Systems

The literature review enabled the identification of a set of 12 core requirements against which voting systems should be analyzed and evaluated in order to judge their adequacy [10], [13], [14], [15], [16], [17], [18], [19], [20], [21], [22], [23], [24], [25].

Table 1 presents those requirements. The order in which requirements are listed intends to signal the importance that researchers have attributed to each one of the requirements, from the most important to the least important, based on the survey of the literature. The table is divided into five columns: the first includes the designation of the requirement, the second briefly describes it and the remaining columns provide a classification of the three voting systems considered in terms of requirements satisfaction. In these last three columns, a + sign indicates that the system generally satisfies the requirement, a - sign indicates that the system falls short of meeting the requirement, and a +/- sign indicates that currently the system does not meet the requirement, but may meet it in the short term.

Table 1. Relationship between Voting Requirements and Voting Systems

Requirement	Description	PBVS	PEVS	REVS
Authenticity	Only persons with the right to vote should be able to cast a vote	+/-	+	+/-
Singularity	Each voter should be able to vote only once	+	+	+
Anonymity	It should not be possible to associate a vote to a voter	+	+	-
Integrity	Votes should not be able to be modified or destroyed	+	+	-
Uncoercibity	No voter should be able to prove the vote that has cast	+/-	+/-	-
Verifiability	Anyone should be able to independently verify that all votes have been correctly counted	+	+	-
Auditability and Certifiability	Voting systems should be able to be tested, audited and certifiable by independent agents	+	+	+
Mobility	Voting systems should not restrict the voting place	-	-	+
Transparency	Voting systems should be clear and transmit accuracy, precision, and security to voters	+	+	+
Availability	Voting systems should be always available during the voting period	+	+	-
Accessibility and Convenience	Voting systems should be accessible by people with special needs and without requiring specific equipment or abilities	+	+	+/-
Detectability and Recoverability	Voting systems should detect errors, faults and attacks and recover voting information to the point of failure	+	+/-	+/-

None of the voting systems satisfies all requirements, with systems that best meet certain requirements falling short of meeting other requirements.

2.3   Trust and Voting

In the realm of voting systems, trust may be conceived as the certainty, held by all electoral stakeholders, that the whole process takes place observing the desired assumptions, specifically with regard to the requirements that voting systems must meet, thus attesting the quality of the system and ensuring compliance with security parameters [20].

If there is no trust by the stakeholders of a voting process, a voting system will hardly succeed and any suspicion that falls on the system precipitates its discredit and may jeopardize the elections. Indeed, several cases of misconduct in EVS led to a significant decrease of citizens' trust on e-voting [26]. The literature provides details about several of those cases. A set of illustrative examples follows. In 1993, during the trial of two EVS, it was found that in an industrial precinct in which there were no registered voters, the system indicated 1,429 votes for the incumbent mayor, who incidentally won the election by 1,425 votes [3]. In 2002, in the realm of a presidential election, an electronic voting machine attributed to a candidate a final vote count of negative 16,022 votes [5]. In the same year, in the second round of a presidential election, the final result of the election was decided by five votes, however it was found that the e-voting system had not registered 78 votes [1]. One year later, an electronic voting system reported results of 140,000 votes, when only 25.000 residents were eligible to vote [5]. In 2006, an election was won by only 386 votes out of about 150.000, losing the trail to 18.000 votes [6]. In 2007, several EVS were tested resulting in tabulations whose values differed from those derived from manual tabulation in 56.1% of the votes counted [27]. Any of these incidents has the potential to undermine the trust that people place in e-voting, raising doubts about its value and increasing people's reluctance to use such systems, in light of the dangers and risks they entail.

Conceptually, trust can be defined as "the willingness of a party to be vulnerable to the actions of another party based on the expectation that the other will perform a particular action important to the trustor, irrespective of the ability to monitor or control that other party" [28, p. 712]. In a trust relationship there is an acceptance of vulnerability to a possible, but not expected, damaging action [29].

The concept of trust requires that there has to be a risk to the parties involved in the trust process and an interdependence between the parties since at least the interests of one of the parties can only be achieved if there is collaboration from other party [30]. Not being static, trust is situational, evolves based on the ability to predict the behavior of the other and it typically emerges and builds up based on past experiences.

In voting systems, as important as meeting the requirements, systems need to convey that those requirements are effectively satisfied.

In the case of e-voting, there are authors who advocate the printing of electronic votes and the transparency of the system by opening the source code as a way to transmit the necessary confidence to voters [1], [16].

For remote electronic voting systems, the difficulties of ensuring and demonstrating trust seem to become more acute. In a 1999 study, 69% of the voters surveyed believed that secure Internet voting would take many years to become reality or perhaps would never be achieved [10]. One decade later, there is still no EVS architecture able to reasonably provide a sufficient degree of trust to the electoral stakeholders. In fact, the simple consideration of the differences in terms of the scaling of voting systems structure shows that an attack in PBVS usually affects a limited number of ballots (those circumscribed to a ballot box), whereas in the case of EVS a simple modification may change the content of thousands of votes [31].

After pondering on e-voting literature, we advance the following issues as potentially influencing trust in electronic voting systems:

- Information made available – the quantity and quality of information and briefings sessions about the e-voting system may influence the voters' confidence in the system
- History of use – the number of times an electronic voting system was used without presenting significant errors may influence the voters' confidence in the system
- Open source code – the ability to inspect the source code of the system may influence the voters' confidence in the system
- Scope of election – different elections will make voters trust differently in the system
- Tests – the quantity and quality of the tests made to the system may influence the voters' confidence in the system
- Audits and Certifications – the existence of audits and certifications from the system development process up to the elections may influence the voters' confidence in the system

- Development team – the recognition and reputation of the team that developed the system may influence the voters' confidence in the system
- Ability to meet requirements – the ability of a system to meet requirements, especially those related to the anonymity of the voter's ballot, may influence the voters' confidence in the system

This list of issues forms the starting point for the identification and analysis of the factors that may influence the confidence in EVS. It will be important to determine whether the proposed issues are relevant to voters and whether there are other factors that voters consider imperative.

3   Research Design

The purpose of this study is to identify the factors influencing voters' confidence in EVS. This goal could only be accomplished through the involvement of voters. Since the focus is on trust in EVS, it would be important that the study's subjects possessed experience of using these systems as this would allow drawing conclusions based on the use of EVS rather than on the intention to use EVS.

To this end, it was necessary to identify individuals who already had used EVS in situations of real elections. The authors knew a Portuguese university that had developed and regularly used a remote electronic voting system. After granting access to this research site, the inquiry was designed based on the existence of that population of voters.

The first version of the aforementioned remote e-voting system was developed ten years ago and the system has been used in several internal elections at the departmental and school levels of the university, with a number of voters ranging from few tens to half a thousand. The typical users of the system are the professors of the institution. The system was one of the first of its kind to obtain the positive opinion of the Portuguese Data Protection National Commission and it is equipped with a set of security mechanisms that aim to instill transparency in the system.

Methodologically, the study consisted in a case study. For the delimitation of the case we defined as subjects of interest all the professors who, belonging to the engineering school of that university, had used at least once the remote e-voting system to exercise their voting rights in the context of a real election.

In carrying out the study we applied two research techniques: collection of documents and semi-structured interviews. The first technique involved the collection of documentation on the system in order to understand its architecture, features, and functionality. The second technique was the main instrument to generate data on the factors that may influence the confidence of voters in EVS.

Previously to conduct the interviews, we developed the interview script, tested the quality of the script by asking two voters to review its wording, and elaborated a preliminary version of the codebook that would support the coding stage.

The script of the interview was structured around the following five themes:

- Assessment of the use of the remote electronic voting system
- Opinion on EVS before using an electronic voting system and after its use

- Key requirements that remote electronic voting systems should satisfy
- Use of EVS at national elections or referendums
- Main factors influencing the confidence in EVS

The preparation of the preliminary codebook involved the definition of a set of codes based on the literature review and on the questions that made up the interview script.

It was also decided that the first four interviews would serve as pilot, to ensure that the script enabled the generation of data with enough quality to feed analysis.

At the beginning of each interview we would request the respondent if we could audio record the interview. Then, interview records would be transcribed and coded. In order to facilitate mechanical procedures associated with coding and analysis we would use Atlas.ti qualitative data analysis software.

4   Description of Study

The documents on the remote e-voting system were obtained from the system development team, which was composed of technical elements from the IT area and elements from the legal area.

Regarding the interviews, 259 emails were sent to the faculty of seven departments of the school with an invitation to participate in the study. The emails asked professors an interview related to their use of the system. Of the 259 invitations sent, 26 were directed to the department faculty where the system best fit in terms of scientific area, namely the department of information systems and technologies. We attempted to promote a significant number of interviews with professors pertaining to other departments, in order to avoid that findings would be based on a too technical view of the system.

In the invitation email we described the study, emphasized the importance of voters' collaboration, and assured the anonymity of the participants and that the data collected would only be used in the study. Although we asked for an individual interview in person, we also suggested as an alternative the possibility of interviews being conducted with the use of online communication tools, or as a last resort to the possibility to send the questions by email and receive the answers also by email.

Of the 259 invitations sent, we got 51 acceptances to participate, 24 indications from professors who so far had not used the system (and therefore did not constitute subjects of the study), six responses from professors who were not available to schedule the interview for the period stipulated for the interviews and 14 system messages of email undelivered due to inexistent or full mailboxes.

Most interviews were conducted in person at the professors' offices during June and July 2011. The distribution of the 51 respondents by scientific area of the department is as follows: 15 (29.4%) from information systems and technologies, 9 (17.6%) from electronics, 9 (17.6%) from civil engineering, 9 (17.6%) from production engineering, 5 (9.8%) from mechanical engineering, and 4 (7.8%) from textile engineering (one of the departments to which we had sent 23 invitations provided no feedback).

At the beginning of each interview we recalled the aim and scope of the study, reinforcing that the answers would be treated anonymously and solely for purposes of the work, and the absence of any linkage between the researchers and the development, maintenance, or promotion of the system. Next, we requested permission to audio record the interview.

Fifty interviews were in person and one was held via Skype. Four respondents did not allow the audio recording of the interview. Interviews amounted to a total of about 10 hours, with an average of 40 minutes per interview, and originated 434 pages of transcripts.

As already mentioned, we started the coding stage with a provisional codebook, since it was not possible to establish a priori all the categories in which the responses of participants would be classified. Therefore, as the analysis of the interviews progressed, we extended the codebook as required, in a process inspired by Grounded Theory. Whenever a new issue arose in the interview, a new code was created and defined in the codebook. Sometimes the addition of the code to the codebook required the review of previous classifications, especially when the introduction of this new code led to an explosion of an existing code into subcodes (the readiness of retrieving previously coded units of text with a certain code provided by Atlas.ti greatly simplified this task). At the end of the coding stage, the codebook contained 166 codes, of which 35 were super codes.

5   Results

The presentation of the main results of the study will follow the five structural themes listed in the research design section.

Overall, the respondents assessed positively the remote electronic voting system they had used. Regarding the usability of the system, 82.7% of the interviewees were satisfied. Those that criticized the system pointed to difficulties in finding the email message they had received with details regarding the election, to prefer that this message had been sent from an institutional email address, and to issues with the web browser interface or the need to install a browser add-on for the system to work properly.

With regard to the information provided about the voting process, 70.6% of the interviewees did not retain much more than basic information about the system (username, password, and URI). Still, 84.4% considered to be perfectly clear with the information received.

On the composition of the system development team, there was unanimity among respondents that the team should include elements from the legal area, in addition to elements from the IT area. In what concerns the need to integrate into the team elements from other areas, 61.1% of respondents did not consider that additional areas of knowledge were in need in the development team, 16.7% claimed that it would make sense to integrate elements from psychology, and 11.1% suggested the inclusion of elements from sociology and ethics.

Given that the Portuguese Data Protection National Commission had issued an opinion on the system, we tried to find out if voters knew it and how they regarded it. Only 9.8% knew the opinion and its contents, 78.4% were unaware of its existence, and 11.8% knew of its existence, but were unaware of its contents. After informing the voters about that opinion and its positive result, 74.5% of the participants considered it very positive and important for promoting confidence in the system.

In order to increase the transparency of the voting process, the system allows the provision to the voter of a numeric code for confirmation of the vote cast in the system. Questioned about this system's feature, 48.6% of the interviewees stated to be unaware of it. Among those who knew it, 21.6% resorted to this mechanism and verified that the system correctly indicated the voting option they had expressed, and 16.2% did not experiment the functionality. Concerning the importance of this mechanism, 65.7% of the interviewees considered it an important measure, 14.3% classified it as a minor feature. However, of the remaining 20% respondents who disagreed with the usefulness of the measure, 8.6% peremptorily argued that this feature might indicate an insecure system, since it allowed to associate codes, to voters and to votes.

The second theme of the interview script concerned the participants' opinions on EVS before using an e-voting system and after its use. Regarding the opinion prior to the use of such a system, 44.6% stated they had never thought about it before the use, 28.6% indicated having a favorable opinion, and 26.8% reported some suspicion and apprehension. After using the system, 93.0% of the respondents considered that they felt so confident using EVS as if they had used the traditional voting system. This view is reinforced by the fact that only 8.3% of the participants would select the traditional voting system if they could choose between the two systems. Curiously, when questioned whether the vote may be more compromised when EVS are used instead of the traditional system (in the sense of a third party knowing the voting option of a voter), 14.6% of the interviewees considered that the vote is no more compromised in the case of e-voting, 43.8% thought it may be more compromised, and 33.3% stated that although personally they did not think so, they conceived that this could be the understanding of other people.

Regarding the main requirements that an e-voting system should satisfy (the third theme of the interview), the respondents provided 118 indications categorized as illustrated in Table 2.

Table 2. Main Requirements of e-Voting Systems

Requirement	n	%
Anonymity	38	32.2
Mobility	27	22.9
Integrity	17	14.4
Usability	14	11.9
Accessibility and Convenience	12	10.2
Verifiability, Auditability and Certifiability	8	6.8
Singularity	2	1.7

Still concerning the requirements of EVS, we asked if respondents had verified or tried to verify if the remote electronic voting system that they had used met the requirements they pointed to. Only 11.1% stated they had examined, albeit very superficially, some of the requirements. The remaining 88.9% asserted they had not carried out any verification.

The fourth theme relates to the possibility of using EVS at the national level. With regard to the use of REVS, half of the participants believed that their use would not be desirable, mainly because there is a set of requirements that can not be met due to the existence of various risks, such as those related to the technical infrastructure, coercion, large scale, and voters' authentication. On the other hand, 35.4% of respondents considered that using EVS would be possible and 4.2% considered it possible, but as an alternative method operating in parallel to the traditional voting system. In the case of PEVS, 23.9% replied negatively to the application of these systems since they would add little value to the voting process, 41.3% provided a positive response, 4.3% considered it possible, but as an alternative method to the traditional voting system, and 30.4% had no opinion.

We also asked participants if they would be willing to give up of some requirements, such as anonymity, integrity of the vote, or uncoercibility, in order to have mobility, increased speed, and reduced costs with the voting process. Surprisingly, 75.6% of respondents answered affirmatively.

The fifth and final theme was related to the factors that would influence voters' confidence in EVS.

With regard to the availability of the system source code, 40.4% of respondents believed that the code should be closed, except for the auditors, 25.0% advocated open source systems, and 25.0% stated to be indifferent.

On the nature of EVS certifications, and given that the Data Protection National Commission's opinion reflected a strictly legal assessment without relying on a technical (IT) evaluation of the system, 77.6% participants stated that the legal evaluation should be complemented by a technical evaluation, while 22.4% considered that the technical evaluation was not needed or was not essential.

Another question aimed to establish if the electoral commission which promotes and monitors the electoral process could influence the confidence in the system, i.e., if the reputation and idoneity of its members could instill in voters greater confidence. Faced with this question the opinions were divided: 56.3% of respondents believed that this could be the case, while 43.8% considered that those were independent factors.

Interviewees were also asked whether they were aware of negative past experiences with other EVS and whether these negative experiences could shake the confidence of voters, particularly during the debate on the possible adoption of EVS at national level. Approximately 70% of respondents were not aware of those experiences. Faced with factual accounts of some of the experiments, 70.2% reported that such information might adversely affect public opinion and demolish any attempt to implement EVS at national level. On the other hand, 29.8% of the respondents believed that each system should be treated as a separate system, and although these experiences might be used as political weapons in a debate on the adoption of EVS, people would be able to distinguish between the situations.

Regarding the main factors that influence the confidence of respondents in EVS, the analysis of the interviews led to the aggregated results in Table 3.

Table 3. Main Factors Influencing Trust in EVS

Trust Factor	n	%
Different types of elections require different security levels	38	33.6
Audits to the system and certifications awarded to the system	21	18.6
Reputation and competency of the system development team	13	11.5
Various uses of the system without errors	12	10.6
Monitoring committee of the electoral process	11	9.7
Information and explanations about the system	8	7.1
Tests made to the system	5	4.4
Guarantee of anonymity	3	2.7
Transparency of the system	1	0.9
Open source code	1	0.9

6   Discussion

The positive assessment of the electronic voting system is supported in a large majority of respondents that claimed to trust the system. To this general opinion we may oppose the fact that a significant number of respondents did not check if the system met the requirements, was unaware of certain features of the system and that the system had been certified by the Data Protection National Commission. The explanation for this apparent inconsistency may rest on participants placing their confidence in the system development team and in the electoral commission, and on the acknowledgment that they did not have major concerns on using the system given the limited scope of the elections.

Before using the system, many participants had not formed an opinion on e-voting since they had never reflected on this subject, others indicated they had some apprehension about this particular technology and the risks it entails, still others were more receptive to the use of e-voting, perhaps because they had greater propensity to the use of IT. After using the system, the majority of participants were more confident in this type of systems, with less apprehension, but revealed that after going through the process it remained the feeling that the freedom to vote may be more compromised in EVS than in the traditional system. Therefore, a perception that when using EVS something can go wrong and that the vote that was expressed may be revealed and so the voter may suffer the consequences does persist.

The possibility of using e-voting in broader elections also raises divisions. On the one hand, there is a more conservative line of participants that advocated a gradual transition, from the traditional voting system to PEVS and then to REVS. On the other hand, a large proportion of respondents considered that PEVS are no longer attractive. Finally, there is a large group that thinks it is very difficult to use REVS in national elections.

By comparing the five core requirements of EVS that were extracted from the literature with the five requirements most cited by participants we find significant differences, as illustrated in Table 4.

Table 4. Comparison of Core Requirements of EVS

Rank	Literature	Study
1	Authenticity	Anonymity
2	Singularity	Mobility
3	Anonymity	Integrity
4	Integrity	Usability
5	Uncoercibility	Accessibility and Convenience

Although a definitive conclusion might not be possible (the ordering of requirements extracted from the literature resulted from the authors' interpretation of the relative importance researchers attribute to the requirements and the participants' ordering is limited to the case analyzed), we find that only two requirements are common. Albeit respondents may have taken for granted certain requirements, it stands out the importance attributed to anonymity and mobility, as well as the emphasis placed on REVS usability, a requirement less stressed in the literature.

The issues initially proposed as potentially influencing voters' confidence in EVS were expressed by participants as relevant to the process of building trust in EVS.

The most cited factor by voters during the interviews was the scope of the elections: elections with different scope and relevance demand different levels of trust in the system, so that the degree of confidence in the system will vary with the election in question.

In the second place come system audits and certifications. For the other factors which influence confidence in EVS opinions are divided. One example concerns if the system source code should be open or closed. A large group of participants argued that the code should be closed, except for audit purposes. Another significant group of respondents (closest to the IT area) only conceived confidence in this type of systems if the source code was open.

The factors that were identified as influencing trust in EVS are inherently different. The first factor – the scope of the election – acts as a moderator of trust: the larger the electorate and the more important elections are the greater the demands of voters to trust the system. Other factors, such as the system development team and the monitoring committee, represent sources of trust, i.e., entities that directly instill voters with trust in the system. The remaining factors may ne viewed as carriers of trust, i.e., technologies and procedures that convey confidence in the system. These carriers serve as propagators or transmitters of trust from the sources of trust. Hence, in the case of audits and certifications, the sources of trust are the agencies that assess and certify the electronic voting systems, the audit reports and the certificates are the vehicles (carriers) of trust of those sources.

Applying this interpretation regarding the nature of trust factors leads to the characterization shown in Table 5, where each factor was classified in terms of type (moderator, source of trust, or carrier of trust). For the carrier factors, we suggest the corresponding sources of trust.

Underlying these factors there is a set of beliefs held by people. For instance, regarding the scope of the election there is the belief that elections with higher number of voters have higher levels of complexity and increased risks. Given this escalation, voters require stronger evidence that the system remains worthy of trust. The case of open source code is also illustrative: it can be argued that underlying this factor is the belief that if the system source code is made publicly available, the community as a whole (actually a very limited and specialized subset of that community) may scrutinize it, or if an individual of that community modifies the code, the community will detect it and react against the modification. An alternative belief is that if the code is open is can be more easily exploited by malevolent individuals who will then be able to attack the system. According to this belief, source code should be carefully protected, namely by keeping it closed.

Table 5. Characterization of EVS Trust Factors

Trust Factor	Type	Source of Trust
Different types of elections require different security levels	moderator	-
Audits to the system and certifications awarded to the system	carrier	audit agencies certification agencies
Reputation and competency of the system development team	source	-
Various uses of the system without errors	carrier	past voting communities
Monitoring committee of the electoral process	source	-
Information and explanations about the system	carrier	monitoring committee development team
Tests made to the system	carrier	system testers
Guarantee of anonymity	carrier	monitoring committee development team
Transparency of the system	carrier	development team
Open source code	carrier	community at large

In the end, we may be able to reduce the phenomenon of trust in EVS to the credibility that voters attach to the sources of trust and to the reliability they recognize carriers of trust possess. The sources of trust that a voter chooses and the carriers of trust that a voter favors both depend on the beliefs of the voter. Isolating these beliefs, identifying the sources of trust, and assessing the carriers of trust may be the way to understand the degree of confidence voters place in an e-voting system and to provide the means to build and deploy trustworthy EVS.

7   Conclusion

In this study we identified the factors that influence voters' confidence in electronic voting systems by undertaking a case study on the use of a remote electronic voting system in which 51 voters were interviewed.

The main contribution of this work is the list of factors that voters consider influence their confidence in EVS, in order of relevance and characterized according to the role they play in the process of instilling trust in voters. Another contribution of this study is the set of requirements that respondents claimed to be essential to EVS to satisfy, and its comparison with the set of requirements extracted from the literature.

The findings of the case study embody a set of recommendations to be taken into account in the implementation of voting processes using IT systems.

We also argue that by considering the nature of each of the factors – moderator of the degree of trust, source of trust, or carrier of trust – we are better equipped to understand the degree of confidence that voters place in this type of systems, as well as the processes underlying the formation of voters' attitudes in what concerns the adoption and use of EVS.

The work enriches the literature by focusing on the factors that electors favor as definers of their confidence in EVS. This complements several propositions of EVS architectures found in the literature that seek to address specific security requirements from a technical point of view. Hence, the findings provide context for the use of EVS by voters. By knowing what fosters trust on EVS from the perspective of voters, we will be in a better position to design trustworthy voting processes and systems, as well as to devise improved procedures to verify and audit their technical properties.

The study has several limitations. Although it is not easy to find voters who have already used remote electronic voting systems, a larger number of interviews would allow a deeper understanding of the processes and conditions that lead to the establishment of a relationship of trust between voters and EVS.

Another limitation relates to the characteristics of the case study, since the elections analyzed refer to a small universe of voters, have a restrict scope and were promoted within a controlled and culturally homogeneous environment. In addition, the participants in this study are extremely qualified individuals with a high cultural level, so this group of voters is not representative of the electorate.

This paper reports an exploratory study on EVS trust factors which leaves open many opportunities for future work. We restricted the study's subjects to voters and it would be worthy to obtain a view of other stakeholders in the process of EVS adoption, such as developers and auditors, and to find out whether the factors that these groups recognize as influencing trust in e-voting differ from those found in this study.

Another work would be to build a variance model based on the trust factors identified and test the causal relationships with a research design that involved a representative sample of the electorate at the national level.

A more qualitative research would be to build a model to explain the process of formation, maintenance, and deterioration of stakeholders' trust in EVS.

Besides these proposals for future work, there are specific issues that arose during the study and that require a better explanation, such as the reasons that led some voters to consider that the vote might be more compromised in EVS than in the traditional voting system and the extent to which voters are willing to sacrifice certain requirements of the voting process in favor of other requirements.

These are research opportunities worth pursuing so that we can better understand trust in e-voting systems and to improve the chances of EVS being successful.

References

1. Dill, D.L., Schneier, B., Simons, B.: Voting and Technology: Who Gets to Count Your Vote? Communications of the ACM 46(8), 29–31 (2003)
2. Granneman, S.: Electronic Voting Debacle. Security (2003),
   http://www.securityfocus.com/columnists/198
3. Mercuri, R.: Electronic Vote Tabulation: Checks & Balances. PhD Thesis, University of Pennsylvania, USA (2001)
4. Schneier, B.: Getting Out the Vote: Why is it so hard to run an honest election? San Francisco Chronicle, October 31 (2004)
5. Schneier, B.: What's wrong with electronic voting machines? OpenDemocracy (2004),
   http://www.opendemocracy.net/media-voting/article_2213.jsp
6. Schneier, B.: Did Your Vote Get Counted? (2006),
   http://www.schneier.com/essay-133.html
7. Antoniou, A., Korakas, C., Manolopoulos, C., Panagiotaki, A., Sofotassios, D., Spirakis, P., Stamatiou, Y.C.: A Trust-Centered Approach for Building E-Voting Systems. In: Wimmer, M.A., Scholl, J., Grönlund, Å. (eds.) EGOV. LNCS, vol. 4656, pp. 366–377. Springer, Heidelberg (2007)
8. Grove, J.: ACM Statement on Voting Systems. Communications of the ACM 7(10), 69–70 (2004)
9. Randell, B., Ryan, P.Y.A.: Voting Technologies and Trust. IEEE Security and Privacy 4(5), 50–56 (2006)
10. Jones, B.: A Report on the Feasibility of Internet Voting, California Internet Voting Task Force, Sacramento, USA (2000)
11. McDaniel, P., Aviv, A., Balzarotti, D., Banks, G., Blaze, M., Butler, K.: EVEREST – Evaluation and Validation of Election-Related Equipment, Standards and Testing (2007),
    http://www.patrickmcdaniel.org/pubs/everest.pdf
12. Jones, D.W.: Voting and Elections, The University of Iowa, USA (2001),
    http://www.divms.uiowa.edu/~jones/voting/
13. ACE: Opportunities, risks and challenges of e-voting. ACE Project, The Electoral Knowledge Network (2001), http://aceproject.org/
14. Antunes, P. (ed.): Voto Electrónico – Discussão técnica dos seus problemas e oportunidades, Edições Sílabo, Lisboa (2008)
15. CE: Legal, Operational and Technical Standards for e-Voting. Recommendation Rec. (2004) of the Council of Europe. Council of Europe Publishing (2005)
16. Crane, R.E., Keller, A.M., Dechert, A., Cherlin, E., Mertz, D.: A Deeper Look: Rebutting Shamos on e-Voting (2005), http://www.acm.org/crossroads/xrds2-4/voting.html
17. Cranor, L.F., Cytron, R.K.: Sensus: A Security-Conscious Electronic Polling System for the Internet. In: Proceedings of the Hawai International Conference on System Sciences, Wailea (1997)
18. Frith, D.: E-voting security: hope or hype? Network Security 11, 14–16 (2007)
19. Gritzalis, D.A.: Principles and requirements for a secure e-voting system. Computers & Security 21(6), 539–556 (2002)
20. Hall, J.L.: Policy Mechanisms for Increasing Transparency in Electronic Voting. PhD Dissertation. University of California at Berkeley, USA (2008)
21. Mercuri, R.: Questions for Voting System Vendors (2000),
    http://www.notablesoftware.com/checklists.html

22. Monteiro, A., Soares, N., Oliveira, R.M., Antunes, P.: Sistemas Electrónicos de Votação. Technical Report, Universidade de Lisboa, Portugal (2001)
23. Neumann, P.G.: Security Criteria for Electronic Voting. In: Proceedings of the 16th National Computer Security Conference, Baltimore (1993)
24. Shamos, I.: Electronic Voting – Evaluating the Threat. In: Proceedings of the Third Conference on Computers, Freedom and Privacy, Burlingame, pp. 3.18–3.25 (1993)
25. Strauss, C., Mertz, D., Dopp, K.: Electronic Voting System Best Practices (2005), http://electionmathematics.org/em-voting-systems/Best_Practices_US.pdf
26. Neumann, G.: Special Issue: The problems and potentials of voting systems. Communications of the ACM 47(10) (2004)
27. OpenRightsGroup: May 2007 Election Report – Findings of the Open Rights Group Election Observation Mission in Scotland an England (2007), http://www.openrightsgroup.org/wp-
   · content/uploads/org_election_report.pdf
28. Mayer, R.C., Davis, J.H., Schoorman, F.D.: An Integrative Model of Organizational Trust. Academy of Management Review 20(3), 709–734 (1995)
29. Schlienger, T., Teufel, S.: Information Security Culture: The socio-cultural dimension in information security management. In: Ghonaimy, A., El-Hadidi, M.T., Aslan, H.K. (eds.) Proceedings of the IFIP TC11 International Conference on Information Security, pp. 191–202. Kluwer (2002)
30. Brei, V.A., Rossi, C.A.V.: Confiança, valor percebido e lealdade em trocas relacionais de serviço: um estudo com usuários de Internet Banking no Brasil. Revista de Administração Contemporânea 9, 145–168 (2005)
31. Mercuri, R.: A better ballot box? IEEE Spectrum 39(10), 46–50 (2002)

ERP Post-adoption: Use and Value –
An Empirical Study on Portuguese SMEs

Pedro Ruivo, Tiago Oliveira, and Miguel Neto

ISEGI, Universidade Nova de Lisboa, Campus de Campolide, 1070-312 Lisbon, Portugal
{pruivo,toliveira,mneto}@isegi.unl.pt

Abstract. Both academics and practitioners have a growing interest in information technology (IT) value. This is particularly important in cases of systems such as enterprise resource planning (ERP), as the use of these systems involves significant investment. In this study we seek to measure and examine determinants of ERP use and value. Based on the diffusion of innovation (DOI) literature to explain ERP use and resource-based view (RBV) theory to explain ERP value, we develop a research model, on which nine hypotheses are postulated for measuring ERP in post-adoption stages and its consequences on Portuguese small and medium enterprise (SME) performance. The model was tested through structural equation modelling (SEM) on a dataset of 134 firms web-surveyed. We find that compatibility, best practices, complexity, efficiency, training, and competitive pressure are important determinants of ERP use. Together with use, collaboration and analytics capabilities will contribute to 'ERP value'. Even though this study provides insight into how SMEs use and extract value from ERP, unlike the typical focus on ERP adoption reported in the literature, this study focuses on post-adoption stages, linking actual usage with value creation.

Keywords: ERP, use, value, post-adoption, diffusion of innovation, resource-based view, SMEs, Portugal.

1 Introduction

Innovation is more and more identified as the transformative force that creates and shapes new economies in today's digital world. Firms often adopt information technology (IT) to improve their competiveness and business performance (Ho and Tai 2004). Davenport (1998) qualified *enterprise resource planning* (ERP) systems as the most important development in the enterprise use of IT. By supporting the execution of operational transactions and advanced planning; alongside real–time data access, ERP's main purpose is to integrate as many enterprise functions as possible (Klaus et al. 2000). It is known that the European economy is composed mainly of small and medium sized enterprises (SMEs), and Portugal adheres to this profile. Although SMEs are fundamentally different compared to large enterprises, ERP systems play a critical role in both segments, as the need to manage both information and managerial resources are important factors to increase productivity and gain a competitive advantage (Hitt *et al.* 2002, Buonanno *et al.* 2005, Raymond and

H. Rahman et al. (Eds.): MCIS 2012, LNBIP 129, pp. 67–81, 2012.
© Springer-Verlag Berlin Heidelberg 2012

Uwizeyemungu 2007, Chuang *et al.* 2009). As suggested in the literature, there is a great interest among researchers and practitioners in measuring the bottom-line benefits of these systems. Since the impact of IT systems on a firm's performance is mostly long term and indirect, measures of the value to business are linked primarily to system usage (Devaraj and Kohli 2003, Nicolaou 2004, Zhu and Kraemer 2005). This area of investigation explores an alternative way to understand and measure IT value by studying ERP in its post-adoption stages; use, and value. In this study we develop and test a model based on the *diffusion of innovation* (DOI) model and *resource-based view* (RBV) theory to explain ERP use and value. The theoretical perspectives are outlined in the next section. The appropriateness of the model is then tested using a sample of 134 Portuguese firms. Findings support the model.

2   Literature Review

Nicolaou and Bhattacharya (2008) find out that there is a positive relationship between ERP implementation and firm efficiencies and pointed out that "firms which implement an ERP system must be conscious of and circumspect enough to realize that ERPs are different from other IT systems. They bring about strategic changes to firms' business processes and as such their deployment presents not a finale but the start of post-implementation activities" critical when competitive advantage is a goal to pursuit. Prior evidence suggests that ERP benefits accrue over periods of time as opposed to one-time windfall gains and that a time-lag of few years is necessary before ERP adopters begin to demonstrate positive differential (Nicolaou, 2004).

Whereas ERP implementation refers to the stage of system planning, configuration, testing, and going-live, ERP use means ERP utilization. It refers to the experience of managing the operation of the system software throughout the system's post-implementation stages (Nah *et al.* 2004; Nicolaou, 2004). In accordance with literature (Nicolaou and Bhattacharya, 2006; Zhu and Kraemer, 2005) we consider ERP to be a type of innovation that is implanted in a firm's core business processes in order to leverage performance. Not only does it extend basic business and streamline integration with suppliers and customers, it also directs system usage to the firm's performance. DeLone and McLean (2003) model aims to explain user satisfaction as the key measure of computer system success, whereas Rogers (1995) DOI model aims to explain and predict if and how an innovation is used within a social system, with regard to performance at the firm level. Accordingly with Oliveira and Martins (2011) study, both DOI and Technology-Organization-Environment (TOE) framework explains firm performance at firm level. While TOE dependent construct is based on likelihood to adopt IT, DOI is based on implementation success for IT use. Research conducted by Bradford and Florin (2003) verifies DOI determinants regarding successful ERP usage. Taking the above reflections, it ours believe that DOI has the potential to provide a more favourable framework that covers the IT adoption processes of SMEs, reflecting the SMEs heterogeneity.

Whereas ERP use refers to the production stage of system usage among firms actually using ERP in their daily business activities, ERP value refers to firms' ability to utilize ERP to create a competitive advantage. It refers to the ERP impact on a firm's performance, throughout the system life in the post-adoption stages (Nicolaou and Bhattacharya, 2008; Rhodes *et al*, 2009). Since ERP value relies on how firms strategically exploit the system, firms' performance in a competitive environment is a subject that draws much attention and attempts to build explanatory theories. While Industrial Organization (IO) theory states that external pressures and the ability to respond to it are the major determinants of firm's success, RBV states that firm specifics sets of resources determine firm's performance. Although both IO and RBV are interested in competitive advantage approach to strategic management, RBV can explain sustained advantages (Hedman and Kalling, 2003). In the IS literature, the RBV has been used to analyse IT capabilities as a resource and to explain IT business value. That is, IT business value depends on the extent to which IT is used in the key activities of the firm. The greater the use, the more likely the firm is to develop unique capabilities from its IT business applications (Bharadwaj 2000, Zhu and Kraemer, 2005, Antero and Riis 2011, Ruivo *et al.* 2012). Studies by Hedman and Kalling (2003) and Fosser *et al.* (2008) used RBV and extended Mata *et al.*'s (1995) framework for organizational and business resources, concluding that ERP systems are IT resources that can lead to sustained, competitive advantages. With this in mind, our theoretical model for ERP value will include variables that input value to ERP and positively impact the predisposition to extract value from the system.

3   Research Model and Hypothesis

In this section we present the model, explain the key elements, and postulate the hypotheses. Our model focuses on two post-adoption stages; use and value, where RBV key activity in post-adoption is value creation through use rather than simply adoption and penetration (Zhu and Kraemer 2005). Our model, illustrated in Figure 1, suggests that DOI will influence ERP use and its actual usage contributes to ERP value, which in turn, has an impact on the firm's performance (Devaraj and Kohli 2003). The upper tier shows the extent of ERP use, influenced by six specific factors embedded in the DOI context: compatibility, complexity, efficiency, best practices, training, and, competitive pressure. Toward the bottom we postulate that ERP leverages unique characteristics of the IT to improve business performance. We define as unique: collaboration and analytics. Together with usage, we believe that these two IT-enhanced capabilities will contribute to ERP value.

Based on DOI literature, compatibility and complexity have shown consistent associations with IS adoption. O'Leary (2000) and Bradford and Florin (2003) report that best practices, training, and competitive pressure are also important dimensions for ERP use. We contribute to this research by including the level of transactional efficiency as an important dimension that will influence ERP usage and therefore postulate six hypotheses. From the RBV perspective, some (albeit few) researchers have shown amount of use to be associated with firm performance (Mabert *et al.* 2001). We contribute to this research by considering collaboration and analytics to be additional important dimensions that will influence ERP value. Justification of our nine hypotheses follows.

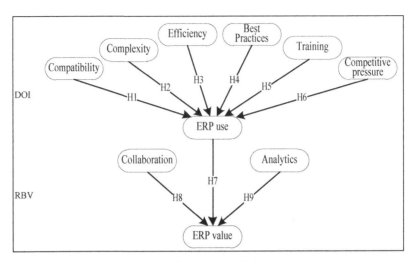

Fig. 1. Research Model

Compatibility

Compatibility is measured by the degree to which the ERP system matches IT features, such as compatibility with hardware and other software. Bradford and Florin (2003) and Elbertsen *et al.* (2006), concluded that the degree of compatibility of ERP systems with existing software and hardware will have a positive relationship with implementation success (system adoption and use). We thus formulate the first hypotheses:

Hypothesis 1. Firms having systems with greater compatibility are more likely to use ERP more.

Complexity

Cooper and Zmud's (1990) research indicates that system usage enhances job performance. Studies conducted by Kositanurit *et al.* (2006) and Chang *et al.* (2011) conclude that ERP complexity is a major factor affecting user performance. Bradford and Florin (2003) concluded that ERP complexity is a critical factor for successful implementation. When it is not easy for users to get the ERP to do what they wish it to do, frustration and unwillingness to use the system generally result. When users are comfortable using ERP, it scales up the users' knowledge of the system and, consequently, their skills in manipulating the system in effective ways. Furthermore, it prepares users to comprehend the system trends sufficiently and comprehensively (Chian-Son, 2005). Based upon this, the second hypothesis is:

Hypothesis 2. Firms having systems that are perceived to be complex are more likely to use ERP less.

Efficiency

Bendoly and Kaefer (2004) assessed that transactional efficiency on data posting and found that its communication over the ERP improves the firm's overall performance. Rajagopal (2002) found that transactional efficiency has a direct influence on ERP use. Business process benefits of ERP investment include transactional efficiency, where reliability effectiveness on the application improves user confidence. Along the same lines, Gattiker and Goodhue (2005) found that coordination improvements and efficiency are significant benefits of ERP use. Taking this background into account, we construct our third hypothesis:

Hypothesis 3. Firms having systems of greater transactional efficiency are more likely to use ERP.

Best Practice
From the perspective of business process reengineering, there are two main options in implementing ERP systems: modify (customization) the ERP package to suit the firm's requirements (with high costs), or the implementation of an ERP package with minimum deviation from the standard settings (with lower costs) (Davenport, 1998). According to Velcu (2007) and Chou and Chang (2008) the reason for adopting 'best practice' is the belief that ERP design does things in the right way. In line with Wenrich and Ahmad (2009), firms that implement industry best practices dramatically reduce risk and time consuming project tasks such as configuration, documentation, testing, and training. Thus, we postulate that firms that opt to implement ERP based on standard best practices will use the system more. Based on these considerations, we formulate the fourth hypothesis:

Hypothesis 4. Firms with standard best-practices in their systems are more likely to use ERP.

Training
Several researchers, including O'Leary (2000) and Bradford and Florin (2003), state that one of the main determinants for successfully adopting, using, and benefiting from ERP systems is the training of the users. The state of preparedness of users to meet situations and carry out a planned sequence of actions without upstream errors has an instantly positive impact on business. Providing knowledge and skills to employees on how to use the system will improve familiarity and boost its use. We therefore postulate that firms with a higher degree of training tend to enjoy greater readiness to use ERP. In line with research, we construct the fifth hypothesis:

Hypothesis 5. Firms with greater users training are more likely to use ERP.

Competitive Pressure
Competitive pressure has long been recognized in the innovation diffusion literature as an important driver of technology diffusion (Bradford and Florin 2003, Zhu and Kraemer 2005). These studies have shown that innovation diffusion is accelerated by the competitive pressure in the environment. Thus, we postulate that competitive pressure plays an important role in pushing firms toward using ERP systems. In line with research, we construct the sixth hypothesis:

Hypothesis 6. Firms facing higher competitive pressure are more likely to use ERP.

ERP Use

The link between ERP use and ERP value is a measure of how users work with the system and of decision-making based on analytical indicators. To explain the connection between usage and value we grounded our proposition on RBV; the greater the extent of ERP use, the greater the likelihood that firms will create capabilities that are rare, inimitable, valuable, and sustainable, thereby contributing to value creation. A study conducted by Shahin and Ainin (2011) found that user fit on ERP is critical in explaining the ERP usage, and a successful adaptation with firms' processes and data flow from other IS systems makes ERP worthwhile. With ERP systems (and their integration capability with other systems) firms can form a specific resource that guides both internal and external collaboration and provides the repository to perform business analyses. As a result, it is only when firms are actually using ERP systems to conduct business that ERP can have an impact on firm performance. Obviously, without system usage it is impossible for ERP to generate any impact on firm performance. Zhu and Kraemer, 2005, and Devaraj and Kohli, 2003) all demonstrate that there is a strong link between system use and system impact. In line with literature, we formulate the seventh hypothesis as:

Hypothesis 7. Firms with greater ERP use are more likely to generate higher ERP value.

Collaboration

Calisir and Calisir (2004), Gattiker and Goodhue (2005), and Ruivo and Neto (2011) studies support the conclusion that ERP systems help users to collaborate; up, down, and across their department, company, and industry ecosystem, increasing their productivity and the health of their firms and business partners. ERP is a kind of gateway to unique functions. That is, ERP is the *sine qua non* factor for others (both humans and applications) to collaborate with ERP – from meeting service-level agreements to promoting enterprise performance. ERP systems provide users with a structured communication channel with the right information at the right time, resulting in increased efficiency and effectiveness. We believe that partnering with ERP and cross-group collaboration amplifies the ERP value. Therefore, and in line with RVB theory, we postulate the eighth hypothesis:

Hypothesis 8. Firms' greater collaboration systems are positively associated with higher ERP value.

Analytics

Davenport and Harris (2007) state that "analytics is not new" but that not many firms give them priority. Firms generally use business analytics to leverage the investment they have made in ERP systems over the last few years. In seeking to gain competiveness, firms use integrated data and set analytics as a strategic initiative. The common data model and visibility across functional departments allows firms' metrics to be unified and consistent. Although ERP systems are essentially transaction-focused on internal data, those firms that have ERP-embedded analytics capabilities can easily and quickly use data for managerial decision making and seize an advantage in their pursuit of sustainable performance (Chiang 2009, Ruivo and Neto 2011). In line with RVB theory and literature, we believe that analytics provides users with unique business insight information, and therefore postulate the ninth hypothesis:

Hypothesis 9. Firms having greater analytics capacity embedded in their system are positively associated with higher ERP value.

ERP Value Measurement

A study conducted by Zhang *et al.* (2005) and Bradford and Florin (2003) concluded that ERP value output can be measured by user satisfaction. Studies conducted by Park et al. (2007) and Chang *et al.* (2011) defined ERP value proposition as: individual productivity, customer satisfaction, and management control. In our study, we assess the positive impact of an ERP system on firm performance by user satisfaction, individual productivity, customer satisfaction, and management control.

4   Research Method and Data

A survey methodology is proposed for data collection to validate the research model and test its nine hypotheses. Each survey item-question was reviewed for content validity by ERP experts (three academics and two consultants). The initial questionnaires were pilot tested on 10 firms and some items were revised for clarity. The finalized questionnaire was designed to be answered in 15 minutes (Malhotra and Birks 2007). With the assistance of International Data Corporation (IDC) we conducted a web survey during September and October 2011. To ensure the generalization of the survey results, the random sampling was stratified by firm size (small and medium; between 10 and 250 employees) and by industry (finance, distribution, manufacturing, and professional services). In total, 400 Portuguese firms received the email survey, and 134 valid responses were obtained (33.5%). Table 1 shows the sample characteristics, where respondents were chief executive officers, managers, and firm owners, representing a wide range of industry types, suggesting the good quality of the data source.

Table 1. The characteristics of the Portuguese sample (N=134)

Characteristics	Frequency	Percentage
Industry type		
Distribution	38	28.4
Manufacturing	32	23.9
Finance	33	24.6
Services	31	23.1
total	134	100.0
Respondent type		
CEO, owner	28	20.9
IT/IS manager	37	27.6
Finance manager	27	20.1
Sales manager	31	23.1
Manufacturing	11	8.2
total	134	100.0

The constructs were operationalized and measurement items used on the basis of a literature review (shown in Appendix A), following a reflective model. While the ERP use construct was measured by two question items calling for responses in percentages, all other constructs were measured by three question items responding on a five-point Likert scale. The control variables used were size and industry type.

5   Data Analysis

We conducted a structural equation model to empirically assess the constructs theorized above, because our propose is to exam the validity of the constructs and does not require normal distribution for the variables, we used the partial least squares (PLS) as implemented in the software SmartPLS[1]. We performed the Kolmogorov-Smirnov test and confirmed that none of the items measured are distributed normally (p<0.001). CB3, CX1, TN1, CP2, and ERPU1 question-items of appendix A were excluded from our research model after the PLS model estimation due low loadings. Table 2 shows that except for BP1 (0.691) all other items have loadings above 0.7 and are significant at (p<0.001). In accordance with Chin (1998), factor loadings should be at least 0.6 and preferably greater than 0.7. We therefore retain all items shown in Table 2.

Furthermore, Table 2 shows that composite reliability (CR) and average variance extracted (AVE) for each construct are above the cut-off of 0.7 and 0.5, respectively. In accordance with Hair et al. (1998), the CR measures the internal consistency of the construct and the extent to which each item explains the corresponding construct and the AVE signifies the amount of indicator variance that is accounted for by the corresponding construct. In summary, our measurement model satisfies reliability and validity criteria. Consequently, the constructs developed can be used to test the conceptual model and its hypotheses.

The results are shown in Figure 2, where path coefficients with significance levels (t-statistics) are presented in parentheses, as well the R^2 values for dependent constructs. Analysis of the hypotheses was based on the examination of the standardized paths. For 'ERP use', all six DOI determinants – compatibility, complexity, efficiency, best practices, training, and competitive pressure – have positive and statistically significant paths leading to the dependent construct. The path associated with complexity is statistically significant and negative, as we expected, and therefore, all hypotheses (H1 to H6) dealing with 'ERP use' are supported. In addition, the model shows a significantly positive link from usage to value (0.210), thereby supporting H7. Although collaboration (H8) has a stronger relationship (0.518) with 'ERP value' than analytics (H9), both H8 and H9 are supported.

---

[1] SmartPLS is a software application for (graphic) path modelling with latent variables (LVP). The partial least squares (PLS)-method is used for the LVP-analysis. More can be found at http://www.smartpls.de

Table 2. PLS factor loading, composite reliability, and average variance extracted (N=134).

Construct / Item	Loading	t-Stat*	CR	AVE
Compatibility			0.958	0.919
CB1	0.925	7.360		
CB2	0.991	12.141		
Complexity			0.925	0.860
CX2	0.936	97.797		
CX3	0.919	93.032		
Efficiency			0.847	0.649
EF1	0.764	32.003		
EF2	0.768	26.920		
EF3	0.880	61.194		
Best Practices			0.834	0.628
BP1	0.796	33.578		
BP2	0.691	18.552		
BP3	0.880	60.196		
Training			0.957	0.917
TN2	0.954	269.978		
TN3	0.961	345.770		
Competitive Pressure			0.882	0.791
CP1	0.983	161.226		
CP3	0.784	23.648		
ERP Use			0.878	0.782
ERPU2	0.894	137.936		
ERPU3	0.875	84.041		
Collaboration			0.902	0.754
CO1	0.898	188.766		
CO2	0.887	156.042		
CO3	0.818	53.113		
Analytics			0.915	0.782
AN1	0.875	111.851		
AN2	0.903	103.026		
AN3	0.874	84.742		
ERP Value			0.886	0.664
ERPV1	0.747	52.967		
ERPV2	0.927	225.381		
ERPV3	0.862	87.722		
ERPV4	0.703	34.468		

Furthermore, through R^2 value examination the ascendants (Compatibility, Complexity, Efficiency, Best-practices, Training and Competitive Pressure) can explain 'ERP use' in 52.9% and (ERP use, Collaboration and Analytics) explain 'ERP value' in 58.2%, implying a good fit of the model. Overall, the above results provide support for the determinants shaping ERP usage in which firms adopt IT, and support our theoretical argument presented in Section 3, where we postulated that, as more firms use ERP (together with collaboration and analytics IT-enhanced capabilities) more value is created by ERP.

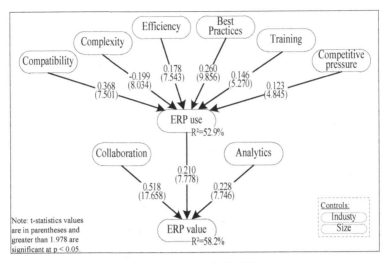

Fig. 2. Path model (N=134)

6 Discussion

The purpose of this paper is to identify the determinants that explain ERP usage and value among Portuguese SMEs. Empirical results support our theoretical model and all hypotheses are supported. Both academic and managerial implications are discussed below.

Among the DOI determinants, compatibility and best practices are found to have significant impact on the degree of 'ERP use', followed by complexity and transactional efficiency, while training and competitive pressure have less of an impact. That is, firms having systems that are more compatible with other hardware and software and also have low levels of customization in their ERP tend to use ERP more, as do firms with less complex systems and greater transactional efficiency. In turn, our interpretation for organizational elements is that firms with better trained users tend to use ERP more, as do firms facing higher levels of competitive pressure. Then, technological characteristics such compatibility and efficiency are dependent on the system stability, which requires time from IT and often from suppliers. ERP with fewer customizations (using standard protocols and best practices) is more fitted to users get familiar with ERP and make low investment in terms of training and proficiency in manipulating the system in effective ways and obtaining value from it. The results show that both users and functional manager's satisfaction are closely linked to the technological features of the ERP adoption (Bradford and Florin, 2003). Hence, the underlying reasoning is that technological product characteristics are the main drivers of ERP usage among Portuguese SMEs.

The 'ERP use' and 'ERP value' relationship are found to be significant and positive links from use to value, supporting our research design, in which use and value are important links in post-adoption stages and are evaluated together in one model. This means that higher degrees of ERP use are associated with firm performance. The underlying reasoning is that use is a missing link to value if not included (Devaraj and Kohli, 2003).

Both collaboration and analytics IT-enhanced capabilities are found to be significant and positive links to 'ERP value'. Firms with good collaboration systems contribute to value creation, as do firms with greater embedded analytics capacity. As discussed in Section 3, while collaborating with colleagues, system, suppliers, partners, and customers all increase productivity, analytics provides greater business insight for a better decision-making process. As a result, these two ERP capabilities help firms to improve performance because they are firm specific, difficult to imitate, and less mobile across firms, which is consistent with the RBV theory. Although both paths associated with collaboration and analytics are significantly positive, collaboration is much stronger. This is probably true because good compatible systems provide firms with a real-time collaboration framework that is fact oriented. The underlying reasoning would be that Portuguese firms perceive greater value and advantage in a collaboration system, because it provides a prolific field for internal organizational changes in order to improve firm performance. Furthermore, as SMEs face high levels of competitive pressure and hold great ERP transactional efficiency, business analytics becomes critical for gaining competitive advantage. It shows that firm's performance benefits typically accrue to ERP adoption only after some years of use (Buonanno et al., 2005; Nicolaou and Bhattacharya, 2006). These results are in line with Nicolaou and Bhattacharya, (2008) study where they have shown that firms who has been use ERP system to manage activities have a positive financial performance differential effect on firms' incremental return on investment (ROI), return on assets (ROA), return on sales ratio (ROS), the cost of goods sold over sales ratio, and the employee efficiency ratio. As well use ERP to extract business analytical data by enhancing ERP through the form of either add-ons[2] or upgrades, possessing an analytic capability in the form of a Business Intelligence (BI) system.

These results have several important implications for management. They offer a useful framework for managers to assess both the organizational and technological conditions under which ERP add value to business. As internet technologies diffuse through greater breadth and depth of use, and become necessities over time, IT-enhanced capabilities such collaboration and business analytics will become even more critical. In particular, our results reveal collaboration to be a major source of ERP value. Our model shows that support for transactional efficiency has been an important determinant to ERP use and that both collaboration and business analytics are important to ERP value. Therefore, we contribute to the research of IT value by including them.

Finally, our study also offers implications for software makers. While compatibility, transactional efficiency, and embedded best practices are perceived as ERP necessities, complexity (in opposite to familiarity and user-friendliness) is found to be an important inhibitor for ERP use, and collaboration and business analytics functionalities have emerged as important facilitators for ERP value.

---

[2] Add-ons are usually not original-vendor supported; they typically improve the ERP systems' functionality in customer specific ways. (Nicolaou and Bhattacharya, 2006)

7   Conclusion

This study explores the notion that ERP post-adoption is a key determinant of firm performance. Grounded on DOI and RBV, we develop and empirically evaluate a research model for assessing ERP use and value at the firm level. While these are usually studied separately, our study proposes that usage and value are closely associated with the post-adoption stages. Our model contributes to the literature by moving beyond dichotomous "adoption versus non-adoption", and link actual use to value creation. Our model also includes transactional efficiency as an important determinant for ERP usage, and together with collaboration and business analytics, contributes to firm performance. Empirical data collected via a web survey of Portuguese SMEs is used to check the measurement validity and to test the hypothesized research model. We find support for our research model; for ERP use, our study examines six DOI determinants (compatibility, complexity, efficiency, best practices, training, and, competitive pressure), in which some of these determinants play different roles for system usage. For ERP value (and consistent with RBV), our study demonstrates that the degree of ERP use and IT-enhanced capabilities, such collaboration and analytics, contribute to value creation from ERP. Moreover, our results indicate that careful attention must be paid to the capabilities that firms use to achieve competitive advantages through ERP systems, paying special attention to collaboration and analytics.

8   Future Work and Limitations

We believe that one limitation of this study is that it applies only to Portuguese SMEs. Future work should address cross-country variation in usage and value. Furthermore, since our dataset is cross-sectional in nature, we cannot analyse longitudinal processes, such as the evolution of ERP usage and value in a dynamic context. We cannot speak empirically on the issue of whether value is sustained, because this requires a longitudinal study. Probably post-adoption stages show a differential performance ratios such as on ROI and ROA depending on the number of years of ERP use (Nicolaou, 2004). Moreover, future work would be to study early stages (i.e. the implementation or shakedown phase) and later stages (post-adoption, i.e. the post-implementation or acceptance phase) (Chou and Chang, 2008; Häkkinen and Hilmola, 2008). Hence, our empirical results show only that relationships exist among the ERP use and value determinants.

References

Antero, M., Riis, P.H.: Strategic Management of Network Resources: A Case Study of an ERP Ecosystem. International Journal of Enterprise Information Systems 7(2), 18–33 (2011)

Bendoly, E., Kaefer, F.: Business technology complementarities: impacts of the presence and strategic timing of ERP on B2B e-commerce technology efficiencies. Omega 32(5), 395–405 (2004)

Bharadwaj, A.S.: A resource-based perspective on information technology capability and firm performance: An empirical investigation. MIS Quarterly 24(1), 169–196 (2000)

Bradford, M., Florin, J.: Examining the role of innovation diffusion factors on the implementation success of enterprise resource planning systems. International Journal of Accounting Information Systems 4(3), 205–225 (2003)

Buonanno, G., Faverio, P., Pigni, F., Ravarini, A., Sciuto, D., Tagliavini, M.: Factors affecting ERP system adoption: A comparative analysis between SMEs and large companies. Journal of Enterprise Information Management 18(1), 384–426 (2005)

Calisir, F., Calisir, F.: The Relation of Interface Usability Characteristics, Perceived Usefulness, and Perceived Ease of Use to End-User Satisfaction with Enterprise Resource Planning (ERP) Systems. Computers in Human Behavior 20(4), 505–515 (2004)

Chang, H.-H., Chou, H.-W., Yin, C.-P., Lin, C.I.: ERP Post-Implementation Learning, ERP Usage and Individual Performance Impact. In: PACIS 2011 Proceedings, paper 35 (2011)

Chou, S.W., Chang, Y.C.: The implementation factors that influence the ERP (enterprise resource planning) benefits. Decision Support Systems 46(1), 149–157 (2008)

Chiang, A.: Creating Dashboards: The Players and Collaboration You Need for a Successful Project. Business Intelligence Journal 14(1), 59–63 (2009)

Yu, C.-S.: Causes influencing the effectiveness of the post-implementation ERP system. Industrial Management & Data Systems 105(1), 115–132 (2005)

Chuang, T., Nakatani, K., Zhou, D.: An exploratory study of the extent of information technology adoption in SMEs: An application of Upper Echelon Theory. Journal of Enterprise Information Management 22(2), 183–196 (2009)

Cooper, R., Zmud, R.: Information Technology Implementation Research: A Technological Diffusion Approach. Management Science 3(2), 123–139 (1990)

Davenport, T.H.: Putting the enterprise into the enterprise system. Harvard Business Review 76(4), 121–131 (1998)

Davenport, T.H., Harris, J.G.: Competing on Analytics: The New Science of Winning. Harvard Business School Press (2007)

Devaraj, S., Kohli, R.: Performance impacts of information technology: Is actual usage the missing link? Management Science 49(3), 273–289 (2003)

Elbertsen, L., Benders, J., Nijssen, E.: ERP use: exclusive or complemented? Industrial Management & Data Systems 106(6), 811–824 (2006)

Fosser, E., Leister, O.H., Moe, C.E.: Organizations and vanilla software: What do we know about ERP systems and competitive advantage? In: 16th European Conference on Information Systems, vol. 8(11), pp. 2460–2471 (2008)

Gattiker, T.F., Goodhue, D.L.: What happens after ERP implementation on plant-level outcomes. MIS Quarterly 29(3), 559–585 (2005)

Hair, J., Anderson, R., Tatham, R., Black, W.: Multivariate Data Analysis. Prentice Hall, Upper Saddle River (1998)

Häkkinen, L., Hilmola, O.P.: Life after ERP implementation: Long-term development of user perceptions of system success in an after-sales environment. Journal of Enterprise Information Management 21(3), 285–310 (2008)

Hedman, J., Kalling, T.: The business model concept: theoretical underpinnings and empirical illustrations. European Journal of Information Systems 12, 49–59 (2003)

Hitt, L.M., Wu, D.J., Zhou, X.: Investment in enterprise resource planning: business impact and productivity measures. Journal of Management Information Systems 19(1), 71–98 (2002)

Ho, C., Tai, Y.: Strategies for the adaptation of ERP systems. Industrial Management & Data Systems 104(3), 234–251 (2004)

Klaus, H., Rosemann, M., Guy, G.G.: What is ERP? Information Systems Frontiers 2(2), 141–162 (2000)

Kositanurit, B., Ngwenyama, O., Osei-Bryson, K.: An exploration of factors that impact individual performance in an ERP environment: An analysis using multiple analytical techniques. European Journal of Information Systems 15, 556–568 (2006)

Low, C., Chen, Y., Wu, M.: Understanding the determinants of cloud computing adoption. Industrial Management & Data Systems 111(7), 1006–1023 (2011)

Mabert, V., Soni, A., Venkataramanan, M.A.: Enterprise resource planning: measuring value. Production Inventory Management Journal 42(3), 46–52 (2001)

Malhotra, N., Birks, D.: Marketing Research: An Applied Approach, 3rd edn. Financial Times Press, Edinburg (2007)

Mata, F.J., Fuerst, W.L., Barney, J.B.: Information technology and sustained competitive advantage: A resource-based analysis. MIS Quarterly 9(4), 487–505 (1995)

Nah, F., Tan, X., The, S.H.: An Investigation on End-Users Acceptance of Enterprise Systems. Information Resources Management Journal 17(3), 32–53 (2004)

Nicolaou, A.I.: Firm Performance Effects in Relation to the Implementation and Use of Enterprise Resource Planning Systems. Journal of Information Systems 18(2), 79–105 (2004)

Nicolaou, A., Bhattacharya, S.: Organizational performance effects of ERP systems usage: the impact of post implementation changes. International Journal of Accounting Information Systems 7, 18–35 (2006)

Nicolaou, A.I., Bhattacharya, S.: Sustainability of ERPs performance outcomes: the role of post-implementation review quality. International Journal of Accounting Information Systems 9, 43–60 (2008)

Oliveira, T., Martins, M.F.: Understanding e-business adoption across industries in European countries. Industrial Management & Data Systems 110(9), 1337–1354 (2010)

Oliveira, T., Martins, M.F.: Literature Review of Information Technology Adoption Models at Firm Level. The Electronic Journal Information Systems Evaluation 14(1), 110–121 (2011)

O'Leary, D.: Enterprise resource planning: systems, life cycle, electronic commerce, and risk. Cambridge Univ. Press, New York (2000)

Park, J.H., Suh, H.J., Yang, H.D.: Perceived absorptive capacity of individual users in performance of enterprise resource planning (ERP) usage: The case for Korean firms. Information & Management 44, 300–312 (2007)

Rajagopal, P.: An innovation-diffusion view of implementation of enterprise resource planning (ERP) systems and development of a research model. Information & Management 40, 87–114 (2002)

Raymond, L., Uwizeyemungu, S.: A profile of ERP adoption in manufacturing SMEs. Journal of Enterprise Information Management 20(4), 487–502 (2007)

Rhodes, J., Lok, P., Yang, S., Bambacas, M.: Resource based view of intangibles on ERP systems implementation and organizational performance in China. Journal of Global Strategic Management 5, 87–96 (2009)

Rogers, E.M.: Diffusion of innovations, 4th edn. The Free Press, New York (1995)

Ruivo, P., Neto, M.: Sustainable enterprise KPIs and ERP post-adoption. In: 6th Iberian Conference on Information Systems and Technologies (CISTI), vol. 1, pp. 1–7 (2011)

Ruivo, P., Oliveira, T., Neto, M.: ERP post-adoption: value impact on firm performance. In: 7th Iberian Conference on Information Systems and Technologies (CISTI), paper 162 (2012)

Shahin, D., Ainin, S.: The influence of organizational factors on successful ERP implementation. Management Decision 49(6), 911–926 (2011)

Straub, D.: Validating instruments in MIS research. MIS Quarterly 13(2), 147–169 (1989)

Velcu, O.: Exploring the effects of ERP systems on organizational performance: evidence from Finnish companies. Industrial Management & Data Systems 107(9), 1316–1334 (2007)

Wenrich, K., Ahmad, N.: Lessons learned during a decade of ERP experience: A case study. International Journal of Enterprise Information Systems 5(1), 55–73 (2009)

Zhang, Z., Lee, M.K.O., Huang, P., Zhang, L., Huang, X.: A framework of ERP systems implementation success in China: An empirical study. International Journal of Production Economics 98(1), 56–80 (2005)

Zhu, K., Kraemer, K.L.: Post-adoption variations in usage and value of e-business by organizations: Cross-country evidence from the retail industry. Information Systems Research 16(1), 61–84 (2005)

Appendix A. Items Measurements

Variable	Indicators	Literature support
	Using a five-point scale, where 1 means 'low' and 5 'high', respondents were asked to rate their perception.	
Compatibility	Please rate the degree to which… CB1 …is your ERP system compatible with others' software. CB2 …is your ERP system compatible with others' hardware. CB3… is your ERP system compatible with others' networks.*	Bradford and Florin ,2003; Elbertsen et al., 2006.
Complexity (reverse code)	According to users, please rate… CX1… how easy it is to them to learn the system.* CX2 …the intuitiveness of system. CX3 …how comfortable they feel using it.	Cooper and Zmud, 1990; Kositanurit et al., 2006; Chang et al., 2011
Efficiency	According to users, please rate the… EF1 …effectiveness in executing repetitive tasks. EF2 …effectiveness of user interface. EF3 …speed and reliability of system.	Rajagopal et al., 2002; Bendoly et al., 2004; Gattiker et al., 2005
Best Practice	According to standard ERP best practices, please rate the degree… BP1 … to which is for users setup the application. BP2 … to which can map workflows based on local requirements. BP3 …of system adaptability to business needs.	Chou and Chang, 2008; Wenrich and Ahmad, 2009; Maguire et al., 2010
Training	According to users program training, please rate the degree of how … TN1 …was training them on the system.* TN2 …was their understanding the content training material. TN3 …worth is navigating through the topics after training and applied in daily tasks.	O'Leary, 2000; Bradford and Florin, 2003; Maguire et al., 2010
Competitive Pressure	Please rate the degree to which … CP1 …has your firm experienced competitive pressure to use ERP? CP2 …would your firm have experienced competitive disadvantage if ERP had not been adopted?* CP3 …does the ERP usage in your firm's competitors affect your landscape market?	Bradford and Florin, 2003; Zhu et al., 2004; Oliveira and Martins, 2010
ERP Use	Accordingly with ERP usage how… ERPU1 …many employees use the system daily? (#)* ERPU2 …much time per day do employees work with the system? (%) ERPU3 …many reports are generated per day? (%)	Bradford and Florin, 2003; Devaraj and Kohli, 2003; Zhu et al., 2004
Collaboration	According to users, please rate the degree of how easy is to them … CO1 … collaborate with colleagues. CO2 … collaborate with system. CO3 … communicate with suppliers, partners, and customers.	Calisir and Calisir, 2004; Gattiker and Goodhue, 2005; Ruivo and Neto, 2010
Analytics	According to users, please rate the degree of… AN1 …comprehensive reporting (KPIs, Dashboards, etc.). AN2 …real-time access to information. AN3 …data visibility across departments.	Davenport et al., 2007; Chiang et al., 2009; Ruivo and Neto, 2010
ERP Value (firm performance)	Accordingly with firm performance, please rate the degree of ERP impact on… ERPV1 …user satisfaction. ERPV2 …individual productivity. ERPV3 …customer satisfaction. ERPV4 …management control.	Bradford and Florin, 2003; Devaraj and Kohli, 2003; Zhu and Kraemer, 2005; Shahin and Ainin, 2011

* CB3, CX1, TN1, CP2, and ERPU1 question-items were excluded after PLS model estimation due to low loadings.

Architectural Coordination of Transformation: Implications from Game Theory

Ralf Abraham and Stephan Aier

Institute of Information Management, University of St. Gallen, Mueller-Friedberg-Strasse 8,
9000 St. Gallen, Switzerland
{Ralf.Abraham,Stephan.Aier}@unisg.ch

Abstract. Enterprise Architecture Management (EAM) is considered a means
to support coordination in enterprises. However, coordination between heterogeneous stakeholder groups with different interests is a challenging task to
achieve. In this paper, we take a game-theoretic perspective on coordination in
organizations. We identify three coordination games from literature: (1) Matching game, (2) Battle of the sexes game, and (3) Assurance game. For each
game, we then provide an example and discuss which EAM deliverables can be
employed to support coordination and which implications for the design of
EAM can be derived. From the analysis of coordination games, we derive a
proposition outlining further EAM evolution along two paths: as an active decision support discipline, but keeping its focus in the IT domain; or moving out of
the IT departments and becoming a strategic decision support discipline for enterprise transformation.

Keywords: Game Theory, Coordination, Enterprise Architecture Management.

1 Introduction

Enterprises face an increasingly complex environment which forces them to undergo
radical change, in other words transform themselves [1, 2] The causes for such transformation efforts range from business- or IT-driven initiatives inside the enterprise to
outside events such as the emergence of new technologies or the introduction of new
regulatory requirements. The increasing complexity in the environment leads to an
increasing complexity of the enterprises themselves.

Large-scale transformation efforts affect multiple domains and layers within an enterprise [3], performed simultaneously in different projects and programs. Providing
coordination in the course of enterprise transformation aims to ensure that the overall
transformation targets are met, that the enterprise as a whole evolves in a consistent
way [4]. The rationale behind this is that an approach focusing solely on local optimi-
zation within projects, without having an overarching coordination mechanism, will
not necessarily lead to—or in the worst case even hamper—the development of the
enterprise in the intended direction.

A discipline that has been proposed to support the coordination of enterprise transformation is Enterprise Architecture Management (EAM) [4, 5, 6]. Descriptively,

H. Rahman et al. (Eds.): MCIS 2012, LNBIP 129, pp. 82–96, 2012.

EAM provides a high-level blueprint of an enterprise, addressing both business and information technology (IT) aspects and particularly the interdependencies between them [7]. Prescriptively, it provides principles and guidelines governing an enterprise's evolution [8]. However, EAM is currently used in very different ways by enterprises, with its impact more often than not limited to a documentation function for the IT domain [9]. Analysts company Gartner predicts that the IT "home grown star" EAM will and has to be moved outside IT departments in order to deliver on its promise and actually evolve towards an enterprise-wide decision support discipline, either as a discipline by itself or its practices becoming integrated into both business and IT strategy [10].

Since organizational transformation is concerned with fundamental change covering many facets of an enterprise, it involves and affects a large number of stakeholders with heterogeneous concerns, organizational tasks and individual interests. Therefore, it is essential to understand individual stakeholder's preferences and the potential conflicts that may arise between them in the course of transformation. However, this is seen as one of the current shortcomings with EAM [11].

In an organizational context, stakeholders are mutually dependent on each other's actions: To achieve an organizational goal, each stakeholder has to choose a particular action. The organizational goal, e.g. the intended transformation result, is reached only if all involved stakeholders choose the appropriate action, i.e. if they coordinate on cooperative behavior. However, stakeholders' individual goals may agree or conflict with organizational goals and may also be influenced by the actions of their peers: For example, a group of line managers may want to choose a particular action only if they believe their peers will do the same.

A way to describe coordination situations between stakeholders, while particularly taking into account stakeholders' actions mutually influencing each other in an organizational context, is provided by game theory. Next to its formal description of the behavior of players, a main contribution of game theory is providing a classification system for decision situations between people [12]. By describing coordination situations in terms of games played between players and analyzing the different payoff matrices, requirements for coordination support in different scenarios may be deducted. Based on these requirements, the possible contributions on EAM in these situations can be delineated.

Our research questions are the following:

1. Which requirements must be met by EAM in each coordination situation?
2. What are the implications for the design of EAM in each coordination situation?

The remainder of this paper is organized as follows. In the next section, we will provide foundations of game theory and game-theoretic representations of common coordination problems based on organizational literature. Section 3 gives a brief overview on EAM and shows requirements and possible contributions in each coordination game. Section 4 discusses our findings and points out possible EAM evolution paths. The paper ends with a summary section discussing limitations and providing a brief conclusion.

2   Game Theory and Coordination Games

Game theory is concerned with the analysis of interactions among rational decision makers. Each player's gain is defined by the combination of his own decision as well as those of other players: his own benefit also depends on the action chosen by the other player. An important function of game theory, next to its formal description of rational players, is providing a classification system of social interactions and decision situations [12]. By doing so, game theory offers a clear language and representation form to describe and compare social interaction between rational participants.

The assumption of rationality has often been criticized: people usually do not behave in a purely rational fashion, but often base their decisions on emotions or instincts as well. Rationality alone cannot fully explain or predict an individual's decisions. However, in groups and in reoccurring situations, as is the case in an enterprise setting, people tend to move towards rational decision making [12]. Therefore, game theory is considered a useful approach in describing organizational coordination situations [13, 14].

For the purpose of this paper, two concepts from game theory are central: Nash equilibrium (NE) and Pareto efficiency. A NE is reached when no player can realize a higher gain by unilaterally deviating from a set of chosen strategies. It is a set of mutual best responses—no rational player has an incentive to change his strategy under the condition that the other player sticks with his strategy.

Another important concept for the analysis of coordination needs is Pareto efficiency. In a Pareto efficient solution, no player can increase his utility without decreasing the other player's utility. Contrarily, in a Pareto inefficient solution, both participants could be better off. While a NE constitutes an individual optimum, a Pareto efficient solution constitutes a social optimum.

To further illustrate the two concepts, consider the classic prisoner's dilemma game. It describes a game between two criminals accused of a particular crime, who are both questioned separately and therefore have to make independent decisions: From each combination of decisions, a different sentence arises for the individual player. The respective payoff matrix is given in Fig. 1.

	Cooperate	Defect
Cooperate	(2,2)*	(0,3)
Defect	(3,0)	(1,1)

Note: NE are marked in grey, an asterisk (*) denotes Pareto efficiency

Fig. 1. Payoff matrix for the prisoner's dilemma

Both players confessing the crime (defecting) results in each player receiving a longer prison sentence than both players denying the crime (cooperating). Hence both players' payoff for cooperating (2,2) is higher than their payoff for defecting (1,1). However, if one player betrays the other by defecting (e.g., turning state's evidence), he receives an even higher payoff (walking free: payoff of 3) at the expense of the other player who receives an even lower payoff (getting the maximum sentence: payoff of 0). These two options are given as (3,0) or (0,3), depending on the row or column player's perspective.

From Fig. 1, the essence of the prisoner's dilemma can be seen: Both a NE and a Pareto-efficient solution exist, but they result from different strategy combinations: Both players cooperating would be Pareto efficient, but the NE purely rational players will converge upon is both players defecting.

Camerer and Knez [14] argue that most organizational situations are not prisoner's dilemmas, but games of coordination instead. Their rationale is based on the idea that in organizations, players know each other and play games repeatedly, i.e. over a long period of time. Moreover, players are not forgetful and remember past actions of their peers. Therefore, strong social control exists, and experimental data have shown that players wish to reciprocate nice behavior: they are willing to sacrifice some personal utility to work towards a common goal [15]. In many organizational situations, players can realize a higher benefit by collaborating (whereas in the prisoner's dilemma, the highest individual benefit is achieved by defecting).

Coordination games—unlike the prisoner's dilemma—have multiple pure strategy NE. This property of coordination games in particular is also the rationale for choosing game theory as a theoretic foundation to describe coordination situations in organizations: With multiple NE available, organizations will aim at coordinating players on the Pareto efficient outcome or find a way of balancing if the NE cannot be Pareto ranked.

In the following, a summary of three organizational impediments to coordination and a game-theoretic expression for each of them will be given. The selection of coordination impediments and games is based on Camerer and Knez [14]. Fig. 2 provides the respective payoff matrices.

	Low	High		Football	Opera		Hare	Stag
Low	(1,1)	(0,0)	Football	(2,1)*	(0,0)	Hare	(1,1)	(1,0)
High	(0,0)	(2,2)*	Opera	(0,0)	(1,2)*	Stag	(0,1)	(2,2)*
	(a) Matching Game			(b) Battle of the sexes Game			(c) Assurance Game	

Note: NE are marked in grey, an asterisk (*) denotes Pareto efficiency

Fig. 2. Payoff matrices for the coordination games

The matching game (Fig. 2 a) has two pure strategy NE, with the (High,High) equilibrium Pareto dominating the (Low,Low) equilibrium. The corresponding organizational impediment to coordination is failures in teams. The term "team" is used in organizational literature [16] to characterize a group in which each member has the same preference over the outcome of the game. In this game, there is no conflict of interest, but players still need to exchange information to coordinate on the mutually desired outcome—in particular, they must be aware of the existence of the Pareto-efficient (High, High) strategy.

In the battle of the sexes game (Fig. 2 b), there are two pure strategy NE which are both Pareto efficient. No NE Pareto dominates the other since players have different preferences over the outcome of the game, and by changing to the other NE, one player would concede some of his payoffs to his counterpart. The associated impediment to coordination is a bargaining problem, caused by a mixed-motive conflict between players: Every player prefers a different outcome (in the classical game theory example of a couple, one prefers the football match, while the other prefers the opera), but both players prefer giving in to the other's demand to not coordinating at all. In the organizational context, participants prefer finding some solution, but each solution gives one player a higher payoff than the other, due to their different preferences. Players agree, however, that finding no solution is the worst possible outcome.

The assurance or stag hunt game (Fig. 2 c) also has two pure strategy NE with one Pareto dominating the other. It describes a situation where coordinating on the higher outcome is associated with some risk: As in the matching game, the optimum outcome will only materialize if all players do indeed cooperate (which would yield a payoff of 2 by both going for the stag), but in contrast to the matching game, individual players have the option to play a safe strategy which guarantees them a lower payoff (going for the hare guarantees a payoff of 1). The associated organizational problem is stakeholders supporting transformation (e.g. by making investments in learning new skills or adopting new processes) only if they know and trust other stakeholders to do the same. Stakeholders who do not believe in the common goal or trust their peers to work towards it have the option to stick with the status quo, so they will not have invested "in vain" should the transformation eventually fail.

This situation essentially models a trade-off between individual safety and collective cooperation. Therefore, it is also referred to as a situation of "risky coordination". The game basically breaks down to trust and the convergence of expectations [17]. In order to coordinate on the Pareto optimum, players must choose the riskier strategy themselves and must also trust other players to do the same. Whereas the matching game discussed earlier requires participants only to know about the Pareto efficient outcome, the assurance game introduces an additional condition: Players must know that their peers also know about the collectively optimal strategy and, moreover, they must trust each other to work towards it. The main difference to the matching game, as evident when comparing the payoff tables, is that non-coordination offers the individual player a risk-free alternative in the assurance game. Therefore, merely communicating an organizational goal and making sure everybody knows about it as in the matching game is not enough: The goal must be credible enough so that players trust others to risk going for it [17].

3   Enterprise Architecture Management in Coordination Games

This chapter will briefly outline EAM, before discussing its contributions to each of the aforementioned coordination games.

3.1   Enterprise Architecture Management

Enterprise Architecture (EA) involves both a descriptive and a prescriptive dimension: In a descriptive sense, EA describes the fundamental structure of an organization by providing a high-level overview on the structure of and dependencies between strategic goals, organizational processes and the underlying software and infrastructure systems. In a prescriptive sense, EA is concerned with establishing guidelines and principles governing an enterprise's evolution by restricting design freedom [8, 18, 19]. This notion of architecture, both representing structure and guiding change, corresponds to the ISO/IEC/IEEE Standard 42010, which defines architecture as "the fundamental organization of a system, embodied in its components, their relationships to each other and the environment, and the principles governing its design and evolution" [20].

In the field of EA, a multitude of methods and frameworks have been developed to address modeling and planning of current and target states of the enterprise [21, 22, 23]. Providing transparent documentation on organizational structure, information flows and implementation of software systems is seen as a key deliverable of EA [7, 24, 25]. Transparency means displaying information in a manner that enables effective decision-taking [26]. This poses a two-fold challenge: on the one hand, supplying complete documentation that covers all relevant aspects (strategy, organization, technology) of an enterprise's current state, yet on the other hand presenting this information to stakeholders with a scope that enables managing this overwhelming amount of information, thus making order out of chaos. Transparency is seen as a key antecedent for EAM to be able to support strategic change [27].

Enterprise Architecture Management (EAM) addresses the establishment and continuous development of EA. It controls the evolution of EA and business change from an architectural perspective. EAM has thus been proposed as a means of coordinating enterprise transformation [4, 5, 6]. EAM is driven by business- or IT-related scenarios [28], based on stakeholder goals [29]. However, the variety of stakeholders and their conflicting goals create "wicked problems" [30], i.e. problems that are characterized by confusing formulation and conflicting values of many decision makers.

Consequently, identify conflicting stakeholder needs and perspectives and coordinating between them is seen as one of the current issues with EAM [11]. By providing a game-theoretic perspective on stakeholder motivations and payoffs, this paper aims at better understanding stakeholder behavior and deriving insights for the evolution of EAM.

3.2   Matching Game

In the matching game, players do not have conflicting interests and are willing to cooperate. However, especially in large enterprises with complex structures, coordination is still far from trivial. Players need to be aware of each other and their options. Organizational examples for such a situation are reuse of software components or business services, or finding the right person in the enterprise for collaborating on a project that is beneficial to all partners. The benefits of the individual players are at the same time the benefits of the enterprise: Increased consistency by reuse of existing functionalities and avoiding duplicate work. The essence in this situation is that improving player's information supply will help steer them towards the Pareto efficient solution.

In order to support this coordination game, EAM must create transparency. The main determinants here are information supply and its visibility. Information supply means providing up-to-date models of the structure and relationships between processes and information systems from a high level perspective. To maintain the quality of the information supply, keeping the documentation models updated in the event of organizational changes and providing an appropriate form of representation is vital. EAM essentially provides a common language for multiple stakeholder groups.

However, both the information supply and visibility aspects need to be further developed: To support enterprise-wide coordination, EAM must address the information needs of a broad variety of stakeholders. EAM predominantly provides models on business processes, software systems and the data flows and interdependencies between them. This information caters for the needs of EAM stakeholders like business and IT departments [31]. However, information needs of other stakeholders are currently not readily provided by EAM. Extending the information supply to financial performance indicators or competence profiles associated with processes, and integrating these with traditional EAM models, may increase the EAM value for a wider number of stakeholders like management accounting or human resource management.

For the visibility aspect, the organizational positioning of a coordination function like EAM is critical. If EAM is deployed inside an IT or business department, appropriate communication measures must be pursued to ensure that all relevant stakeholders are aware of its existence and services. Having EAM deployed on a global level, as a corporate support discipline, will increase its visibility. Consequently, its information supplying capability becomes more likely to be actually noticed and used by stakeholders.

3.3   Battle of the Sexes Game

In contrast to the matching game, players in the battle of the sexes game have different preferences. This is the only of the three games that has two Pareto efficient NE. As a consequence, merely providing transparency will not solve this coordination problem. From an organizational perspective, non-coordination is the most detrimental option that is to be avoided. While the overall payoff for the enterprise is equivalent in both NE, each possible coordination option will offer one player a higher benefit than the other. Eventually, a balancing action needs to be taken.

The conflict between business and IT departments regarding standardization issues is an example of such a coordination problem: While business departments wish to have systems customized to their specific requirements in order to increase operational flexibility, IT departments strive for standardization as a means of controlling costs and complexity [31]. Similarly, Murer et al. [32] describe a trade-off between business value and agility, where a one-sided focus on either objective will eventually lead to hardly maintainable systems on the one hand or solutions that are too inflexible to meet business unit's demands on the other hand. In the long run, a balancing action needs to be taken, for example efforts to reduce the heterogeneity of IT systems if the landscape has become too fragmented. Murer et al [32] refer to this balancing as "managed evolution".

When the battle of the sexes game is played repeatedly, as is the case in an enterprise context, a simple and fair solution would be to alternate between player's objectives: In the classic game theory description of the battle of the sexes game, the couple could take turns in going to the football match or the opera. In the organizational context, a similar balancing function is called for in such battle of the sexes conflicts. However, finding the right moment to carry out the balancing action is a challenging task. Eventually, management is responsible for resolving such conflicts by making deliberate architectural decisions.

Providing transparency on the status quo is an essential requirement in this situation, but it is not sufficient. EAM may support this coordination situation by providing an organizational history in the form of a record of organizational decisions. A sense of predictability and justification may thus be established, eventually increasing stakeholder's acceptance of the decisions taken. This could be implemented by incorporating rationales for decisions in the supply of information. In the conflict between business flexibility and IT standardization, providing organizational history may also help management determine when a re-balancing action is needed. Research has shown that managerial decisions are in fact influenced by organizational history [33]. Aveiro et al. [34] also argue for organizations to be aware of their past decisions in order to guide future changes.

Since EAM is to provide decision support in this situation, it should be positioned accordingly in the organization [26, 35], i.e. reporting to management and not be located in the line organization. This currently poses a problem for EAM approaches that are deeply rooted in the IT departments and have little impact beyond [9]. However, in practice a small number of cases can be observed where an EAM function for exactly this reason is located outside the IT department, reporting to the chief operating officer, for example. In this situation, EAM may ultimately support coordination and balancing over time.

3.4   Assurance Game

Like in the matching game, there is only one Pareto efficient NE, so organizations have a target to coordinate upon. However, the key difference in the assurance game is the issue of trust: Players unwilling to take a risk in trusting other players to work towards global goals as well will prefer a locally optimized, safe solution [36].

An organizational example is the introduction of an enterprise-wide artifact, like a planning or review process for business unit projects or an integration platform covering or replacing various individual software systems. Such artifacts – if widely adopted – may provide synergies for the enterprise as a whole as well as for the individual business units by reducing heterogeneity and redundancy. A concrete case might be a superordinate planning and review process covering individual business unit's project proposals, to avoid the provision of parallel systems (for example, each business unit developing and maintaining its own time management system).

In contrast to the battle of the sexes game, where motivation is intrinsically different and players see no greater benefit giving up their own preference and coordinating on the global goal, players in this situation are aware of potential long term benefits. However, they also see a loss of individual autonomy associated with supporting the globally optimum solution. Players see the benefit only materialize if a critical mass of their peers cooperates as well. Thus, the willingness to cooperate for each player depends on his perception of the overall cooperation rate. Players who do not wish to cooperate may instead play the safe alternative of sticking with the status quo; but the enterprise pays the long-term price by not moving to the Pareto efficient solution.

Basically, coordination in this situation may be fostered by either incentives or sanctions: Cooperating business units or early adopters may be financially rewarded, and success stories may be communicated in order to create a bandwagon effect. On the other hand, strong principles and guidelines may be employed to mandate adoption of the new solution. This alternative, however, requires strong governance structures as well in order to actually enforce compliance [37]. In practice, a mix of both alternatives is likely to take place, e.g. providing incentives while at the same time making players aware of the existence of sanctions. The eventual mix is dependent on various contingency factors like existing governance structures or organizational culture.

In either case, displaying top management awareness and support in a credible way is essential in this coordination game [17]. To support the sanctioning alternative, EAM can provide architectural principles and guidelines (e.g., granting exceptions only when participants give convincing rationales or requiring payment of a price premium for sticking with the old solution). To support the incentive alternative, EAM can provide transparency on the status quo, a history of organizational decisions (including rationales for these decisions) and success stories: Communicating success stories to a wide audience and making stakeholders' commitments transparent to each other may give players the motivation to coordinate on the Pareto optimum outcome. An important factor here is mutual trust. Pirson and Malhotra [38] suggest that for stakeholders with deep, internal relationships to the organization, i.e. employees, transparency is a significant predictor of trust. EAM deliverables related to transparency like up-to-date documentation, as well as a record of organizational history can therefore support coordination in this game by fostering trust. However, they are just one component in coordinating such a situation, next to organizational culture and communication.

Credibility of management interventions is a key requirement here to make stakeholders' expectations converge [17]. In order to support this coordination situation, EAM should not have an IT-centered focus (and possibly bias), but be perceived as a corporate function. Ultimately, if organizations manage to decrease the payoff of the safe solution by either providing incentives or sanctions, the assurance game may be turned into a matching game. Here, the Pareto efficient outcome can be coordinated upon more easily.

4   Discussion

EAM can support coordination in both a passive and an active way. In the passive way, its function is creating transparency by providing documentation on the structure of the enterprise's business processes and underlying IT infrastructure. In the active way, EAM serves as a decision support function and helps management address the battle of the sexes and assurance game. Table 1 provides a summary of the findings for EAM in respect to each coordination game.

Table 1. Requirements for EAM from coordination games

	Matching game	Battle of the sexes game	Assurance game
EAM Function	• Documentation	• Leadership support • Balancing	• Leadership support • Building trust
EAM Deliverables	• Transparency	• Transparency • History and rationales of organizational decisions	• Transparency • Guidelines • History and rationales of organizational decisions
EAM Design Implication	• IT-centered EAM still possible, however stakeholder awareness is critical • Suitable form of representation for stakeholders outside IT is necessary	• Developing EAM into a decision support function for management	• Developing EAM into a decision support function for management • Only feasible with a high EAM maturity, i.e. a "track record"

Our analysis of the coordination games yields two important dimensions for the development of EAM into a coordination support for enterprise transformations. Fig. 3 depicts these two dimensions and evolution paths of EAM within each dimension.

Dimension one, on the vertical axis, describes the way EAM influences an enterprise—in a passive, documentation-oriented way or in a way of active design and decision support. Dimension two on the horizontal axis describes the scope and therefore the positioning of EAM—being either an IT-focused approach (typically positioned within the IT department) or being an enterprise-wide function positioned outside IT.

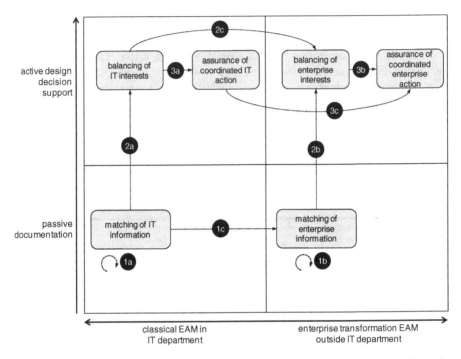

Fig. 3. Development paths of classical passive (IT-)EAM to an active enterprise transformation EAM

EAM may evolve from its historical starting point (step 1a) as an IT-rooted, passive documentation approach along these two dimensions on two evolution paths: (1) becoming an active design decision support in the IT domain (step 2a), then taking its services out of the IT department to an enterprise-level (steps 2c or 3a and 3c), or (2) first take the step out of the IT department (step 1c) and then moving from a documentation role to a design decision support discipline (steps 2b or 2b and 3b). A direct leap from classical IT-driven EAM in a passive, documentation-centered role (lower-left quadrant) to an active decision-support function with enterprise-wide focus (upper-right quadrant) would be a radical step that is unlikely to be taken directly. Instead, enterprises can build on their experiences of applying EAM to the IT domain when extending EAM to an enterprise-wide function [27].

If EAM keeps its classical role in the IT department, it can only coordinate in an IT context. In its reactive role, it may provide information support in matching games (step 1a). If it evolves into a design support discipline for IT issues, it may help balance in a battle of the sexes game, e.g. between developers and maintenance personnel (step 2a), or help establish mutual trust in an assurance game, e.g. between different development teams (step 3a).

If EAM is to support enterprise-wide coordination, the coordination games it supports are much wider in scope: instead of balancing local interests or building trust between players from one single domain as in the IT context, EAM takes an enterprise-wide scope. The games it supports are played between players from different domains across the enterprise. They include battle of the sexes games such as balancing between business-specific requirements and IT standardization goals described as "managed evolution" by Murer et al. [32] or as business/IT alignment by others [39, 40, 41]. Even more challenging are enterprise-wide assurance games of building convergent expectations and mutual trust between business, IT and corporate functions. In order to provide these services, EAM has to move out of the IT department and take one of the paths envisioned for instance by Gartner [10]: Become a corporate decision support discipline, or merge its products and processes into business strategy. In the latter case, EAM may evolve along path 1c, merging its information supply capabilities into other strategic disciplines that eventually provide active design decision support.

Independent of which development path EAM eventually takes, key requirements for enterprise-wide coordination games can only be fulfilled if EAM (1) manages to provide transparency and (2) is perceived as a corporate discipline. Visibility to stakeholders and providing organizational history from a credible, domain-independent perspective cannot be achieved if EAM is perceived as covering only a domain-specific viewpoint instead of having an enterprise-wide scope.

From our analysis of coordination games in enterprises, two main propositions for EAM may be derived:

P1a: EAM successfully supporting the matching game is a precondition for EAM successfully supporting the battle of the sexes game.

P1b: EAM successfully supporting the battle of the sexes game is a precondition for EAM successfully supporting the assurance game.

P2: In order for EAM to generate impact outside the IT domain, EAM has to be positioned outside the IT department.

Proposition P1 may be intuitive because it conforms to the experiences in maturing EAM or other coordination functions. Proposition P2, however, seems more interesting since it can be observed in practice, that enterprise architects constantly struggle with their role, tasks, and success outside their domestic IT department. While trying to better understand the requirements and also the habits of their business stakeholders is a necessary task, the emancipation from their "IT birthplace" may only be observed in very few places, yet.

5   Summary

5.1   Limitations

The results of this paper must be interpreted considering a number of limitations: First, game theory makes strong assumptions that include rational players and information asymmetry. Therefore, the applicability of game theory to real-life situations heavily depends on the degree to which these assumptions actually hold.

Moreover, in order to limit complexity, we have focused on 2-player games in this paper. However, repeatedly played games with more than two players (n-player games) can provide a more realistic yet considerably more complex description of organizational conflicts.

Additionally, many types of organizational coordination situations could involve elements of several of the games discussed herein, or may not be covered fully by the games discussed (e.g., to which extent does a pure battle of the sexes game exist in a real-world enterprise with a plethora of stakeholders and their inter-linked interests).

These limitations will particularly come forward during validation, i.e. when mapping concrete organizational situations to one of the games discussed in this paper and applying the EAM design implications. Nevertheless, applying game theory in a simplified form does provide a first classification scheme of organizational coordination situations. However, it needs to be considered that the true complexity of real-life organizations can at best be approximated by two-by-two payoff matrices.

5.2   Conclusion

In this paper, we have taken a game-theoretic look on coordination situations in enterprises and derived design implications for EAM from three coordination games. The major findings are that (1) transparency and visibility of EAM information to stakeholders are a key requirement in all coordination games, that (2) EAM must pass a maturing cycle, with rising requirements from supporting matching game situations to supporting coordination in the assurance game, and that (3) in order to support enterprise transformation, i.e. transformation cutting across single domains, EAM should be positioned as an enterprise-level support function outside the IT departments, in order to increase its visibility.

Further research should look into more specific coordination and transformation situations (like Mergers & Acquisitions, the launch of new products or regulatory changes mandating changes in information systems) and more specific EAM deliverables such as certain types of models (e.g., on dependencies, decision rationales, goals) or principles (e.g., on different levels of granularity). The role of EAM in coordinating such transformation efforts could be analyzed in case studies. The propositions derived in the previous section may thus be tested for validity, reliability and generalizability.

The current work provides as its main contribution a theoretically founded set of propositions and evolution paths for EAM in the course of enterprise transformation.

Acknowledgement. This work has been supported by the Swiss National Science Foundation (SNSF).

References

1. Rouse, W.B.: A Theory of Enterprise Transformation. Systems Engineering 8(4), 279–295 (2005)
2. Purchase, V., Parry, G., Valerdi, R., Nightingale, D., Mills, J.: Enterprise Transformation: Why Are We Interested, What Is It, and What Are the Challenges? Journal of Enterprise Transformation 1(1), 14–33 (2011)

3. Rouse, W.B.: Enterprises as systems: Essential challenges and approaches to transformation. Systems Engineering 8(2), 138–150 (2005)
4. Harmsen, F., Proper, H.A.E., Kok, N.: Informed Governance of Enterprise Transformations. In: Proper, E., Harmsen, F., Dietz, J.L.G. (eds.) PRET 2009. LNBIP, vol. 28, pp. 155–180. Springer, Heidelberg (2009)
5. Pulkkinen, M., Naumenko, A., Luostarinen, K.: Managing information security in a business network of machinery maintenance services business - Enterprise architecture as a coordination tool. Journal of Systems and Software 80(10), 1607–1620 (2007)
6. Ross, J.W., Weill, P., Robertson, D.C.: Enterprise Architecture as Strategy. Creating a Foundation for Business Execution. Harvard Business School Press, Boston (2006)
7. The Open Group: TOGAF Version 9.1 (2011)
8. Proper, E., Greefhorst, D.: The Roles of Principles in Enterprise Architecture. In: Proper, E., Lankhorst, M.M., Schönherr, M., Barjis, J., Overbeek, S. (eds.) TEAR 2010. LNBIP, vol. 70, pp. 57–70. Springer, Heidelberg (2010)
9. Aier, S., Gleichauf, B., Winter, R.: Understanding Enterprise Architecture Management Design – An Empirical Analysis. In: Proceedings of the 10th International Conference on Wirtschaftsinformatik WI 2011, Zurich, pp. 645–654 (2011)
10. Gartner Inc.: The Future of EA in 2020; EA Is Integral to Strategic Planning (2011)
11. Lucke, C., Krell, S., Lechner, U.: Critical Issues in Enterprise Architecting – A Literature Review. In: AMCIS 2010 Proceedings, Paper 305 (2010)
12. Aumann, R.J.: What is game theory trying to accomplish? In: Arrow, K., Honkapohja, S. (eds.) Frontiers of Economics, pp. 28–76 (1985)
13. Weber, R., Camerer, C., Rottenstreich, Y., Knez, M.: The Illusion of Leadership: Misattribution of Cause in Coordination Games. Organization Science 12(5), 582–598 (2001)
14. Camerer, C., Knez, M.: Coordination in organizations: A game-theoretic perspective. In: Shapira, Z. (ed.) Organizational Decision Making, pp. 158–188. Cambridge University Press, New York (1997)
15. Rabin, M.: Incorporating Fairness into Game Theory and Economics. The American Economic Review 83(5), 1281–1302 (1993)
16. Marschak, J., Radner, R.: Economic Thoery of Teams. Yale University Press, New Haven (1972)
17. Camerer, C., Knez, M.: Coordination, Organizational Boundaries and Fads in Business Practices. Industrial and Corporate Change 5(1), 89–112 (1996)
18. Fischer, C., Winter, R., Aier, S.: What is an Enterprise Architecture Design Principle? Towards a Consolidated Definition. In: Lee, R. (ed.) Computer and Information Science 2010. SCI, vol. 317, pp. 193–205. Springer, Heidelberg (2010)
19. Stelzer, D.: Enterprise Architecture Principles: Literature Review and Research Directions. In: Dan, A., Gittler, F., Toumani, F. (eds.) ICSOC/ServiceWave 2009. LNCS, vol. 6275, pp. 12–21. Springer, Heidelberg (2010)
20. ISO/IEC/IEEE: Systems and software engineering – Architecture description (ISO/IEC/IEEE 42010:2011). Springer, Heidelberg (2011)
21. Spewak, S.H., Hill, S.C.: Enterprise Architecture Planning - Developing a Blueprint for Data, Applications and Technology. John Wiley & Sons, New York (1993)
22. Spewak, S.H., Tiemann, M.: Updating the Enterprise Architecture Planning Model. Journal of Enterprise Architecture 2(2), 11–19 (2006)
23. Pulkkinen, M.: Systemic Management of Architectural Decisions in Enterprise Architecture Planning. Four Dimensions and Three Abstraction Levels. In: Proceedings of the 39th Annual Hawaii International Conference on System Sciences (HICSS 2006), pp. 179a (171–179). IEEE Computer Society, Honolulu (2006)

24. Jonkers, H., Lankhorst, M.M., Doest, H.W.L., Arbab, F., Bosma, H., Wieringa, R.J.: Enterprise architecture: Management tool and blueprint for the organisation. Information Systems Frontiers 8(2), 63–66 (2006)

25. Lankhorst, M.: Enterprise Architecture at Work: Modelling, Communication and Analysis. Springer, Berlin (2005)

26. Strano, C., Rehmani, Q.: The Role of the Enterprise Architect. International Journal of Information Systems and e-Business Management 5(4), 379–396 (2007)

27. Radeke, F.: Toward Understanding Enterprise Architecture Management's Role in Strategic Change: Antecedents, Processes, Outcomes. In: Wirtschaftinformatik Proceedings 2011, Paper 62 (2011)

28. Winter, R., Bucher, T., Fischer, R., Kurpjuweit, S.: Analysis and Application Scenarios of Enterprise Architecture - An Exploratory Study (Reprint). Journal of Enterprise Architecture 3(3), 33–43 (2007)

29. Niemi, E.: Enterprise Architecture Stakeholders - A holistic view. In: The 13th Americas Conference on Information Systems (AMCIS 2007), Keystone, CO (2007)

30. Pries-Heje, J., Baskerville, R.L.: The Design Theory Nexus. MIS Quarterly 32(4), 731–755 (2008)

31. Boh, W.F., Yellin, D.: Using Enterprise Architecture Standards in Managing Information Technology. Journal of Management Information Systems 23(3), 163–207 (2007)

32. Murer, S., Bonati, B., Furrer, F.J.: Managed Evolution: A Strategy for Very Large Information Systems. Springer, Heidelberg (2010)

33. Brunninge, O.: Using history in organizations: How managers make purposeful reference to history in strategy processes. Journal of Organizational Change Management 22(1), 8–26 (2009)

34. Aveiro, D., Silva, A.R., Tribolet, J.: Towards a G.O.D. Organization for Organizational Self-Awareness. In: Albani, A., Dietz, J.L.G. (eds.) CIAO! 2010. LNBIP, vol. 49, pp. 16–30. Springer, Heidelberg (2010)

35. Kluge, C., Dietzsch, A., Rosemann, M.: How to realise corporate value from enterprise architecture. In: ECIS 2006 Proceedings, Paper 133 (2006)

36. Asfaw, T., Bada, A., Allario, F.: Enablers and Challenges in Using Enterprise Architecture Concepts to Drive Transformation: Perspectives from Private Organizations and Federal Government Agencies. Journal of Enterprise Architecture 5(3), 18–28 (2009)

37. Brown, A.E., Grant, G.G.: Framing the Frameworks: A Review of IT Governance Research. Communications of the Association for Information Systems 15, 696–712 (2005)

38. Pirson, M., Malhotra, D.: Foundations of Organizational Trust: What Matters to Different Stakeholders? Organization Science 22(4), 1087–1104 (2011)

39. Henderson, J.C., Venkatraman, N.: Strategic alignment: Leveraging information technology for transforming organizations. IBM Systems Journal 32(1), 4–16 (1993)

40. Aier, S., Winter, R.: Virtual Decoupling for IT/Business Alignment – Conceptual Foundations, Architecture Design and Implementation Example. Business & Information Systems Engineering 1(2), 150–163 (2009)

41. Chan, Y.E., Reich, B.H.: IT alignment: an annotated bibliography. Journal of Information Technology 22(4), 316–396 (2007)

Executing Enterprise Dynamic Systems Control with the Demo Processor: The Business Transactions Transition Space Validation

Sérgio Guerreiro[1], Steven J.H. van Kervel[2], André Vasconcelos[3,4], and José Tribolet[3,4]

[1] Universidade Lusófona de Humanidades e Tecnologias, Escola de Comunicação, Artes, Arquitectura e Tecnologias da Informação, Campo Grande 376, 1749-024 Lisbon, Portugal
sergio.guerreiro@ulusofona.pt
[2] Formetis BV, Hemelrijk 12 C, NL 5281PS, Netherlands
steven.van.kervel@formetis.nl
[3] CODE, Center for Organizational Design & Engineering, INOV,
Rua Alves Redol 9,Lisbon, Portugal
[4] Department of Information Systems and Computer Science,
Instituto Superior Técnico, Technical University of Lisbon, Portugal
andre.vasconcelos@dei.ist.utl.pt, jose.tribolet@inesc.pt

Abstract. Business transactions models are useful to share a common understanding between the stakeholders in a process-based organization; however alone they do not guarantee that the actors perform their actions correspondingly. This paper proposes and exemplifies a solution to the Enterprise Information Systems (EIS) generation and operation using a Model Driven Engineering (MDE) approach founded and derived from Enterprise Ontology (EO) theory. The obtained EIS are (i) descriptive information systems that monitor and deliver a truthful representation of the enterprise on a software engine: the DEMO processor and (ii) prescriptive information system supported by an ontology specifically researched for controlling the operation of business transactions: the enterprise dynamic systems control (EDSC). The achieved benefits are (i) partially automatic validation of EDSC ontology; (ii) self-contained environment to test and validate the DEMO processor and (iii) full workflow capabilities calculated from DEMO models, with formal rigor, minimizing anomalies and minimizing the programming effort.

Keywords: Business transactions, Control, DEMO, Enterprise ontology, Runtime, Simulation, Validation.

1 Introduction

Business transaction models establish the design freedom restrictions prescribed for an organization, and are used to share a common understanding between the stakeholders in a process-based organization. We therefore introduce the notion of an enterprise, an abstraction of a company or an organisation. An enterprise is a social system, composed of human actors. The actors co-operate for the production

H. Rahman et al. (Eds.): MCIS 2012, LNBIP 129, pp. 97–112, 2012.

of the enterprise and they communicate with each other about their production parts. The business transaction model is a model of the enterprise that specifies how the actors should co-operate and communicate to produce the production in an optimal way. However, usually, business transactions models do not guarantee that the business actors perform the transactions accordingly in real life and this problem must be addressed. Business actors while playing an active role in business transactions are simultaneously the essentials elements of the enterprise dynamic systems control (EDSC), because they individually and/or collectively observe the reality and autonomously produce new control acts that result in facts. Without actor's activity there are no performed acts thus the organisation, which is a social system, does not exist. In the scope of process-based organisations, to guarantee that the prescribed business transactions are respected, it is necessary to continuously control the misalignments between the prescribed business transactions and the observed operation in the organisation; at the atomic level. The EDSC proposal presented in this paper consists on a set of concepts that are designed to enforce control[1] of the enterprise in the run-time business transactions. The EDSC ontology discussion is relevant to share a common understanding about its application domain. But, besides this discussion the capability to generate and control an information system directly derived from models allows an agile adaptation of the enterprises to the rapid requirements change. This endeavour has been pursued in the software engineering field for decades, for instance, by agile methodologies [1] from the software development point of view. This paper addresses this issue but concerning in the scope of Enterprise Engineering (EE), based on enterprise ontology [2][3], more specifically in the capability of validating DEMO models prior to its implementation phase. The result is that different scenarios of business transactions might be simulated, in run-time, regarding its consistency and completeness before implementing the software artefacts that supports its operation in production. DEMO ontological models validation has been a research field in the EE. Joseph Barjis [4][5] uses Petri net theory to simulate DEMO business transactions models. This approach enables the inconsistencies identification. However, a conversion between DEMO process structure diagram and Petri nets is still required. Tokyo Institute of Technology is actually working in this field [6], future developments are expected.

To introduce the solution, an enterprise information system (EIS) is herein considered as an information system that is driven by DEMO models under execution by software engine, the DEMO processor. Moreover, we consider that an EIS is a *descriptive* information system that delivers a precise representation of the dynamic state of enterprise at the atomic transaction step level and at any time. An EIS is also a control system, according to the control systems theory [7] that enforces model compliance or obedience of a system to some external specification, in this case a DEMO enterprise model specification. In this way an EIS is also a *prescriptive* information system, with a similar functionality as a workflow system [8] that executes a business procedure. In [9] a number of problems and anomalies in BPM (1.0) and workflow are reported; lack of ontological completeness; construct excess, construct overload, construct redundancy, lack of construct clarity. In our EIS' workflow capabilities are calculated directly with formal rigor, ontological

---

[1] The notion of control is here the compliance to a model of the enterprise.

completeness and lack of anomalies from DEMO models, they are not modelled separately. In this paper we show that these problems are solved using the DEMO processor (section 4). The formal correctness, validation of the EIS as a DEMO model driven control system for enterprises is subject of investigation in this paper. In detail this paper presents and discusses the results obtained by the EDSC transition space validation phase [10][11][12]. A transition space is considered as the set of allowable sequences of transitions in a state space of a system. EDSC ontology is solid founded in EE, more specifically, on the business transaction concept defined in Enterprise Ontology (EO) [13][14]. The validation is supported by other ongoing research effort for run-time generation and control of business transactions: the DEMO processor [15][16]. Combining the EDSC research with the DEMO processor research has a two-way advantage: a partially automatic validation of EDSC ontology and a self-contained environment to test and to validate DEMO processor. The business transaction concept is defined as a model representation of a given organisational reality that is valid within a specific timeframe. As proposed in EO, a business transaction involves (i) actor role definitions, in order to specify who[2] is responsible for each part of the transaction, who initiates it and who executes it, (ii) a transition space definition, and (iii) a state space definition. When we refer to run-time business transactions, we are referring to the instances of a business transactions model that are executing[3] at a precise and single instant in time. An enterprise has a set of transactions that are arranged by the composition axiom, as presented in [13]: '...*a business process is a collection of causally related transaction types, such that the starting step is either a request performed by an actor role in the environment (external activation) or a request by an internal actor to itself (self-activation)*'.

The domain of interest presented in this paper is on deriving the EIS directly from the theory of EO using a model driven engineering (MDE) approach [17], the theoretical foundation is the GSDP-MDE (Generic Systems Development Process and Model Driven Engineering) methodology [18]. EO is an ontology that complies with the formal definition of ontology, *"a formal, explicit specification of a conceptualisation shared between stakeholders"* [19]. Ontology delivers a conceptualisation of phenomena in reality, in this case for EO conceptualisations about enterprises that operate in reality. Essential quality criteria of an ontology are *truthfulness* and *appropriateness* for a specific domain [20]. EO has good empirical evidence of appropriateness and truthfulness, supported by many case studies [21][22]. There are two valuable advantages of the use of a 'high quality' ontology[4] as a foundation for information systems; the formal rigor of the conceptualisations and specifications on one side, and the ontological truthfulness and appropriateness qualities on the other side. The ontological truthfulness quality is required to ensure

---

[2] DEMO models specify only actor's roles but not a specific natural person. The link between an actor role and a specific person is outside our scope of interest.

[3] It implies that in a large-scale production environment with many production instances there is an equal number of DEMO model instances in execution; each DEMO model uniquely linked to a specific production instance.

[4] An ontology may be truthful but less appropriate; in this case any results, model specifications, are true but less useful for our purpose. An ontology that is not truthful is not only 'not appropriate' but any model specifications and derived calculated results may not be true, with very limited value. Similarly, any set of conceptualizations that fail to deliver a formal specification is not an ontology and is also of a very limited value.

that an information system delivers always a truthful representation of the enterprise. The ontological appropriateness quality is required to ensure that an information system delivers appropriate results, in line with our purposes. With these qualities we may obtain models of a domain that are truthful and appropriate, for our purpose. This addresses the problem of lacking business-IT alignment [23]; IT systems that do not support the operation of the enterprise as expected. The other side is the formal rigor of models; ontological models are represented by objects, attributes linked to objects, relations between objects and there are rules that govern the existence of objects, attributes, attribute values, and relations. Models can be expressed using a formal language, composed of a set of symbols, a vocabulary and a set of rules, a grammar that constitute an ontological language L. Guizzardi [24] delivers the foundations for high quality ontological languages. If a specific cardinality law is followed then important advantages are achieved; lack of software anomalies, lack of construct excess, lack of construct overload and ontological completeness. These advantages address the problems and anomalies of BPMN (Business Process Modelling Notation) described by Van Nuffel [2009]. The construction of an ontological language L and the construction of a software engine that is capable to read, write, construct, destroy and execute models expressed in L is a MDE approach. We use the EO theory and the DEMO methodology for enterprise [13][14] to construct DEMO enterprise models. The formal DEMO specifications is composed by four DEMO aspect models expressed in four graphical formal languages and are used as the foundation of a MDE approach in software. A sentential language in XML representation (DMOL, DEMO Modelling Language) has been designed to capture DEMO models, represented by the four DEMO aspect models. A software engine (DEMO Processor) that reads, writes, constructs, destroys and executes DMOL model specifications has been designed and implemented. This document is organized as follows. Section 2 introduces how business transactions are ontological described in DEMO ontology. Section 3 details the case study to be validated by DEMO processor. Section 4 describes the DEMO processor. Section 5 presents the performed experiments and identifies the correspondingly outcomes. Finally, section 6 concludes the paper and points to future work.

2   DEMO Business Transactions

The EO theory and the DEMO methodology for enterprise are proposed by Dietz in [13][14]. It consists of an essential ontology (EO) that is compatible with the communication and production, acts and facts that occur in reality between actors in the different layers of the organisation. EO is a rigorous formal theory that provides a solid understanding of organisations, based upon three theories; the -theory or Fact-information theory (FI), the τ-theory that stands for Technology, Architecture and Ontology (TAO), and the Ψ-theory that stands for Performance in Social Interaction (PSI). DEMO is founded on four distinct axioms and a theorem: (i) the Operation Axiom, (ii) the Transaction Axiom, (iii) the Composition Axiom, (iv) the Distinction Axiom, and (v) the Organisation Theorem. The world is composed of: (i) the enterprise, which is a social system which includes state space and transition space, and (ii) the entire surrounding environment. This paper only addresses the validation of the transition space.

Focusing in the Ψ-theory, the DEMO basic transaction pattern is depicted by Fig. 1. Two distinct actor roles are identified in this transactional pattern: the Customer and the Producer. The goal of performing such a transaction pattern is to obtain a new fact. The transactional pattern is performed by a sequence of coordination and production acts that leads to the production of the new fact, encompassing three phases: (i) the order phase (O-phase) that encompasses coordination and production acts of request, promise, decline and quit, (ii) the execution phase (E-phase) that includes the production act of execution and the execution of the new fact itself and (iii) the result phase (R-phase) that includes coordination and production acts of state, reject, stop and accept.

Firstly, when the Customer desires a new 'production' or 'product', he requests it. After the request for the production, (usually) a promise to produce the production is delivered by the Producer. Then, after the production, the Producer states that the production is available. Finally, the Customer (usually) accepts the new fact produced. This basic DEMO basic transaction pattern is universal in the sense that it summarises all the co-ordination and production acts that could occur between persons to persons, machines to machines and also between persons and machines. Sometimes, parts of this transaction pattern are performed tacitly. DEMO basic transaction pattern aims at specifying the transition space of a system that is given by the set of allowable sequences of transitions. Every state transition is exclusively dependent from the current states of all surrounding transactions. There is no memory of previous states.

The organisational actors are the ones that are responsible for performing the production and/or co-ordination acts in the scope of a business transaction. A production act (P-act) contributes to bringing the goods and/or services (material or immaterial) that are delivered to the environment of the enterprise, and a co-ordination act (C-act) enters into and complies with commitments toward each other regarding the performance of the production acts. The P-acts and C-acts have effect in the correspondingly two separate worlds: the production world (P-world) and the coordination world (C-world) [13]. Referring to Fig. 1, co-ordination acts lies outside the elementary actor roles because communication always happens through a communication channel that exists in the surrounding environment. The most primitive form of communication is verbal speaking. A more technological form is, for instance, an electronic mail message or a web service invocation. When a co-ordination act is designed with a bold line then it means that is a final co-ordination act where the transaction pattern ends. When a production act is designed with a bold line then it means that is an initial production act.

The DEMO basic transaction pattern is a conversational pattern to be used between actors and not a set of activities within the scope of business transactions. The DEMO transaction pattern lies in the ontological world; hence its implementation requires more detail and analysis. A single transactional process step, e.g. TX/request, would be implemented by a web-based software application.

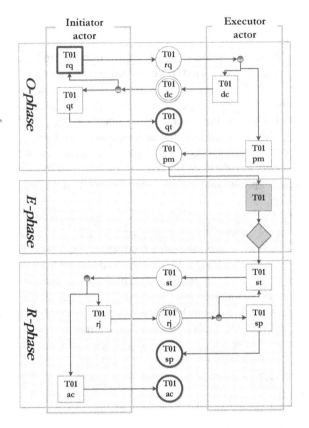

Fig. 1. The DEMO standard pattern of a transaction between 2 actors with separation between communication and production acts (Adapted from [13])

3   Run-Time Business Transactions Control Description

Business transactions models, as introduced in section 2, prescribe the design freedom restrictions of the business transactions dynamics but *per se* do not guarantee that organisational actors perform them accordingly, which is needed. To solve this problem, we propose the usage of EDSC that is actually composed by the set of concepts that guarantees that the prescriptions are followed in the operation by performing a continuously cycle of observation, decision and control action [25][26]. Control action actuates with a change in the business transaction models prescription to avoid the recurrence of unintended operations or a change in the control rules if the deviation from prescription is recognized as being innovative. Usually, control in organisations is strictly considered as a black-box perspective that lies inside the actor's capabilities, and the models of the business transaction specify what the actors should do. Then, the organisation trusts that control is tacitly implemented [27][28]. This paper identifies that this perspective is valid but only represents a partial coverage of control in organisations. In a black-box perspective, control is thus only identified by the result of the actors in the reality which can only be seen as a whole but not by its parts. Thereafter, in this scope, this solution defeats that besides the capability of the individual and collective actors to decide and take control actions, also autonomous mechanisms of observing and acting should be completely understood by ontology and then enforced in the operation of an organisation.

This section proposes a transition space of a DEMO-based ontology to enforce EDSC in the run-time operation of business transactions. At operational level, the solution checks misalignments between prescribed business transactions models and observed operations in the organisation. These observations are used to trigger actions by the organisational control. Organisational control checks if the historical business transactions comply with the prescribed business rules. The control action results in changes in the prescribed business transactions models or changes in the business rules. In the first case of control action, the prescribed business transactions are changed to avoid the recurrence of unintended operations. In the second case of control action, innovation is recognized as positive and the deviations from the prescribed transactions models are incorporated in the new prescription. The proposed ontology combines enterprise governance (EG) concepts [2] with concepts defined on dynamic systems control (DSC) field [25][26]. DSC defines observation as [26]: '...a system is completely observable if every state variable of the system affects some of the outputs. It is often desirable to obtain information on the state variables from the measurements of the outputs and the inputs. If any one of the states cannot be observed from the measurements of the outputs, the state is said to be unobservable and the system is not completely observable or simply unobservable...'. EG defines decision as [29]: '...is the organisational competence for continuously exercising guiding authority over enterprise strategy and architecture development, and the subsequent design, implementation and operation of the enterprise...'. DSC defines control action as [26]: '...a process is said to be completely controllable if every state variable of the process can be controlled to reach a certain objective in finite time by some unconstrained control u(t). If any one of the state variables is independent of the control u(t), there would be no way of driving this particular state variable to a desired state in finite time by means of a control effort. Therefore, this particular state is said to be uncontrollable, and as long as there is as least on uncontrollable state, the system is said not to be completely controllable or simple uncontrollable...'.

In our proposal, a control cycle encompasses observation, decision and control action. Where the observation and the control action are concepts both taken from DSC field and decision is taken from EG field. In line with this consideration, four sets of transactions are identifiable to control the run-time business transactions operated by the organisational actors (human-based or computer-based), and summarized on **Table 1: Observation** of the operation: (T04), **Prescribed definitions,**

Table 1. Transaction result table presenting the transactions types and the obtained result types

Transaction Type	Result type
T01 Business rule definition	R01 Business rule BR has been defined for period P
T02 Model definition	R02 Model M has been defined for period P
T03 Access definition	R03 Access A has been defined for period P
T04 Observation of run-time session	R04 Session S has been observed for period P
T11 Business rule management	R11 Business rules BR have been managed for period P
T12 Model management	R12 Model M has been managed for period P
T13 Access management	R13 Access A have been managed for period P
T05 Run-time control	R05 Session S has been controlled for period P
T06 Run-time access control	R06 Access A has been controlled for period P
T07 Run-time business rule control	R07 Business rule BR has been controlled for period P
T08 Run-time ID control	R08 Identification ID has been controlled for period P

regarding the business rules, the business transaction models and the accesses: (T01, T02 and T03), **Management** of the business rules, business transactions models and accesses: (T11, T12 and T13), and **Control** regarding the actual session, the accesses and the business rules: (T05, T06, T07 and T08). Each transaction is valid within a specific period of time.

Within the EDSC boundary, on Fig. 2, exists the responsibility for the observation of the operation of the enterprise and to act when needed. In detail, the business rule manager (A01) is responsible to self-initiate the business rule definition transaction (T01) and also to initiate the business rule management transaction (T11). Similarly, the model manager (A02) is responsible to self-initiate the model definition transaction (T02) and also to initiate the model management transaction (T12). Access controller (A03) is responsible to self-initiate the access definition transaction (T03) and to initiate the access management transaction (T13). The idea of having a self-initiate transaction is to enable the definition of the controller references before run-time. If no references are established then no control can be performed. References are considered herein as the control bootstrap. The control actuation is performed by initiating one of the following transactions: business rule management (T11), model management (T12) or access management (T13). From the EG kernel functional perspective, the control of the run-time business transactions is performed by observing all the process steps operated by the users (CA04) and when needed T11, T12 or T13 are triggered.

The observation initiates the observation of run-time session transaction (T04). A user might be a person or a machine. Ontologically, transaction T04 means the connection of the EG kernel with the operation of a given business transaction that is compatible with a DEMO model. In practice, it means that observation is a mandatory requirement to enable EG. Once the observation over the DEMO artifacts is established then decision is a matter of evaluating the observations and deciding the correct actions to be performed. Then, every business transaction execution that we want to control must be connected with the boundary of the EG. The idea, is that the coordination and production, acts and facts, keeps being executed outside the EG.

Therefore, EG is observing the operation and acting accordingly with its predefined definitions that were made by the business manager, model manager and access controller. Elementary actor role Interceptor (A04) initiates T05 which is named as the run-time controller and that creates a new fact in the ontology that is "Session S has been controlled for period P". The run-time controller executes T05 initiating three parallel transactions: **Run-time access control** (T06), control if the access to the sessions should be granted or revoked, **Run-time business rule control** (T07), control if the ex-ante defined business rules are satisfied, and **Run-time ID control** (T08), control if each DEMO artifact in the session has an unique identification. The artifacts that are being considered are: Elementary actor roles, Transaction kind, Action rule, Fact type, Object class and Result type. Transactions T06, T07 and T08 are performed by the correspondingly actors: the run-time access controller (A06) and the business rules engine (A07).

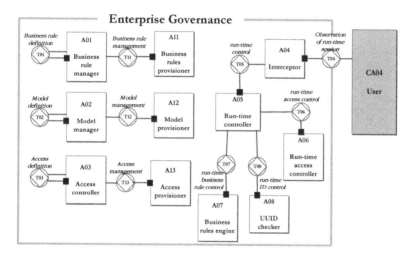

Fig. 2. Actor Transaction Diagram presenting the interaction of the enterprise governance with the surrounding environment. Two main sets of transactions are identified: the enterprise governance provisioning (T01, T02, T03, T11, T12, T13) and the run-time control (T04, T05, T06, T07, T08).

In detail, the transition space of transactions T04, T05, T06, T07 and T08 follows the diagram depicted in Fig. 3, named as process structure diagram (PSD) in DEMO. The presented PSD uses the DEMO standard pattern of a transaction (see Fig. 1) applied to 3 actors: initiator, intermediate and executor. The intermediate requests a second transaction to the executor after receiving a request from the initiator, e.g., in Fig. 3 T05 is requested by A04 after A04 receives a T04 request from CA04. Conversely, the T04 is only stated after the state of T05. This pattern is called promise after request (PaR). Moreover, disagreements patterns between 3 actors are added to the DEMO standard pattern of a transaction, which are presented by red lines in Fig. 3.

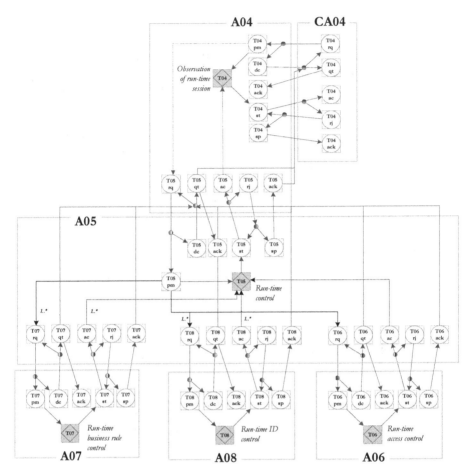

Fig. 3. Process structure diagram of the access control combined with business rules and universal identifier, using the DEMO standard transaction pattern as depicted in **Fig. 1.**

4   The DEMO Processor

The DEMO processor constructs and executes DEMO models, expressed in XML DMOL (DEMO Modeling Language) enables model simulation, model validation and incremental model improvement during development (Fig. 4). The development process starts with the modeling stage for an enterprise (nested in enterprises etc.) that delivers the four graphical DEMO aspect models. Then the models are entered -translated (not programmed) on the DEMO processor in a 1:1 process. The DEMO processor renders a representation of the models in the XML DMOL language. The DEMO processor calculates and executes the enterprise model dynamically and delivers simulation results for model validation. The execution involves all communication and coordination in a *prescriptive* way between all (human) actors (1..n) of the enterprise, similar to a workflow system, shown in Fig. 4. If model validation fails the model under execution can be edited (model parts construction and destruction) and the simulation – validation cycle is repeated. After successful validation – acceptance by the stakeholders - the model is rendered as a DMOL (DEMO Modeling Language) XML file with full state information and stored in a model repository. At any time the original model, in its current state, can be parsed and rebuild for further simulation. A model representation rendered in (near) natural language enables the (re-) construction of the four DEMO aspect models. This process is repeated until we have a complete model repository of all elementary enterprises of a production chain, each of them producing an elementary production component. In production (Fig. 5) for each elementary production component a production model instance for that elementary enterprise is created from the model repository by a copy operation. Production instances are aggregated by the DEMO processor into a model under execution that represent the production of all aggregated enterprises A and B. Model building, aggregation and optional destruction is executed at runtime. In production the DEMO processor executing the aggregated model delivers all communication and coordination for each actor in each enterprise, as a **workflow system. For each production step** *descriptive* **data can be delivered to a MIS (Management Information System). At any time an aggregated model can be decomposed into its aggregating DMOL file components, stored in the production database. When the production resumes the original production model reconstructs itself, with full state information and continues communication and coordination**. The DEMO models can be unlimited large and are being executed in a formal correct way; the anomalies and shortcomings of BPMN (section 1) [9] are eliminated.

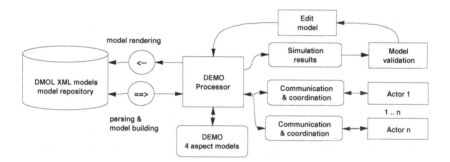

Fig. 4. DEMO model simulation and validation of an enterprise model

The first DEMO processor application in production is a case management system for a company that delivers energy and utility services, water and electricity, to citizens. Its production is a tailor-made contract between the citizen, who is an active co-producer, and the company. The case management system is composed of the EIS, the DEMO processor that executes DEMO models, and a closely integrated document information system and interfaces to legacy IT systems. The contract covers issues such as type of services provided, costs, costs calculation procedures, conditions for payments, letters, mails, instructions for the subcontractors, etc. There is enforced compliance of legal procedures, policies, conditions, approvals etc. The quality of the system is high; incomplete transactions, deadlocks, deadline overflow, violation of procedures etc, are eliminated. The practical experiences until now are: (i) the domain

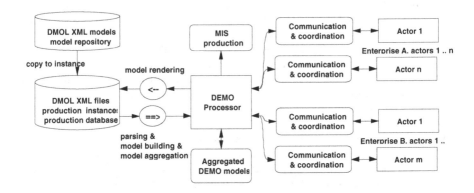

Fig. 5. DEMO processor in production environment

knowledge of key personnel was leading in the design stage. The early and easy model validation steps assured a total acceptance of the software application at acceptance tests, (ii) the efforts for implementation in software are already less than the efforts dedicated to the modeling stages and (iii) the company appreciates the structured way of working and the elimination to deviate from procedures.

5   Experiment and Outcomes

This section validates the EDSC ontology previously described in section 3 using the DEMO processor (section 4). The aim is to identify any incompleteness and inconsistencies introduced during the design phase of EDSC DEMO models. The advantage of using the DEMO processor to validate a set of business transactions specified with DEMO ontology is to foresee its inconsistencies before applying to a real organisation or EIS software system. DEMO processor instantiates the ontology and thus allows the modeller to validate and learn if the transition space is correctly designed.

The approach is based in a strategy of separating the distinct business transactions of the ontology. The transition space of each business transaction is validated separately in the DEMO processor and then integrated in the overall solution. The identified inconsistencies are then considered to correct the models. This procedure is repeated until every business transaction of the model validates successfully, in an iterative approach. Formally, the following validation procedure is followed: (i) design a single business transaction, (ii) execute the designed business transaction in DEMO processor, (iii) if any violation to the DEMO standard pattern of a transaction including disagreements is identified, then the transition space is redesigned, and restart step (i). The different business transactions are then integrated in order to validate the execution of the overall solution. Following this experimental approach, the PSD of EDSC ontology (see Fig. 3) is separated into three distinct business transactions: *access control* (T06), *business rules* (T07) and *universal identification* (T08). After the individual validation step is performed successfully, *access control* is combined with business rules and then universal identification is added to the formers. All the process steps depicted in Fig. 3 are triggered during the validation process. The benefit of such a fine-grained validation is the ability to establish a step-by-step confidence that the transactions are well designed and that encompasses all the possible coordination acts combinations as defined in Fig. 1. Because of readability purposes only three business transactions are considered from the overall EDSC ontological definition. DEMO standard pattern validation is out of the scope of this paper.

Table 2. Business transactions validation and outcomes obtained by the experiments

Experi ment	Business Transactions	Identified outcomes from experiment
1	*Access control* (T06)	- Full decomposition of transactions - Disagreements patterns inclusion - Concatenated transactions
2	*Business rules* (T07)	- Parallel transactions
3	*Universal identification* (T08)	- The need to further specify the action model (ARS)
4	*Access control* (T06) with *Business Rules* (T07)	- Negative-policy enforcement
5	*Access control* (T06) with *Business Rules* (T07) and *Universal identification* (T08)	- Negative-policy enforcement

Table 2 explains the outcomes, or learning, that are obtained while the business transactions transition space of EDSC is iteratively executed in DEMO processor.

Full decomposition of transactions refers to the obligation of designing the production of a single new fact along with each business transaction. Otherwise, the design is not possible to be executed in the DEMO processor. Each business transaction process step is related 1:1 to each action rule. Action rules specification (ARS) is the DEMO representation for detail design of each business transaction process step, using SBVR specification [29]. The learned criterion to stop the decomposition is when each action rule only produces one fact type.

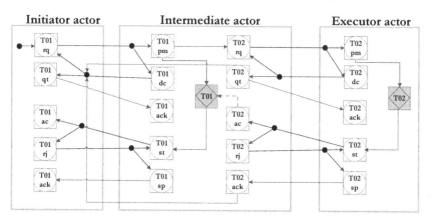

Fig. 6. Standard pattern of a transaction with disagreements patterns between 3 actors

Regarding the outcome of disagreements patterns inclusion, experiment 1 identified that designing DEMO business transactions compatible with classical two-phase commits when three or more actors are involved requires the addition of the disagreements patterns to the initial DEMO standard transaction pattern (Fig. 1). Regarding this specific implementation concern, Fig. 6 depicts the full pattern between 3 actors that is actually being executed by the DEMO processor. In EDSC, the disagreements patterns are needed because of the following: **Rejections**, not all statements are accepted. If the result of a state is not proper in the eyes of an intermediate actor then he would be able to reject it, by the mean of a decision point; **Declinations**, not all requests could be promised. And, if the request of a transaction is declined then a new decision is posed to the initiator actor, which might request again or quit the transaction and **Commit or rollback mechanism**, regarding the run-time control, the transaction T04 is only finished successfully if T05 is stated successfully. On the other hand, T05 is only finished successfully if T06, T07 and T08 are stated successfully. If any of those transactions are quitted, rejected or declined then a consequence is made to maintain the consistency between the initiator and the executors, meaning that the transaction do not succeed.

Regarding the outcomes of concatenated/parallel transactions, these two different kinds of topology are used to define the scheduling of the business transactions. Where, concatenated means that the transactions are scheduled to start after finishing the former, by other words, using the promise after request (PaR) pattern. The first transaction always depends on the second. This pattern is used between the T04 and T05. And where parallel transactions means that multiple transactions could start concurrently. N transactions might be executing at the same time. Parallel transactions pattern is used for T06, T07 and T08.

Finally, with experiments 4 and 5, the policy that is used in EDSC is to have a negative security policy enforcement where the T04 starts to be revoked and, only and only if, all the transactions (T05, T06, T07 and T08) are accepted then the access is granted. This policy should be followed in organisations where granting is stricter that revoking.

6   Conclusions and Future Work

This paper presents and discusses the results obtained by the transition space validation phase of an ontology specifically researched for controlling the operation of business transactions. We achieved a partially automatic validation methodology of the demo processor and a self-contained environment to do this. The ultimate goal is to demonstrate the capability of directly deriving an EIS (enterprise information system) from EO theory using a MDE approach, to monitor and control enterprises. The solution is grounded in the assumption, supported by empirical evidences, that EO theory delivers domain models (DEMO models) that have the qualities of appropriateness and truthfulness. A DEMO model of an enterprise is being executed on a software engine, called DEMO processor. The advantage of using DEMO processor to validate a designed ontology is assess the quality of a specified model, re-engineer the model if needed (model validation by stakeholders using shared reasoning) before applying it to a real organisation. The fine-grained validation operated by DEMO processor, allows a step-by-step confidence that the transactions are well designed and that encompasses all the possible co-ordination acts, performed by actors, as defined in the DEMO standard pattern. Combining EDSC research with DEMO processor research has a two-way advantage: a partially automatic validation of EDSC ontology and a self-contained environment to test and to validate DEMO processor. The specific outcomes obtained with the EDSC ontology are useful to clarify the purpose that DEMO processor is able offer: full decomposition of transactions, disagreements patterns inclusion, concatenated / parallel transactions identification, further detail required in the action rules specification and negative-policy enforcement. The main advantage of this approach is that, if DEMO models executed on the DEMO processor pass the EDSC validation, then the DEMO processor delivers workflow-like business procedures that are completely calculated from DEMO enterprise models, with formal rigor, absence of anomalies and guaranteed ontological completeness. Despite the concepts that are put forward in this paper, further research is needed to (i) validate the state space using modal logic based approaches, (ii) to validate this approach with other real case study from industry (in addition to the one mentioned), (iii) to full identify the delivered outcomes in other case studies and (iv) to develop the EDSC implementation.

Acknowledgments. The first author would like to state that this work was supported by a PhD scholarship: SFRH / BD / 43252 / 2008, and also by a national project: PTDC / CCICOM / 115897 / 2009, MOBSERV, Sistemas Facilitadores da Utilização de Serviços por Dispositivos Móveis, from Fundação para a Ciência e a Tecnologia, Ministério da Ciência, Tecnologia e Ensino Superior, Portugal.

References

1. Sommerville, I.: Software Engineering, 9th edn. Addison-Wesley (2011)
2. Albani, A., Dietz, J., Hoogervorst, J., Mulder, H., Tribolet, J.: Enterprise engineering: the concise manifesto. In: CIAO Network Meeting Minute, version 7 (2010)
3. Dietz, J.L.G., Hoogervorst, J.A.P.: The Principles of Enterprise Engineering. In: Albani, A., Aveiro, D., Barjis, J. (eds.) EEWC 2012. LNBIP, vol. 110, pp. 15–30. Springer, Heidelberg (2012)
4. Barjis, J.: Automatic business process analysis and simulation based on demo. Enterp. Inf. Syst. 1, 365–381 (2007)
5. Barjis, J.: The importance of business process modeling in software systems design. Sci. Comput. Program. 71, 73–87 (2008)
6. Liu, Y.: Enterprise knowlegde based collaborative business process simulating and reasoning. In: 11th CIAO Doctoral Consortium, Antwerpen (2011)
7. Elgerd, O.: Control systems theory. McGraw Hill Text (1967) ISBN 13: 9780070191747
8. Van der Aalst, W., van Hee, K.: Workflow management, models, methods, and systems. MIT Press (2004) ISBN 978-0-262-72046-5
9. Van Nuffel, D., Mulder, H., Van Kervel, S.: Enhancing the Formal Foundations of BPMN by Enterprise Ontology. In: Albani, A., Barjis, J., Dietz, J.L.G. (eds.) CIAO!/EOMAS 2009. LNBIP, vol. 34, pp. 115–129. Springer, Heidelberg (2009)

10. Guerreiro, S., Vasconcelos, A., Tribolet, J.: Enforcing control in the run-time business transactions. In: Proceedings of 5th International Conference on Research and Practical Issues of Enterprise Information Systems (CONFENIS 2011), Center for Industrial Production, Aalborg University, Fibigerstraede 16, DK-9220 Aalborg, Denmark (2011a) ISBN: 978-87-91831-42-3

11. Guerreiro, S., Vasconcelos, A., Tribolet, J.: Dynamic business transactions control, an ontological example: organizational access control with DEMO. In: Proceedings of the International Conference on Knowledge Engineering and Ontology Development (KEOD 2011), Paris, France, pp. 549–554 (2011b); Special Session on Enterprise Ontology (SSEO 2011)

12. Guerreiro, S., Vasconcelos, A., Tribolet, J.: Enterprise Dynamic Systems Control Enforcement of Run-Time Business Transactions. In: Albani, A., Aveiro, D., Barjis, J. (eds.) EEWC 2012. LNBIP, vol. 110, pp. 46–60. Springer, Heidelberg (2012)

13. Dietz, J.L.G.: Enterprise Ontology – Theory and Methodology. Springer, Heidelberg (2006)

14. Dietz, J.L.G.: Architecture: building strategy into design. Nederlands Architectuur Forum. Academic Service (2007)

15. van Kervel, S.: Enterprise ontology driven information system engineering. Presentation given at CIAO! (2009)

16. van Kervel, S.J.H.: High Quality Technical Documentation for Large Industrial Plants Using an Enterprise Engineering and Conceptual Modeling Based Software Solution. In: De Troyer, O., Bauzer Medeiros, C., Billen, R., Hallot, P., Simitsis, A., Van Mingroot, H. (eds.) ER Workshops 2011. LNCS, vol. 6999, pp. 383–388. Springer, Heidelberg (2011)

17. OMG: Model Driven Architecture ® specifications, The OMG (2001)

18. van Kervel, S., Dietz, J., Hintzen, J., van Meeuwen, T., Zijlstra, B.: Enterprise Ontology Driven Software Engineering. In: Proceedings of the 7th International Conference on Software Paradigm Trends (ICSOFT 2012) (2012)

19. Gruber, R.: A Translation approach to portable Ontology Specifications. Knowledge Acquisition 5(2), 199–220 (1993)

20. Krogstie, J.: Evaluating UML: A practical Application of a Framework for the understanding of Quality in Requirements Specifications and Conceptual Modeling. In: Norwegian Informatics Conference (NIK) (2000)

21. Op't Land, M.: Applying Architecture and Ontology to the splitting and Allying of Enterprises, PhD thesis, University of Technology Delft (2008) ISBN: 978-90-71382-32-1

22. Mulder, F.: Rapid Enterprise Design. PhD Thesis, University of Technology Delft, The Netherlands (2007) ISBN 90-810480-1-5

23. ITGI: The IT Governance Institute (2012), http://www.itgi.org/

24. Guizzardi, G.: Ontological Foundations for Structural Conceptual Models. PhD thesis, University of Twente, The Netherlands (2005) ISBN 90-75176-81-3

25. Franklin, G.F., Powell, J.D., Emami-Naeini, A.: Feedback Control of Dynamic Systems, 2nd edn. Addison-Wesley Publishing Company (1991)

26. Ribeiro, M.: Análise de sistemas lineares, vol. 1 e 2. IST Press (2002)

27. Jaeger, A., Baliga, B.: Control systems and strategic adaptation: Lessons from the japanese experience. Strategic Management Journal 6, 115–134 (1985)

28. Nieminen, A., Lehtonen, M.: Organisational control in programme teams: An empirical study in change programme context, pp. 63–72. European Academy of Management (EURAM) (2008)

29. OMG. Semantics of business vocabulary and business rules (2008), http://www.omg.org/spec/SBVR/1.0/PDF (accessed in June 2011)

Towards Value-Oriented Enterprise Engineering – Relativity in Service System Networks

João Pombinho[1,2], David Aveiro[3], and José Tribolet[1,2]

[1] CODE - Center for Organizational Design & Engineering, INESC INOV,
Rua Alves Redol 9, Lisbon, Portugal
[2] Department of Information Systems and Computer Science, Instituto Superior Técnico
Technical University of Lisbon, Portugal
[3] Exact Sciences and Engineering Centre, University of Madeira, Funchal, Madeira, Portugal
jpmp@ist.utl.pt, daveiro@uma.pt, jose.tribolet@inesc.pt

Abstract. Defining the purpose of a system is non-trivial as, by definition, it arises from the relation with its environment. In this paper, we analyze relevant state of the art in the areas of General Systems Theory, Enterprise Engineering, Value Modeling, Enterprise Architecture and Business Modeling. Their main shortcoming essentially resides in lack of flexibly dealing with relativity of enterprise frontier definition. To address this issue, our research is focused on modeling different perspectives of enterprises as systems, namely construction, function and contribution. The approach presented in this paper involves 1) distinguishing the three mentioned perspectives and 2) articulating the concepts of each perspective so that an end-to-end, integrated, model is provided. To this end, we propose a conceptual framework that supports recursive contribution definition, by design. Specifying the value in a contribution perspective allows improved specification of the rationale behind value network establishment and system/subsystem bonding. We can now specify how each component of a system S contributes (provides value) not only to the purpose of S but to other purposes present in the value chains S participates in.

Keywords: Enterprise Engineering, Value, Contribution, Purpose.

1 Introduction

Business complexity and the change pace of enterprise environments, coupled with increasing ICT support, turn the gap between strategy and its implementation into a major challenge. Studies indicate as much as 90 percent of organizations fail to succeed in applying their strategies [1]. Misalignments between the *business* and its support systems is frequently appointed as a reason of these failures [2, 3].

The mechanisms humans use to manage the complexity inherent to these *systems of systems* and their dynamics pose various challenges, as they are not based on a transversal, coherent and concise model. The hinge between the business vision of a system and its implementation by supporting systems is not modeled in a way that adequately supports the development and evolution of a system and its positioning in a value network. We believe the origin of these issues is essentially structural.

H. Rahman et al. (Eds.): MCIS 2012, LNBIP 129, pp. 113–124, 2012.

Therefore, a paradigm shift in the way of modeling and developing systems should occur so that they can be increasingly developed with their dynamic context in mind.

Formal organizations are generally created as providers of a *repeatable* solution to a given demand. There is reasonable belief that the elements providing a solution will be continuously available; so much, that they are considered part of the organization. However, with the current change pace, stability is a luxury unavailable to most organizations as both offer and demand continuously change. With the aim of providing agility, the rationale behind value network establishment and system/subsystem bonding must be modeled regardless of value chain positioning.

This paper is structured as follows: section 2 presents research scoping, with Enterprise Engineering as ground and the Library example for problem clarification. Current challenges are then identified and grouped in three problem areas, with a brief related work review in section 3. Our solution proposal based on value definition, relativity and recursivity is presented next and the paper closes with conclusions.

2   Base Theory and Problem Statement

2.1   Enterprise Engineering

By enterprise engineering we mean the whole body of knowledge regarding the development, implementation, and operational use of enterprises [4]. Enterprise ontology [4] includes both a sound theory and a sound method for supporting enterprise engineering. It goes beyond traditional function (black-box) perspective and aims to change organizations based on the construction (white-box) perspective, were they are considered as systems composed of social actors and their interactions in terms of social commitments regarding the production of business facts.

From the Transaction Axiom of Enterprise Ontology, we find that actors perform two kinds of acts. By performing production acts (P-acts), the actors contribute to bringing about and delivering services to the environment of the organization. By performing coordination acts (C-acts), actors enter into and comply with commitments. In doing so, they initiate and coordinate the performance of production acts. Examples of C-acts are requesting and promising a P-fact. The result of successfully performing a C-act is a C-fact. The result of successfully performing a P-act is a P-fact. A P-fact in the case Library (see next section) is "loan L has been started". An actor role is defined as a particular, atomic 'amount' of authority, viz. the authority needed to perform precisely one kind of production act. P-acts and C-acts occur in generic recurrent patterns, called transactions. Every transaction process is some path through this complete pattern, and every business process in every organization is a connected collection of such transaction processes. This holds also for processes across organizations, like in supply chains and networks. That is why the transaction pattern is universal and must be taken as a socionomic law: people always and everywhere conduct business (of whatever kind) along this pattern [4].

From the Distinction Axiom of Enterprise Ontology's PSI-theory, we find that we can categorize all acts of an organization in 3 categories - *ontological*, *infological* and *datalogical*, related, respectively with the 3 human abilities: *performa* (deciding, judging, etc.), *informa* (deducing, reasoning, computing, etc.) and *forma* (storing, transmitting, etc.). By applying both axioms, Enterprise Ontology's Design and Engineering Methodology for Organizations (DEMO) is able to produce concise, coherent and complete models with a reduction of around 90% in complexity, compared to traditional approaches like flowcharts and BPMN [13].

Two aspects of a system are clearly differentiated: *Teleological*, concerning its function and behavior, a black-box; and *Ontological*, about its construction and operation, a white-box [5]. This distinction is crucial as it implies 1) separating these concerns and 2) articulating them. The *Generic System Development Process* (GSDP) addresses the hinge between teleological and ontological modeling, beginning with the need by a system, the *using system* (US), of a supporting system, called the *object system* (OS). From the white-box model of the US, one determines the functional requirements for the OS and then the white-box model towards implementation.

2.2   Library Example and Issues Identification

In order to clarify the problem space, the classical DEMO Library case [4] will be used. In Fig. 1, system elements dealing with membership (solid line-bounded area) do not seem to bring value to the customer, who only wants to get hold of a book. However, this is all but clear in the ontological (construction) model:

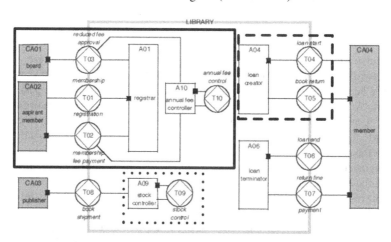

Fig. 1. Library example (Actor Transaction Diagram) – Construction analysis

Other remarks can be made about modeling issues regarding the Library's core business, *providing reading content*: 1) the core service is concealed in the area marked by a dashed line, obscured inside a loan transaction; 2) the area within points encloses a support process that may need revision, for instance, in a change scenario of going digital; 3) inside the solid black line, a sacrifice of the customer in obtaining the book: the Membership Management subsystem. Do customers really *want* a membership or is it a strategy to get a fixed amount of income to face, for instance, stocking management? Is it done for profit or simply as a response to the cost of keeping a large library? Under what conditions this decision should be reviewed? In trying to answer these questions, three problem areas where isolated:

Value Definition. What is the core value-providing transaction? Should it be named "Loan book" or "Provide (limited-time) access to (reading) content"? Is the "Membership registration" service interesting *per se*, or is it only in the way of getting a book, particular to this library construction? An independent value structure which is not subordinate to the system specifics, but the other way around, is needed.

Support for Dynamic System Construction Modeling. The construction of a system resulting from the development process is a compiled structure that obscures the system/subsystem relations and their motivation. It is hard to separate a subsystem from its owner system, especially if it was modeled from a flat description of the operation of the organization, instead of incremental design steps. How does a Library compare to a Bookstore or a Publisher, from the customer's perspective?

System Intervention Rationale Modeling. The rationale of choices made during the system development process is frequently not clear. For instance, regarding the Membership Management subsystem: 1) What is its purpose – is it mitigating the risk of non-return? What were the design and constructional principles, assumptions and constraints applied? Do they hold for other kinds of content, e.g., e-books? It is also not clear what to do with the objects supporting the rationale of the decisions made during the process, such as: 1) assumptions, e.g., the customer is necessarily a reader; 2) constraints, e.g., available technology to offer books such as physical or digital.

2.3   Problem Statement

We conceive enterprises as artificial [4, 6] service systems [7] which are actors in value networks [8]. During the process of changing an enterprise one needs to constantly be aware of value conditions imposed by stakeholders in the past, present and future. At times such conditions will be obvious just by looking at an organization component and at times they will not. These value conditions show how each and every part of an organization contributes to the purpose of the organization itself and/or to the purposes of other elements in the organization's environment (market). While engineering any organization one should be aware of all the value threads that influence the existence of the components target of change.

Current research approaches don't model value in a formal way that is relatable to the composition of the value providing system. Also, it is not clear how to structurally model system/subsystem relations. This makes it impossible to define the rationale of system intervention systematically for improving analysis and future change handling.

3   Related Work – State of the Art Approaches

3.1   Value Modeling

All kinds of enterprises have in common bringing about *value* to their *environment*, either directly or indirectly, so it is a unifying concept. Also, it is increasingly recognized that the concept of value assists in improving communication between stakeholders of related systems, particularly Business and IT [9].

e3Value [8] is an ontological approach for modeling networked value constellations. It is directed towards e-commerce and analyses the creation, exchange and consumption of economically valuable objects in multi-actor networks. An enterprise is modeled as an *actor*, which is perceived by his or her environment as an economically independent entity exchanging Value Objects. The demand and offer market concepts are a natural consequence of the economic context of Value Objects.

We propose to apply e3Value in a way that improves system and subsystem value modeling: inside the boundaries of organizations, instead of limited to e-commerce relations between formal organizations, as will be presented in section 4.1.

3.2   Enterprise Architecture

Archimate is a modeling language with broad practical application. In its architecture framework, three enterprise layers are distinguished: business, application and technology. The contents of application and technology layers are regarded as implementation and, thus, not directly modeled in DEMO. Archimate's business layer relates to all three B-I-D layers of DEMO, without clear distinction [10].

Archimate began addressing motivation since the release of its 2.0 specification [11]. However, this important step forward is about representing the motivation within the scope of a single system. While it has value in itself, in order to reap the full benefits of addressing the motivation layer, it must go further into *engineering* the business itself across multiple, connected, systems. Moreover, Archimate does not embody the concept of *intention*, a characteristic of the so called third wave of approaches, like DEMO [10]. In order to fruitfully combine both approaches, the whole business layer should conform to DEMO, positively constraining the modeling activity. Enforcing the rigorous semantics of DEMO into Archimate's business layer is a promising starting point to perform Archimate-based value modeling.

3.3   Business Modeling and Requirements Engineering

In a system's lifecycle, the concept of Value Proposal [12] is only realized during operation. Still, the way it is achieved and supported must be addressed at the scope of system development. The Business Model Canvas (BMC) [12] offers a systematic approach to developing business models. It comprises 9 key-concepts, presented next. The demand for a *Value Proposition* is modeled by Customer Segments, Customer Relationships and Channels, which make up the Revenue Streams. The infrastructure needed to support a Value Proposition comprises Key Activities, Key Resources and Partner Network. Together, they make up the Cost Structure behind the Value Proposition. While BMC had widespread success as an innovative approach to business model generation, being a top-down and relatively informal approach, it lacks constructional depth even from a business perspective [13]. Accordingly, the potential benefits of combining with a more formal approach, specifically e3Value, have been recognized by Osterwalder and a comparison is presented in [14].

The question is how to reach towards formality in business model definition. From literature review, it appears the origin of high-level business requirements is mostly traceable to *strategy*. But, then, strategy must be defined clearly and in articulation with the other elements of the solution development. Oliver provides a working definition for strategy as *the process of understanding the industry, the firm's position in that industry, and taking action either to change the industry's structure or the organization's position to improve organizational results* [15]. While it addresses fundamental concepts, its obvious problem is that it lacks structure.

In order to perform a rational and meaningful analysis it is necessary to make these forces more objective. In the Library example, *Improve Customer Experience*, *Decrease risk of non-return* or *Reduce storage space* are goals that should be decomposed and unambiguously refer to other model constructs, such as transactions and their production facts. The Strategy-Oriented Alignment in Requirements Engineering approach [16] recognizes this gap and aims at addressing it by explicitly stating business strategy, identifying high-level business objectives and tracing them to low-level system requirements. However, the bidirectional connection to functional perspective and, in turn, to the construction of the system is still missing. More importantly, it bypasses the formal modeling of the relation to external systems - the main influencers of a given strategy.

Business Analysis Body of Knowledge [17] provides context and methodology but lacks in formal constructs that can be used for bidirectional integration with the following development stages. Requirement specification is commonly guided by templates and standards that prescribe how requirement specification documents are structured. However, their informality results in both functional and constructional requirements to be included in the descriptions.

Goal-oriented Requirements Engineering approaches, such as I* and KAOS (for early and late requirements, respectively) address the teleological perspective, allowing to trace requirements to goals. ARMOR [18] is an example of a motivation-focused requirements modeling language, resulting from their combination. Despite being an advance in expressing goal structure and tracing, s goal is defined as a direct consequence of a certain strategy. However, the strategy itself or the motivation and reasoning behind it are not modeled in an integrated way. As we will see in the following section, specifying motivation in term of the needs of another system in successive engineering processes brings a greater level of objectiveness.

4   Towards a Solution: A New Perspective

Our approach fundamentally differs from the state of the art by following three lines:

- Formally defining the *value* of a system as a relation with other systems;
- Distinguishing three perspectives of a system: construction (white-box), function (black-box) and *contribution* (environment relations);
- Defining purpose by 1) decomposing a system into its components and 2) recursively modeling the development of each system component.

4.1   Systematically Defining Value

In the Library example introduced in section 2, the system may be used by a customer to solve an *information need* problem, but it can also solve a *gifting* problem. According to the demand segments the system's owner wishes to address, and competing offers, different system design and engineering decisions are made. Returning to the example, the *Obtain Book* service abstracts away implementation choices or provisioning mechanisms. Hence, it brings the Library's production to an essential level, which is the first step in allowing comparison to other alternatives of bringing about such item. Some examples are internet ordering, borrowing from a friend, acquiring a digital version or even downloading an illegal copy. Each of these variations introduces an offer at the solution market level with specific pricing, dependencies and risks, which end up providing different end-user experiences.

We consider combining the essential modeling of the business organization, in DEMO, with its value model, in e3Value, as a crucial step towards formal value definition. Both approaches were related in [19] but no detailed ontological matching was provided nor apparently intended. As we have seen, the elements of the business layer of state of the art approaches have undesirable large degrees of modeling freedom, resulting in incompleteness and incoherencies. For instance, Archimate's definition of Business Services lacks DEMO's B-I-D distinction. DEMO would provide completeness by matching with the Transactional Pattern and isolating essential (ontological, i.e. B-) transactions, as presented in [20, 21]. Their alignment is critical, since it relates a production fact and the value object it pertains to.

The service value concept is based on e3Value by relating the buyer/seller dual-party semantics to DEMO's Using System and Object System. *Actors* are the active elements of both social systems and value networks. An actor is a *subject* fulfilling an *actor role* in a *transaction type*. The *initiator* and *executor* actor roles are bound by their common interest in bringing about a *production result*. In e3Value, both actors (*provider* and *requester*) are bound by the willingness to share value objects. A *value object* is specifiable as the combination of an access right to some resource and a transformation enabled by this resource [22]. The alignment between a *production fact* (DEMO's Transaction Result) and *value object* is critical, as the production of a system determines its effective contribution to the value chains it participates in. A *transaction* represents the relationship between actors by associating *value ports* of different directions. A unitary DEMO transaction relates to a *value exchange* in e3Value. A *value transaction* involves at least two, according to the principle of *economic reciprocity* - the actor is only willing to exchange objects via all ports (incoming and outgoing) of its value interface, or none at all.

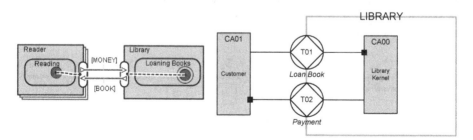

Fig. 2. e3Value and DEMO simplified Library examples

In the simplified Library example, Fig. 2, the requested production facts are:

- R01 – book loan (possession of a **physical book copy**) has started
- R02 – book loan was paid (**money**)

Relating production fact and value object is trivial in this case: the implicit value objects of R01 and R02 are now explicit, in bold, inside brackets. However, it can be hard if value-orientation is not present in transaction definition.

In summary: function, supported by construction, is exposed as a service in a market through one or more Value Interfaces. DEMO's transactions correspond to Value Exchanges, which are aggregated in e3Value's Value Transaction (with economic reciprocity). Decomposing value exchanges down to these primitives explicitly connects the value model of the system with its construction.

4.2   A Matter of Perspective: Relativity and Recursivity

Dietz [4] defines something as a system if and only if it has: *composition* – a set of elements of some category (grey nodes in Fig. 5); *environment* – a set of elements of the same category, disjoint from the composition (white nodes); *production* – things produced by elements in the composition and delivered to the environment; *structure* – a set of influence bonds among the elements in the composition, and between them and the elements in the environment (connections between white and grey nodes). Together, these properties are called the *construction* of a system.

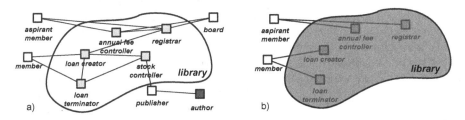

Fig. 3. Construction (a) and Function (b) perspectives of the Library

The Library's construction perspective is shown if Fig. 3 a). Notice the grey nodes are part of the composition, the white are the environment and the black is not part of the system. In Fig. 3 b), we can see the partial functional perspective of the member (including aspirant member, which is an earlier mandatory state).

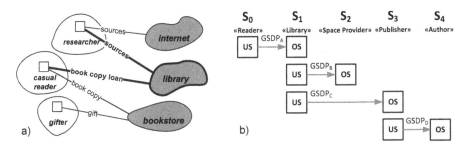

Fig. 4. Contribution perspective of the Library (a) and recursive GSDP application (b)

Fig 4. a) shows the contribution perspective, comprising boundary and relations with its using systems. Let us designate our using system by *reader*, while noting that the service system only provides him with *temporary possession of a book copy*. He may choose to lend it, for instance, or even re-loan it. What he may do with the book copy – value activities in e3Value terminology – should be addressed as another formal system. Modeling purpose as the contribution of a given system's production to its environment, as described in [21], is a powerful teleological concept. It is important to note that the goal is subordinate to the concept of purpose. The latter is as much of a strategic concern for a given system as it is a need by its using system.

As presented in section 2, designing and building a single super system made up of individual system parts is not a solid solution as it does not provide enough flexibility in dealing with change. Porter's Value Chain differentiates core and support business processes [23], which are *relative* concepts – every component of a business can potentially be a business by itself. The system should, thus, be freed from the formal boundaries of a firm as there is no real reason to have that limitation during enterprise design steps. Thus, it is necessary to have the theory to decompose system into more granular systems and chain them together with explicit value-oriented rationale.

To address this design issue, besides system positioning relativity, we use a GSDP cycle for each problem/solution pair, as shown in Fig 4. b). Value-based problem/solution chains are set up, where value objects are requested from suppliers to fulfill the needs of customers, implying multiple function/construction cycles. Each individual system performs value activities that transform and increase object system value. For instance, in $GSDP_D$, a Publisher system requests the Author to provide content, because of the need by the Library to loan books which, in turn, originates from the need of a customer to read. This way, a particular problem is either trivially solved at the market, if a complete solution exists, or split into a set of new problems, recursively. In this way, the functional requirements that led to the choice of a particular solution can now be registered as relating to particular value exchanges, revealing the structure behind business bonding. Conversely, the motivation of a given component can be determined by analyzing its chain of using systems.

4.3   Library Example: The Threat of Disintermediation

To illustrate the concepts presented in the previous sections, a new stage of the Library organization follows. *Disintermediation* is defined as *the elimination of an intermediary in a transaction between two parties*. In the Library's business, one threat is the Publisher bypassing the channels direct to reader. In this scenario, some relevant questions are 1) how prepared is our Library do deal with these new forces and 2) what are the essential Library components that differentiate it from other alternatives to providing similar services, let us designate it by *reading experience*.

Besides the Publisher, the Library faces tough competition from other more directly comparable solutions for providing access to books, such as bookstores. As a research result, it is now possible to distinguish the *start book loan* function, which is the functional perspective, from the value that function has for specific segments, which is the contribution perspective. At a first modeling iteration, the value object can be identified as the *book copy*, but the fact that different customer segments, *using systems*, demand it prompts for a revision of the value object definition. Investigating what each using system does with the value object, i.e., which value activities are carried through, one finds that the researcher and the casual reader have different valuations for the Library's contribution: the first regards it as a *research source* and the second as a way of obtaining access to a book copy. The casual reader also differentiates the Library's contribution from the Bookstore's because the Library provides *reading space* so that the book can be enjoyed in the beautiful building and atmosphere. The Publisher alone cannot possibly provide this *reading experience*.

To model this important difference, physical space must be defined as a component that improves the Library system contribution. In turn, this implies modeling:

- a new value object, *physical space*;
- a new actor role, *physical space provider*;
- a value exchange between the Library and the *physical space provider*;
- a transaction supporting the value exchange, thus defining it ontologically;
- the process model that chains transactions related by value object dependencies, so that physical space provision supports reading experience, e.g., devices for e-book reading or lightning conditions for physical books;

The first four bullets follow from the previous section. The last one, however, is based on production dependencies, such as the Result Chain presented in [24] and, in a more narrow but formal sense, DEMO's Result Structure [4]. This part is not yet fully incorporated in the model and is regarded as a next step, particularly specifying how these concepts are created during a GSDP iteration. In this example, should the Library consider switching from physical books only to both physical and digital, it must be investigated if the value of the *reading experience* production fact is preserved. This follows from earlier GSDP iterations that defined the contribution of the *physical space provider* subsystem as an enabler to *reading experience* value.

It is also now interesting to note that, from the point of view of the Library's customer, the membership management sub-system identified in section 2.2 turns out to be quite valuable in the sense that it is by becoming a member of the library that she gains the right to access the library space and enjoy a unique reading experience. If some manager would decide to eliminate the membership system part of the Library for some reason (no need to worry anymore with the risk of losing books) he could be losing essential business activity and income. By specifying all value objects exchanges (in this case, membership fee is exchanged for the right to use library's physical space) in all value chains crossing a certain organization construction we are better equipped to justify and specify organization change rationale.

We conclude this brief example by noting that, by distinguishing the function and contribution perspectives, it is possible to improve and align the overall enterprise model. The Library is now more prepared to identify the aspects that differentiate its value proposal. However, the Publisher organization itself should not be unconcerned, as retail giants such as Amazon may bypass it [25] in the relation with the authors! This is a clear example of the importance of essential value network analysis and its influence on functional and constructional development of a system.

5 Conclusion

We focused on the problem that current approaches of EE, Enterprise Architecture, Business Modeling and Value Modeling do not give a complete nor objective picture of how system components contribute to the system's purpose.

Our contribution is a framework for value system analysis and development funded on sound theory. Effectively integrating the *contribution* (why), *function* (what) and *construction* (how) dimensions of a system. Focusing on value as the bottom line supports traceability between every element of the model and purpose, improving communication between stakeholders. Additionally, the contribution perspective allows explicitly defining the contribution of each p-fact of a system to its using systems, as the value of a certain p-fact can differ when integrated in different value chains - relativity. Other distinguishing aspect of this approach is defining system environment as a set of (more) objective sibling systems instead of stakeholders.

Next, we addressed the fact that adaptability and innovation capabilities of an enterprise are as good as the reusable information from the rationale behind the design and engineering process. Value is critical in establishing this rationale but is not enough by itself to provide a uniform way to express an arbitrary number of purpose levels (*why* dimension) of a chain of systems. We propose recursive applications of the GSDP, alternating function and construction, modeling problem/solution cycles for each system/subsystem relation while specifying the subsystem contributions.

As a challenge, we note that the detail level that can easily be reached by recursive application of the GSDP is quite high, which calls for improved synthesis mechanisms. Furthermore, enforcing the definition of value at design time is challenging as it forces formal specification of issues commonly regarded as subjective. Additionally, regarding practical application, domain-specific frameworks are needed to provide design and construction principles for detailed implementation.

A practical case on Business Case support for specifying the value proposals at an IT Demand Management scenario is currently underway, where challenges such as multi-criteria satisfaction and other interesting issues are likely to arise.

References

1. Kaplan, R.S., Norton, D.P.: Strategy Maps: Converting Intangible Assets Into Tangible Outcomes. Harvard Business School Press, Boston (2004)
2. Henderson, J.C., Venkatraman, N.: Strategic alignment: leveraging information technology for transforming organizations, vol. 32(1), pp. 4–16 (1993)
3. Laudon, K.C., Laudon, J.P.: Management Information Systems: Managing the Digital Firm. Prentice Hall (2011)
4. Dietz, J.L.G.: Enterprise Ontology: Theory and Methodology. Springer (2006)
5. Dietz, J.L.G.: Architecture - Building strategy into design. Netherlands Architecture Forum, Academic Service - SDU, The Hague, The Netherlands (2008)
6. Skyttner, L.: General Systems Theory: Problems, Perspectives, Practice, 2nd edn. World Scientific Publishing Co. Pte. Ltd., Singapore (2005)
7. Maglio, P.P., Vargo, S.L., Caswell, N., Spohrer, J.: The service system is the basic abstraction of the service science. Information Systems and eBusiness Management (2009)

8. Gordijn, J.: Value-based requirements Engineering: Exploring innovatie e-commerce ideas. Vrije Universiteit Amsterdam, Amsterdam (2002)
9. Cameron, B., Leaver, S., Worthington, B.: Value-Based Communication Boosts Business' Perception of IT. Forrester Research (2009)
10. Ettema, R., Dietz, J.L.G.: ArchiMate and DEMO – Mates to Date? In: Albani, A., Barjis, J., Dietz, J.L.G. (eds.) CIAO!/EOMAS 2009. LNBIP, vol. 34, pp. 172–186. Springer, Heidelberg (2009)
11. The Open Group, Archimate 2.0 Specification. Van Haren Publishing (2012)
12. Osterwalder, A., Pigneur, Y.: Business Model Generation: A Handbook for Visionaries, Game Changers, and Challengers. Self-Published (2009)
13. Rosenberg, A., von Rosing, M., Chase, G., Omar, R., Taylor, J.: Applying Real-World BPM in an SAP Environment. SAP Press (2011)
14. Gordijn, J., Osterwalder, A., Pigneur, Y.: Comparing two Business Model Ontologies for Designing eBusiness Models and Value Constellations. In: 18th Bled eConference - eIntegration in Action, Bled, Slovenia (2005)
15. Oliver, R.W.: Real-Time Strategy: What Is Strategy, Anyway? Journal of Business Strategy 22(6), 7–10 (2001)
16. Bleistein, S.J., Aurum, A., Cox, K., Ray, P.K.: Strategy-Oriented Alignment in Requirements Engineering: Linking Business Strategy to Requirements of e-Business Systems using the SOARE Approach. Journal of Research and Practice in Information Technology 36(4), 259–276 (2004)
17. International Institute of Business Analysis, The Guide to the Business Analysis Body of Knowledge Version 2.0 (2009)
18. Quartel, D., Engelsman, W., Jonkers, H., van Sinderen, M.: A goal-oriented requirements modelling language for enterprise architecture. In: IEEE International Enterprise Distributed Object Computing Conference, Auckland, New Zealand (2009)
19. Weigand, H., Heuvel, W.-J.V.D.: A Conceptual Architecture for Pragmatic Web Services. In: First International Conference on the Pragmatic Web, Stuttgart, Germany (2006)
20. Pombinho, J., Tribolet, J.: Modeling the Value of a System's Production – Matching DEMO and e3Value. In: 6th International Workshop on Value Modeling and Business Ontology, Vienna, Austria (2012)
21. Pombinho, J., Aveiro, D., Tribolet, J.: Towards Objective Business Modeling in Enterprise Engineering – Defining Function, Value and Purpose. In: Albani, A., Aveiro, D., Barjis, J. (eds.) EEWC 2012. LNBIP, vol. 110, pp. 93–107. Springer, Heidelberg (2012)
22. Weigand, H., Johannesson, P., Andersson, B., Bergholtz, M., Edirisuriya, A., Ilayperuma, T.: On the Notion of Value Object. In: Martinez, F.H., Pohl, K. (eds.) CAiSE 2006. LNCS, vol. 4001, pp. 321–335. Springer, Heidelberg (2006)
23. Porter, M.E.: Competitive Advantage: Creating and Sustaining Superior Performance. Free Press (1998)
24. Boehm, B.: Value-Based Software Engineering. SIGSOFT Software Engineering Notes 28(2), 4 (2003)
25. Streitfeld, D.: Amazon Signing Up Authors, Writing Publishers Out of Deal. New York Times, A1 (2011)

Intra-transactional Interaction in Internet Auctions: The Impact on Outcomes

Ananth Srinivasan and Liu Fangxing

ISOM Department, University of Auckland Business School
Private Bag 92019, Auckland 1142, New Zealand
a.srinivasan@auckland.ac.nz, fliu048@aucklanduni.ac.nz

Abstract. We report results from empirically examining the effect of intra-transactional interaction in internet auctions on auction outcomes. A widely reported problem with internet auctions is the issue of information asymmetry between sellers and buyers resulting in adverse selection. We argue that rich information exchange among buyers and sellers while an auction is in progress ("live interaction") can address this problem. Live interaction can have significant benefits toward achieving successful outcomes such as meeting the auction reservation price and obtaining price premiums. This is particularly true in the case of products that have relatively high value and possess a complex set of product attributes. Using data from a popular internet auction site, we test this proposition with a data set of 990 used car auctions. A particular feature of this site is that the interactions are publicly viewable, thereby enhancing the likelihood of increased participation in the auction. The proposition is tested using logistic regression models. The results show that the ability of participants to engage in intra-transactional conversations with sellers is significantly related to achieving positive outcomes such as meeting the auction reservation price and obtaining price premiums.

Keywords: Internet auctions, Internet auctions, On-line marketplaces, On-line Platform design, Auction participant behavior.

1 Introduction and Problem Statement

Internet auctions, as a part of e-commerce market activity, has grown even more quickly than the online retail sector (Bajari & Hortacsu, 2004). With the specific case of internet auctions, the issue of information asymmetry leading to adverse selection is a central issue that has been investigated by several researchers. Issues such as trust building and authentication of participants, and their impact on resulting price premiums and whether the auction reserve price was met have received a lot of attention. The key questions here are: how well can the information asymmetry issue be mitigated through the mechanisms that the auction sites offer; how can we better understand the key determinants of the outcomes of online auctions; and how can we improve the design of the market mechanisms to improve efficiency and prevent market failure in the long run.

H. Rahman et al. (Eds.): MCIS 2012, LNBIP 129, pp. 125–138, 2012.

Some research in this space has emphasized the usefulness of studying online auctions of used cars. For example Andrew and Benzing (2007) realized that many previous studies examining the effect of factors such as reputation system and auction characteristics on the price premium were based on relatively low priced homogenous products. The authors argued that the usefulness of the studies were limited, and extended the research on online auction to higher value items such as used cars. They established the argument that the seller and auction characteristics play a greater role in determining the auction outcome for higher priced heterogeneous products. Lewis (2010) also examined the used car online auction market. He proposed that product uncertainty and risk can be reduced by allowing the seller to disclose private information so that an explicit contract can be entered into.

In this research, we focus on one particular channel of information disclosure in online auctions namely publicly viewable interactions between a seller and potential buyers while an auction is in progress. We contend that publicly viewable, intra-transactional, buyer-seller interaction has several advantages over other forms of information disclosure, in terms of affecting the auction outcome. First the questions are asked before the conclusion of an auction thus the interaction is 'live' and more relevant to the current auction. Second, such live interactions can help enforce explicit contracts and therefore reduce uncertainty about the auction. Third, and perhaps most importantly, such interactions represent an approach to information disclosure where the buyers actively participate in the generation of disclosure. This can greatly improve the quality of disclosure and may be preferable to the traditional approach where buyers passively consume disclosure information provided by the seller. In situations where relatively higher value second-hand items are auctioned online, the presumed inherent complexity of the items would need better disclosure to adequately address the information asymmetry concern. This study proposes that the facilitation of such disclosure can positively affect auction outcomes by increasing transaction efficiency and thereby benefitting the stakeholders of the auction. In this paper we test this proposition by examining data from internet auctions of used cars in a popular auction site where live interaction, as described above, is supported.

2 Background

2.1 Influence of Textual Online Word-of-Mouth

Word-of-mouth can serve as an indicator of a product's success, when measured by its degree of penetration and dispersion (Godes & Mayzlin, 2004). It also serves as a leading driver of consumer behaviour and applies a strong influence on consumer judgment and choice of products by affecting consumer awareness and preferences (Herr, Kardes & Kim, 1991). Dellarocas (2003) argues that the online version of word-of-mouth has been given new significance since the internet's capability of bidirectional communication enables individuals to not only receive information from organizations but also make their thoughts and opinions accessible to the global community and therefore create a large-scale network where opinions about a large pool of topics are shared. Dellarocas, Awad and Zhang (2004) point out that word-of-mouth had been given the unprecedented scalability and speed of diffusion, as well as persistence and measurability. The online version of word-of-mouth leaves a digital footprint that can be traced, measured and analysed. Online word-of-mouth is spread through a variety of electronic forms, such as email, e-newsletters, instant messaging such as chat rooms (Gelb & Sundaram, 2002), online community or discussion forums (Hagel & Armstrong, 1997; Bickart & Schindler 2001; Rheingold, 2000; Kozinets, 2002). The most prominent types of online word-of-mouth studied in the e-marketplace are product reviews and seller feedback. They have been argued to have substantial influence over consumers in the buying decision process (Weinberg & Davis, 2004).

Several researchers have looked at the relationships between online product reviews and their influence on consumer choices, product sales, revenue forecasting and planning (e.g. Senecal & Nante, 2004; Chevalier & Mayzlin, 2006; Dellarocas, Awad & Zhang 2007). The positive impact of seller feedback on trust building, quality assurance and effectiveness of online market mechanisms has been reported in the literature (e,g, Dellarocas, 2003; Pavlou and Gefen, 2005; Lucking-Reiley, Bryan & Reeves, 2007). Grant (2002) and Hof (2001) suggest that while there are many reasons explaining the success of online auctions, feedback as examples of reputation systems is a crucial contributor.

Until recently, although the potential utility of studying the textual content of user feedback has been suggested (Ba & Pavlou, 2002), many researchers have focused on numerical online word-of-mouth information such as star rating reviews and polarized seller/buyer feedback ratings. This might be attributed to the difficulty in characterising and assigning meaning to different textual content (Pavlou & Gefen, 2005). Recent work by Hu, Pavlou and Zhang (2006) and Ghose and Ipeirotis (2007) are examples of research that suggest that a careful examination of the textual content of feedback can provide useful results to researchers.

2.2 Performance of Online Auction Sites

Another stream of literature, which is closely related to this paper, investigates market place design elements contributing to the successful outcome of a more specific type of electronic markets: online auctions. The issue of information asymmetry and adverse selection that results from uncertainty has been widely reported in the literature (Akerlof, 1970). Wolf & Muhanna (2005) argue that the information asymmetry and adverse selection is more pronounced in online auctions. Spatial and temporal separation between sellers and the potential buyers exacerbates this problem (Pavlou, Liang & Xue, 2007). Gefen, Karahanna & Straub (2003) state that such separation inhibits buyers using social cues such as physical interaction and body language to assess seller quality and buyers in the online context can only assess product quality through the internet interface rather than testing product quality by "kicking the tires". Several approaches to the design of mechanisms to mitigate the ill effects of information asymmetry in online auction sites are suggested in the literature. Almost all these approaches focus on enhancing trust among auction stakeholders by proper information disclosure about sellers, buyers, and products. We explore the issue of disclosure in more detail in the next section.

2.3 Information Disclosure in Online Auction Sites

Information Disclosure: Seller Initiated. Dimoka and Pavlou (2008) developed a framework to classify product information that can be disclosed by a seller in an online auction site through adopting the information signalling theory. Categories of disclosure in the framework include: 1) product description; 2) third-party product certification; 3) posted auction prices; and 4) intrinsic product characteristics. They argue that high quality combinations of textual, visual and multi-media based product description can competently reveal the details of the item being sold, and therefore benefit the seller from investing more time and cost for extra explanations, and benefit the buyers with sufficient product information. Jin (2005) suggests that the accurate disclosure of information about products encourages the determination of both monetary profits and seller goodwill. In a second-hand product auction situation, the product description has even more significance, as Lewis (2010) argues that the disclosure of seller private information can help to form a verifiable and enforceable contract between the seller and the buyer and therefore reduce the uncertainty in the auction.

Information Disclosure: Seller Initiated. The first category of buyer-initiated information disclosure is seller feedback from the reputation systems, which most online auction websites have. The feedback mechanisms have been well studied by previous researchers, and so has the information disclosed in such mechanisms. User feedback data is the outcome of a completed transaction (Richins, 1983), through which the buyers express their experiences and feelings about the completed transaction. The feedback information disclosed can be a numerical star rating, or it can be textual comments that identify the seller's outstanding or abysmal behaviour (Pavlou & Dimoka, 2006). The impact of such feedback information is significant in establishing trust and fostering cooperation, as well as affecting other buyers' purchasing decisions (Friedkin, 1998).

Another channel through which buyers can disclose information in online auctions is the questions that they pose to the seller. Some online auction sites offer potential buyers the chance to engage the seller with questions about the particular transaction. In their study of the online conversations, Godes & Mayzlin (2004) recognized the need to understand such interactions because they proposed that the environment where the conversations take place can be apprehended better by directly observing the interpersonal communication flow. However, from a researcher's point of view, such interaction typically takes place privately (in which case the nature of the interaction is not observable) or it occurs after the transaction is concluded (in which case its impact on the current transaction is negated).

2.4 Quality of Information Disclosure

The main motivation behind the choice of buyer-initiated intra-transactional questions in an online auction as the focus of this work is that buyer questions are deemed to serve as a means of influencing the quality of information disclosure by the seller and enhances information value to all potential buyers. The reason for this impact can be explained from three aspects: explicit contract formation, the live timing of current transaction, and the nature of bi-directionality as well as the consequent ability to trigger active information disclosure.

Contract Formation with Disclosed Information. Many researchers have focused their studies on the role of seller feedback mechanisms in the auction websites (Resnick & Zeckhauser, 2005; Houser & Wooders, 2006), where they proposed that reputation systems can predict sellers' future actions. While some evidence was found to support this argument, certain problematic aspects of this approach are noted. For example, Resnick and Zechhauser (2005) state that the net seller feedback statistic from eBay is far from the best predictor of future performance (Resnick & Zeckhauser, 2005). Lewis (2010) argues that while feedback systems can foster buyer-seller cooperation, the contracts that such systems help to enforce are implicit contracts. There are no enforceable contractual obligations on the seller to perform to the historical standard. On the other hand, a buyer-posed question requires the seller to respond and thus make a verifiable disclosure on the particular auction webpage. Lewis (2010) argues that this emphasis on the seller's private information shifts the focus from the feedback system and the associated implicit contract towards the role of disclosure and the explicit contract it defines.

Timing of Information Disclosure. Numerous papers provide evidence of the fact that word-of-mouth communication is an outcome of consumer actions (Richins, 1983; Anderson, 1998; and Bowman and Narayandas, 2001). Anderson (1998) proposed a U-shaped model while examining the positive and negative experience. He argues that the two extremes: the very satisfied and the very un-satisfied are more likely to engage in word-of-mouth communications. In contrast to the interaction information from feedback mechanisms, the interactions represented by the buyer-posed questions and seller responses provide a much more timely and relevant impact to the current transaction. The questions are asked and are to be answered before the auction closes and therefore the information disclosed from such interaction is influential on the current auction. This disclosure is therefore likely to be a better performance predictor for the particular transaction, because the questions and seller responses are focused and transaction-oriented.

Active Disclosure of Information. While voluntarily disclosed product information can be used to form explicit contracts and mitigate product uncertainties, it has some disadvantages compared to buyer initiated disclosure. First, the nature of product description is not 'bi-directional' and thus the description can hardly be referred as interaction between buyers and sellers. In this sense, voluntary information disclosure by the seller can be considered as 'passive' information from the perspective of potential buyers in online auction markets. It is what the seller deems to be important about the product, or what the seller wants to show the potential buyers. Such information is not actively triggered by potential buyers and thus may not be a true representation of what product information a buyer considers necessary to be disclosed. On the other hand, questions asked during an auction are true bidirectional interactions which are initiated by the buyers. They represent the perfect example of buyer driven active disclosure and are hypothesized to have the ability to improve the overall information disclosure, since they facilitate the disclosure of information that buyers really desire.

Conceptual Framework. The building block of this conceptual framework comes from the two ways of mitigating the adverse selection problem in online auction sites: establishing trust and facilitating information disclosure. In addition to the elements that have been discussed in the literature, this work proposes that an additional factor which we refer to as "Live Interaction" will be significant in terms of influence on the final auction outcome. The term "Live Interaction" stands for online interactions that have been triggered by buyer-initiated questions while an auction is in progress. Compared to other formats of information disclosure, it has the ability to form explicit and enforceable contracts; it takes place during a particular transaction therefore is relevant to and has impact on the current transaction; and it is bidirectional communication initiated by the buyer and thus facilitates active information disclosure. This study explicitly acknowledges the importance of textual data of online word-of-mouth. Therefore the textual characteristics of live interaction during an auction are considered along with other factors that have been previously reported: the pre-set auction configuration (auction length, end time, etc.); voluntary disclosure of information (photo, text, etc.); and the reputation system (feedback star rating, etc.) in the comprehensive conceptual framework (Figure 1). The dotted section of the figure segments the particular focus of this research.

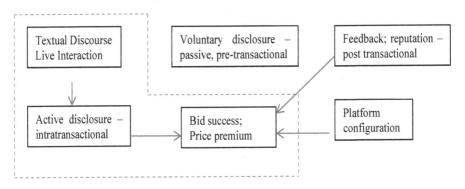

Fig. 1. The Conceptual Model

3 Research Design

3.1 Data Collection Site

TradeMe is the second most visited auction website in New Zealand after Google New Zealand. It is ranked 4th in New Zealand and 1500th in the world by Alexa Internet (Alexa Internet, 2011). The site accounts for a billion page views per month and is responsible for 68% of all internet web-page traffic originated from New Zealand servers (MacManus, 2006). TradeMe has about 2.8 million active registered members, with more than 1.67 million auctions and around 10,000 people online at any given time (TradeMe, 2011). A key feature of the TradeMe auction site is its "Ask seller a question" forum which incorporates both the live timing of interaction between sellers and buyers and the public viewability of the content. In a particular auction page, if a potential buyer has any question regarding the product, seller, or transaction as a whole, he or she may pose questions to the seller during the auction and the seller in turn is able to respond. Once a question has been answered by the seller, the original question and the answer will be shown in the forum on the auction page along with the other information such as the questioner's user ID and rating score (TradeMe, 2011). An example of such interaction is shown in Appendix A.

3.2 Car Auctions in TradeMe

The product category that we focused on was car auctions. The main reasons for doing this were:

- TradeMe Motors is one of the most important categories within the website's operation. There are over 60,000 used car auctions currently online, this gives us a relatively large data pool (TradeMe, 2011).
- The value of the items in used car auctions is relatively high. The typical potential buyer will seek as much information as is necessary before making an expensive bid. This in turn highlights the importance of high quality disclosure to achieve successful auction outcomes.
- Used cars represent a category where there is a high level of product attribute complexity. Therefore the quality of information disclosure is vital to address any information asymmetry in order to deal with adverse selection and prevent subsequent market failure.

These characteristics would foster higher participation in a live interaction forum thereby generating a substantial level of intra-transactional information exchange.

3.3 Data Collection

Data required from TradeMe is collected via a software agent using TradeMe's authenticated API service. This service allows 1000 API calls per hour to the TradeMe auction site. Relevant listings are identified by an API call to the search feature. Results are parsed and added to a watch list in a database. The application revisits each listing periodically and stores the raw results in XML format in the database. New listings are automatically identified from the search method which gets called once every 2 hours. For a two-week period (from 1st April to 15th April 2011), the software agent compiled a dataset containing 990 used car auctions which were closed. Of these, there were 295 listings with at least one bid and 170 listings where the reserve price was met representing a success rate of just over 17%.

4 Model

The basic question that we intend to empirically test is: what aspects of internet auction based intra-transactional (live) interaction among sellers and buyers are influential in determining auction outcomes. As per the conceptual model from Figure 1, the basic model that we test can be expressed as: *Auction Outcome = f (live interaction variables; "other relevant" variables)*.

4.1 Dependent Variables

We define the dependent variable, outcome, in a couple of different ways. First, we look at whether the reserve price of the auction was met or not – a preliminary indicator of auction success. Second, we look at whether a price premium was achieved in a successful auction – a refined measure of auction success. Both these dependent variables are used as binary indicators. The resulting model that we test is a logistic regression model.

The price premium indicator is computed by comparing the final auction price with "market value" of the product. The market value is determined by looking at the valuation of comparable cars using the Price Check service offered by Turners Auction, New Zealand. This is the largest (offline) auction house in the country with an annual auction capacity of 120000 vehicles. The service provides market price indicators for cars rated as being excellent, average or poor. We classified each car from a successful auction in our dataset into one of these categories based on the guidelines offered by the service. A comparison of the final selling price of the car in our dataset with the market value price from the service provides the price premium indicator for the auction.

4.2 Independent Variables

The first set of independent variables in the model is obtained by examining the live interaction records from the transactions. These essentially consist of counts of questions and answers where buyers can engage sellers about the specifics of an auction, as well as the characteristics of these questions and answers. The general purpose of doing this is to actively bring about higher quality disclosure about the transaction. The following make up the live interaction count variable set.

QuestionCount – this is a count of the number of questions posted by the buyer during the auction.

UnansweredQuestion – this is a count of the number of questions posted by the buyer but not responded to by the seller.

SellerCommentsCount – the seller has the option to post comments to provide additional information to the description given in the auction. This variable refers to the number of comments added voluntarily (not trigged by a buyer question) by the seller.

ThreadCount – this is the number of threads in the auction's "ask seller a question" section. A thread is defined as a back-and-forth conversation between the seller and one particular buyer, for example if one buyer posts multiple questions in an auction which are responded to by the buyer, they constitute one thread.

AvgQuestionLength – this is the average length in words of the questions posted by the buyer in one auction.

AvgResponseLength – this is the average length in words of the answers posted by the seller in response to the questions in one auction.

AvgResponseTime_Seconds – this represents the average time elapsed (in seconds) between a buyer's question being posed and the seller's response to that question.

The other independent variables in the models are the structural variables outside the live interaction set, which were considered to be important determinants of auction outcomes based on prior research. The first three of these variables represent a more passive set of disclosure items and are those that are driven entirely by the seller. The case of seller ratings is slightly different in that they are accumulated ratings by several buyers based on past experiences with a particular seller.

PhotoCount –this represents the number of photos that the seller has posted in the specific auction

SellerRating – this measures the feedback rating that the seller has. TradeMe uses a star-rating system, in which a seller can receive positive, neutral, and negative feedback. The final score for a seller is obtained by subtracting the number of negative feedback points from the total number of positive feedback points received from individual members.

OptionalAttributes – this is the number of optional descriptive variables, provided by the seller in an auction, which are not mandatory.

Features – TradeMe allows sellers to tick a number of appropriate features for the listed car from a total selection of 10. This variable measures the number of features chosen by the seller in a particular auction.

5   Results

We test the logistic regression model with the following variants:

- Independent variables are included in the model in both raw and log transformed versions. The transformation is used to address concerns regarding the distribution of these variables.
- The set of independent variables include live interaction variables by themselves as well as these variables embedded in a larger model that includes other structural variables. This will partial out the effects of independent variables that influence outcomes but are not measures of live interaction.

Therefore, we produce four sub-models for each of the two dependent variables. The results are presented in the following sections.

5.1 Dependent Variable: Reserve Met Indicator

The results from the four models are shown below in Table 1. The number of auctions in these models is 990. (Full model results are available on request - the results have

Table 1. Logistic Regression models – Dependent variable: Reserve Price Met (n=900)

Model	Description	Nagelkerke R^2	Significant independent variables
Model 1a	Live interaction variables	0.486	Question count: B=0.682, p<0.001
			Unanswered questions: B=-1.67, p<0.001
			Average response length: B=-0.007, p=0.016
			Thread count: B=-1.142, p=0.001
Model 1b	Log transformed variables	0.498	Question count: B=3.175, p<0.001
			Unanswered questions: B=-2.391, p<0.001
			Average Question Length: B=0.919, p=0.013
			Average Response Speed: -0.376, p<0.001
			Thread count: B=-1.445, p=0.009
Model 1c	Variables from Model 1a with additional non-live interaction structural variables	0.600	Question count: B=0.814, p<0.001
			Unanswered questions: B=-1.823, p<0.001
			Average response length: B=-0.007, p=0.032
			Thread count: B=-1.410, p<0.001
			Seller Rating: B=0.003, p=0.02
			Optional Attributes: B=0.278, p=0.018
			Features: B=0.446, p=0.001
Model 1d	Log transformed variables	0.586	Question count: B=3.347, p<0.001
			Unanswered questions: B=-2.153, p=0.001
			Average response length: B=-0.426, p=0.049
			Thread count: B=-1.473, p=0.012
			Seller Rating: B=0.353, p=0.004
			Optional Attributes: B=2.747, p=0.025
			Features: B=2.067, p=0.012
			Average Response Speed: B=-0.283, p=0.01)

been summarized in this table in the interest of brevity). Models 1a and 1b show the main results from the models for live interaction variables with and without log transformations. Models 1c and 1d show the main results for live interaction variables embedded within a larger structural model with and without log transformations. All models show chi-squared values significant at p<0.000.

All four models exhibit reasonable levels of predictive power. The significance of live interaction variables demonstrates the value of this aspect of auction design. The

Table 2. Logistic Regression models - Dependent variable: Price Premium (n=170)

Model	Description	Nagelkerke R^2	Significant independent variables
Model 2a	Live interaction variables	0.425	Question count: B=0.354, p<0.001
			Unanswered questions: B=-2.076, p=0.002
			Thread count: B=-0.896, p=0.006
Model 2b	Log transformed variables	0.426	Question count: B=2.176, p<0.001
			Unanswered questions: B=-3.468, p<0.000
			Thread count: B=-1.393, p=0.018
Model 2c	Variables from Model 2a with additional non-live interaction structural variables	0.518	Question count: B=0.340, p<0.001
			Unanswered questions: B=-1.817, p=0.007
			Thread count: B=-0.853, p=0.012
			Seller Rating: B=0.001, p=0.007
Model 2d	Log transformed variables	0.504	Question count: B=2.122, p<0.001
			Unanswered questions: B=-3.178, p=0.001
			Thread count: B=-1.601, p=0.014
			Seller Rating: B=0.364, p=0.006

ability of participants to engage in intra-transactional discourse contributes positively to meeting the reserve price. Unanswered questions, verbose responses and extended engagement (evidenced by thread counts) all carry penalties toward successful outcomes. It is interesting that quick responses carry a negative coefficient perhaps indicating that buyers prefer thoughtful and considered answers to their questions. While Models 1c and 1d that included other structural variables improved the overall performance of the models, the significance of the live interaction variables remained more or less unchanged.

5.2 Dependent Variable: Price Premium Indicator

Following the presentation convention from Section 5.1, we now present model results where the dependent variable is price premium indicator. Recall that price premiums are achieved when the final auction price exceeds the market value of the car. Again, all models show chi-squared values at p<0.000. The number of listings for these models is 170.

Consistent with the results from Models 1a-1d, facilitating live interaction has an influential effect on achieving price premiums. An increased number of questions indicate an enhanced level of buyer interest in the auction leading to better outcomes. Unanswered or verbose responses are penalized. The larger structural models (2c and 2d) improve model performance but the significance of live interaction remains largely unchanged.

6 Discussion and Conclusion

The basic premise in this paper is that the design of internet auction platforms can achieve good quality outcomes if the right design features are built in to them. High value auctions are susceptible to the occurrence of information asymmetry among auction participants leading to the well-known adverse selection problem. Methods of mitigating information asymmetry need to be carefully investigated when auction platforms are design. A useful mechanism that has been underutilized in auction platforms is the provision of intra-transactional information exchange among auction participants. The auction platform that is discussed in this paper is one of the few that employs a particular method of such information exchange. The modelling results clearly show that when participants have the opportunity to indulge in such exchange, better outcomes as measured by meeting auction reserve prices and achieving price premiums follow. As a next step, it would be useful to compare these results with auction sites where intra-transactional interaction is not present. This would take the form of a controlled field experiment.

In this paper, we looked at the existence (through counts) of live interaction. The next step in the research is to investigate the actual content of information exchange in order to see what types of information lead to better quality outcomes. This will become increasingly more valuable as internet auctions rapidly move toward deployment on mobile platforms that require rich and quick information being made available to participants.

Acknowledgments. We are grateful to Mr. Jason Tung for his assistance with data preparation for this project.

References

1. Alexa Internet Inc. Alexa The Web Information Company (2011),
   http://www.alexa.com/ (retrieved March 24, 2011)
2. Anderson, E.W.: Customer Satisfaction and Word of Mouth. Journal of Service Research 1(1), 5–17 (1998)
3. Andrews, T., Benzing, C.: The Determinants of Price in Internet Auctions of Used Cars. Atlantic Economic Journal, International Atlantic Economic Society 35(1), 43–57 (2007)
4. Ba, S., Pavlou, P.A.: Evidence of the Effect of Trust Building Technology in Electronic Markets: Price Premiums and Buyer Behavior. MIS Quarterly 26(3), 243–268 (2002)
5. Bajari, P., Ali, H.S.: Winner's Curse, Reserve Prices and Endogenous Entry: Empirical Insights from eBay. Rand Journal of Economics 34, 329–356 (2003)
6. Bickart, B., Shindler, R.M.: Internet forums as influential sources of consumer information. Journal of Interactive Marketing 15(3), 31–40 (2001)

7. Bowman, D., Farley, J.U., Narayandas, D.: Managing Customer-Initiated Contacts with Manufacturers: The Impact on Share of Category Requirements and Word-of-Mouth Behavior. Journal of Marketing Research 38, 281–297 (2001)
8. Chevalier, J., Mayzlin, D.: The Effect of Word of Mouth on Sales: Online Book Reviews. Journal of Marketing Research 43(3), 9 (2006)
9. Dellarocas, C.: The digitization of word of mouth: promise and challenges of online feedback mechanisms. Management Science 49(10), 1407–1424 (2003)
10. Dellarocas, C.N., Awad, N.F., Zhang, X.: Exploring the Value of Online Product Reviews in Forecasting Sales: The Case of Motion Pictures. Journal of Interactive Marketing 21(4), 23–45 (2007)
11. Dimoka, A., Pavlou, P.: Understanding and Mitigating Product Uncertainty in Online Auction Marketplaces. 2008 Industry Studies Conference Paper (2008), http://ssrn.com/abstract=1135006 (retrieved April 05, 2011)
12. Friedkin, N.E.: A Structual Theory of Social Influence. Cambridge University Press, Cambridge (1998)
13. Gefen, D., Karahanna, E., Straub, D.W.: Trust and TAM in online shopping: An integrated model. MIS Quarterly 27(1), 51–90 (2003)
14. Gelb, B.D., Sundaram, S.: Adapting to word of mouth. Business Horizons 45(4), 21–25 (2002)
15. Ghose, A., Ipeirotis, P.G.: Designing Novel Review Ranking Systems: Predicting the Usefulness and Impact of Reviews. In: International Conference on Electronic Commerce 2007, pp. 19–22 (2007)
16. Godes, D., Mayzlin, D.: Using Online Conversations to Measure Word of Mouth Communication. Marketing Science 23(4), 545–560 (2004)
17. Hof, R.D.: The people's company. Business Week, pp. EB10-11, EB14-17 December 3 (2001)
18. Houser, D., Wooders, J.: Reputation in auctions: Theory, and evidence from eBay. Journal of Economics & Management Strategy 15, 353–369 (2006)
19. Hu, N., Pavlou, P.A., Zhang, J.: Can online reviews reveal a product's true quality? Empirical findings and analytical modeling of online word-of-mouth communication. In: Proceedings of the 7th ACM Conference on Electronic Commerce (EC 2006), pp. 324–330 (2006)
20. Jin, G.: Competition and disclosure incentive: an empirical study of HMOs. RAND Journal of Eonomics 26, 93–113 (2005)
21. Kozinets, R.V.: The Field Behind the Screen: Using Netnography for Marketing Research in Online Communities. Journal of Marketing Research 39(2), 61–72 (2002)
22. Lewis, G.: Asymmetric Information, Adverse Selection and Online Disclosure: The Case of eBay Motors (2010), http://ssrn.com/abstract=1358341 (retrieved May 07, 2011)
23. Lucking-Reiley, D., Bryan, D., Prasad, N., Reeves, D.: Pennies from eBay: The Determinants of Price in Online Auction. Journal of Industrial Economics 55(2), 223–233 (2007)
24. Pavlou, P.A., Dimoka, A.: The Nature and Role of Feedback Text Comments in Online Marketplaces: Implications for Trust Building, Price Premiums, and Seller Differentiation. Information Systems Research 17(4), 392–414 (2006)
25. Pavlou, P.A., Gefen, D.: Psychological Contract Violation in Online Marketplaces: Antecedents, Consequences, and Moderating Role. Information Systems Research 16(4), 372–399 (2005)

26. Pavlou, P.A., Liang, H., Xue, Y.: Understanding and Mitigating Uncertainty in Online Environments: An Agency Theory Perspective. MIS Quarterly 31(1), 105–136 (2007)
27. Resnick, P., Zeckhauser, R.: Trust among Strangers in Internet Transactions: Empirical Analysis of eBay's Reputation System. In: The Economics of the Internet and E-commerce. Advances in Applied Microeconomics, vol. 11. JAI Press (2002)
28. Richins, M.L.: Negative Word-of-Mouth by Dissatisfied Consumers: A Pilot Study. Journal of Marketing 47, 68–78 (1983)
29. Senecal, S., Nantel, J.: The influence of online product recommendations on consumers' online choices. Journal of Retailing 80, 159–169 (2004)
30. Straub, D., Gefen, D., Boudreau, M.C.: The ISWorld Quantitative, Positivist Research Methods Website (2004), http://dstraub.cis.gsu.edu:88/quant/ (retrieved April 07, 2011)
31. Weinberg, B.D., Davis, L.: Exploring the WOW in online-auction feedback. Journal of Business Research 58, 1609–1621 (2005)
32. Wolf, J.R., Muhanna, W.A.: Adverse Selection and Reputation Systems in Online Auctions: Evidence From Ebay Motors. In: Twenty-Sixth International Conference on Information Systems (2005)

Appendix 1: TradeMe's Questions and Answers Section

Note: Member IDs and phone numbers have been replaced to preserve their privacy.

Questions and answers

Q do you have a BUY NOW price please? member1 (64 ⭐) 8:17 pm, Fri 11 Mar
A Please call me and we can try to find a suitable price for both of us Mark 021XXXXXXX 8:27 am, Sat 12 Mar

Q why was it re registered? member2 (496 ⭐) 3:45 pm, Sun 13 Mar
A Please call me and i can explain 021XXXXXXX. 7:19 am, Mon 14 Mar

Q Hi, why was it re registered. Thanks. member3 (21 ⭐) 9:58 pm, Wed 16 Mar
A Please call me and I can explain. 021XXXXXXX 9:10 am, Thu 17 Mar

Q Hi, I have a hearing problem, you are going to have to answer here. Cheers. member3 (21 ⭐) 9:37 am, Thu 17 Mar
A As below 9:45 pm, Thu 17 Mar

Q i also would like to know why it was reregisteredbut would like the answer for all to see i dont see a problem if all is ok. the car is in your family so you know the history. member4 (3 ⭐) 9:22 pm, Thu 17 Mar
A Car was deregistered as it was accident damaged.It was hit slightly in the rear.As it was so new and so low in the kms the insurance company gave the owner a new vehicle.The one i own was deregistered and sold.Any check welcomed.It has run perfectly for me the last two years and 30 000 kms. Damage was repaired for about 1500 and certified by an engineer.I doubt anyone could see any repair signs . 9:45 pm, Thu 17 Mar

Q Hi - do you have any photos before repairs were done? member5 (50 ⭐) 4:47 pm, Mon 21 Mar
A Sorry no.It was some time ago.The damage was quite small and as it was you could still drive it.In the event you buy it and are not happy with the small repair I will give you a full refund on the car .The repair was certified by an engineer as all cars reregister must be returned to factory specification. 8:49 am, Tue 22 Mar

Semiotics Perception towards Designing Users' Intuitive Web User Interface: A Study on Interface Signs

Muhammad Nazrul Islam

Turku Centre for Computer Science (TUCS)
Department of Information Technologies,
Åbo Akademi University, 20520 Turku, Finland
nazrulturku@gmail.com

Abstract. Web interface signs (e.g., navigational link, button, image, command affordance, thumbnails, etc.) are complicated as well as crucial elements of web user interfaces. Interface signs act as a means of users' interaction and communication artifacts with a web application. Designing intuitive interface signs contributes to improve the users' understanding, satisfaction, communicability of web interfaces, and the like. Sign design principles are semiotics by nature; since semiotics is the doctrine of signs. Therefore, the fundamental objective of this study was to reveal the features of user intuitive interface signs for boosting web usability from a semiotics point of view. In order to achieve this research goal, a systematic empirical study was conducted on 404 web signs and revealed a number of semiotics considerations for designing user intuitive web interface signs to improve applications' usability.

Keywords: Semiotics, web interface, web usability, interface design, web sign ontology.

1   Introduction

An increasing number of internet applications and services compete for users' attention, time, and satisfaction. Usability, which measures the easiness with which users interact with web interfaces, contributes to users' satisfaction, happiness, as well as pleasure; and on the contrary lack of usability contributes to users' dissatisfaction and frustration, and thus eventually will result in total abandonment of the system. Therefore, designing intuitive interface signs for the users is essential to maintain the user satisfied, to ensure understanding, and to provide the means to communicate, e.g., [1], [2], [3], [4], [5]. In other words, designing intuitive interface signs for the users is essential for improving applications' usability. These design principles focus on sense production and interpretation and thereby implicate semiotics, the doctrine of sign, that is, the science of signs [6].

The web interface provides the medium of interaction between the human and the computer in web applications and plays a vital role in the systems' usability. Web interface design and its usability evaluation are employed along a number of

H. Rahman et al. (Eds.): MCIS 2012, LNBIP 129, pp. 139–155, 2012.
© Springer-Verlag Berlin Heidelberg 2012

dimensions. Bolchini et al. [1] include content, information architecture, navigation, layout and the interface signs (e.g., command affordances, labels, icons, symbols, etc.) in these dimensions (Figure 1). If two applications are identical with respect to content, information, navigation and graphical layout but different in terms of interface signs, then we can assume that more intuitive interface signs will contribute positively to the usability.

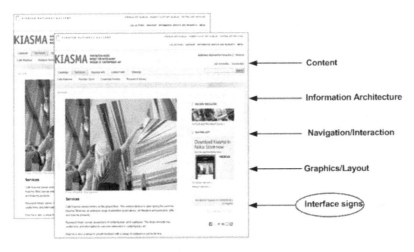

Fig. 1. Web interface design and usability evaluation dimensions

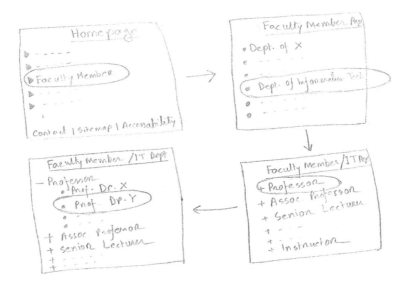

Fig. 2. An example of users' interactions with web signs

Let us place (see figure 2) a simple example (i) to provide an idea of web signs, and also (ii) to show how all the content and functions are directed by web signs in a web application. For instance, a user wants to know about *'Prof. Dr. Y'* (e.g., contact details, research interest, etc.), who worked at the department of Information Technology at 'X' university. To perform/obtain this task/information, a user needs to interact with a number of signs, which seems more intuitive to him/her. One possible way to perform this task could be to click (i) firstly on a web sign 'Faculty Member' on *Homepage*, (ii) then on 'Dept. of Information Tech.' on *Faculty Member* page, (iii) after that on '+ Professor' on *Faculty Member/IT Dept.* page, and (iv) finally on '• Prof. Dr. Y' on *Faculty Member/IT Dept.* page.

Moreover, intuitiveness of interface signs affects communicability, and communicability subsequently affects on application's usability [7], [8], [9]. As Salgado et al. [7] stated: "Communicability problems tend to lead to usability problems, since usability tacitly requires that users 'get the system's logic through interface signs' before they can possibly learn to use them, retain them, and be satisfied with interaction" [7]. In previous work, a study was conducted to observe how users' interpretations of web interface signs affect web usability. The study concluded that users' inaccurate interpretations of interface signs significantly aligned to produce the usability problems and as a consequence its affects overall web usability [10], [11]. Another study [12] focused on the usability evaluation of interface signs' intuitiveness in order to assess the value of integrating semiotics perception in usability evaluation. The results of this study showed that integrating semiotic perception in usability testing yielded a number of benefits that contributed to the application's usability evaluation. Nevertheless, semiotics research on web interface in particular focuses mainly on the language of the web interface and its usability.

Therefore, this research focuses on web interface signs to investigate issues related to design/redesign web interface signs, so that end users may easily interpret a sign to retrieve its meaning properly. One fundamental research question with such research is *"What semiotics considerations are needed to design users' intuitive web interface signs for boosting the web usability?"* To attain this research goal, this study was conducted on 404 web interface signs retrieved from 20 websites (10 websites from educational web domain and 10 from cultural heritage web domain) and their archived versions; this study revealed a number of semiotics considerations to design the web signs to be intuitive to the end users. It is important to mention here that an earlier version of this work is published in [13], where the study was conducted on 272 web interface signs of educational websites.

This paper is structured as follows. Semiotics, web interface sign, and web sign ontology are discussed to provide an overview of the research background in section 2. In section 3, the study method is presented. Study results and a discussion on study results are discussed in sections 4 and 5 respectively. The conclusion and ideas for future work are provided in the final section.

2   Research Background

2.1   Semiotics and Web Interface Sign

Signs take the form of words, images, flavors, odors, acts, objects, sounds, and the like, with an intrinsic meaning. Without having an intrinsic as well as intended meaning these things are not treated as signs and for treating these as signs designers need to invest them with meaning [14]. Hence, a sign is considered as a sign when it is interpreted by someone as such [15]. The user interface of a web application generally consists to a large extent of interface signs, whether we call them links, indexes, images, buttons, icons, or even animations [16].

The study of signs, symbols, and signification is called semiotics. Semiotics is considered an account of representation, signification, meaning, as well as reference [17]. A complete definition of semiotics could be presented as "the study of signs, signification, and signifying systems" [18]. A theory and a model of semiotics are presented here to provide a concise idea about semiotics, interface signs and their interpretations.

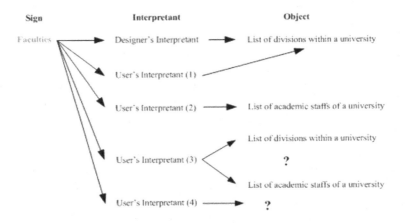

Fig. 3. Possible Interpretation of a web interface sign

Peirce's semiotics model [6] consists of a triadic relationship with the representamen (representation or sign), the object and the interpretant. The representamen stands to somebody for something in some respect or capacity. It addresses somebody and creates in the mind of that person an equivalent, or perhaps a more developed sign; the object (referent) is the actual thing the sign stands for. The interpretant (meaning) is therefore the sign created in the mind of the perceiver or the reaction caused by the object in the perceiver [19]. For these, a sign requires the concurrent presence of these three constituents. According to Gottlob Frege, the sign is a logical triad consisting of: *Zeichen* (sign) for the symbol, *Sinn* (sense) for the concept, and *Bedeutung* (reference) for the object [20]. As an example, Frege cited the terms '*morning star*' and '*evening star*'. Both terms refer to the planet Venus as their meaning, but their senses are very unlike the way in which the planet is presented (one term refers to a star seen in the morning, and other one refers to a star seen in the evening). An example of Pierce's model depicted in figure 3, observes that the same sign may refer to different objects by different interpretants. Frege's theory depicted in figure 4, observes that different signs may lead to the same object by different interpretants.

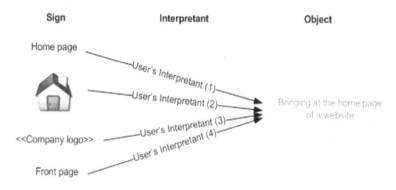

Fig. 4. Different signs referring to the same object

In the above discussion, some important properties can be discerned. For instance i) there is no one-to-one link between the object and the sign; various signs may have a single meaning in spite of several meanings, ii) the end users usually guess the sign meanings through the *creation and interpretation* of 'signs', iii) the intended meaning of a sign depends on the socio-cultural context, and iv) the end users communicate with an application to perform their desired tasks by interacting with interface signs. Due to these properties, users can perform the desired task properly when the end user's interpretant matches the referential object of the interface signs with the designer's interpretant, and incorrectly otherwise. That is why, it is important to investigate why some signs are more intuitive to the users and some are not. This research particularly focused on this point to reveal the semiotics considerations to design interface signs to be intuitive to the users.

2.2   Web Sign Ontology

According to the Speroni [21], the term 'ontology' is defined as the set of concepts and skills that the user should own for understanding the referential meaning of an interface sign. From the users' perspective, ontology is the knowledge or concepts that are needed to understand and properly interpret the meaning of an interface sign. From the designers' perspective, it is the knowledge or concepts presupposed and pointed by an interface sign. A proper users' interpretation of interfaces sign depends on a matching between ontologies presupposed by the interface sign and the ones owned by the user. Followings are the most common ontologies (see figure 5) that are used in many websites [1], [21], [22]:

InterLocutor/Institution Ontology (ILO): each website talks on behalf of its owner (institution/organization) or interlocutor. Therefore, it is very common to have interface signs in website that refers to the world of the owner. ILO refers to the

Fig. 5. Examples of Ontologies showed in University Technology Malaysia's Homepage

knowledge concerning the organization behind the website. In a university website signs like "university administration", "About us", etc. are the instances of ILO.

Internet Ontology (IO): this ontology refers to the knowledge of the world of web, web browsing and its concepts and conventions. For example, the signs "back", "home", "add to cart", etc. in web interface.

Website Ontology (WO): there are interface signs which are specific enough to a particular website. Knowledge concerning this specific signs is referred as WO. User could properly interpret the meaning of this signs only he or she is familiar with this website. For example, a specific sign could be used in a university website to represent the departments and this could be intuitively understandable only to the users who are familiar with this particular website.

Topic Ontology (TO): the knowledge concerning the concepts belonging to the particular topics the website talks about. In a university website any interface sign referring to concepts strictly related to professor, courses, etc. are examples of signs referring to the topic ontology.

Common Sense Ontology (CSO): This ontology refers to the knowledge concerning concepts belonging to common background of users and uses the common sense. A sign "calendar" in a university website could be an example of CSO. Since it makes use of the common concept of calendar from the real world and it stands for providing the list of university events grouped by date.

Web Domain Ontology (WDO): there are interface signs which are specific enough to a particular web domain (e.g., cultural heritage web domain, e-commerce web domain, etc.). Knowledge concerning this specific signs is referred as WDO. User could properly interpret the meaning of these signs only if he or she is familiar with this web domain. For example, signs like "Departments", "Research", "Faculties", etc. could be used in a university website of educational web domain and this could be intuitively understandable only to the users who are familiar with this particular web domain.

3   Study Methodology

3.1   Steps of Study Method

This research investigates issues related to the interface sign re-design and its intuitiveness through a comparative study of web interface signs before and after re-design. The following three sequential steps were followed to attain the research goal of this study.

Step 1: Websites selection and retrieval of its archival version. To obtain the research objective, which websites were chosen was not important but important was what kind of changes were made in interface sign redesign and how these issues of re-design affect on web sign interpretation. Therefore, this empirical study was conducted on (i) university websites of education web domain and (ii) museum websites of cultural heritage web domain to demonstrate the feasibility and soundness of this research. A total 10 university websites and 10 museum websites (see the appendix) were selected. After that, historical versions of these websites were retrieved using web archival software named *'Wayback Machine'* (http://www.archive.org). A small set of heuristics were employed to select the websites and its archival version. For instance, (i) archival version should be available for the selected websites; (ii) archival homepage was properly retrieved by the *'Wayback Machine'*, e.g., without any retrieval failure message; (iii) if a website has more than one archival version then chose (analytically) a suitable one that seemed more suitable for this study, e.g., sufficient changes made in version update; and the like. The study was conducted only on the homepage of selected websites and their archived versions, i.e., a total of 40 homepages were considered for this study.

Step 2: Data collection. An inspection was carried out very meticulously for each of the interface signs in archived version's homepages to discover the signs that were re-designed in the current version. A total of 202 signs were discovered from 20 homepages that were redesigned. After that, both the re-designed signs and its old version's signs were investigated to obtain the study data (e.g., if it was found that an interface sign S in archived version webpage was re-designed as S' in the current version webpage, then this study investigated both the S and S' to collect the study data). Thus, a total of 404 signs (202 archived version's signs plus 202 redesigned signs) from 40 homepages were considered in this comparative study. This study produced the following types of data-

a. *Level of difficulty or intuitiveness experienced* in interpreting the sign properly. The level of complexity was given in a scale of 1 to 5, where 1 refers to 'very easy/intuitive' and 5 refers to 'extremely difficult/not intuitive at all' to interpret the intended meaning of an interface sign.

b. *Type of sign* indicates whether an interface sign was linguistic or iconic. A linguistic sign refers to the web sign that uses words only, e.g., "Contact", "Calendar", "About us", etc. Web Sign that are represented by an icon, thumbnail, image, etc. (other than only words/letters) are referred to iconic sign, e.g., , , etc.

c. *Web sign ontology* indicates the ontologies (ILO, TO, CSO, WDO, WO, and IO) to which web signs belonged; that is, which ontology was presupposed and pointed out by a web sign. A web sign could belong to multiple ontologies and in such case the most significant one (ontology) was considered for that particular sign. For instance, a sign "Contact" belongs to CSO and IO but this sign seemed more relevant with the IO in hypermedia (web context). Thus the sign was considered as an IO sign.

d. *Other features* observed related to the interface sign redesign. For instance, whether a small text / icon / symbol / thumbnail / image was appended or removed in interface sign redesign, relational signs, position, font, graphics, and the like.

Step 3: Data Analysis and Synthesizing. Study data were analyzed as well as synthesized to draw the semiotics implications to design or re-design the web interface signs. These were carried out mainly to obtain results for a set of specific questions to attain the research goal, e.g., (i) how does sign redesign affect on sign's intuitiveness (or interpretation difficulties)? (ii) Which ontology's signs were more difficult to interpret its intended meaning? (iii) How do *ontology changes* in sign redesign affect on sign's complexity to interpret its meaning? (iv) How do *label changes* and *type changes* in sign redesign affect on sign's intuitiveness? and the like.

3.2   Focus Group Discussion

A light weight focus group discussion was organized to amend the data and its collection process due to three main reasons: (i) data related to (a) and (c) are quite subjective, (ii) one single author acts as a semiotic expert to retrieve the study data, and (iii) one web sign may belong to multiple ontologies, thus choosing the most relevant one was also a subjective matter. Author chose a number of signs and retrieved data for these signs and then asked the focus group discussion's participants (1 doctoral researcher in HCI, 1 researcher plus practitioner in UX and usability, 4 graduate students considered as end users) to make comments, criticize, as well as advise on author's retrieved data to amend this data and its collection process. Although no significant differences were observed compared to authors extracted data, a few adjustments were performed. These adjustments were kept in author's mind to collect the study data.

3.3   An Example of Data Extraction

An example of data extraction of an interface sign (see figure 6) of University Malaysia Sabah (UMS) website is presented in table 1. Both the archival version's sign and its redesigned sign (sign indicated by an arrow in figure 6) stand for referring to the page for accessing the library information/services. Both signs are iconic as they consist of a small text and image. In archival version sign, the text "WEB VIRTUA" is not a familiar term to represent library in educational web domain and not even in internet world. This term also does not refer to the existing real world library. Users who are not familiar with this website will feel difficulties to interpret this sign. Again, the image of this icon representing a few books and a magazine/newspaper may make sense to guess its meaning, but users might be confused with the text ("web virtua") of this iconic sign. On the other hand, the text and image of redesigned sign were very easily interpretable by the users as these are very common terms for educational web domain and also make a clear sense to link with the real world library. That is why, complexity/intuitiveness score is given for the old and redesigned sign as 3 and 1 respectively. The old version sign belongs to website ontology (WO) and redesigned one belongs to web domain ontology (WDO). Both signs were iconic. The sign was redesigned by changing the text label and icon redesign.

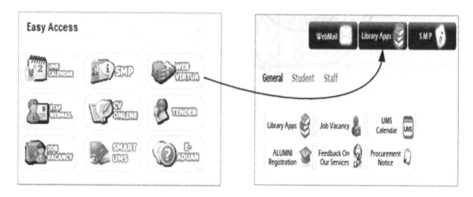

Fig. 6. Screenshot of UMS's homepage: archival version (left one) and current version (right one)

Table 1. An example of data extraction

Data	Web sign stands for providing library information/services	
	Old sign	Redesigned sign
Complexity/intuitiveness	3	1
Type of sign	Iconic	Iconic
Sign ontology	Website Ontology	Internet Ontology
Other features related to sign redesigned	Label changes, Icon redesign	

4   Results

A total of 202 signs ($N = 202$) were redesigned in current version's homepages. Thus, a total of 404 signs were considered in this comparative study. This section discusses the analysis and synthesis of collected data and remarks its outcome.

(i) Intuitiveness differs in sign redesign: This study showed that 41% ($N = 82$) of redesigned signs did not change in terms of sign intuitiveness, 42% ($N = 86$) of redesigned signs' level of intuitiveness increased, and 17% ($N = 34$) of redesigned signs' sign intuitiveness decreased (see figure 7). Table 2 presents a few examples of web sign redesign and their effects on sign's intuitiveness. This study also showed that mean (M) and standard deviation (SD) value for the old and current version's sign intuitiveness were, case I: 2.95[1.19] and 1.19[0.45] respectively for the signs ($N = 86$) where intuitiveness increased, and case II: 1.26[0.57] and 2.71[0.97] respectively for the signs ($N = 34$) where intuitiveness decreased.

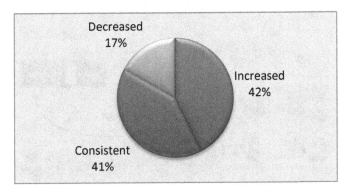

Fig. 7. Interface sign redesign affects on level of complexity/intuitiveness in users' interpretations

Table 2. Web sign redesign and its affects on sign's intuitivemess

Web Signs		Sign stands for	Sign Intuitiveness
Old	Redesigned		
"Search"	🔍	To search information within the website.	Not changed
🔲ADUAN	Feedback On Our Services	To get users feedback/suggestions about the web services.	Reduced
SMP	SMP	To access university's web portal to write, collaborate and share information with other users.	Increased

An unpaired t-test that compares the means of two groups (mean value of old version's signs vs. current version's signs) in sign intuitiveness for both cases showed (statistically) significant differences (case i: $t = 12.82, p < 0.0001$ and case ii:

$t = 7.51, p < 0.0001$). Since a significant percentage of signs' intuitiveness was consistent in sign redesign, and signs that increased and decreased in sign intuitiveness also make a statistically significant difference, the results indicate that (i) redesign of interface signs does not always reduce the interpretations difficulties, and (ii) the significance of revealing the semiotics considerations to web signs redesign, so that designers may get the concepts about factors need to consider in web sign redesign to make a sign more intuitive.

ii) *Complexity belongs to different ontological signs:* This study indicated that signs which belonged to Website Ontology (WO) showed comparatively higher level of difficulties (mean complexity = 3.92) and signs which belonged to Internet Ontology (IO) showed comparatively lower level of difficulties (mean complexity = 1.10) in interpreting the referential meaning of web signs. Mean complexities to understand the meanings of signs that belong to different ontologies are presented in figure 8. This result indicated that strive (i) to avoid Website Ontological (WO) signs, and (ii) to use Internet Ontological (IO) and Web Domain Ontological (WDO) signs in web interfaces may increase the sign intuitiveness to interpret its referential/intended meaning properly.

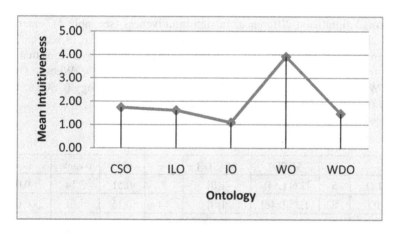

Fig. 8. Mean complexity belongs to different ontology

(iii) Label changes in sign redesign: This study observed that about 44% of total web signs were redesigned only by changing its label/wording. An unpaired t-test showed the significant differences in sign intuitiveness ($N = 39$, old signs $M[SD] = 2.87[1.42]$, redesigned signs $M'[SD'] = 1.36[0.74], t = 5.89, p < 0.0001$) while signs were redesigned only by label changes and with changed ontology. Again, no significant differences in sign intuitiveness was observed ($N = 50, M[SD] = 1.24[0.48], M'[SD'] = 1.28[0.70], t = 0.17, p = 0.86$) while signs were redesigned only by label changes and with no changed ontology. Table 3 presents a few examples of label changes in web sign redesign and their effects on ontology changes and sign intuitiveness. This result indicated that label changes were very common and mostly followed in sign redesign but it does not generally affect on complexity experiences in interpretations of web signs unless it changes the ontology too.

Table 3. Examples of label changes in sign redesign and their affects on sign intuitiveness

Web Signs		Ontology		Sign stands for	Sign intuitiveness
Old	Redesigned	Old	Redesigned		
'About us'	'The University'	ILO	ILO	To provide information (overview) related to the university itself.	Not changed
'Communication & Public Affairs'	'Contact'	CSO	IO	To provide the contact details.	Changed

(iv) Ontology changes in sign redesign: Study data showed that 33.17% (N= 67) of total signs changed ontology in sign redesign and these changes also increased the sign intuitiveness to interpret the meaning of a sign by 43.89%. Again, redesigned a sign that changes the ontology from WO to IO, WO to WDO, CSO to ILO, and CSO to IO showed significant differences in sign intuitiveness (see table 4). Examples of ontology changes from WO to IO and WO to WDO are shown in section 3 using figure 5 and table 1. This result indicated that strive to redesign web signs that change ontology from Website Ontology (WO) to Internet Ontology (IO), Website Ontology (WO) to Web Domain Ontology (WDO), Common Sense Ontology (CSO) to Internet Ontology (IO) may reduce the interpretations' difficulties.

Table 4. Examples of ontology changes

OC	N	M[SD]	M´[SD´]	DF	SED	t-value	p-value
CSO -ILO*	5	2.6[1.14]	1[0]	8	0.51	3.14	0.0138
CSO - IO*	8	1.75[0.46]	1[0]	14	0.16	4.61	0.0004
CSO-WDO	7	1.43[0.79]	1.57[0.53]	12	0.36	0.39	0.704
ILO -IO	3	2[1]	1[0]	4	0.58	1.73	0.158
WO -IO*	11	3.91[1.22]	1.18[0.40]	20	0.39	7.05	< 0.0001
WO -WDO*	16	3.94[1.12]	1.38[0.50]	30	0.31	8.35	< 0.0001

OC: Ontology Changes in sign redesign   N: Number of sign
M[SD]: Mean & Standard Deviation of intuitiveness (old signs)
M´[SD´]: Mean & Standard Deviation of intuitiveness (redesigned signs)
DF: Degree of freedom;   SED: Standard error of difference;   *: Statistically significant

(v) Type changes in sign redesign: This study observed that 10.4% ($N = 21$) of signs were redesigned by changing its type. An unpaired t-test showed the significant differences in sign intuitiveness *($N = 21$, old signs $M[SD] = 2.05[0.92]$, redesigned signs $M'[SD'] = 1.38[0.80], t = 2.22, p = 0.03)* while signs were redesigned by

changing its type. This result indicated that type changes affect mostly on difficulty experienced in understanding the meaning of web sign.

(vi) Other observed features affect mostly in sign intuitiveness: This study showed that about 19% ($N = 38$) of total web signs append a small text and/or icon in sign redesign. Though, an unpaired t-test showed no significant differences in sign intuitiveness ($N = 38$, old signs $M[SD] = 1.71[1.11]$, redesigned signs $M'[SD'] = 1.42[0.89]$, $t = 1.26$, $p = 0.21$) but it reduced 14% of interpretation difficulties while a sign was appended an icon/small text in redesign. This study also showed that appending an icon/small text did not usually change the ontology and type of a web sign. Thus, this result indicated that (i) appending a small text/icon does not significantly affect on complexity experiences in interpretations of web signs since it generally did not change the ontology or type of a web sign, (ii) when it is not possible to change ontology and type for a particular web sign then it might be a good choice to append a small text or icon with this sign to increase its intuitiveness.

5   Discussions

This section summarizes the main findings of the study, and discusses the implications for research and practice, and limitations of this study.

5.1   Main Findings

This study provides a set of semiotics considerations to design and evaluate user intuitive web signs for boosting the web usability. This research mainly showed (i) the significance of considering semiotics perception to design web signs to be intuitive to the end users, (ii) how web sign may belong to different ontology (knowledge domain), and (iii) the idea of complexity associated to different ontological signs. The study findings are briefly summarized as follows:

> Redesign of interface signs does not always reduce interpretation difficulties. Thus designers need to employ semiotics perception to design users' intuitive web signs.
> End users experience comparatively (i) higher level of difficulties with signs that belong to Website Ontology(WO), (ii) average level of difficulties with signs that belong to Common Sense Ontology (CSO) and InterLocutor Ontology (ILO), and (iii) lower level of difficulties with signs that belong to Internet Ontology (IO) and Web Domain Ontology (WDO)in interpreting the signs' meaning properly.
> Interface sign redesign only by label changes is very common and mostly followed in sign redesign but it does not generally affect on interpretation difficulties unless it changes the ontology too.
> Redesigned web signs that changed ontology from (i) Website Ontology (WO) to Internet Ontology (IO), (ii) Website Ontology (WO) to Web Domain Ontology (WDO), (iii) Common Sense Ontology (CSO) to InterLocutor Ontology (ILO), and (iv) Common Sense Ontology (CSO) to Internet Ontology (IO) provide significant differences in sign intuitiveness.

> ➢ Type changes and ontology changes affect mostly on sign's intuitiveness to be interpreted properly.
> ➢ For cases where the ontology and type changes are not possible by only label changes and icon redesign, it is better to append a small icon/thumbnail/small text to reduce the interpretation complexities.

For cases where the ontology and type changes are not possible by only label changes and icon redesign, it is better to append a small icon/thumbnail/small text to reduce the interpretation complexities.

5.2   Implication for Practice

This research provides a number of semiotics considerations for HCI practitioners. Practitioners may use these considerations as design guidelines and also as evaluation checklists in designing and/or evaluating users' intuitive web interface. Few example guidelines based on this study outcome could be:

- Strive to avoid Website Ontological (WO) signs in web interface.
- Change sign label/wording in web sign redesign so that it eventually also changes its ontology.
- Try to use Internet Ontological (IO) and Web Domain Ontological (WDO) signs in web interface.
- Strive to redesign web signs that change ontology from Website Ontology (WO) to Internet Ontology (IO).
- Append a small text / icon with a web sign to make it more intuitive if needed, etc.

These guidelines might play four major roles in web interface design and evaluation. These roles are: (i) raising awareness of concepts, (ii) assisting in design choice, (iii) offering strategies for solving design choice, and (iv) providing support in evaluation. Let us take a simple example which illustrates how guidelines raise awareness of concepts: a semiotic guideline may introduce a concept that the practitioners (designers) may have not encountered before, e.g., *"strive to avoid Website Ontological (WO) signs in web interface"* and by this guideline designer may gain concept of avoiding WO's signs for designing user intuitive web interfaces.

5.3   Implication for Research

For researchers, this study showed the significance of semiotics perceptions to design and evaluate web interfaces. Thus to provide a complete set of semiotics considerations becomes essential for designing user intuitive web interface. Several ways of productive future research remain. For instance: (i) conducting an empirical study to obtain data from the end users to improve the value and applicability of research outcome, (ii) comparing extracted data (e.g., complexity score, ontology) by the end users to those extracted by the author as a semiotics expert in this study would be another fruitful area for future work, (iii) extending this study method to other web domains (e.g., e-commerce, e/government, etc.) to obtain more generalize outcome, (iv) assessing the significance of considering cultural issues in semiotics research to design and evaluate the web interface, (v) focusing on mobile web/app interface might be another appealing area of further research, (vi) action research or an extensive empirical research to validate research findings would be a logical next step in extending this research, and the like.

5.4   Limitations of This Study

There were a few limitations to this study. This study was conducted by a single author. Moreover, two (web sign ontology and intuitiveness score) out of four types of study data were completely subjective, thus the main limitations of this study was inaccuracy of data extraction. Author tried to alleviate this threat of data extraction not only by his expertise (more than 6 years of experience on semiotics research in user interface design and evaluation) but also by employing a focus group discussion to amend the extracted data and its collection process. The types of data chosen for this study might also fail to notice some other important factors of sign redesign from semiotic point of view.

6   Conclusion and Future Work

This research conducted an empirical study web interface signs and reported a number of semiotics consideration for designing the users' intuitive web interface. For HCI researchers, several ways of fruitful future research still remain to provide a complete and generalized set of semiotics considerations for designing users' intuitive web interface. For practice, this research provides a number of semiotics considerations, so that practitioners may use these considerations as design guidelines or evaluation checklists in designing or evaluating users' intuitive web interface.

However, author is fully acknowledged the limitation of this research as stated in section 5.4. This can be overcome either by conducting an empirical study to collect data directly from the end users or by conducting similar studies by (at least) two more semiotic experts and then compare/analyze the test data with the current one.

Therefore, author intends to conduct an extensive empirical study by user tests not only to amend this finding but also to provide a more complete set of semiotics considerations to design and evaluate user intuitive web interfaces. The findings of these (comparative study, user tests) studies will be converged to propose a meaning-based user interface design and evaluation framework.   In the final phase, practitioners will be involved to validate the research results and alleviate the subjectivity of the sign assessment method.

Acknowledgments. HPY:nTutkimussäätiö (Elisa Oyj) and Research and Training Foundation of TeliaSonera in Finland provided the grants that has made this research possible. For this, Elisa and TeliaSonera are gratefully acknowledged. To Franck Tétard, thank you for your feedback and suggestions for strengthening this paper.

References

1. Bolchini, D., Chatterji, R., Speroni, M.: Developing heuristics for the semiotics inspection of websites. In: 27th ACM International Conference on Design of Communication (SIGDOC 2009), Indiana, USA, pp. 67–71. ACM Press (2009)
2. de Souze, C.S.: The Semiotic Engineering of Human-Computer Interaction. The MIT Press, Cambridge (2005)
3. de Souza, C.S.: Semiotic engineering: bringing designers and users together at interaction time. Interdisciplinary Journal of Human-Computer Interaction - Interacting with Computers 17(3), 317–341 (2005)
4. de Souza, C.S., Barbosa, S.D.J., Prates, R.O.: A semiotics engineering approach to user interface design. Journal of Knowledge Based System 14(8), 461–465 (2011)
5. Islam, M.N., Ali, M., Al-Mamun, A., Islam, M.: Semiotics Explorations on Designing the Information Intensive Web Interfaces. International Arab Journal of Information Technology 7(1), 45–54 (2010)
6. Peirce, C.S.: Collected Writings. In: Hartshorne, C., Weiss, P., Burks, A. (eds.). Harvard University Press, Cambridge (1932-1952)
7. de Castro Salgado, L.C., de Souza, C.S., Leitão, C.F.: A semiotic inspection of ICDL. In: de Lucena, C.J.P. (ed.) Monografias em Ciência da Computação, No. 31/09, Brazil (2009) ISSN: 0103-9741
8. de Souza, C.S., Leitão, C.F., Prates, R.O., da Silva, E.J.: The Semiotic Inspection Method. In: VII Brazilian Symposium on Human Factors in Computing Systems (IHC 2006), Natal, RN, Brazil, pp. 148–157. ACM Press (2006)
9. de Souza, C.S., Cypher, A.: Semiotic Engineering in Practice: Redesigning the CoScripter Interface. In: Working Conference on Advanced Visual Interfaces (AVI 2008), pp. 165–172. ACM Press, Napoli (2008)
10. Islam, M.N.: Beyond Users' Inaccurate Interpretations of Web Interface Signs: A Semiotic Perception. In: The IFIP 13th International Conference on Informatics and Semiotics in Organizations (ICISO 2011), Leeuwarden, Netherlands, pp. 31–40 (2011)
11. Islam, M.N.: A Semiotics Perspective to web Usability: An Empirical case Study. In: IADIS International Conference on Interface and Human Computer Interaction (IHCI 2011), pp. 19–28. IADIS Publisher (2011)
12. Islam, M.N., Tétard, F., Reijonen, P., Tarkkanen, K.: Integrating Semiotics Perception in Usability Testing: A Light Weighted Experiment on an e-Health Application. In: IADIS International Conference on Interfaces and Human Computer Interaction 2012 (IHCI 2012), pp. 141–148. IADIS Publisher (2012)
13. Islam, M.N.: Towards Designing Users' Intuitive Web Interface. In: 6th International Conference on Complex, Intelligent, and Software Intensive Systems (CISIS 2012), Italy, pp. 513–518. IEEE Computer Society (2012)
14. Morris, C.: Foundations of the Theory of Signs. In: International Encyclopedia of Unified Science, vol. 1(2). University of Chicago Press (1938)
15. Ferreira, J., Barr, P., Noble, J.: The Semiotics of User Interface Redesign. In: 6th Australasian User Interface Conference (AUIC 2005), Newcastle, NSW, Australia (2005)
16. Neumuller, M.: Hypertext Semiotics in the Commercialized Internet, unpublished doctoral dissertation, Wirtschaftsuniversität Wien (2001)
17. Saussure, F.D.: Course in General Linguistics (trans. Harris, R.). Duckworth, London (1983)
18. Robert, S., Robert, B., Sandy, F.L.: New Vocabularies in Film Semiotics: Structuralism. Post-Structuralism and Beyond. Routledge, Taylor &Francies, London (1992)

19. Andersen, P.: Computer Semiotics. Scandinavian Journal of Information Systems 4, 3–30 (1992)
20. Frege, G.: Begriffsschrift (1879); English Translation. In: van Heijenoort, J. (ed.) From Frege to Gödel, pp. 1–82. Harvard University Press, Cambridge (1967)
21. Speroni, M.: Mastering the Semiotics of Information-Intensive Web Interfaces, unpublished doctoral dissertation, Faculty of Communication Sciences, University of Lugano, Swizerland (2006)
22. Triacca, L., Speroni, M., Ramani, C.: Understanding semiotics issues in usability evaluation of cultural heritage websites: the DICE case study. Studies in Communication Sciences 5(1), 75–92 (2005)

Appendix: List of Websites, and Dates of Archival Versions

University	URL	Date of archival version
University of Helsinki	www.helsinki.fi/university	15.08.2004
University of Turku	www.utu.fi	19.07.2004
University of Tampere	www.uta.fi	07.12.2005
University of Oulu	www.oulu.fi	07.06.2004
Jyväskylä University of Applied Sci.	www.jamk.fi	14.11.2007
UniversitiMalaysiaSabah	www.ums.edu.my	07.02.2010
UniversitiSains Malaysia	www.usm.my	15.10.2004
Universiti Technology Malaysia	www.utm.my	14.06.2004
Universiti Malaysia Pahang	www.ump.edu.my	12.02.2007
Universiti Utara Malaysia	www.uum.edu.my	21.04.2004
Museum of Contemporary Art	www.kiasma.fi	06.12.2004
Museum of Finnish Architecture	www.mfa.fi	05.02.2005
Retretti Art Centre	www.retretti.fi	16.04.2004
Amos Anderson Art Museum	www.amosanderson.fi	02.02.2004
Turku City Art Museum	www.wam.fi	05.02.2004
Alvar Aalto Museum	www.alvaraalto.fi	12.12.2005
Spy Museum	www.vakoilumuseo.fi	24.08.2010
Design Museum	www.designmuseum.fi	11.10.2006
Islamic Art Museum Malaysia	www.iamm.org.my	11.02.2005
PusatSains Negara Museum	www.psn.gov.my	11.03.2005

Towards E-mail Prevalence in Media Repertoires: Evidence and Explanations for Knowledge Workers of a Public Organization

François de Corbière[1], François-Charles Wolff[2],
Sophie Bretesché[1], and Bénédicte Geffroy[1]

[1] Ecole des Mines de Nantes, LEMNA, 4 rue Alfred Kastler, 44300 Nantes, France
{sophie.bretesche,francois.de-corbiere,
benedicte.geffroy}@mines-nantes.fr
[2] IEMN-IAE, LEMNA, chemin de la censive du tertre, 44300 Nantes, France
francois.wolff@univ-nantes.fr

Abstract. E-mail is and remains widely used by knowledge workers in organizations. The objective of this paper is twofold. On the one hand, it aims at verifying e-mail is the most used medium by knowledge workers within their communication media repertoires. On the other hand, we try to understand which factors influence e-mail use. A public organization was selected to realize an in-depth case study with both quantitative and qualitative data. Quantitative analysis shows that e-mail is the preferred medium of knowledge workers to exchange documents and information. Moreover, individual characteristics poorly explain media use, and in particular e-mail use. Qualitative analysis of interviews with senior executives proposes organizational explanations of e-mail prevalence in this organization. Indeed in a moving, fuzzy and political organization, e-mail is preferred for several reasons that are advanced in this paper.

Keywords: media repertoires, e-mail use, individual factors, organizational context, case study.

Introduction

Communication is time consuming for knowledge workers since they spend a large part of their time communicating (Te'eni, 2001; Davenport, 2005). Organizations have to provide knowledge workers appropriate communication technologies for them to improve communication performance. In MIS, communication performance is referred to as mutual understanding (Dennis et al., 2008). Even if technology adoption and appropriation by users have long been studied in MIS, the question of media choice by knowledge workers remains a big question mark. This is particularly true since the number of communication technologies that can be used in organizations is constantly growing. Theoretically, the medium providing the best communication performance should be chosen by knowledge workers (Daft and Lengel, 1986; Dennis

H. Rahman et al. (Eds.): MCIS 2012, LNBIP 129, pp. 156–168, 2012.

et al., 2008). However, a large range of communication technologies may foster information overload and so threaten communication performance (Jones et al., 2004; Massey and Montoya-Weiss 2006; Huang and Lin, 2009). Therefore, current organizations face a paradox: on the one hand, a large range of communication technologies should allow knowledge workers to choose the most appropriate medium in order to communicate efficiently; On the other hand, it should induce technology and information overload and so threaten communication performance.

Nowadays, some technologies, such as instant messaging and social networks, are presented as alternative or complementary communication tools to those already used in organizations (Lowry et al., 2011; Suh et al., 2011). However e-mail is still mainly used for communication tasks and we can hypothesize it will stay the preferred medium of knowledge workers in the next decades (Markus, 1994, Ducheneaut and Watts, 2005; Huang and Lin, 2009). Following Weber (2004), we consider that there is a lack of research investigating the use of mature technologies, those that have already been infused in modern organizations for individuals to communicate with each others. At first, this paper aims at identifying if e-mail is substituting other media. In other words we question the wide use of e-mail compared to the other media available for different communication tasks. We thus analyze communication media repertoire, defined as "the collection of communication channels and identifiable routines of use for specific communication purposes within a defined community" (Watson-Manheim and Bélanger, 2007, p.268). Secondly, it seems particularly important and valuable both for researchers and managers to understand the factors explaining e-mail selection and use by knowledge workers within their communication media repertoire.

After the literature review on media choice and media use by knowledge workers, the research framework is presented. Then the methodology is explained. A case study is conducted in order to identify in a specific organization the main factors influencing the wide use of e-mail. Results from both quantitative and qualitative analysis lead us to discuss the influence of organizational context on media use within media repertoires.

1   Theoretical Background

1.1   Theories of Media Choice for Communication Performance

For explaining and discussing media choice, the media richness theory (MRT, Daft and Lengel, 1986) is widely mobilized in the literature. It postulates that a medium has intrinsic characteristics that make it more or less adapted to a communication task. In particular, the more the medium fosters strong interactions (voice, gestures...), the more it is suitable for tasks requiring strong interactions between actors. In that sense, face-to-face interactions and telephone are presented as richer than e-mail. In this theory and major part of the theories of media choice, the task-medium fit provides communication performance that is evaluated in terms of shared understanding (Te'eni, 2001).

Culnan and Markus (1987) have quickly pointed out a failure of MRT, because of its lack of considerations about the synchronous property of media. A medium such as e-mail may be richer than the telephone because it allows the sender to be discharged from the receiver availability (Straub and Karahanna, 1998). In the criticisms of MRT, Markus (1994) and Lee (1994) have also explained that e-mail can be a rich medium in some contexts. In particular, social processes in organizations sometimes induce a heavy use of e-mail, even for equivocal communications tasks for which e-mail is not the most appropriate and efficient medium in MRT (Markus, 1994).

The media synchronicity theory (MST, Dennis et al, 2008) appears as a useful complement of MRT to explain the influence of media characteristics on communication performance. The authors clarify the fit between communication processes and media capabilities. They refer to information theory of Shannon and Weaver (1949) for the analysis of media capabilities by distinguishing two different forms of communication processes:

- "Conveyance focuses on the transmission of large amounts of raw information and subsequent retrospective analysis, suggesting that individuals will have less of a need to transmit and process information at the same time."
- "Convergence focuses on the transmission of higher-level abstractions of information and negotiations of these abstractions to existing mental models, suggesting that individuals will have a greater need to quickly transmit and process smaller volumes of information to develop a shared understanding."

Both MST and MRT aim at defining the fit between media and tasks for communication performance. Thus, these theories are useful to identify an appropriate medium for achieving a given task. They are referred to as single medium theories (Lee et al., 2007; Boukef and Kalika, 2009). In particular, these theories allow for a distinction between communication tasks and between technological characteristics of the medium analyzed. But they insufficiently take care of the communication context for explaining effective choice and use of media by knowledge workers (Markus, 1994; Straub and Karahanna, 1998; Watson-Manheim and Bélanger, 2007).

1.2   Media Use in Media Repertoires

The objective of the paper is not to identify the most appropriate medium for a communication task, but rather to identify the frequency of use of diverse media for diverse communication tasks. A literature review on media repertoires is thus needed.

Nowadays, there is a growing development of communication tools in organizations. Instant messaging and social networks are current instantiations of additional communication tools to those already used in organizations (Lowry et al., 2011; Suh et al., 2011). The question of substitution and complementarities between media of repertoires is therefore an important research question (Lee et al., 2007; Isaac et al., 2008). In particular, a large range of communication technologies generally induces additional communicating activities and sometimes conducts to information overload and threatens communication performance (Jones et al., 2004; Massey and Montoya-Weiss 2006; Huang and Lin, 2009). In this context, for a specific communication task, users may choose to use a single medium, or several media simultaneously, sequentially, or repetitively (Watson-Manheim and Bélanger, 2007; Lee et al., 2007; Boukef and Kalika, 2009).

Within communication media repertoires, contextual factors significantly influence the decision to use a medium (Watson-Manheim and Bélanger, 2007): timeliness of the communication task; familiarity with technology and task; users' role; users' hierarchical position; physical and cognitive distance between users; organizational structure; social and organizational encouragement... Among these factors, one can identify factors that refer to communication tasks and media characteristics that are close to those presented in single medium theories. However, other factors are issued from individual and organizational characteristics.

1.3   Factors Influencing Media Use within Media Repertoires

Consistently with the research question, this paper aims at analyzing frequency of use of different media included in media repertoires (Watson-Manheim and Bélanger, 2007). For that purpose, we select three categories of factors influencing media selection and use within media repertoires by knowledge workers: communication tasks, individual and organizational characteristics.

Media choice depends on the communication tasks knowledge workers have to perform (Daft and Lengel, 1986; Te'eni, 2001; Dennis et al., 2008). From conveyance and convergence definitions of communication processes (Dennis et al., 2008), we can extract the nature of information exchanged, the interdependency between actors, and the actors involved as three important variables characterizing the communication tasks. Following single medium theories and their criticisms, these variables have an impact on media choice and use by knowledge workers.

- The nature of information can refer to the volume or the formalization of information to convey.
- Communication tasks may reflect different interdependencies between actors involved. In particular, urgency level of the task is a well-known factor influencing media choice since it creates a more or less timely interdependency between actors. Moreover, coordination modes of information exchanges may reflect sequential or reciprocal interdependency between actors. Indeed, communication tasks may involve transmission from one actor to other ones or sharing and co creation between several actors.
- The actors involved in communication also characterize communication tasks. For the individual that communicates, cognitive and physical distance with his/her correspondents is determinant (Te'eni, 2001). In particular, the hierarchical and geographical position of the correspondents influences medium choice and use.

To analyze media use within media repertoires for achieving communication tasks, individual characteristics are variables to integrate. Taking care of individual factors influencing adoption and use of technologies, we focus on individual characteristics such as gender, age, experience with media, expertise and hierarchical position.

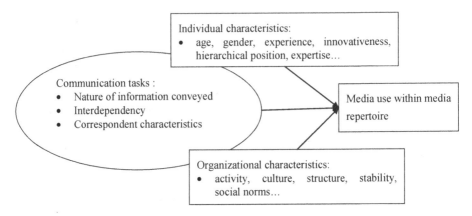

Fig. 1. The research framework

Finally, following the synthesis of van den Hooff, Groot and de Jonge (2005), social environment also influences medium use. For the purpose of this paper which is to analyze medium use frequency within media repertoires, we extend social environment considerations to organizational characteristics. We thus include considerations about organizational factors such as activity, culture, structure and stability for instance. Figure 1 represents the research framework of the paper.

2   Methodology

2.1   A Case Study in a Public and Moving Organization

A case study (Yin, 2009) was conducted in a French local authority, including 7500 agents. During the past ten years, this organization has experienced a changing organizational environment. The support services are shared between the entities of the city and those of the urban community. Moreover, public policies have generated forms of cooperation based on project mode. Compared to private organizations, public organizations face the influence of politics on their activities. The previous contextual elements were strong justifications for the case selection (Eisenhardt, 1989): the analyzed organization appears as an extreme case for which organizational factors may have a great impact on knowledge workers activity, especially in terms of communication tasks.

The case study conducted associates both quantitative and qualitative data (Benbasat et al., 1987). They are collected to confirm e-mail prevalence within media repertoires and to identify the factors, both individual and organizational, that influence e-mail use by knowledge workers.

2.2   Quantitative Analysis

We built the survey instrument with IT managers of the local authority. We first interviewed the CIO, members of the team designing collaborative tools, and members of the team managing the development and maintenance of the collaborative tools. The main objective was to identify media repertoires provided to knowledge workers for achieving communication tasks. We propose a first draft of the survey instrument that was discussed and validated during a meeting conducted with the IT managers.

In the instrument, communication tasks are distinguished considering the nature of information conveyed, the interdependency between actors, and categories of correspondents. To be consistent with the organization analyzed, we distinguished the nature of information conveyed towards its degree of formalization (documents and information). Interdependency of the communication tasks can be sequential for transmission of documents and information, or reciprocal for mutual adjustments in document co-creation or discussion. Moreover, we identified five categories of correspondents for individuals of the studied organization with whom actors have different physical and cognitive distance (hierarchical superiors, team members, other colleagues, external partners, and elected officials).

Consistently with the framework, we used a five points Likert scale to measure the frequency of use of each suitable medium for the 20 communication tasks previously described. Indeed, respondents are questioned on their use of media within the media repertoire associated to a communication task. Answers ranging from "never" to "all the time", we associate a score to each modality, respectively 1 for "never", 2 for "rarely", 3 for "sometimes", 4 for "often" and 5 for "all the time".

Concerning media repertoire, for all the categories of correspondent, knowledge workers can use:

- Intranet, Network, e-mail, Paper, and FTP (File Transfer Protocol) for transmission of documents
- Intranet, Network, e-mail, and Paper for co creation of documents
- Intranet, e-mail, Paper, Face-to-Face meeting and phone call for transmission of information
- Intranet, e-mail, Paper, Face-to-Face meeting and phone call for discussion

The following individual characteristics were included in the survey instrument: age (under 40; between 40 and 50, more than 50), gender (male, female), hierarchical position (executive or director, service manager, other knowledge workers), nature of activity (dominance of managerial or expertise activity), entity attachment (city or urban community), shared activity between city and urban community (or not). All the media provided by the local authority have been implemented for at least eight years. We thus did not integrate individual characteristics such as experience with the media and innovativeness of individuals.

For data collection, the survey was anonymously administered in February 2011 to the 844 knowledge workers of the local authority. 351 usable responses are analyzed (sample of 42%).

2.3   Qualitative Analysis

In addition to the quantitative data collection, semi-structured interviews were conducted over a period of two months (March and April 2011) with the 12 senior executives of the local authority. Since the survey instrument did not include organizational characteristics that should explain media use within media repertoires, the main objective of the interviews with senior executives was to develop a deep understanding of the organizational context (Eisenhardt, 1989). Indeed, it seemed difficult to integrate organizational factors in the survey instrument since the literature has not sufficiently emphasized, from our point of view, the explaining role of organizational context on media use. The interview guide encompasses four main themes: the individual courses, the organizational context, the description of the function and activity especially in terms of communication tasks, and media use. The 18 hours of interviews were transcribed for data analysis. A thematic analysis was performed (Miles and Huberman, 1994) on e-mail use compared to other media and on organizational context in order to understand organizational factors influencing e-mail prevalence in this organization.

3   Results

3.1   E-mail as the Preferred Medium of Knowledge Workers

We begin our empirical analysis with a description of the prevalence of e-mail compared to other media inside the organization. While the associated scores to each modality have no meaning in themselves, they allow us making some comparisons in the intensity of use of the various media. In Table 1, we report average scores by communication activity (transmission of documents, co creation of documents, transmission of information, discussion), and by communication correspondents belonging to the organization (hierarchical superiors, team members, other colleagues).

When considering all activities, we find that the highest score is associated to the use of e-mail, with an average value of 4.02. It is followed by face-to-face meeting (3.91), and then by network and phone call (the average score is around 3 in both cases). Conversely, FTP and intranet are the less used media inside the organization.

Table 1. Average scores of media use

Media	Intranet	Network	E-Mail	Paper	FTP	Meeting	Phone
Communication activity							
• Transmission of documents	1.57	3.10	4.33	2.95	1.25	-	-
• Co creation of documents	1.45	2.97	3.92	2.77	-	-	-
• Transmission of information	1.35	-	4.11	2.81	-	3.84	3.04
• Discussion	1.14	-	3.76	2.20	-	3.99	3.10
Communication correspondent							
• Superiors	1.36	2.73	4.02	2.82	1.20	3.89	2.83
• Team members	1.38	3.37	3.95	2.73	1.19	4.15	2.86
• Other colleagues	1.48	2.99	4.09	2.51	1.28	3.72	3.47
All activities	1.43	3.02	4.02	2.69	1.25	3.91	3.07

Next, we find substantial differences depending on the communication activity. On the one hand, e-mail is a very common medium when considering transmissions or co-creations of documents. The possibility of easily sending attached documents undoubtedly explains the success. Electronic documents also circulate very often through network, but documents in paper format are far from having disappeared. More complex tools (intranet and FTP) seem less attractive for knowledge workers in their daily activities. On the other hand, we observe that the average scores are very high both for face-to-face meeting and e-mail for tasks associated to information exchanges (either transmission or discussion). E-mail is first in terms of ranking for transmission (with a score of 4.11), while face-to-face meetings appear to be the most frequently used medium for discussion. Phone calls are at the third rank, the average score corresponding to a sometimes category.

We also investigate whether the use of media is influenced by the communication correspondent. As shown in Table 1, we find few differences whether the respondents interact with superiors, with team members, or with other colleagues. E-mail is the first medium used except for team members. Face-to-face meeting is at first rank in that case, which could be explained by a higher proximity, both in terms of cognitive and physical distance. This pattern is consistent with a more frequent use of phone calls with other colleagues.

3.2   The Low Influence of Individual Characteristics on Media Use

To investigate the role of individual characteristics on the use of different media, we turn to an econometric analysis. For each activity, we estimate a linear model to explain the corresponding score. Since uses of the various media are likely to be correlated, we consider a seemingly unrelated regression. We consider the following explanatory variables: being a woman, age with three categories (40 or less, between 41 and 50, above 50), working at the urban community and being a manager (executives, directors, service managers, and other knowledge workers with a dominant activity of management. The reference category being other knowledge workers with a dominant activity of expertise). Estimates are reported in Table 2.

The main finding is that individual characteristics poorly explain the different outcomes. Except for network, R^2 associated to each media remains low, less than 0.1 on average. We can conclude that individual factors have low influence on media selection and use.

However, we still note some interesting results in Table 2. First, there is no clear gender difference except for intranet (at the 10 percent level) and face-to-face meetings. On average, women are more likely than men to have physical meetings with their colleagues. Secondly, e-mail use is less frequent among employees aged above 50. These could be linked to a generational effect, as the oldest knowledge workers have grown up inside the organization without having access to this medium during the first part of their career. A similar negative coefficient is found for network, meeting and phone calls, while the reverse pattern is found for intranet. This result is amazing since intranet is the most recent medium introduced in the organization. As almost all media are concerned, we deduce that older workers have fewer interactions with other inside the local authority on average. Thirdly, e-mail and phone use is slightly less frequent among those working at the urban community.

Table 2. SUR model of media use, by type of medium

Variables	Intranet	Network	E-Mail	Paper	FTP	Meeting	Phone
Constant	1.258*** (14.75)	2.653*** (15.81)	4.190*** (50.48)	2.924*** (24.76)	1.310*** (16.14)	3.796*** (44.74)	3.200*** (26.46)
Woman (ref: man)	0.111* (1.65)	0.155 (1.16)	-0.101 (-1.54)	-0.075 (-0.80)	-0.093 (-1.44)	0.177*** (2.63)	-0.132 (-1.38)
Age 41-50 (ref: ≤40)	0.041 (0.48)	-0.207 (-1.26)	-0.132 (-1.62)	-0.165 (-1.42)	0.212*** (2.65)	-0.143* (-1.71)	0.142 (1.20)
>50	0.249*** (3.07)	-0.389** (-2.44)	-0.280*** (-3.55)	-0.097 (-0.86)	0.006 (0.08)	-0.156* (-1.94)	-0.232** (-2.02)
Working at the urban community (ref: city)	-0.018 (-0.26)	0.691*** (5.08)	-0.119* (-1.77)	-0.198** (-2.07)	-0.043 (-0.65)	0.083 (1.20)	-0.311*** (-3.18)
Director or manager (ref: expertise)	-0.147** (-2.21)	-0.066 (-0.51)	0.123* (1.90)	-0.104 (-1.13)	-0.096 (-1.51)	0.078 (1.18)	0.212** (2.24)
R^2	0.054	0.130	0.066	0.030	0.045	0.060	0.085

Note: modèle SUR (Seemingly unrelated regressions). Significance levels are respectively 1% (***), 5% (**), and 10% (*).

Conversely, the results show that those working at the urban community use much more often networks (the average score increases by 0.69 points), the relationship being highly significant. An explanation could be that specific tools such as networks have been developed in the context of the urban community rather than the one of the city. In fact, the proportion of experts among knowledge workers is highly more important at the urban community than at the city (72% versus 59%). Thus, the results are concordant with the last one: we find that compared to experts, managers and directors slightly more often rely on e-mail and phone calls whereas experts use more often the intranet. One of the interesting conclusions is that managers need higher interactions with others and thus prefer e-mail and phone to more sophisticated media, whereas experts need more sophisticated media for some of their communication tasks.

3.3   Towards an Organizational Explanation of E-mail Use

Descriptive analysis of quantitative data shows that e-mail is the preferred medium of knowledge workers within media repertoires for achieving diverse communication tasks. Moreover, econometric analysis shows that, overall, individual characteristics of knowledge workers poorly explain the frequency of use of the different media within media repertoire. The qualitative analysis aims at better understanding organizational factors explaining the intensive use of e-mails by knowledge workers. To start, the analysis of interviews with senior executives, who are board members, provides a better understanding of the organization itself.

First, the organization is presented as being very partitioned between its departments: "The first point is partitioning. The vertical system, completely vertical." This first characteristic involves an important volume of communication tasks within the local authority. Indeed, bureaucratic organizations induce unneeded communication tasks. For example, a senior executive says: "we often validate by e-mail decisions that I found in the evening in the paper mail. I have to do it twice."

Then, several interviewees tell us that the development of public policy encourages organization by project. In 2011, there were 5000 projects, with different boundaries, budgets, and delays... In particular, the number of projects promotes a growing number of communication tasks within the organization. One senior executive: "When you participate to several projects, you multiply the meetings, and you multiply exchanges with your colleagues belonging to the same projects than you. After, as you work with colleagues physically splitted in the whole territory, e-mail imposes itself as the dominant method of communication". This is particularly true in this organization since entities are distributed in a lot of buildings within the administrative territory of the urban community.

In addition, project management and bureaucracy are presented as incompatible according to an interviewee: "There are plenty of people who talk about project management here, but there is none. Because a project manager should manage all components of one project. Since the organization is partitioned, he/she is responsible of the part of the project belonging to his/her department. And we must go after the other to ask them complements. And when you see the project presented, it is a parade. This is not the project manager that presents the project. The project manager, if here, he/she presents the component X. After there is a guy who present the social aspect of the project, so that he belongs to a different department. After there is another guy in another department who presents the transportation component... So there is no project manager. This is crazy."

In fact, when combining project management and bureaucratic organization, patterns of communication are not simplified but complexified. Finally, this creates fuzzy responsibilities concerning the project: "Sometimes, it becomes incredible when you see e-mails moving, we say: Is there somebody who is responsible for that?" Finally, the fuzzy organization and e-mail exchanges scheme are incresed by the sharing movement. Indeed, some departments, such as Human Resources, IS, Finance, are shared or being shared between the urban community and the city. "The sharing movement increases the fuzzy impression of an organization where processes are not enough formalized. But sharing movement would normally be stabilized over time. Conversely, the issue of process, I think it's a permanent problem."

Overall, the different aspects of the organization evolution induce an increased volume of communication tasks, and in particular the use of e-mail to exchange, coordinate, make decisions... In addition, agents are in a political organization, in which elected officials have an important role and are not present in everyday worklife. They send orders, often by e-mail, and knowledge workers repeat this communication mode to organize actions. "The pressure is imposed by the politicians."

The Executive Director summarized communication management in his organization according to the peculiarity of the business, or rather the dual activity. "Here you are not in a classic productive organization. You are in a political organization, and for any political organization, it is critical to understand that you have two objectives: a production one and a representation one. The representation dimension is fundamental, and it is more difficult to plan, organize this type of activity. When the mayor should visit an area, this is something you can not easily organize, formalize. It depends on the neighborhood, the social climate, the period of the year, the reason ... and this results in permanent information exchanges between the different people involved in the event organization."

To conclude, qualitative analysis gives a set of organizational explanations for e-mail use within media repertoires. In particular, in a fuzzy, moving and public organization, formalization and standardization are low and conduct knowledge workers to use intensively e-mail within their communication repertoires.

4   Discussion and Conclusion

In this paper, we have analyzed frequency of use of different media within media repertoires (Watson-Manheim and Bélanger, 2007). Media choice, and thus frequency of media use within media repertoires, should depend on the communication task knowledge workers have to perform (Daft and Lengel, 1986; Dennis et al., 2008). The results in the analyzed organization do not provide so clear conclusions. Indeed, even if there are significant differences between transmission of documents and discussions, we have provided empirical evidence that e-mail is widely use by knowledge workers for all communication tasks with all categories of correspondents. Indeed, consistently with previous researches (Markus, 1994, Ducheneaut and Watts, 2005; Huang and Lin, 2009), e-mail should remain the preferred medium of knowledge workers. This is particularly true since e-mail has intrinsic characteristics for knowledge workers to easily adapt its use for a set of different communication tasks. In addition, e-mail also allows knowledge workers to achieve other tasks, such as decision making, coordination, traceability, memorization, files and discussion classification, etc. Even if e-mail is widely used, it does not totally substitute other media, since other media of repertoires are still used. The next question is therefore about the value of including new media in media repertoires. The performance needs to be further investigated. In particular, how to define a good or a well-appropriated media repertoire? Does it refer to a large range of media, so that individuals may use a medium or a combination of media that clearly fit with their needs? In that case, introducing new media in media repertoires should conduct to a better communication performance. Conversely, in which cases the introduction of new media within media repertoires conducts to information overload and so threaten communication performance (Jones et al., 2004; Massey and Montoya-Weiss 2006; Huang and Lin, 2009)? Investigating how media repertoires and media use within repertoires influence knowledge workers performance is a relevant area of future research. This should be conducted with the analysis of communication performance, but also with the analysis of the effect class of problems issued from the size of media repertoires and from the intensity of media use. Effects of media use and repertoires size on the transformation of knowledge workers activities are not enough investigated (Weber, 2004).

The results have also shown that individual characteristics do not sufficiently explain media use by knowledge workers, whatever the communication activity (formalization of information conveyed, sequential or reciprocal coordination, cognitive and physical distance). This conclusion issued from the quantitative analysis is particularly interesting. One can find in the literature (see van den Hooff et al., 2005 for a review) that individual characteristics such as age, gender, hierarchical position, experience, expertise (etc) influence media choice. From the case study conducted, this conclusion is mitigated. Indeed, with media repertoires constituted by media that have already been infused in an organization, individual characteristics poorly explain media use. Furthermore, as an interesting result, managers use e-mail and phone more frequently than experts, whereas experts use complex media more frequently than managers. This result should be developed in future research to provide arguments for organizations to adapt media repertoires by considering knowledge workers activities.

Finally, the qualitative analysis is a valuable complement of previous literature since it provides organizational explanations of e-mail heavy use by knowledge workers. Social norms (Markus, 1994) in the public organization analyzed probably derive from impulsion of the elected officials that send orders by e-mails. This partially explains organizational influence on media use. However, we also found that the fuzzy, moving and public traits of the local authority analyzed influence e-mail selection and use by knowledge workers. An area of future research is to perform a set of case studies to better understand the influence of organizational traits on media use within media repertoires. In particular, it is not clear that organizational traits influence directly media use by knowledge workers within their media repertoires (Watson-Manheim and Bélanger, 2007). Organizational traits may also moderate the influence of communication tasks or individuals characteristics on media use.

References

Benbasat, I., Goldstein, D.K., Mead, M.: The Case Research Strategy in Studies of Information Systems. MIS Quarterly 11(3), 369–386 (1987)

Boukef, N., Kalika, M.: New lenses to investigate media use: The layering process perspective. In: ECIS 2009 Proceedings, Paper 184 (2009)

Carlson, J.R., Zmud, R.W.: Channel expansion theory and the experiental nature of media richness perceptions. Academy of Management Journal 42(1), 153–170 (1999)

Culnan, M.J., Markus, M.L.: Information technologies. In: Krone, K.J., Jablin, F.M., Putman, L.L. (eds.) Handbook of Organizational Communication. Sage Publications (1987)

Daft, R.L., Lengel, R.H.: Organizational information requirements, media richness and structural design. Management Science 32, 554–571 (1986)

Davenport, T.H.: Thinking for a living: How to get better performance and results from knowledge workers. Harvard Business School Press, Boston (2005)

Dennis, A.R., Fuller, R.M., Valacich, J.S.: Media, Tasks, and communication processes: a theory of media synchronicity. MIS Quarterly 32(3), 575–600 (2008)

Ducheneaut, N., Watts, L.A.: In search of coherence: a review of email research. Human-Computer Interaction 20(1&2), 11–48 (2005)

Eisenhardt, K.M.: Building theories from case study research. Academy of Management Review 14(4), 532–550 (1989)

Huang, E., Lin, S.: Do Knowledge Workers use e-mail wisely? Journal of Computer Information System 50(1), 65–73 (2009)

Isaac, H., Kalika, M., Boukef Charki, N.: An empirical investigation of e-mail use versus face-to-face meetings: Integrating the Napoleon effect perspective. Communications of the Association for Information Systems (22), 501–514 (2008)

Jones, Q., Ravid, G., Rafaeli, S.: Information Overload and the Message Dynamics of Online Interaction Spaces: A Theoretical Model and Empirical Exploration. Information Systems Research 15(2), 194–210 (2004)

Lee, A.S.: Electronic mail as a medium for rich communication: An empirical investigation using hermeneutic interpretation. MIS Quarterly 18(2), 143–157 (1994)

Lee, C.S., Watson-Manheim, M.B., Ramaprasad, A.: Exploring the relationship between communication risk perception and communication portfolio. IEEE Transactions on Professional Communication 50(2), 130–146 (2007)

Lowry, P., Cao, J., Everard, A.: Privacy Concerns Versus Desire for Interpersonal Awareness in Driving the Use of Self-Disclosure Technologies: The Case of Instant Messaging in Two Cultures. Journal of Management Information Systems 27(4), 163–200 (2011)

Markus, M.L.: Electronic Mail as the medium of managerial choice. Organization Science 5(5), 502–527 (1994)

Massey, A.P., Montoya-Weiss, M.M.: Unravelling the temporal fabric of knowledge conversation: A model of media selection and use. MIS Quarterly 30(1), 99–114 (2006)

Miles, M.B., Huberman, A.M.: Qualitative data analyses. Sage Publications (1994)

Shannon, C., Weaver, W.: The Mathematical Theory of Communication. Univ. of Illinois Press (1949)

Straub, D., Karahanna, E.: Knowledge worker communications and recipient availability: toward a task closure explanation of media choice. Organization Science 9(2), 160–175 (1998)

Suh, A., Shin, K.S., Ahuja, M., Kim, M.S.: The Influence of Virtuality on Social Networks Within and Across Work Groups: A Multilevel Approach. Journal of Management Information Systems 28(1), 381–386 (2011)

Te'eni, D.: Review: A cognitive–affective model of organizational communication for designing IT. MIS Quarterly 25(2), 251–321 (2001)

Van den Hooff, B., Groot, J., de Jonge, S.: Situational influences on the use of communication technologies: A meta analysis and exploratory study. Journal of Business Communication 41(2), 4–27 (2005)

Watson-Manheim, M.B., Bélanger, F.: Communication repertoires: Dealing with the multiplicity of media choices. MIS Quarterly 31(2), 267–293 (2007)

Weber, R.: The Grim Reaper: The Curse of e-mail. MIS Quarterly 28(3), 3–14 (2004)

Yin, R.K.: Case Study Research: Design and Methods, 4th edn. Sage Publications, Thousand Oaks (2009)

An Indicator Function for Insufficient Data Quality –
A Contribution to Data Accuracy

Quirin Görz[1] and Marcus Kaiser[2]

[1] FIM Research Center, University of Augsburg, Universitätsstr. 12, 86135 Augsburg, Germany
`quirin.goerz@wiwi.uni-augsburg.de`
[2] Senacor Technologies AG, Erika-Mann-Str. 55, 80636 Munich, Germany
`marcus.kaiser@senacor.com`

Abstract. Owing to the fact that insufficient data quality usually leads to wrong decisions and high costs, managing data quality is a prerequisite for the successful execution of business and decision processes. An economics-driven management of data quality is in need of efficient measurement procedures, which allow for a predominantly automated identification of poor data quality. Against this background the paper investigates how metrics for the DQ dimensions completeness, validity, and currency can be aggregated to derive an indicator for accuracy. Therefore existing approaches to measure these dimensions are analyzed in order to make explicit, which metric addresses which aspect of data quality. Based on this analysis, an indicator function is designed returning a measure for accuracy on different levels of a data resource. The indicator function's applicability is demonstrated using a customer database example.

Keywords: Data quality, data quality management, measurement, accuracy.

1   Introduction

Poor data quality (DQ) usually is associated with wrong decisions and high costs [3], [16], [19]. For instance, a study conducted by the Data Warehouse Institute revealed that in 67% of the involved organizations poor DQ causes high costs [38]. Moreover, 75% of the interviewees in an international study on DQ admitted wrong decisions due to incorrect data [23]. These findings are complemented by a survey conducted by CSO Insights, where 47% of the responding senior marketing executives had seen either a noticeable or severe impact on their marketing campaigns from poor DQ [13]. Consequently, high quality data are prerequisite for executing business and decision processes. Ensuring DQ hence constitutes a relevant problem for organizations [4], [38]. To solve this problem in an economics-oriented manner, efficient instruments are necessary to measure and subsequently detect insufficient DQ [22], [24], [37].

Literature indicates that DQ is a multidimensional concept [35], [42]. One of the most cited DQ dimension is accuracy [32], [40]. To measure accuracy of an attribute value exactly, two pieces of information must be available: The attribute value as it is stored in a data resource and its real-world counterpart. In many cases, determining

H. Rahman et al. (Eds.): MCIS 2012, LNBIP 129, pp. 169–184, 2012.

the latter is time- and cost-intensive [20]. Thus, there is a need for other DQ dimensions which allow for deriving information on an attribute value's quality without knowing its (costly to determine) real-world counterpart. DQ dimensions which can be used to indicate an attribute value's accuracy are completeness, validity, and currency. However, these DQ dimensions only give an indication on an attribute value's accuracy and do not represent its exact accuracy. Moreover, each of these dimensions only represents one particular aspect of the accuracy of an attribute value. Thus, an aggregated view of these three dimensions would yield a more complete indication of an attribute value's accuracy.

Although it is well known that there are interdependencies between particular DQ dimensions [2], [10], DQ dimensions and especially their measurement are usually discussed independently from each other. So far, three approaches exist to aggregate metrics for different DQ dimensions, which will be discussed in this paper. This discussion will reveal that there is no approach to estimate in a consistent, meaningful way, how accurate data stored in a data resource are, even if the attribute values are already evaluated via metrics for different DQ dimensions. This is the more astonishing, as many papers in the area of DQ management rely on a variable representing the overall level of DQ without defining this variable in a formal way (e.g. [18]). Within this paper we aim to close this research gap by designing an indicator function for accuracy. Therefore we investigate the following research question: *How can accuracy of an attribute value be measured by aggregating metrics for the DQ dimensions completeness, validity, and currency?*

The paper is organized as follows: Section 2 sums up the relevant literature dealing with defining and measuring the DQ dimensions accuracy, completeness, validity, and currency as well as on approaches for aggregating metrics for different DQ dimensions. Afterwards, an indicator function for indicating accuracy is designed in Section 3. In Section 4 the indicator function's applicability is demonstrated by means of a customer database example. Results and limitations are summarized in Section 5.

2   Background and Related Work

Literature provides several definitions for DQ. For instance, according to Orr [34] DQ "is the measure of the agreement between the data views presented by an information system and that same data in the real-world" and Parssian et al. [36] state that "the terms information quality and data quality have been used to characterize mismatches between the view of the world provided by an IS and the true state of the world". To characterize these "mismatches" in more detail, several DQ dimensions have been introduced. According to Lee et al. [32], the dimensions accuracy, completeness, validity, and currency are most relevant in the context of measuring the quality of attribute values. One important feature of these four dimensions is, that they refer to a quality of conformance (QoC) perspective[1] and hence can be measured by metrics in an inter-subjectively verifiable manner [30]. In the following we discuss definitions

---

[1] More details on the two perspectives "quality of conformance" (QoC) and "quality of design" (QoD) can be found in Heinrich et al. [25] and Juran [29].

and metrics for these four dimensions, relate them to each other with respect to their measurement costs, and give a brief overview on several approaches to aggregate DQ dimensions. From this discussion, we deduce the research gap to be investigated in this paper.

2.1   Definitions and Measurement Procedures

To get an overview which aspects of DQ the four DQ dimensions accuracy, completeness, validity, and currency cover and how these aspects can be measured by means of metrics, we discuss their definitions and the respective measurement procedures in the following. Thereby we focus on metrics, which have been formally defined and can be measured in a predominantly automated way. Other well-known approaches (for an overview, please refer to Batini et al. [5]) like the AIMQ-Method [32] or the Total Data Quality Methodology [41] are hence not in the scope of this paper as they do not provide formally defined metrics which allow for a predominantly automated measurement.

Accuracy. According to Eppler [15], 'accuracy' can be defined as "how closely information matches a real-life state", which is a common definition in DQ literature and will be used in the following. That is, accuracy of an attribute value measures the distance between the attribute value $v_I(t_n.a_m)$ stored in the data resource and the corresponding value in the real-world $v_W(t_n.a_m)$ at the moment of measuring DQ [6]. If these two values are identical, the stored attribute value $v_I(t_n.a_m)$ is correct. Thereby, t_n ($n \in IN$) stands for a tuple which represents a real-world entity by storing its attribute values $t_n.a_1, t_n.a_2, ... t_n.a_M$. Accuracy is thus determined by means of a distance measure [20]:

Let $d(v_I(t_n.a_m), v_W(t_n.a_m))$ denote a domain-specific distance function for attribute a_m. It quantifies the closeness between $v_I(t_n.a_m)$ and $v_W(t_n.a_m)$ and normalizes its results to the interval $[0; 1]$, where 0 connotes perfect congruence and 1 connotes no congruence at all[2]. Based on these definitions we can define the metric for accuracy on the level of attribute values as follows [25]:

$$Q_{Accu}(v_I(t_n.a_m), v_W(t_n.a_m)) = 1 - d(v_I(t_n.a_m), v_W(t_n.a_m)) \tag{1}$$

So, to measure accuracy, not only the attribute value $v_I(t_n.a_m)$ stored in a data resource is needed, but also its counterpart in the real-world $v_W(t_n.a_m)$ at the moment of measurement. This necessity of having to know the real-world counterpart $v_W(t_n.a_m)$ is a shortcoming in practical application [20], which can only be solved at high cost in certain areas – if at all [24]. Taking the example of customer data, each customer has to be contacted and asked for the correct value which holds at the moment of asking. Although this is an extreme example, acquiring the real-world counterpart nearly always occasions high costs. On the other hand, after such a comparison of the attribute value stored $v_I(t_n.a_m)$ to its real-world counterpart $v_W(t_n.a_m)$, the latter is

---

[2] Please refer to Heinrich et al. [26] for examples of normalized distance functions and illustrations for the effects of not normalized distance functions.

known and as a result, $v_I(t_n.a_m)$ can be updated and should therefore be perfectly accurate.

Completeness. Literature on DQ uses the term 'completeness' in different contexts. As this paper deals with the quality of attribute values in a data resource which is assumed as given (cf. QoD perspective), an attribute shall be defined as complete in this paper (in accordance with Fox et al. [20] and Batini and Scannapieco [6]), if it semantically differs from *NULL*. *NULL* is equivalent to "missing value" [39] and means "value at present unknown" [12]. This is in contrast to Fox et al. [20], who – in addition – perceive "value does not exist" as *NULL*. If it is however known, that no value exists for an entity's attribute (e.g. a customer has no telephone and therefore no value can be stored for the attribute 'phone number'), this attribute should be considered as complete in terms of the definition above. Hence, it is represented by a corresponding (standardised) attribute value in the data resource (e.g., 'N/A' for "property inapplicable" [12] or "nothing" [39]).

To measure the completeness of an attribute value, one has to determine a set of attribute values $S_{Incomp}^{a_m}$ for each attribute a_m, considered as incomplete. The elements in this set are thus semantically equivalent to *NULL*. Once $S_{Incomp}^{a_m}$ is determined, a metric for completeness (slightly adapted from the metric defined by Heinrich et al. [25]) of an attribute value $v_I(t_n.a_m)$ can be defined:

$$Q_{Comp}(v_I(t_n, a_m)) = 0 \Leftrightarrow v_I(t_n, a_m) \in S_{Incomp}^{a_m} \tag{2a}$$

$$Q_{Comp}(v_I(t_n, a_m)) = 1 \Leftrightarrow v_I(t_n, a_m) \notin S_{Incomp}^{a_m} \tag{2b}$$

In comparison to measuring accuracy it is not necessary to determine the real-world counterpart of the attribute value $v_I(t_n.a_m)$ stored in the data resource. Instead it is sufficient to know the attribute value $v_I(t_n.a_m)$ and the set of attribute values $S_{Incomp}^{a_m}$, which are considered as incomplete. Thus, it is possible to measure completeness repeatedly and – at least, to a large extent – automatically. This is why it should cause less effort to measure completeness than accuracy.

Validity. An attribute value "is invalid if its contents are not within the pre-specified value domain [...] and is valid otherwise" [17], a definition which shall also be used in this article. Moreover, 'validity' is also known as 'domain integrity' which means that "all values of an attribute must be drawn from a specified domain" [31]. Hence, from a QoC perspective, validity refers to the question, whether an attribute value $v_I(t_n.a_m)$ is part of a (pre-specified) value domain $S_{Vali}^{a_m}$ or not. As with the set of incomplete values, defining the value domain $S_{Vali}^{a_m}$ for the particular attribute a_m is a prerequisite for measuring its validity. The value domain $S_{Vali}^{a_m}$ can also be defined by means of several rules or constraints [27]. Moreover, the validity of an attribute value is measured by means of a Boolean variable [20]. According to Heinrich et al. [27], an attribute value is thus either *valid* or *not valid*. With $S_{Vali}^{a_m}$ being the value domain, that is, the set of all values which are valid for attribute a_m, we define the metric for validity on the level of attribute values as follows:

$$Q_{Vali}(v_I(t_n, a_m)) = 0 \Leftrightarrow v_I(t_n, a_m) \notin S_{Vali}^{a_m} \qquad (3a)$$

$$Q_{Vali}(v_I(t_n, a_m)) = 1 \Leftrightarrow v_I(t_n, a_m) \in S_{Vali}^{a_m} \qquad (3b)$$

Thus, the value domain $S_{Vali}^{a_m}$ can be deduced from business rules or domain-specific functions [27]. The valid value domain of an attribute value $v_I(t_n.a_m)$ can also be derived from another attribute value $v_I(t_n.a_o)$ for attribute a_o of the same tupel t_n (we use the term 'tupel' instead of 'record set' to avoid confusion with respect to the variables, as we will use r for 'relation' later on). However, if such cross-attribute logical dependencies shall be taken into account, it is necessary to analyze the validity of the determining attribute value $v_I(t_n.a_o)$ first. This is because restricting the value domain for the dependent attribute value $v_I(t_n.a_m)$ based on the determining value $v_I(t_n.a_o)$ for another attribute is only reasonable if the determining value $v_I(t_n.a_o)$ is valid itself. Taking the example of an address, it does not make sense to derive the 'city' from the 'zip code', if the latter value is for instance negative, i. e. not valid. Owing to this restriction, we leave aside cross-attribute logical dependencies for this paper, but such effects are subject to further research.

Completeness and validity have in common, that a set of values has to be defined in advance so that the two dimensions can be measured. In general, the effort for defining the corresponding set should be higher for validity, as all valid values have to be defined for a particular attribute, whereas completeness requires only listing of those values which are semantically equivalent to *NULL* for each attribute. Comparing the effort for measuring validity to the one for accuracy, the effort for the former can be considered by far lower, as it does not require a real-world test and – after the initial definition of $S_{Vali}^{a_m}$ – the measurement can be repeated in an automated way.

Currency. Recent papers on DQ define 'currency' (often used synonymously with timeliness) as the probability that an attribute value $v_I(t_n.a_m)$, which was accurate at the instance of its storage, is still congruent with its real-world counterpart $v_W(t_n.a_m)$ at the moment of measurement [24]. This definition shall also hold for this article. That is, currency represents the probability that an attribute value is still up-to-date and has not become outdated due to a temporal decline. Thus, in contrast to measuring accuracy, measuring currency provides a probability and not a verified statement under certainty.

Let hence $s^{v_I(t_n.a_m)}$ be the time period which has passed since the accurate storage of the attribute value $v_I(t_n.a_m)$ in the data resource. Furthermore, S^{a_m} denotes the shelf life of an attribute a_m. That is, it represents the time period which passes before the – originally accurately stored – attribute value $v_I(t_n.a_m)$ does no longer correspond to its real-world counterpart, as $v_W(t_n.a_m)$ has changed in the meantime. As shelf life S^{a_m} is usually unknown, it is considered a random variable. Moreover, according to Heinrich et al. [24], we define a distribution function $F^{a_m}\left(s^{v_I(t_n.a_m)}\right) = P\left(S^{a_m} \leq s^{v_I(t_n.a_m)}\right)$ specifically for each attribute a_m. This distribution function returns the probability that the shelf life of a particular attribute value is shorter than the time period which has passed since its storage in the data resource; or – to put it another way – the probability that an attribute value became outdated in the meantime due to a temporal decline. Based on these definitions the general metric for currency can be defined as follows [24]:

$$Q_{Curr}(s^{v_I(t_n,a_m)}) = 1 - F^{a_m}(s^{v_I(t_n,a_m)}) \tag{4}$$

In contrast to completeness and validity, the metric for currency is not based on a set of values defined for each attribute, but on the distribution function $F^{a_m}\left(s^{v_I(t_n.a_m)}\right)$ which has to be specifically determined for each attribute a_m. To do this, statistical procedures are necessary as, for instance, discussed in Heinrich et al. [24]. This investment has to be made once before the first measurement, but the resulting distribution function can then be used several times. As a result, the recurring costs for measuring currency are usually less than for measuring accuracy.

Summing up, the definition of the DQ dimension accuracy seems to be the closest to the definitions of DQ: By measuring accuracy insufficient DQ is certainly detected and the DQ dimensions completeness, validity, and currency are measured simultaneously. But when measuring accuracy, not only the attribute value $v_I(t_n.a_m)$ stored in a data resource is needed, but also its real-world counterpart $v_W(t_n.a_m)$ at the instance of measurement. In contrast, measuring completeness, validity, and currency can be realized by means of metrics without comparing the stored attribute value $v_I(t_n.a_m)$ to its real-world counterpart $v_W(t_n.a_m)$. Although, determining a set of incomplete attribute values $S_{Incomp}^{a_m}$, a value domain $S_{Vali}^{a_m}$, and a distribution function $F^{a_m}\left(s^{v_I(t_n.a_m)}\right)$ occasions initial costs, measuring accuracy usually is much more expensive in the long run. This is because the parameters for measuring completeness, validity, and currency have to be determined once and can afterwards be used for multiple automated measurements with no or little adaptions, while the real-world counterpart for measuring accuracy has to be determined for each measurement at high cost anew. Owing to these high costs, indicating an attribute value's accuracy, without knowing its real-world counterpart, would be of high value, especially in recurring measurements. Thus, taking into account metrics for completeness, validity, and currency – which are less cost intensive in the long run – seems to be economically reasonable. As each of these metrics measures a specific aspect of an attribute value's accuracy (see below) an aggregated view of these three dimensions would yield a more complete indication of an attribute value's accuracy and hence of its insufficiency. Consequently, approaches to aggregate DQ dimensions are discussed in the following.

2.2   Approaches to Aggregate Different DQ Dimensions

Existing interdependencies between particular DQ dimensions are analysed in several publications. For instance, interdependencies between DQ dimensions like accuracy and timeliness (not currency) as well as completeness and consistency are modelled as trade-offs [1], [2]. In addition, logical connections between DQ dimensions are discussed [21] and approaches are developed to quantify existing interdependencies by means of correlations [14], [32]. Besides, the dependencies and the interactions between different DQ dimension are analysed based on the complexity of the problem [7]. None of these papers addresses the topic of formally aggregating DQ dimensions. So far, only three publications do so:

The first [9] designs a formal approach for combining the results of metrics for different DQ dimensions to one aggregated DQ measure. It is defined based on a weighted average:

$$Q_{Over} = w_{Accu} \times Q_{Accu} + w_{Comp} \times Q_{Comp} + w_{Vali} \times Q_{Vali} + w_{Curr} \times Q_{Curr} + w_{Inter} \times Q_{Inter} + w_{Acc} \times Q_{Acc} \tag{5}$$

This aggregation takes into account the dimensions 'interpretability' (Q_{Inter}) and 'accessibility' (Q_{Acc}), which refer to Quality of Design (QoD) and not to QoC. Hence, these dimensions are not relevant in our context. Nevertheless, the idea of using a weighted average might still be appropriate to aggregate metrics for different DQ dimensions, as also Pipino et al. [37] propose to do so. However, using a weighted average comes along with several shortcomings, which are discussed by Helfert et al. [28]. They mainly stress that a weighted average assumes independence of the metrics to be aggregated. As will be revealed in section 3, this assumption does not hold in the given context: for instance, an incomplete value should not be valid; consequently, independence is not given.

Besides, Even and Shankararayanan [16] suggest an aggregation function which shall reflect the overall utility reduction caused by different quality defects. They propose the algebraic product:

$$Q_{Cons} = Q_{Accu} \times Q_{Comp} \times Q_{Vali} \times Q_{Curr} \tag{6}$$

On the one hand, this aggregated quality of an attribute value is perfect ($Q_{Cons} = 1$) if no defect is present (i.e. $Q_{Accu} = Q_{Comp} = Q_{Vali} = Q_{Curr} = 1$) and on the other hand, it is absolutely imperfect ($Q_{Cons} = 0$) if at least one of the components has a zero value. However, within the paper of Even and Shankararayanan [16], completeness refers to a QoD and not to a QoC definition: It is defined as the inclusion or exclusion of an attribute value in the data specification. This makes sense from a utility based point of view, but not for indicating an attribute value's accuracy.

In addition, Calero et al. [8] develop a DQ model for web portals (the so called PDQM). That is, they develop a model to determine overall DQ of a web portal based on probabilistic theory. Therefore, Calero et al. [8] use an approach that employs Bayesian networks and Fuzzy logic in order to aggregate several DQ dimensions. These DQ dimensions mostly rely on a QoD definition (e.g. applicability, availability, believability, flexibility, etc.) rather than a QoC definition. Furthermore, they also do not measure accuracy by a real-world test but give a discrete indication of accuracy (good, medium, bad) based on the number of duplicates presented on a web portal. The approach is feasible for determining overall DQ of web portals and has been partly tested in a real-world setting [11] but is insufficient for other domains such as corporate data sets as several DQ dimension (e.g. accuracy, completeness, etc.) have been adapted to the web portal domain [8].

Moreover, in these approaches another problem arises by including the dimension accuracy itself: As argued earlier, it is necessary to determine the real-world value $v_W(t_n.a_m)$ in order to measure accuracy, so that it can be compared to the attribute value stored in the data resource $v_I(t_n.a_m)$. Thereby, accuracy can be determined exactly – whereas the other three dimensions only return an indication on the accuracy of the attribute value. If the real-world value is known, the metric for accuracy should be used and there is no need for the other dimensions or their aggregation at all.

2.3   Research Gap

So far, there exists no approach to aggregate metrics for completeness, validity, and currency enabling an indication on the accuracy of an attribute value by considering dependencies between the different DQ dimensions and representing them adequately. To close this research gap, we design an indication function which makes use of metrics for the DQ dimensions completeness, validity, and currency to indicate an attribute value's accuracy in an economics-oriented way.

3   Design of an Indicator Function for Accuracy

The indicator function is an artefact which is to be designed. To guide the search process for this artefact in a scientifically founded way, we state eight requirements which shall be fulfilled by the indicator function.

First, we demand five requirements which were already used in existing DQ literature to derive metrics to measure the four DQ dimensions considered in this paper: completeness [25], validity [27], currency [24], and accuracy [26]. That is, the metrics to measure these dimensions (represented by formulas 1 to 4) also meet the following requirements:

(R1) Normalisation: The results of the indicator function must be normalised to ensure that they can be compared to each other (e.g. to compare different levels of DQ over time [37]). In this context, DQ metrics are often ratios with a value ranging between 0 (perfectly bad) and 1 (perfectly good) [16], [37].

(R2) Interval scale: The difference between two results of the indicator function must be interval scaled (i.e. must have a defined meaning which remains the same independent from the height of the results). Only then the results can be input parameters to economic considerations.

(R3) Interpretability: Only if the meaning of the results of the indicator function are comprehensible, they are "easy to interpret by business users" as demanded by Even and Shankaranarayanan [16].

(R4) Aggregation: It shall be possible to quantify DQ on the level of attribute values, tupels, relations, and the whole (relational) database in a way, so that the values have consistent semantic interpretation (interpretation consistency, [16]) on each level. In addition, the metrics must allow aggregation of values on a given level to the next higher level (aggregation consistency, [16]).

(R5) Applicability: For the purpose of enabling their application, the metrics are based on input parameters that are determinable. When defining metrics, measurement methods should be defined and in cases when exact measurement is not possible or cost-intensive, alternative (rigorous) methods (e.g. statistical) shall be proposed. From an economic point of view, it is also required that the measurement procedure can be accomplished at a high level of automation.

Requirements (R1) to (R3) characterise the results of the indicator function, whereas (R4) and (R5) address the applicability in the context of an economics-oriented DQ management.

The further requirements define how the different DQ dimensions considered impact the result of the indicator function on the level of attribute values. Hence, we are looking for a function $Q_{Ind}^{v_I(t_n.a_m)}(Q_{Comp}(v_I(t_n.a_m)), Q_{Vali}(v_I(t_n.a_m)), Q_{Curr}(s^{v_I(t_n.a_m)}))$, which returns an indicator on the accuracy of the attribute value $v_I(t_n.a_m)$ based on its metric results for completeness $Q_{Comp}(v_I(t_n.a_m))$, validity $Q_{Vali}(v_I(t_n.a_m))$, and currency $Q_{Curr}(s^{v_I(t_n.a_m)})$.

Again, we start with completeness: An incomplete attribute value cannot be accurate by definition; if no attribute value is stored, it is different from the real-world counterpart (if the latter exists – cf. section 2.1.2). Consequently, it cannot be valid or current either and it would therefore seem inappropriate if the metric results for validity and currency had any influence. Hence, in case of an incomplete attribute value, the metric for completeness fixes the value of the indicator function at 0:

(R6) $Q_{Comp}(v_I(t_n.a_m)) = 0 \Rightarrow Q_{Ind}^{v_I(t_n.a_m)}(0, Q_{Vali}(v_I(t_n.a_m)), Q_{Curr}(s^{v_I(t_n.a_m)})) = 0$.

Note that the metric for currency might return a value greater than 0, as it relies only on the shelf life $s^{v_I(t_n.a_m)}$ and does not take into account the actually stored value. This indication is however overruled via (R6), so that solely completeness determines the overall value of the indicator function.

If an attribute value is however complete, the result of the indicator function depends on the dimensions validity and currency. As an invalid value is also inaccurate by definition, currency is not relevant here either and it shall hold:

(R7) $Q_{Comp}(v_I(t_n.a_m)) = 1 \wedge Q_{Vali}(v_I(t_n.a_m)) = 0 \Rightarrow Q_{Ind}^{v_I(t_n.a_m)}(1, 0, Q_{Curr}(s^{v_I(t_n.a_m)})) = 0$

Again, (R7) ensures that currency is overruled and has no impact on the overall indication.

In case of a complete and valid attribute value, its DQ will be judged in addition based on its currency, because only in this case the attribute value can be accurate and the metric for currency indeed returns the probability that the stored attribute value still corresponds to its real-world counterpart. Consequently, it shall hold:

(R8) $Q_{Comp}(v_I(t_n.a_m)) = 1 \wedge Q_{Vali}(v_I(t_n.a_m)) = 1 \Rightarrow Q_{Ind}^{v_I(t_n.a_m)}(1,1,Q_{Curr}(s^{v_I(t_n.a_m)})) = Q_{Curr}(s^{v_I(t_n.a_m)})$

Comparing the existing approaches to (R1) to (R8) it can be stated that the weighted average operator (5) meets requirements (R6) to (R8) only if the weights are determined for each attribute value $v_I(t_n.a_m)$ individually based on its completeness, validity, and currency: For instance, if an attribute value is complete, but invalid, the weights for completeness and currency should be 0, whereas the weight for validity should be 1. This procedure seems rather complex and causes additional computation time when applying the indicator function in an automated way. Moreover, the purpose of the weights is not to fully exclude or include one dimension, but to provide a weighting based on the dimensions general relevance. Consequently, the weighted average operator seems not suitable for our purposes. Although, the Bayesian network approach proposed by Calero et al. [8] is based on probabilistic theory it cannot be applied to the metrics introduced in section 2. The PDQM relies on specific (objective and subjective) measures for the Bayesian network's entry nods which form the basis for determining the measures of the specific DQ dimensions (e.g. accuracy) in terms of probability tables.

A mathematical operator fulfilling requirements (R1) to (R8) is the algebraic product, which was also used in (6). Based on it, the indicator function for accuracy can be formulated as follows:

$$
\begin{aligned}
Q_{Ind}^{v_I(t_n.a_m)}(Q_{Comp}(v_I(t_n.a_m)), Q_{Vali}(v_I(t_n.a_m)), Q_{Curr}(s^{v_I(t_n.a_m)})) = \\
= Q_{Comp}(v_I(t_n.a_m)) \times Q_{Vali}(v_I(t_n.a_m)) \times Q_{Curr}(s^{v_I(t_n.a_m)})
\end{aligned}
\tag{7}
$$

The value of this indicator function is 0, if the attribute value is incomplete or invalid or both. In all cases, currency is not taken into account. Only if an attribute value is complete and valid, currency plays a role and determines the result of the indicator function.

Besides (R6) to (R8), the proposed indicator function fulfils the other properties as well: On the level of attribute values, the results of formula (7) are normalized to the interval [0; 1] (R1). As only the value domain for currency is the continuum between 0 and 1, the interval scale property depends on this dimension. Since currency is measured by means of a probability, the results are interval scaled (R2). In addition, a probability can be considered interpretable (R3). Once the initial actions for an automated measurement are taken per attribute (definition of the corresponding sets $S_{Incomp}^{a_m}$ and $S_{Vali}^{a_m}$ for completeness and validity or definition of the distribution function $F^{a_m}(s^{v_I(t_n.a_m)})$ for currency respectively), the measurement can be done repeatedly in an automated way (R5).

To meet requirement (R4), we also develop formulas which give an indication on accuracy on higher levels of a data resource based on formula (7). As the metrics have to be defined specifically for each attribute, the attributes of a relation shall be considered as the next level [33] (in contrast to e.g. Heinrich et al. [25], who consider the tupels of a relation as the next level).

The indicator function on the level of attribute a_m bases on the indicator function values of all $N \in IN$ tupels, which are stored in a relation at the moment of measuring DQ. To measure DQ in an inter-subjectively verifiable way, the tupels t_n shall not be weighted, so that all have the same impact:[3]

$$Q_{Ind}^{a_m} = \sum_{n=1}^{N} Q_{Ind}^{v_I(t_n.a_m)} (Q_{Comp}(v_I(t_n.a_m)), Q_{Vali}(v_I(t_n.a_m)), Q_{Curr}(s^{v_I(t_n.a_m)})) \Big/ N \qquad (8)$$

Also on the level of relations, the indicator function for accuracy can be determined based on the indicator function of the (unweighted) $M \in IN$ attributes by means of the arithmetic mean:

$$Q_{Ind}^{r} = \sum_{m=1}^{M} Q^{a_m} \Big/ M \qquad (9)$$

Assuming the data resource consisting of $P \in IN$ pairwise non overlapping relations and all attributes being represented only once in the data resource, the indicator function for accuracy on the level of the data resource can be defined using formula (9):

$$Q_{Ind}^{d} = \sum_{r=1}^{P} Q^{r} \Big/ P \qquad (10)$$

The designed formulas can now be used to give an indication on the DQ in terms of accuracy on all levels of a data resource in an inter-subjectively verifiable and automated way. Hence, (A4) is met.

4   Demonstration of Applicability

The practical applicability of the indicator function for accuracy shall be demonstrated in a customer database example. We consider a fictive company intending to measure the accuracy of its data at regular intervals. The company preferably conducts e-mail-based direct marketing campaigns. The success of these campaigns depends on the accuracy of the e-mail addresses stored in the customer database. Therefore the company measures at regular intervals the quality of e-mail addresses stored in the customer database. The customer database is built using a relational database schema. For reasons of clearness, we consider one relation "customers", which is shown in Table 1.

Table 1. Exemplary relation for customer data

C_ID	last_name	first_name	e_mail_address	entry_date
1	Hansen	Olaf	O.Hansen@example.com	1998-11-01
2	Parker	Peter	p.parker@world-time.time	2010-01-17
3	Smith	Michael	NULL	2007-09-27

---

[3] Some existing approaches propose to weight attributes and/or tupels. Such a weighting can be useful in particular business situations and can be integrated in the formulas proposed here.

The relation consists of the following five attributes: a distinct identifier (C_ID), a customer's last name (last_name), a customer's first name (first_name), a customer's e-mail address (e_mail_address), and the respective date of data entry (entry_date). To not find out only with the next campaign about the inaccuracy of the e-mail addresses, the company applies the indicator function designed above. At the level of attribute values, the indicator function is designed as a product of the results of the metrics for completeness, validity, and currency. For calculating the indicator function, the company thus has to take the following four steps: (i) calculate the metric for completeness, (ii) calculate the metric for validity, (iii) calculate the metric for currency, and (iv) multiply the metrics' results for each attribute value. All four steps can be performed in a predominantly automated way. This shall be illustrated by describing the measurement of the metrics in terms of the standard data query language SQL (while acknowledging that other ways of implementation are feasible as well).

To measure completeness, formulas (2a) and (2b) are used. In this example, we assume that the set of attribute values which are considered as incomplete $S_{Incomp}^{a_m}$ is equal to *NULL*: $S_{Incomp}^{a_m} = \{NULL\}$. The metric can hence be implemented without much effort by a SQL Statement of the form "SELECT C_ID FROM customers WHERE e_mail_address IS NULL". Thus, the result of the metric for completeness for the records returned by this statement equals 0 and for the remaining records 1.

To determine the validity of an e-mail-address, formulas (3a) and (3b) are applied. An e-mail address shall be considered valid only if its top-level domain (e.g. .com, .de, .it, etc.) corresponds to a given set of top-level domains. Simplifying, we assume that all records which are returned by the following SQL statement are valid and constitute therefore $S_{Vali}^{a_m}$: "SELECT C_ID FROM customers WHERE e_mail_address LIKE ,%.org' OR ,%.com' OR ,%.aero' OR ,%.biz' OR ,%.cat' OR ,%.com' OR ,%.coop' OR ,%.edu' OR ,%.gov' OR ,%.info' OR ,%.int' OR ,%.jobs' OR ,%.mil' OR ,%.mobi' OR ,%.museum' OR ,%.name' OR ,%.net' OR ,%.org' OR ,%.pro' OR ,%.travel". Thus, the result of the metric for validity for the records returned by this statement equals 1. For all other records the result of the metric equals 0.

As mentioned earlier, it is not necessary to define a value range to measure currency. Instead, the distribution function of the shelf-life S^{a_m} has to be determined. The distribution's parameters can be determined in an objective way by statistical methods on the basis of random samples, statistical distributions, and historical data or in a subjective way by expert estimates (a detailed procedure to develop metrics for currency can be found in Heinrich et al. [24]). As soon as a suitable distribution function and parameters have been determined, an automated measurement can be conducted repeatedly. Therefore, the time span which has elapsed since the attribute values' storage in the database, has to be determined first, based on their entry dates. The respective entry dates again can be selected by a SQL statement ("SELECT C_ID, entry_date FROM customers"). The difference between the instant of measuring currency and the e-mail addresses' entry dates results in the time span of interest $s^{v_I(t_n \cdot a_m)}$. Using this time span and the distribution parameters, the respective currency of an e-mail address can be calculated. Hereafter we exemplarily assume that the shelf life of an e-mail address is exponentially distributed with a decline rate of 0.1. The latter indicates how many values of the attribute a_m become out-of-date on average within one period of time. Thus, we obtain the following metric for currency:

$$Q_{curr}(s^{v_{In} \cdot a_m}) := \exp(-0.1 \cdot s^{v_{In} \cdot a_m})$$
(11)

Within the fourth and last step the results from these three metrics have to be multiplied for each e-mail address according to formula (7). For the e-mail addresses from Table 1 we obtain the results for the indicator function depicted in Table 2. We also list the results when using the weighted average as aggregation function (cf. section 2.2) to discuss the differences and exclude thereof the dimensions 'accuracy', 'interpretability' and 'accessibility' for the reasons discussed earlier. Moreover, we assume that the remaining dimensions considered are equally weighted ($w_{Comp} = w_{Vali} = w_{Curr} = 1/3$).

Table 2. Results for the indicator function on 2012-03-15

C_ID	e_mail_address	entry_date	Q_{Comp}	Q_{Vali}	Q_{Curr}	Q_{Ind}	Q_{Over}
1	O.Hansen@example.com	1998-11-01	1	1	0.27	0.27	0.76
2	p.parker@world-time.time	2010-01-17	1	0	0.80	0.00	0.60
3	NULL	2007-09-27	0	0	0.64	0.00	0.21

The results from Table 2 show that two out of the three e-mail addresses are for sure inaccurate, as they are either not valid (C_ID 2) or incomplete (C_ID 3). Consequently, the value for Q_{Ind} is 0 in both cases. In contrast, Q_{Over} is greater than 0 in both cases; for customer 2, the quality is, in fact, judged quite good at a value of $Q_{Over} = 0.6$. The third e-mail address (customer with C_ID 1) could not be identified as inaccurate according to the indicator function. But, the result indicates that the attribute value is only up-to-date with a probability of 27% which is also the value of the indicator function. The weighted average rates the quality of this attribute value however much higher at 0.76, as the relatively low value for currency is compensated by the high values for completeness and validity. The results of the indicator function can be used as an input to formula (8) in order to calculate the DQ of the attribute "e_mail_address". The resulting value of the indicator function is 0.09. That is, the average quality of the attribute "e_mail_address" is only 0.09.

Transferring this comparatively simple example to very large datasets shows the potential of this automated, repeated, and practicable indication of accuracy. Nonetheless, this is just an example, which demonstrates its applicability and advantages compared to existing approaches. Thus, further attempts are needed to evaluate this indicator function in real-world settings to gain further information from an economic point of view.

5   Conclusion

This paper contributes to an economics-oriented DQ management by designing an indicator function for accuracy as well as by defining eight requirements for aggregating metrics for the DQ dimensions completeness, validity, and currency. The indicator function is based on metrics for the DQ dimensions completeness, validity, and currency, which are aggregated by means of the algebraic product. This procedure enables for a predominantly automated measurement of accuracy. Owing to the avoidance of cost intensive real-world test, this is an advantage especially in very large data sets and in recurring measurements. The indicator function results from a requirements-driven design, ensuring an inter-subjectively verifiable and scientifically founded search process. Besides, formulas to indicate DQ on the levels of attributes, relations, and the database itself are developed. The general applicability of the indicator function is demonstrated in a customer database example and its results are compared to existing approaches.

Some limitations provide room for further research. One limitation exists regarding the dimension 'validity'. As described earlier, the valid value domain of an attribute value $v_f(t_n.a_m)$ can also be derived from another attribute value $v_f(t_n.a_o)$ for attribute a_o of the same tupel t_n. That is, interdependencies among different attribute values of the same tuple can be used to determine an attribute value's validity. However, this procedure has one shortcoming which has not been solved yet: Before determining an attribute value's validity depending on another attribute value of the same tuple, the quality of the latter attribute value has to be determined first (cf. section 2.1.3). Consequently, further research is needed to define metrics for measuring validity taking into account such dependencies. Another limitation of this paper is the missing empirical evidence. Currently, only an example demonstrates the indicator function's general applicability. To further validate the indicator function and its results, several case studies should be conducted. The authors are currently working on an application of the indicator function in the context of managing address data. Results from this study may provide further insides on the costs and benefits of the indicator function under real-world conditions.

References

1. Ballou, D.P., Pazer, H.L.: Modeling completeness versus consistency tradeoffs in information decision contexts. IEEE Trans. Knowled. Data Eng. 1, 240–243 (2003)
2. Ballou, D.P., Pazer, H.L.: Designing information systems to optimize the accuracy-timeliness tradeoff. Information Systems Research 1, 51–72 (1995)
3. Ballou, D.P., Tayi, G.K.: Enhancing Data Quality in Data Warehouse Environments. Communications of the ACM 1, 73–78 (1999)
4. Ballou, D.P., Wang, R.Y., Pazer, H.L., Tayi, G.K.: Modeling Information Manufacturing Systems to Determine Information Product Quality. Management Science 4, 462–484 (1998)
5. Batini, C., Barone, D., Cabitza, F., Grega, S.: A Data Quality Methodology for Heterogenous Data. International Journal of Database Management Systems 1, 60–79 (2011)

6. Batini, C., Scannapieco, M.: Data Quality. Concepts, Methodologies and Techniques (Data-Centric Systems and Applications), vol. 1, Berlin (2006)
7. Blake, R., Mangiameli, P.: The Effects and Interactions of Data Quality and Problem Complexity on Classification. Journal of Data and Information Quality (JDIQ) 2, 8 (2011)
8. Calero, C., Caro, A., Piattini, M.: An applicable data quality model for web portal data consumers. World Wide Web 4, 465–484 (2008)
9. Cappiello, C., Comuzzi, M.: A Utility-Based Model to Define the Optimal Data Quality Level in IT Service Offering. In: Proceedings of the 17th European Conference on Information Systems (ECIS), Verona (Italy), pp. 1062–1074 (2009)
10. Cappiello, C., Francalanci, C., Pernici, B.: Time-Related Factors of Data Quality in Multichannel Information Systems. Journal of Management Information Systems 3, 71–91 (2004)
11. Caro, A., Calero, C., Piattini, M.: Development Process of the Operational Version of PDQM. In: Benatallah, B., Casati, F., Georgakopoulos, D., Bartolini, C., Sadiq, W., Godart, C. (eds.) WISE 2007. LNCS, vol. 4831, pp. 436–448. Springer, Heidelberg (2007)
12. Codd, E.F.: Extending the database relational model to capture more meaning. ACM Transactions on Database Systems (TODS) 4, 397–434 (1979)
13. CSO Insights: 2005 Executive Report: Target Marketing Priorities Analysis (2005)
14. De Amicis, F., Barone, D., Batini, C.: An analytical framework to analyze dependencies among data quality dimensions. In: Proceedings of the 11th International Conference on Information Quality (ICIQ), Cambridge, MA (USA), pp. 369–383 (2006)
15. Eppler, M.J.: Managing information quality, vol. 1, Berlin (2003)
16. Even, A., Shankaranarayanan, G.: Utility-Driven Assessment of Data Quality. The DATA BASE for Advances in Information Systems 2, 75–93 (2007)
17. Even, A., Shankaranarayanan, G.: Value-driven data quality assessment. In: Proceedings of the 10th International Conference on Information Quality (ICIQ), pp. 221–236. MIT Press, Cambridge (2005)
18. Even, A., Shankaranarayanan, G., Berger, P.D.: Economics-Driven Data Management: An Application to the Design of Tabular Datasets. IEEE Transactions on Knowledge and Data Engineering 6, 818–831 (2007)
19. Fisher, C.W., Chengalur-Smith, I.N., Ballou, D.P.: The Impact of Experience and Time on the Use of Data Quality Information in Decision Making. Information Systems Research 2, 170–188 (2003)
20. Fox, C., Levitin, A., Redman, T.C.: The Notion of Data and Its Quality Dimensions. Information Processing & Management 1, 9–19 (1994)
21. Gackowski, Z.J.: Logical interdependence of data/information quality dimensions—A purpose-focused view on IQ. In: Proceedings of the Ninth International Conference on Information Quality (ICIQ 2004), Cambridge, MA, USA (2004)
22. Görz, Q.: An Economics-Driven Decision Model for Data Quality Improvement – A Contribution to Data Currency. In: Proceedings of the 17th Americas Conference on Information Systems (AMCIS), Detroit, Michigan, USA (2011)
23. Information Workers Beware: Your Business Data Can't Be Trusted, http://www.sap.com/about/newsroom/businessobjects/20060625_005028.epx
24. Heinrich, B., Kaiser, M., Klier, M.: A Procedure to Develop Metrics For Currency and its Application in CRM. ACM Journal of Data and Information Quality 1, 5:1–5:28 (2009)
25. Heinrich, B., Kaiser, M., Klier, M.: Does the EU Insurance Mediation Directive help to improve Data Quality? - A metric-based analysis. In: Proceedings of the 16th European Conference on Information Systems (ECIS), Galway, Irland (2008)

26. Heinrich, B., Kaiser, M., Klier, M.: How to measure data quality? – a metric based approach. In: Proceedings of the 28th International Conference on Information Systems (ICIS), Montreal, Canada (2007)
27. Heinrich, B., Kaiser, M., Klier, M.: Metrics for measuring data quality – Foundations for an economic data quality management. In: 2nd International Conference on Software and Data Technologies (ICSOFT), Barcelona, Spain (2007)
28. Helfert, M., Foley, O., Ge, M., Cappiello, C.: Limitations of Weighted Sum Measures for Information Quality. In: Proceedings of the 15th Americas Conference on Information Systems (AMCIS), San Francisco, CA, USA (2009)
29. Juran, J.M.: How to think about Quality, New York, vol. 5, pp. 2.1–2.18 (1998)
30. Kahn, B.K., Strong, D.M., Wang, R.Y.: Information quality benchmarks: product and service performance. Commun. ACM 4, 184–192 (2002)
31. Lee, Y.W., Pipino, L., Strong, D.M., Wang, R.Y.: Process-Embedded Data Integrity. Journal of Database Management 1, 87–103 (2004)
32. Lee, Y.W., Strong, D.M., Kahn, B.K., Wang, R.Y.: AIMQ: a methodology for information quality assessment. Information & Management 2, 133–146 (2002)
33. Naumann, F., Freytag, J., Leser, U.: Completeness of Integrated Information Sources. Information Systems 7, 583–615 (2004)
34. Orr, K.: Data Quality and Systems Theory. Communications of the ACM 2, 66–71 (1998)
35. Otto, B., Lee, Y.W., Caballero, I.: Information and data quality in business networking: a key concept for enterprises in its early stages of development. Electronic Markets, 83–97 (2011)
36. Parssian, A., Sarkar, S., Jacob, V.S.: Assessing Data Quality for Information Products: Impact of Selection, Projection, and Cartesian Product. Management Science 7, 967–982 (2004)
37. Pipino, L., Lee, Y.W., Wang, R.Y.: Data Quality Assessment. Communications of the ACM 4, 211–218 (2002)
38. Russom, P.: Taking Data Quality to the Enterprise through Data Governance. The Data Warehousing Institute, Seattle (2006)
39. Vassiliou, Y.: Null values in data base management - a denotational semantics approach. In: Proceedings of the 1979 ACM SIGMOD International Conference on Management of Data (SIGMOD 1979), pp. 162–169. ACM, Boston (1979)
40. Wand, Y., Wang, R.Y.: Anchoring data quality dimensions in ontological foundations. Communications of the ACM 11, 86–95 (1996)
41. Wang, R.Y.: A Product Perspective on Total Data Quality Management. Communications of the ACM 2, 58–65 (1998)
42. Wang, R.Y., Strong, D.M.: Beyond accuracy: what data quality means to data consumers. Journal of Management Information Systems 4, 5–33 (1996)

Improving Robustness of Scale-Free Networks
to Message Distortion

Ofir Ben-Assuli and Arie Jacobi

Ono Academic College, Zahal Street 104,
55000, Kiryat Ono, Israel
{ofir.benassuli,jacobi.arie}@gmail.com

Abstract. Vast numbers of organizations and individuals communicate every day by sending messages over social networks. These messages, however, are subject to change as they propagate through the network. This paper calculates the distortion of a message as it propagates in a social network with a scale-free topology, and suggests a remedial process in which a node corrects the distortion during the diffusion process to improve the robustness of scale-free networks to message distortion. We test a model on a simulation of different types of scale-free networks, and compare different sets of corrective nodes including hubs, regular (non hub) nodes, and a combination of hubs and regular nodes. Using hubs that correct the distorted message while it is diffused are shown to decrease the global error measurement of the distortion, and improve the robustness of the network.

Keywords: Social networks, distortion of information, organizational communication, scale-free networks.

1   Introduction

The Web 2.0 information revolution has led to an exponential growth in the number of organizations and individuals who communicate by sending messages over electronic social networks. Messages can be verbal or written, and the mechanisms for sending messages include real-time chatting applications in an electronic social network, Word Of Mouth (WOM) marketing methods, electronic WOMs [1], or forwarding a message in an email with an additional text. These messages, however, are subject to change as they are diffused in the network. If distorted, advertising messages in an electronic social network for example can undermine the entire marketing mission as was the case for an Apple iPad product. Though very successful, its name was promptly changed on the internet to 'iTampon' and prompted numerous predictable jokes. Twitter's worldwide trending topics ranked 'iTampon' as number two (see http://gizmodo.com/trendingtopics). This highlights the need for practical methods to correct distorted messages during diffusion in social networks.

This paper introduces a mathematical model to calculate the distortion of a message as it propagates in a social network. It compares different sets of corrective nodes to determine which set best improves a global measurement of the distortion.

H. Rahman et al. (Eds.): MCIS 2012, LNBIP 129, pp. 185–199, 2012.

Three different sets composed of hubs or nodes with many links, regular (non hub) nodes, and a combination of hubs and regular nodes were examined.

We tested our mathematical model through a simulation study in which the distortion of a message as it propagates in a social network was calculated based on a random selection of contacts receiving a message from a given node, and a random selection of letters in the message. During the propagation process a global error measurement of the distortion was calculated. After the propagation phase, the global measurement error distortion results for the sets of corrective nodes were compared. The discussion presents practical recommendations for ways to prevent information distortion diffused in social networks.

2   Background and Literature Survey

In the past few years, the discovery of the small-world and scale-free properties of many natural and artificial complex networks has stimulated a great deal of interest in studying the underlying organizing principles of various complex networks, which has led to dramatic advances in this emerging field of research. A comprehensive review can be found in [2], [3], and [4]. These reviews contain basic concepts, important advances, and significant results in current studies of various complex networks. Some fundamental properties and typical network models are described.

In the following sections we review several key studies. We include works on diffusion of information and on distortion and changes in data transmitted through social networks. Then, basic notions of network theory are introduced and an overview of our method is presented.

2.1   Propagation and Data Distortion via Social Networks

Propagation or diffusion refers to the transport on a network from node to node of some quantity, such as information, opinion or epidemics. Propagation in networks has been studied frequently in the social network community since Rapaport's pioneering study on the influence of network characteristics such as transitivity of node linking on disease propagation [5,6]. The spread of socially-transmitted diseases is a canonical example; see [7] for a modeling approach from a theoretical physics perspective and [8] for an up-to-date approach in bio-mathematics, together with references for their study on the propagation of AIDS.

There are few works on the perceived quality of information sent through social networks. O'Reilly [9] conducted several laboratory and field studies investigating antecedents and consequences of the intentional distortion of information by senders in organizational communication networks. His laboratory studies were used to examine the impact of two interpersonal variables (trust in the receiver and perceived influence of the receiver over the sender) and directionality of information flow (upward, lateral, and downward) on senders' propensities to block or suppress information. Field studies established the external validity of these laboratory investigations and related information distortion by senders to job satisfaction and performance. The results of these studies showed that (1) a bias exists towards screening certain types of information from upward transmission; (2) low trust in the receiver of a message results in significantly more suppression of information by senders, especially information which reflects unfavorably on the senders; and (3) a measure of information distortion is significantly and inversely associated with job satisfaction and individual and group performance. These findings differ in several respects from previous studies on organizational communication. Their implications for decision-making are discussed and O'Reilly [9] suggested a model relating antecedents and consequences to information distortion.

Panzarasa et al. [10] examined users' behavior and social interaction patterns, and inferred the processes underpinning the dynamics of use of online communities established over time by online messages. They investigated hubs' responsibilities for holding the system together and facilitating information flow. They also examined how hubs as "opinion leaders" can be exploited by purposefully directing information campaigns to them to spread ideas or fads, thus promoting the diffusion of innovations.

Sarker et al. [11] examined the theoretical linkages between trust, communication, and member performance in virtual teams. They tested three proposed models (additive, interaction, and mediation), and found that their 'mediating' model best explained how communication and trust work together to influence performance. This study, through its adoption of the social network analysis approach, demonstrates the strengths of applying network approaches when examining new organizational forms.

Crucitti and Marchiori introduced a definition of the efficiency of a network to propagate information (see [12] and [13]). They assumed that the efficiency Q_{ij} of the communication between node i and j in a graph G is inversely proportional to the shortest distance: $Q_{ij} = 1 / d_{ij}$, $\forall i, j$. The efficiency Q_{ij} was defined on a global and local scale. The global efficiency of a graph G is defined as

$$E_{glob}(G) = \frac{1}{N(N-1)} \sum_{i \neq j \in G} \frac{1}{d_{ij}},$$

The local efficiency is defined as the average efficiency of local sub-graphs

$$E_{loc}(G) = \frac{1}{N} \sum_{i \in G} E(G_i), \text{ where } E(G_i) = \frac{1}{k_i(k_i - 1)} \sum_{l \neq m \in G_i} \frac{1}{d_{lm}},$$

and G_i is the sub-graph of the neighbors of node i. The two definitions of the global and local efficiency are normalized.

In this paper, we refer to the concept of robustness with regard to the resilience of a network to distortion of information diffused in it, rather than the use of robustness in graph theory and network analysis [12, 14] that measures the resilience of the network to the removal of edges or vertices. To the best of our knowledge there have been no studies on the robustness of different types of social networks to distortion of information.

2.2   Network Background

To calculate the distortion of information transmitted in a social network, we first define some basic terms in graph theory. A network is represented by its mathematical model, a graph. A graph G = (V,E) formally consists of a set of vertices V and a set of edges E between them. An edge e_{ij} connects vertex i with vertex j.

The neighborhood S_i for a vertex V_i is defined as its immediately connected neighbors as follows:

$$S_i = \{v_j : e_{ij} \in E \wedge e_{ji} \in E\}. \tag{1}$$

We define $k_i = |S_i|$ as the number of vertices in the neighborhood S_i of a vertex V_i. The local clustering coefficient C_i for a vertex V_i is given by the proportion of links between the vertices within its neighborhood S_i divided by the maximum number of links that could possibly exist in S_i [15]. For an undirected graph which has the property that E_{ij} and E_{ji} are considered identical, if a vertex V_i has K_i neighbors, it is interconnected by up to $k_i(k_i - 1)/2$ nodes, which is the maximum number of edges within S_i. Therefore, the local clustering coefficient for undirected graphs is defined as

$$C_i = 2|\{e_{ij}\}|/k_i(k_i - 1) : v_i, \ v_j \in S_i, \ e_{ij} \in E \tag{2}$$

On the network level, a network N contains n nodes interconnected by up to a total of $m = n(n-1)/2$ edges. Each node represents a person and each edge that connects two nodes represents a connection between two people. In the networks we used in this study, there was at most only one edge between any two nodes and no node connected to itself.

The connectivity probability p of a network is the average probability that any node is connected to any other node. It is simply the number of edges divided by the maximum possible number of edges:

$$p = \frac{2m}{n(n-1)}.$$

A fully connected network has a probability of p = 1.

2.3   Scale-Free Networks

In this article we only analyze scale-free networks. Scale-free networks (or BA networks, see [16, 17]) are those in which the network starts with m_0 unconnected vertices, and at each time step t, another node is added with m edges ($m \leq m_0$). The probability Π_i of existing node i being connected to the new node is proportional to the connectivity of that node.

$$\Pi_i = k_i / \sum_j k_j . \tag{3}$$

The model incorporates two properties: growth (i.e., an increase in the number of nodes and edges over time) and preferential attachment (i.e., an increased likelihood of high-degree nodes acquiring new edges – "the rich get richer"). Preference is thus given to "earlier" nodes, thereby forming hubs. The BA scale-free model produces networks with a power law degree distribution $p(k) = ak^{-\gamma}$, where typically the exponent γ satisfies $2 \leq \gamma \leq 3$. Albert and Barabási [17] proposed an extended model of network evolution that gives a more realistic description of local processing by taking into account the additions of new nodes and new links, and the rewiring of links.

Scale-free networks display a high degree of resilience to random attacks. In other words, the ability of the nodes in scale-free networks to communicate is unaffected by the failure of some randomly chosen nodes. However, scale-free networks are extremely vulnerable to the removal of hubs, which play a crucial role in maintaining network connectivity [18].

Numerical results have indicated that BA scale-free networks have small average distance between two generic nodes. The average path length of a scale-free model is somewhat smaller, but the clustering coefficient is much higher. This implies that the existence of hubs plays a key role in bringing the other nodes of the network close to each other. However, currently there is no analytical prediction formula for average path length or the clustering coefficient for the scale-free model. In scale-free networks the average clustering coefficient is small, and the clustering-degree function C(k) is constant [19].

3   Methodology

3.1   Overview of Our Method

In this paper we present a study of the robustness of a scale-free network to distortion of information in the form of a verbal or written message, and ways to decrease the total distortion error. A message has a tendency to change when one person transfers it to another person. Our assumption is that this change in the transferred message, what we call its distortion, is usually reflected in different parts of the message, but some of the information remains unaltered. We compare a global measurement of the distortion of the propagated messages in scale-free networks using a simulation.

The simulation involved a model of the network and a model of the distortion process propagating in the network. The propagation model was tailored so as to reflect the realities of the dissemination of information in a social network.

3.2   Proposed Model

Given a network N with n nodes, and a message m which represents a sequence of letters, words, or parts of sentences, without loss of generality in this model we chose to define m as a sequence of letters $\sigma_i \in \Sigma, i = 1,\ldots,k$, where $\Sigma \in \{0,1\}$ is an alphabet. We define the length $k = |m|$ of m to be number of letters in m. We can refer to m as a Boolean vector $\mathbf{v} = [\mathbf{v_0},\ldots,\mathbf{v_k}]^T$ of degree k, where $\mathbf{v}_i \in \{0,1\}$.

Message m represents a message that a person sends to other individuals over a social network. Therefore, each letter σ_i represents a letter in a natural language message.

Initially, message m is transmitted by l different people in network N. These people are called initial propagators. A person P_i in network N forwards message m to $0 \le q \le k_i$ of his contacts (the people that P_i is linked to in the network), where k_i is the degree of P_i and q is chosen randomly.

The first message that a person P_i receives is denoted as m_1^P and this is the message that P_i stores. We denote this message as the "message in memory" $\hat{m}$. Each time P_i receives a mutation of the message m from another contact, $\hat{m}$ will be affected. In order to create a mutated "message in memory" $\hat{m}$, we need to consider all the r messages received by person P, denoted by

$$\left(m_1^P,\ldots,m_r^P\right). \tag{4}$$

For every mutated letter $\sigma_i \in \hat{m}$, $i = 1,\ldots,k$, σ_i is chosen to be the letter that has the maximum number of occurrences among all letters (the mode) at location i in all the r messages $\left(m_1^P,\ldots,m_r^P\right)$. In the case where we have an equal number of different letters, the original letter in message m_1^P is chosen.

Let $\qquad\qquad c^1 = $ number of "1"s in all letters $\sigma_i \in \left(m_1^P,\ldots,m_r^P\right)$,

And let $\qquad\quad c^0 = $ number of "0"s in all letters $\sigma_i \in \left(m_1^P,\ldots,m_r^P\right)$.

We calculate $\qquad\qquad \sigma_i = \begin{cases} 1, & \text{if } c^1 > c^0 \\ 0, & \text{if } c^1 < c^0 \\ \sigma_i \in m_1^P & \text{if } c^1 = c^0 \end{cases}$.

At every transmission of the message in memory $\hat{m}$ from a given person P_i to person P_j in network N, $\hat{m}$ may be distorted (again) into $\hat{m}$, such that some of the letters in $\hat{m}$ which were chosen randomly will change in value. The number of letters that change can differ from person to person in the network.

3.3   Operationalization of the Research Variables

Absolute Error as a Dependent Variable. The absolute error EA^i, for a person P^i, represents the number of mutations from the original message m that was first propagated in the network. It is calculated as follows:

Let $\mathbf{u} = m - m_1^P$ be the difference vector for person P^i. We calculate

$$EA^i = \text{Number of "1"s in } \mathbf{u} . \tag{5}$$

Example: Assuming that the original message $m = \begin{bmatrix}1101111\end{bmatrix}^T$ and the final message $m = \begin{bmatrix}0101001\end{bmatrix}^T$, the difference vector:

$$\mathbf{u} = m - m_1^P = \begin{bmatrix}1101111\end{bmatrix}^T - \begin{bmatrix}0101001\end{bmatrix}^T = \begin{bmatrix}1000110\end{bmatrix}^T .$$

Therefore, $EA^i = 3$ which is the number of "1"s in $\mathbf{u}$.

After the propagation of m in network N that contains n people, we can then calculate the average global absolute distortion value N_A^D for N as

$$N_A^D = \sum_{j=1}^{n} EA^j / n . \tag{6}$$

The absolute error is the primary outcome measure, because it represents the global average error, which reflects the change from the original message m that was first propagated in the network.

3.4   Independent Variables and Node Properties

Degree – The degree of a vertex in a network is the number of edges attached to it. Degree is often interpreted in terms of the immediate risk that a node will contract whatever is flowing through the network (such as a virus, or some information).

Hub – Scale-free networks are characterized by a power law distribution of the number of links connecting to a node, and therefore include nodes which are often called "hubs", which have many more connections than others. In graph theory terms these nodes (vertices) have a degree that exceeds the average degree by an order of magnitude (e.g., [20]).

Original Message – The original message is the message that was first to propagate in the network.

First Propagator – Defines a person (node) in the network that holds the original message and the first to propagate it in the network. There might be a number of First Propagators of the original message.

Message-In-Memory – Message-In-Memory is the message that a person in the network (node) has in memory. This message was formed in two possible ways:

- It was initially received from one of this person's connections in the network, and therefore will be identical to this initial message, called the "Person-Original-Message".

- It already exists, but it is affected and altered by other messages that the person receives from his/her connections in the network. Every letter of the newly affected Message-In-Memory is calculated as the mode (most frequently occurring) of the letters in the same location in all the previous messages that this person received.

Transferred Message – Before transfer of Message-In-Memory, the message might be distorted by the person and then is transferred to some or all of his/her connections in the network.

Mutation – Every time a message propagates in a network, and is transferred from one person (the sender) to another (the receiver), it might be distorted by the sender of the message. The receiver gets a mutated message and each such message is called a mutation.

3.5   Model Simulations

We tested the model on scale-free networks to determine how hubs and/or regular non-hub nodes in the network can diminish the distortion with regard to error (7) by correcting it. Finally, we compared the statistical results using mathematical and statistical tools.

The algorithm we used to traverse the undirected graph that represents the network under simulation is the Breadth First Search (BFS) algorithm for graph search and traversal.

The results presented here used only one First Propagator; each node in the network could be visited a constant number of times, and each simulation of a given network was executed multiple times (twenty times for each type of corrector). At each visited node in every execution cycle, the letters that underwent mutation during the distortion process of a "transferred message" and their location were also chosen randomly.

Breadth First Search (BFS) Algorithm. Breadth First Search (BFS) is a search algorithm defined to find a path from a start node to a destination node in a graph. We used BFS to traverse a given network which is represented using a data structure of the graph. BFS begins at the source node (First Propagator) by checking each of its neighbors. Each of these neighbors checks their neighbors; this continues until all nodes are visited.

We changed the basic BFS algorithm slightly to allow more than one visit at each node. At each node v that BFS visits, BFS checks whether the number of visits did not exceed a given limit of allowed visits per node. In our simulation, BFS checks all the neighboring nodes (note that we did not chose them randomly), and for each of these, the algorithm takes the "message-in-memory" of node v, mutates it, and transfers it to each one of the neighbors. The mutated message affects each of v's neighbors, and its influence is expressed according to equations (4,5) above.

The BFS algorithm is executed for each First Propagator separately and sequentially. Each First Propagator leaves its impressions on every node in the network cumulatively. In other words, the effect that the first of the First Propagators leaves on the messages at each node in the network remains when the second First

Propagator starts to propagate, and the algorithms take into account the previous information on the nodes (the messages that the node received during the propagation executed by the first of the First Propagators).

Data Description. We used the NWB network analysis package developed by Barabási's team at Indiana University [21], and self-written software to produce the different types of networks. The scale-free networks we tested in our simulations have an exponent γ that characterizes human social networks and satisfies $2 \leq \gamma \leq 3$. In addition, we determined which node is a hub using the three sigma criteria.

4   Research Hypotheses

In this paper we tested the following hypotheses:

H1: There is a positive relationship between the number of correcting hubs and a decrease in the absolute error.
H2: There is a positive relationship between the number of corrective regular nodes and a decrease in the absolute error.
H3: The absolute error will be lower after correction using hubs than after correction using regular nodes for the two target numbers of correcting nodes (one or two).
H4.1: The absolute error will be lower after correction using two hubs than after correction using a mix of one regular node and one hub.
H4.2: The absolute error will be lower after correction using a mix of one regular node and one hub than after correction using two regular nodes.

The above hypotheses are based on the assumption that scale-free networks are less sensitive to data distortion after several hubs, regular nodes or a mix of them have corrected the message (to its original values). Moreover, the correction will be more powerful if the correctors are hubs instead of regular nodes. In scale-free networks, hubs and high degree nodes receive the propagated message at an early stage of diffusion, and they deliver it after correction (if they are a corrector node) to many contacts in the network [3, 5, 6, 17]. Therefore, the message path through the network is shorter than via other types of nodes, and as a result fewer message distortions occur in the propagation process.

5   Results

5.1   Descriptive Statistics

In Table 1, we present the descriptive statistics for a given scale-free network with 30,000 nodes and 1,191,718 links. For each set of corrective nodes and without any correction, we ran the simulation twenty times for each type of corrector. The nodes in the network were visited for all types of correctors, so the degree and mutation data are identical for all types of correctors (presented in Table 1). We used the same network and nodes to avoid inconsistency.

Table 1. Descriptive statistics for a scale-free network with 30,000 nodes (identical for all types of correctors)

		Degree	Mutations
N	Valid	30000	30000
	Missing	0	0
Mean		79.45	5.83
Std. Error of Mean		.492	.004
Median		56.00	6.00
Mode		40	6
Range		1662	6

Table 2. The averages and additional descriptive statistics for each type of correctors

		Absolute Error					
		No Corrections	Correction using one hub corrector	Correction using two hubs correctors	Correction using one regular node corrector	Correction using two regular node correctors	Correction using one regular node and one hub
N	Valid	30000	30000	30000	30000	30000	30000
	Missing	0	0	0	0	0	0
Mean		4.5770	3.4414	3.2429	4.2563	3.7178	3.7011
Std. Error of Mean		.00799	.00850	.00832	.00842	.00832	.00808
Median		5.0000	3.0000	3.0000	4.0000	4.0000	4.0000
Mode		5.00	3.00	3.00	4.00	4.00	4.00
Range		10.00	10.00	9.00	9.00	10.00	10.00

5.2   Statistical Analyses

Statistical analyses were performed using SPSS version 20 (SPSS Inc., Chicago, IL, USA) software. To test for differences in our dependent (the absolute error) continuous variable between two groups of correctors, a paired t-test was performed, since we were dealing with the same network and the same nodes. To test for differences in our dependent variable between more than three groups, a General Linear Modeling (GLM) for Repeated Measurements was performed.

As shown in Table 3, there were significant differences between the means of absolute error for all three types of hub correctors (corrections of Hubs: $F=7723.42$, $P < 0.001$; corrections of Regular nodes: $F=2837.93$, $P < 0.001$).

5.3   Testing Our Hypotheses

We also tested for the differences in each pair of correctors to analyze the connections between correctors in light of our hypotheses.

Table Structure. This sub-section describes the structure of the result tables. The first column to the left shows the compared pairs including the means of absolute errors. The second column to the left presents the mean difference for each pair. For instance for the first row of Table 4 the mean difference (1.136) = the mean of No correctors (4.577) – the mean of One Hub Corrector (3.441). The third and fourth columns to the left represent the standard deviation and the T-value respectively. The sixth column to the left presents the p-value of each pair comparison.

Table 3. GLM for Repeated Measurements for the corrections of Hub and of Regular Nodes (0,1,2).

Source		Type III Sum of Squares	Df	Mean Square	F	Sig.
		Tests of Within-Subjects Effects				
		Measure: Hub Difference				
Factor 1	Sphericity Assumed	31088.52	2	15544.26	7723.42	<0.001
	Greenhouse-Geisser	31088.52	2	15551.9	7723.42	<0.001
	Huynh-Feldt	31088.52	2	15550.86	7723.42	<0.001
	Lower-bound	31088.52	1	31088.52	7723.42	<0.001
		Measure: Regular Difference				
Factor 2	Sphericity Assumed	11311.49	2	5655.74	2837.93	<0.001
	Greenhouse-Geisser	11311.49	2	5656.96	2837.93	<0.001
	Huynh-Feldt	11311.49	2	5656.59	2837.93	<0.001
	Lower-bound	11311.49	1	11311.49	2837.93	<0.001

Table 4. The relationship between the number of correcting hubs (0, 1, 2) and a decrease in the absolute error (H1)

Measured Pair (mean absolute error)		Mean difference	Std. Deviation	t	Sig. (2-tailed)
Pair 1	No correctors (4.577) vs. One Hub Corrector (3.441)	1.136	2.01	97.78	<0.001
Pair 2	One Hub Corrector (3.441) vs. Two Hub Correctors (3.243)	.198	2.02	17.01	<0.001
Pair 3	No correctors (4.577) vs. Two Hub Correctors (3.243)	1.334	1.98	116.42	<0.001

As shown in Table 4, the differences between all three pairs of means were significant on a paired-sample t-test. Therefore, there was a positive relationship between the number of correcting hubs and a decrease in the absolute error (H1 accepted).

Table 5. The relationship between the number of correcting regular nodes (0, 1, 2) and a decrease in the absolute error (H2).

Measured Pair (mean absolute error)		Mean difference	Std. Deviation	t	Sig. (2-tailed)
Pair 1	No correctors (4.577) vs. One Regular Corrector (4.256)	.321	1.98	28.02	<0.001
Pair 2	One Regular Corrector (4.256) vs. Two Regular Correctors (3.718)	.538	2.01	46.47	<0.001
Pair 3	No correctors (4.577) vs. Two Regular Correctors (3.718)	.859	2	74.44	<0.001

Table 5 shows that the differences between all three pairs of means were significant on the paired-sample t-test. Therefore, there was a positive relationship between the number of regular nodes correcting the message and a decrease in the absolute error (H2 accepted).

Table 6. The comparison between ability to correct(absolute error) of regular nodes (1, 2) and hubs (1, 2)(H3)

Measured Pair (mean absolute error)		Mean difference	Std. Deviation	t	Sig. (2-tailed)
Pair 1	One Hub Corrector (3.441) vs. One Regular Corrector (4.256)	-.815	2.05	-68.94	<0.001
Pair 2	Two Hub Correctors (3.243) vs. Two Regular Correctors (3.718)	-.475	2.03	-40.52	<0.001

Table 6 shows that the differences between two pairs of means were significant on the paired-sample t-test. Hence, the absolute error was lower after correction using hubs than after correction using regular nodes for the two (one or two) numbers of correcting nodes (H3 accepted).

Table 7. The comparison between ability to correct (absolute error) of a mix of one regular node and one hub vs. two hubs (H4.1) and vs. two regular nodes (H4.2)

Measured Pair (mean absolute error)		Mean difference	Std. Deviation	t	Sig. (2-tailed)
Pair 1	Two Hub Correctors (3.243) vs. One Regular Corrector and one Hub (3.701)	-.458	1.96	-40.49	<0.001
Pair 2	Two Regular Correctors (3.718) vs. One Regular Corrector and one Hub (3.701)	.017	1.95	1.48	0.138

Table 7 shows that the absolute error was lower after correction using two hubs than after correction using a mix of one regular node and one hub (p < 0.001, H4.1 accepted). However, the absolute error was not significantly lower after correction using a mix of one regular node and one hub than using two regular nodes (p =0. 138, H4.2 disconfirmed).

5.4   Summary of the Results

We ran the simulation many times to increase the consistency of our results and obtained very similar results. The generality of our conclusions and their applicability to other sizes of scale-free networks is important but must be considered with the appropriate degree of caution.

In general, our results show significance differences between the means of the three types of node correctors in terms of absolute error. These differences are summarized in Figure 1. All of our research hypotheses were accepted except for hypothesis H4.2, in which the absolute error did not decrease after a correction using a mix of one regular node and one hub, compared to a correction using two regular nodes.

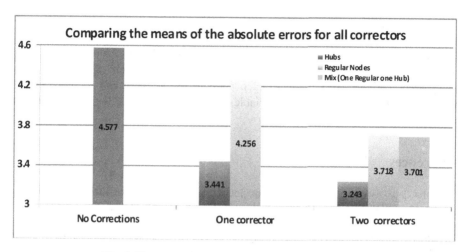

Fig. 1. The mean absolute errors for types of corrections

6 Discussion and Conclusion

In this study we calculated the distortion of a message as it propagates in a social network using a simulated mathematical model. The simulation was executed on a scale-free model using same size networks. We also established a remedial process in which a hub or a regular node, or a combination of both hub and a regular node, could decrease the distortion absolute error during the diffusion process. At the end of the diffusion process of the message in a network, we calculated and compared the results of the average global absolute distortion value N_A^D, for all types of corrective nodes, to measure the extent to which the correction process decreased the global absolute error, and as a result enhanced the robustness of the network to distortion of information.

The results show that when hubs in scale-free networks act as message correctors they are capable of average global absolute distortion error correction. The hubs and the high degree nodes receive messages at an early stage of propagation, and they deliver it to many contacts in the network. Therefore, the message path through the network is shorter than in the other types of networks, and as a result fewer message distortions occur in the propagation process.

A more immediate result from the above conclusion is that to minimize the distortion of a message in a social network, it should be passed as soon as possible to the hubs that can correct the distortion by delivering the original message in the network. If the network does not include hubs, the message should first be passed to the nodes with the highest degree.

The conclusions of this study can be applied in many areas. One example is ensuring that a marketing message will remain as accurate as possible. To minimize the distortion, a marketing strategy should be chosen such that while the marketing message is propagating in the network, chosen hubs will correct the message, which will then be delivered to the rest of the contacts in the network.

Future research will attempt to remedy the limitations of the current study, and enhance the validity of the conclusions. We would like to run the simulation over networks with more than 1,000,000 nodes. We also would like to run the simulation on real scale-free network data. In addition, future research could test more independent variables that relate to each node in the network and globally to the whole network. Examples of such variables are Local Clustering, Degree Centrality and Betweenness Centrality.

References

1. Sohn, D.: Disentangling the Effects of Social Network Density on Electronic Word-of-Mouth (eWOM) Intention. J. Comput.-Mediat. Comm. 14, 352–367 (2009)
2. Strogatz, S.H.: Exploring Complex Networks. Nature 410, 268 (2001)
3. Albert, R., Barabási, A.L.: Statistical Mechanics of Complex Networks. Rev. Mod. Phys. 74, 47–97 (2002)
4. Wang, X.F., Chen, G.: Complex Networks: Small-world, Scale-free and Beyond. IEEE Circ. Syst. Magazine 3, 6–20 (2003)
5. Rapoport, A.: Spread of Information through a Population with Socio-Structural Bias: I. Assumption of Transitivity. B. Math. Biol. 15, 523–533 (1953a)
6. Rapoport, A.: Spread of Information through a Population with Socio-Structural Bias: II. Various Models with Partial Transitivity. B. Math. Biol. 15, 535–546 (1953b)
7. Newman, M.E.J.: Spread of Epidemic Disease on Networks. Phys. Rev. E 66, 016128 (2002)
8. Eames, K.T.D., Keeling, M.J.: Modeling Dynamic and Network Heterogeneities in the Spread of Sexually Transmitted Diseases. Proceedings of the National Academy of Sciences of the United States of America, 13330 (2002)
9. O'Reilly, C.A.: The Intentional Distortion of Information in Organizational Communication: A Laboratory and Field Investigation. Human Relations 31, 173–193 (1978)
10. Panzarasa, P., Opsahl, T., Carley, M.K.: Patterns and Dynamics of Users' Behavior and Interaction: Network Analysis of an Online Community. JASIST 60, 911–932 (2009)
11. Sarker, S., Ahuja, M., Sarker, S., Kirkeby, S.: The Role of Communication and Trust in Global Virtual Teams: A Social Network Perspective. JMIS 28, 273–309 (2011)
12. Crucitti, P., Latora, V., Marchiori, M., Rapisarda, A.: Efficiency of Scale-free Networks: Error and Attack Tolerance. Physica A 320, 642 (2003)
13. Latora, V., Crucitti, P.: Efficient Behavior of Small-world Networks. Phys. Rev. Lett. 87, 198701 (2001)
14. Singer, Y.: Dynamic Measure of Network Robustness. In: 24th IEEE Convention on Electrical and Electronics Engineers in Israel, pp. 366–370 (2006)
15. Watts, D.J., Strogatz, S.H.: Collective Dynamics of Small-world Networks. Nature 393, 440–442 (1998)
16. Barabási, A.L., Albert, R.: Emergence of Scaling in Random Networks. Science 286, 509–512 (1999)
17. Albert, R., Barabási, A.L.: Topology of Complex Networks: Local Events and Universality. Phys. Rev. Lett. 85, 5234–5237 (2000)

18. Scharnhorst, A.: Complex Networks and the Web: Insights from Nonlinear Physics. J. Comput.-Mediat. Comm. 8 (2003)
19. Ravasz, E., Somera, A.L., Mongru, D.A., Oltvai, Z.N., Barabási, A.L.: Hierarchical Organization of Modularity in Metabolic Networks. Science 297, 1551–1555 (2002)
20. Barabási, A.L., Crandall, R.E.: Linked: The New Science of Networks. Am. J. Phys. 71, 409 (2003)
21. NWB Team: Network Workbench Tool. Indiana University and Northeastern University (2006), http://nwb.slis.indiana.edu

Critical Privacy Factors of Internet of Things Services: An Empirical Investigation with Domain Experts

Tobias Kowatsch[1] and Wolfgang Maass[2]

[1] Institute of Technology Management, University of St.Gallen,
Dufourstrasse 40a, CH-9000 St.Gallen, Switzerland
tobias.kowatsch@unisg.ch
[2] Chair in Information and Service Systems, Department of Law and Economics,
Saarland University, P.O. 15 11 50, 66041 Saarbrcken, Germany
wolfgang.maass@iss.uni-saarland.de

Abstract. Internet of Things (IOT) services provide new security and privacy challenges in our everyday life. But no empirical instrument has been developed for the class of IOT services that identifies privacy factors that predict usage intentions and individuals' willingness to provide personal information. The contribution of this paper is to address this lack of research. The proposed research model integrates the Extended Privacy Calculus Model and the Technology Acceptance Model and is pre-tested with 30 IOT experts. Results indicate that intentions to use IOT services are influenced by various factors such as perceived privacy risks and personal interest. It is further assumed that factors such as legislation, data security or transparency of information use influence the adoption of IOT services. Accordingly, further research must focus on a better understanding of these factors to increase the adoption of both useful and secure IOT services.

Keywords: Privacy, Security, Internet of Things, Extended Privacy Calculus Model, Technology Adoption Model, Empirical Study.

1 Introduction

With the increasing amount of Internet of Things (IOT) services, i.e. sensor-based IS services facilitated by identification technologies such as barcode, radio frequency or global satellite communication, people face new security and privacy challenges in their private and business life [23]. For example, mobile applications such as Foursquare, Facebook Places, Google Places or Groupon track the location of their users to provide an added value by the underlying contract: give up a little of your privacy, and you get worthwhile information. In case of the above-mentioned examples, the tracking of location-based information becomes obvious to a user, as she is aware of it by intentionally using them. However, sometimes it is not obvious which kind of information gets tracked at which time,

H. Rahman et al. (Eds.): MCIS 2012, LNBIP 129, pp. 200–211, 2012.

e.g., when those services are running in the background or when the user forgets to terminate them. Serious consequences might be, for instance, when that information is linked to Twitter or Facebook and is then used to commit crimes such as breaking into an empty home. Nevertheless, there exist also situations in which personal information is being intentionally recorded in the background. For example, a health monitoring service must track constantly critical health parameters of an individual without notifying her about it all the time.

In this regard, it is therefore of utmost importance to better understand usage patterns and perceptions from an end-user perspective such that IOT services can be designed with appropriate privacy and security standards in mind. Accordingly, the relevance of privacy and security-related topics has been addressed by prior IS research to a great extent. In particular, an IS Security Design framework, IS security guidelines [21] and IS security objectives [9] have been identified primarily in the context of (business) organizations. An in-depth review of literature on information privacy in the IS field is provided by [5].

However, to the best of our knowledge, no empirical instrument has been developed and tested for the class of IOT services that reveals significant predictors of IOT service usage in business situations and private situations. IOT services differ particularly from other IT-related applications in traditional office or home office situations due to their ubiquitous and embedded characteristics that pervade everyday life. Thus, privacy concerns due to unobtrusive data collection methods are more critical for this class of applications and appropriate evaluation instruments are required.

From a theoretical point of view, we ground the current work on utility maximization theory [3,20] and the privacy calculus model [10,16]. We hereby argue that as long as IOT services are perceived as being useful and the higher the individual or organizational interest in using them are the lower are privacy concerns and thus, the higher are adoption rates of such kind of services.

The contribution of this paper is therefore to present results of an empirical study on privacy concerns, rationales and potential ways of overcoming the privacy fears of IOT services that are currently discussed in the European IOT community. This paper will further provide a detailed plan of how an impact assessment of the initially identified IOT services can be carried out. For that purpose, a corresponding research model is proposed and empirically pre-tested with 31 IOT experts. This research model comprises critical factors that predict usage intentions of IOT services and individuals' willingness to provide personal information in order to use them appropriately.

In the following, the research model and hypotheses are presented. Accordingly, two empirical models from privacy research — the Extended Privacy Calculus Model [10] — and from IT adoption research — the Technology Acceptance Model [7] — are combined and tailored to the concept of IOT services. In a next step, the research methodology is described and the results are then presented. This paper concludes with a discussion of the results and gives an outlook on future work.

2   Research Model and Hypotheses

The research model and hypotheses of the current study are depicted in Fig. 1. The rational for the hypothesized relationships among the constructs is given in the following paragraphs.

The theoretical constructs and their relationships are primarily derived from the Extended Privacy Calculus Model (EPCM) [10]. EPCM has been successfully tested in the domain of electronic commerce and proposes the following privacy factors that influence the willingness to provide personal information for Internet transactions: perceived Internet privacy risk, Internet privacy concerns, Internet trust and personal Internet interest. The underlying assumption of EPCM is grounded in two contradicting predictors that both influence the willingness to provide personal information positively and negatively at the same time. That is, perceived Internet privacy risks and Internet privacy concerns are risk beliefs that negatively influence the willingness to provide personal information for Internet transactions, whereas Internet trust and personal Internet interest have a positive relationship with the willingness of providing personal information. Overall, these constructs from EPCM can be appropriately tailored to the concept of an IOT service as the latter can also trigger transactions of information on the Internet but with the help of interconnected physical objects.

In addition, two constructs from the Technology Acceptance Model (TAM) [7] were considered in the current work. That is, perceived usefulness and the intention to use IT. Having its roots in the Information Systems discipline, TAM describes determinants of technology adoption and was published in various variations in the past [8,13,22]. TAM is rooted in the social sciences, in particular, the theory of reasoned action [2] and its successor, the theory of planned behavior [1]. Both theories fundamentally state that individuals beliefs influence behavioral intentions that, in turn, have an effect on actual behavior. The target behavior of interest in the IS community was then the adoption of IS artifacts and their sustainable usage that might have positive effects on organizational key performance indicators.

Both EPCM and TAM have been incorporated in the current research to address critical privacy factors and technology factors that are relevant to social acceptance and impact evaluation of IOT services. The definitions of the seven constructs are adapted from [10, p.64] and [7, p.320ff] such that they apply to the concept of IOT services. Hereby, IOT services are defined as sensor-based IS services that support people in business situations and private situations. The five definitions as adapted from EPCM to IOT services are listed in the following:

- *Perceived IOT service privacy risk* is a perceived risk of opportunistic behavior related to the disclosure of personal information of IOT service users in general.
- *Privacy concerns against IOT service* are concerns about opportunistic behavior related to the personal information transferred to the IOT service by the individual respondent in particular.

- *Trust in organization providing the IOT service* is a trust belief reflecting confidence that personal information transferred to the IOT service organization will be handled competently, reliably, and safely.
- *Personal interest in IOT service* reflects the cognitive attraction to an IOT service while overriding privacy concerns.
- *Willingness to provide personal information* for IOT service represents the degree to which an individual is likely to provide personal information such as location-based information or financial information required to complete transactions of a particular IOT service.

The following two constructs are adapted from TAM whereby perceived usefulness was reworded as expected usefulness due to the prospective character of the current study on future IOT services:

- *Expected Usefulness of IOT service* is defined as the degree to which a person believes that using this IOT service would enhance his or her overall performance in everyday situations.
- *Intention to use IOT service* reflects behavioral expectations of individuals that predict their future use of the IOT service.

Two modifications were made in order to combine EPCM and TAM. First, intention to use was included as construct that mediates the impact on the willingness to provide personal information. The rationale for this relationship lies in the fact that an individual person would not provide his or her personal information for a particular IOT service without intending to use that service [1]. In line with theory of planned behavior, usage intention predicts therefore actual usage of an IOT service that also involves divulging personal information such as financial information or location-based information. Second, expected usefulness of an IOT service was added as construct that influences intentions to use that service. The rationale here is that IOT services are more likely to be adopted when they are perceived useful. This relationship was directly adopted from TAM [7]. It must be noted that perceived ease of use from TAM is not used in the current work as the focus lies on future IOT services. It is therefore not possible to measure ease of use at this early stage of investigation, i.e. without a prototypical implementation that could be physically tested.

In summary, the eight hypotheses as depicted in Fig. 1 are derived from EPCM, TAM and the assumptions discussed above. Additionally, it is investigated how contextual factors may influence these relationships. Three approaches are considered. First, it was done exploratory by varying the type of situations in which an IOT service is being used. Hereby, we contrast business situations, e.g., using an IOT service for business traveling purposes, with private situations, e.g., using an IOT service in a smart home environment. Second, we further investigate which kind of legislative body should be involved when it comes to privacy policies and data protection. And finally, we also evaluate information transparency, i.e. the detail of information and frequency of notification a user of an IOT service should get such that tracking of personal data is transparent enough.

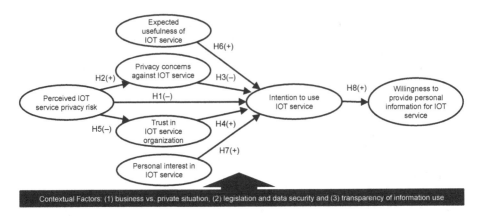

Fig. 1. Research Model

3   Method

In order to pre-test the research model, a questionnaire-based survey was developed. For this reason, four IOT services embedded in two business situations and two private situations were identified from a pool of more than 50 IOT situations [19]. The services have been selected and adapted from several EU projects, including SmartSantander, SENSEI, eSENSE, EXALTED, FLORENCE, PROS-ENSE, LOLA and MIMOSA. The rationale behind the evaluation of situational descriptions of IOT services is based on a design method, in which situational descriptions are evaluated as an early step of the development of a Ubiquitous Information System [12].

The identification of relevant IOT services was conducted in two steps. First, an overall relevance score was calculated for each IOT service based on data from an existing online survey [19]. In that survey, 211 subjects selected some of the proposed IOT services and indicated their (1) degree of interest in that IOT service, (2) the degree to which the IOT service might increase the quality of life, (3) the relevance of that IOT service to society, (4) the relevance of the IOT service to business, (5) the market maturity and finally, (6) the technology maturity related to that particular IOT service. Hereby, five-point Likert scales ranging from low (1) to high (5) were employed. First, the means of each of the six statements were calculated. Then, each mean value was multiplied with the number of responses that reflects the relevance of a particular IOT situation. This intermediary score was then multiplied by one, two or three in case the mean value lies significantly above the neutral scale value of three (neither) at the .05, .01 or .001 level by applying one-sample t-tests. The resulting raw relevance score was therefore higher the higher the mean values of the questionnaire items, the more responses an IOT service had and the higher the significance level was. Finally, the overall relevance score was calculated by the sum of the six scores for each statement as described above.

In the second step, the resulting IOT services were ranked according to the overall relevance score. The following four best-ranked IOT services embedded in business situations and private situations have been chosen for the current study:

1. *Public Transport Payment (PTP) Service:* You are taking the bus to work or during a business trip and you receive a message via your mobile phone that you will be charged once you get off the bus based on the number of zones you cross. The information also displays the cost per zone. Payment is performed automatically via your mobile phone. (Business Situation)

2. *Navigation (Nav) Service:* You just finished your morning routine and are getting ready to leave your home for a business trip. You receive detailed information about traffic conditions including traffic accidents, traffic jams, weather conditions and parking possibilities directly integrated into your personal navigation service. It routs you — including driving, walking, public transport and car-pooling — in the most efficient way and as close as possible to your destination. Persons (incl. you), cars and public transport share their location-based information together with other data relevant for the navigation service in the Internet cloud. (Business Situation)

3. *Smart Home (SH) Service:* The Smart Home service provides the complete control of your house. It switches the lights automatically on when you enter and switches them off when you leave a room. Arriving home after work, your face is recognized at the entrance and the electronic key in your pocket is detected. This service triggers the heating system, by combining data from outdoor and indoor temperature, weather forecast from the Internet, and user preferences. It adjusts the house energy consumption to the real needs of the family, and most importantly it helps you save money. It also recognizes which appliances (washing machine, dishwasher, water heater, heating system, etc.) are turned on at a given time and synchronizes them to ensure the best energy efficiency taking into account the pricing structure of utility companies. (Private Situation)

4. *Health Monitoring (HM) Service:* Recently the doctors have diagnosed that Johns Alzheimer disease is taking a turn for the worse. As a result, his children have decided to upgrade the monitoring solution with sensor applications that enable the monitoring of his locations, posture and mental conditions at home and in the neighborhood. So John retains his private and social life, which is very important for coping with his condition and happiness. (Private Situation)

The questionnaire items of the EPCM constructs were adapted from [10] whereas expected usefulness and intention to use were adapted from [13] and [22]. Items for the contextual factors, i.e. legislative aspects on privacy and data security as well as information transparency, have been developed from scratch for this study (see also Fig. 2, Fig. 3 and Fig. 4). Finally, demographic data was collected. The complete survey instrument for each of the four IOT services can be obtained from [15].

4   Results

Overall, 26 male and 5 female subjects have evaluated the four IOT services during the IOT week in Barcelona in June 2011. This evaluation took 40 minutes on average. The subjects were domain experts as they were involved in IOT-related EU projects IOT-Architecture, IOT-Initiative or SmartSantander. Their age ranged from 25 to 64.

Descriptive statistics of the questionnaire items are listed in Table 1. With one exception, Cronbachs Alpha lies over the recommended threshold of .70 indicating good reliability of the scales employed [18]. Accordingly, aggregated means for each theoretical construct were calculated. Additionally, one-sample t-tests were used for each aggregated variable to indicate whether the means differ significantly from the neutral scale value of three. That is, one-sample t-tests show whether subjects have rated the constructs rather positively, neutral or negatively.

Table 1. Descriptive statistics. Format: Alpha, Mean, Std.Dev; $* p < .05$, $*** p < .001$, p-values from one-sample t-tests with test value $= 3$, N=31.

Construct	1. PTP Service			2. Nav Service			3. SH Service			4. HM Service		
Privacy risk	.866	3.32	0.92	.909	3.39*	0.89	.915	3.15	0.95	.906	2.90	0.94
Privacy concerns	.899	3.33	1.00	.960	3.38*	0.96	.931	3.35	0.96	.907	3.08	0.95
Trust in organization	.778	3.56***	0.69	.839	3.05	0.73	.906	3.27	0.86	.738	3.67***	0.71
Expected usefulness	.940	3.92***	0.90	.961	3.89***	0.72	.934	3.61***	0.77	.892	4.28***	0.55
Personal interest	.889	3.35	1.01	.922	3.35*	0.87	.942	3.25	0.96	.850	4.09***	0.56
Intention to use	.897	3.74***	0.91	.922	3.70***	0.92	.909	3.59***	0.76	.926	4.08***	0.61
Will. to provide info.	.860	3.03	1.13	.806	2.80	1.13	.721	2.89	0.98	.444	n/a	n/a

Consistent with prior research [13,14], partial least squares (PLS) analysis was used for data analysis of our research model. PLS belonging to structural equation modeling (SEM) was chosen over regression analysis, because SEM can analyze all of the paths in one analysis [4,11]. PLS allows analyzing the structural model for assessing the relationships among the theoretical constructs and the measurement model for assessing the validity and reliability of the questionnaire items. In our research, all theoretical constructs were modeled as reflective, because their items are manifestations of them [4] and are expected to correlate with each other [6].

In order to test the validity of our constructs, we performed a confirmatory factor analysis using SEM with the R package PLS-PM (Version 0.1-11) and the bootstrapping resample procedure with 400 iterations. Although one item had a factor loading below the recommended value of .70 (WP2 of the health monitoring service, for details on the item wording see [15]), we retained it to maintain continuity with the other three IOT services. All the other items loaded on their assigned latent variables. Thus, our scales show good convergent validity. The PLS path coefficients together with their significance levels for each hypothesis are shown in Table 2. These results show that only hypotheses H2 and H8 are supported by the empirical data for all four IOT services. H4 is to be rejected. The remaining hypotheses are only partly supported by the data.

Table 2. PLS path coefficients. Note: * $p < .05$, ** $p < .01$, *** $p < .001$, N=31.

Hypothesis	1. PTP Service	2. Nav Service	3. SH Service	4. HM Service	Result
H1: PR x IU	$-.29$	$-.38$*	$-.69$**	$-.03$	(accepted)
H2: PR x PC	.83***	.88***	.82***	.88***	accepted
H3: PC x IU	.08	.03	$-.57$*	$-.14$	(accepted)
H4: TO x IU	.01	$-.02$	.07	.04	rejected
H5: PR x TO	$-.56$**	$-.38$	$-.52$***	$-.44$*	(accepted)
H6: EU x IU	.54***	.36*	.63***	.22	(accepted)
H7: PI x IU	.20	.44*	.15	.55*	(accepted)
H8: IU x WP	.74***	.72***	.67***	.68***	accepted

The explained variances (R^2) for the dependent variables are shown in Table 3. Hereby, the predicting factors of perceived privacy concerns and the intention to use an IOT service explain a high degree of variance.

Table 3. Explained variances (R^2) from PLS analysis

Construct	1. PTP Service	2. Nav Service	3. SH Service	4. HM Service
Privacy concerns	.697	.773	.672	.776
Trust in organization	.345	.186	.288	.222
Intention to use	.805	.817	.735	.670
Will. to provide info.	.556	.523	.457	.469

Furthermore, descriptive statistics related to the questionnaire items on legislation and data security are presented in Fig. 2. Additionally, it was reported by an IOT expert that it is crucial to use only personal information where it is really necessary, i.e. organizations should not request and save personal information for its on sake or potential future use. Moreover, results on the preferred level of detail of notifications on personal information use are depicted in Fig. 3, whereas feedback regarding the frequency of notifications is shown in Fig. 4. One IOT expert reported that details on personal information use should only be made available to the user on request. By contrast, another expert pointed out that the user must confirm actively each transaction that transfers personal information to a third-party organization. With regard to the frequency of notification, one expert discussed the option that users should also be informed when the way of personal information use is being changed. A detailed discussion of these results is presented in the next section.

5   Discussion

5.1   Determinants of IOT Service Use

First, it can be stated that all four IOT services are perceived as relevant by the subjects of this pretest. That is, the values for expected usefulness of the four IOT services and intention to use these services lie all significantly above the neutral test value of three (cf. Table 1).

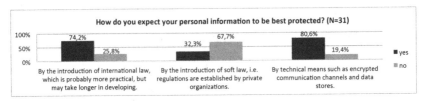

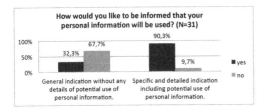

Fig. 2. Legislation and data security

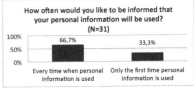

Fig. 3. Detail of notification   **Fig. 4.** Frequency of Notification

Second, though all of these IOT services are perceived as relevant, subjects have no distinct position on whether to provide personal information for those services or not. This fact is based on the construct willingness to provide personal information for IOT use that lies neither significantly above nor below the neutral scale value (cf. Table 1). Therefore, subjects are uncertain in terms of providing access to their personal information in general. It could only be shown for one item of the Health Monitoring service that subjects were willing to provide personal information. However, this result could be explained by the fact that subjects had to rate this item indirectly for another person, i.e. as a family member of John who suffers from Alzheimer disease and is not able to decide for himself.

Third, the current study has adapted the Extended Privacy Calculus Model [10] to the IOT domain with a focus on IOT services. This model describes critical privacy factors and was further extended with two constructs from the Technology Adoption Model [7]. In contrast to the proposed and hypothesized relationships, it could not be shown that the contradicting predictors — i.e. perceived IOT service privacy risk and privacy concerns against an IOT service on the one hand and trust in an organization providing the IOT service, expected usefulness of the IOT service and personal interest in the IOT service on the other hand — have a significant negative or positive impact on the intention to use that IOT service. One reason may be the different purposes of the IOT services. For example, a public transport payment service must be useful in the first instance to be adopted but for a smart home service also privacy concerns must be taken into account. Moreover, it can even be observed that trust in a service providing organization has no influence at all according to these results. That is, trust relative to, for example, expected usefulness is less important for the domain experts of the current pretest. Its effect size is probably too small to be identified by the current sample size of 31, too. Furthermore it is assumed that a more concrete description of the service providing organization would result in different findings.

Fourth, it must be noted that there exists no obvious pattern that distinguishes subjects evaluations of IOT services in business situations from private situations. A potential reason may be the fact that IOT services foster the convergence of both types of situations, i.e. they are permanently available no matter whether a person is at home, at the office or elsewhere. This fuzzy interference of perceptions might therefore also influence the perceptions of privacy risks and privacy concerns.

Finally and with regard to the high variances explained for privacy concerns and usage intentions (Table 3), it is argued that the privacy factors investigated in the current study are good predictors as far as they show a significant relationship in Table 2.

5.2   Legislation, Data Security and Transparency of Information Use

Results on legislation, data security (Fig. 2) and transparency of information use (Fig. 3 and Fig. 4) provide additional guidelines for the design and implementation of IOT services [9,21]. Accordingly, subjects expect their personal information to be primarily protected by international law, which is probably more practical, but may take longer in developing in contrast to soft law introduced by private organizations. In addition to these legislative aspects, personal information should be protected by technical means (Fig. 2). Thus, state of the art encryption and security standards should be incorporated and promoted together with the pure functionality of IOT services as such.

Furthermore, subjects made a point of requesting specific and detailed statements with regard to personal information use. Thus, brief and more general statements should be avoided when an IOT service is deployed or they should at least point to a detailed description such that users are able to request this information on demand (Fig. 3).

The majority of subjects, i.e. 66.7%, stated also that they want to be informed every time when personal information is used by an IOT service. However, also 33.3% of the subjects want to be informed only the first time. The default option should therefore be a trigger that informs users of an IOT service every time personal information is forwarded to a third-party organization. But IOT service providers should also provide the option to change this trigger (Fig. 4).

5.3   Limitations

The current study has several limitations. First, the results are biased in the sense that primarily male and technology-savvy persons have participated, i.e. subjects were experts in the field. But even though experts may adopt the proposed IOT services first, support from a more equally distributed sample is strongly required to increase external validity of the current findings. Second, with 31 subjects the sample size is quite limited to identify small effects. Thus, using PLS for hypotheses testing might not render significant path coefficients even though these coefficients differ obviously from zero (cf. Table 2, H5 of the Navigation Service). And third, because IOT experts can rely on their experience in the field, external validity of the results is limited with regard to the textual descriptions of IOT situations compared to drawings, video clips, or lab experiments that would all increase subjects understanding of the IOT services and thus the quality of evaluations. In particular, the construct trust in organization requires subjects to think about potential providers of those services, which adds a common method bias to the results.

6   Conclusion and Outlook

In this paper on critical privacy factors of future IOT services, the Extended Privacy Calculus Model [10] has been combined with the Technology Acceptance Model [7] and was pre-tested in the IOT domain by conducting a survey with 31 domain experts. As a result, preliminary factors have been identified that influence the adoption of IOT services and thus, might be critical in the design process of those services.

Future work will extend this research by conducting further studies in order to cross-check the current findings and thus, to increase the external validity and quality of implications. In doing so, the guiding research question remains: How can IOT services be designed such that they are not only useful and technically secure but also address privacy concerns of their users?

Acknowledgments. This work was co-funded by the European Union as part of the Internet of Things Initiative (IoT-I, FP7ICT20095257565).

References

1. Ajzen, I.: The theory of planned behavior. Organizational Behavior and Human Decision Processes 50(2), 179–211 (1991)
2. Ajzen, I., Fishbein, M.: Understanding Attitudes and Predicting Social Behaviour. Prentice Hall, Inglewood Cliffs (1980)
3. Awad, N.F., Krishnan, M.S.: The personalization Privacy Paradox: An Empirical Evaluation of Information Transparency and the Willingness to be Profiled Online for Personalization. MIS Quarterly 30(1), 13–28 (2006)
4. Barclay, D., Thompson, R., Higgins, C.: The partial least squares (PLS) approach to causal modeling: Personal computer adoption and use an illustration. Technology Studies 2(2), 285–309 (1995)
5. Bélanger, F., Crossler, R.E.: Privacy in the Digital Age: A Review of Information Privacy Research in Information Systems. MIS Quarterly 35(4), 1017–1041 (2011)
6. Chin, W.W.: Issues and Opinion on Structural Equation Modeling. MIS Quarterly 22(1), vii–xvi (1998)
7. Davis, F.D.: Perceived Usefulness, Perceived Ease of Use, and User Acceptance of Information Technology. MIS Quarterly 13(3), 319–339 (1989)
8. Davis, F.D., Venkatesh, V.: Toward preprototype user acceptance testing of new information systems: Implications for software project management. IEEE Trans. on Engineering Management 51(1), 31–46 (2004)
9. Dhillon, G., Torkzadeh, G.: Value-focused assessment of information system security in organizations. Information Systems Journal 16(3), 293–314 (2006)

10. Dinev, T., Hart, P.: An Extended Privacy Calculus Model for E-Commerce Transactions. Information Systems Research 17(1), 61–80 (2006)
11. Gefen, D., Straub, D., Boudreau, M.-C.: Structural Equation Modeling Techniques and Regression: Guidelines for Research Practice. Communications of the Association for Information Systems 7(7), 1–78 (2000)
12. Janzen, S., Kowatsch, T., Maass, W.: A Methodology for Content-Centered Design of Ambient Environments. In: Winter, R., Zhao, J.L., Aier, S. (eds.) DESRIST 2010. LNCS, vol. 6105, pp. 210–225. Springer, Heidelberg (2010)
13. Kamis, A., Koufaris, M., Stern, T.: Using an Attribute-Based Decision Support System for User-Customized Products Online: An Experimental Investigation. MIS Quarterly 32(1), 159–177 (2008)
14. Komiak, S.Y.X., Benbasat, I.: The Effects of Personalization and Familiarity on Trust and Adoption of Recommendation Agents. MIS Quarterly 30(4), 941–960 (2006)
15. Kowatsch, T., Maass, W., Weber, R., Weber, R.: The Internet of Things Initiative (IOT-I) Deliverable 2.2: Initial Social Acceptance and Impact Evaluation, FP7 ICT project, contract number: 257565 (2011)
16. Laufer, R.S., Wolfe, M.: Privacy as a concept and a social issue: A multidimensional developmental theory. J. Soc. Issues 33(3), 22–42 (1977)
17. Moore, G.C., Benbasat, I.: Development of an instrument to measure the perceptions of adopting an information technology innovation. Information Systems Research 2(3), 192–222 (1991)
18. Nunnally, J.C.: Psychometric Theory. McGraw-Hill, New York (1967)
19. Presser, M., Krco, S.: The Internet of Things Initiative (IOT-I) Deliverable 2.1: Initial report on IoT applications of strategic interest, FP7 ICT project, contract number: 257565 (2011)
20. Rust, R.T., Kannan, P.K., Peng, N.: The Customer Economics of Internet Privacy. Journal of the Academy of Marketing Science 30(4), 455–464 (2002)
21. Siponen, M.T., Iivari, J.: IS Security Design Theory Framework and Six Approaches to the Application of IS Security Policies and Guidelines. Journal of the Association for Information Systems 7(7), 445–472 (2006)
22. Venkatesh, V., Morris, M.G., Davis, G.B., Davis, F.D.: User acceptance of information technology: Toward a unified view. MIS Quarterly 27(3), 425–478 (2003)
23. Weber, R.: Internet of Things - New security and privacy challenges. Computer Law & Security 23(1), 23–30 (2010)
24. Wixom, B.H., Todd, P.A.: A Theoretical Integration of User Satisfaction and Technology Acceptance. Information Systems Research 16(1), 85–102 (2005)

Information Systems Success: Measuring Wiki Implementation Success, Based on the DeLone & McLean Model

João Alexandre[1] and Pedro Isaías[2]

[1] ISEG – Technical University of Lisbon, Rua do Quelhas, 6, 1200-781 Lisbon, Portugal
joao.m.alexandre@gmail.com
[2] Universidade Aberta and ADVANCE Research Center - ISEG – Technical University
of Lisbon, Rua do Quelhas, 6, 1200-781 Lisbon, Portugal
pisaias@uab.pt

Abstract. In all the organizations, the information systems should see the success of its implementation measured. This paper tests the DeLone & McLean (2003) information systems success model using a wiki implementation.

From the model, the measures to be studied were elaborated in diverse questions having a 6-point Likert scale for the answers. Several identifiable validation relationships in the proposed model, on which the study has been based, were summarised as seven hypotheses of relationships between the variables. The paper uses the Structural Equation Modelling (SEM) technique to test the referred hypotheses.

The model has proved its validity and suitability for the measurement of web 2.0 tools, and the model explained an amount exceeding 75% the results obtained.

The results show that the satisfaction of the user is a strong inducer of liquid benefits, at individual and organizational level, in line with other studies in the literature.

Keywords: Information Systems Success, Success Measures, Structural Equation Modelling (SEM), Wiki.

1 Introduction

The success of Information Systems (IS) is one of the oldest subjects of investigation in the IS area. Information systems affect many aspects of the internal and external operations of an enterprise, and the value obtained by the enterprise from the benefits of Information Technologies (IT) is a concern for the performance and survival of the organization (Livari, 2005).

Information systems are understood as computer systems that provide users with information concerning a certain organization in a certain context (Livari, 2005).

H. Rahman et al. (Eds.): MCIS 2012, LNBIP 129, pp. 212–224, 2012.

There are several definitions for the success of information systems and many more for success measures. The definition of success will vary according to the stakeholders involved, since the perspective of the project manager is totally different from that of the programmer, the senior manager or the client, with an emphasis on different factors, such as budget, time, costs, functionality, performance, trust, and security.

Users can define success as the way to obtain satisfaction and increase the productivity of their work. For the organization, success can be, for example, the liquid contribution for profit, or the gaining of competitive advantages and disruptive technologies.

This study aims to measure the success of implementing a web 2.0 tool (wiki) in an organization using the Delone & Mclean success model. This model was chosen because it is already well studied and validated. Another objective of the study was to validate if the relations proposed by the model are suitable for this type of system.

2   Literature Review

In face of the existence of almost as many measures as existing studies, Delone & McLean (1992) tried to systemise the measures, which implied a significant reduction of the number of dependent variables. Also, they proposed a taxonomy that encompassed the majority of the existing studies and that grouped in categories the multiplicity of measures. This taxonomy had the objective of allowing comparisons between the results of different researches, a task which, until then, had been impossible.

The taxonomy proposed by DeLone & McLean (1992) includes six dimensions of IS success: i) system quality – concerning the information processing system, i.e. the desired system characteristics; ii) information quality – the value attributed to the outcomes of the information system, or to the quality of the existing or produced information; iii) usage – the analysis of how and when the system is currently used; iv) user satisfaction – focusing on the satisfaction indicator or the attitude of the user with relation to the system; v) individual impact – referring to the indication of how the information system has been offering users more data and information in the decision-making process, how it has contributed to an improvement of their productivity, or how it has produced a change in the users' activity; and vi) organisational impact – relating to the influence that the individual impact has over the organisation, or the impact that the individual decisions have over the organisation (DeLone & McLean, 1992; Livari, 2005).

DeLone & McLean (1992) thus highlight the multidimensional nature of an information system's success, suggesting that these dimensions are interdependent. This model (Figure 1) assumes that the quality of the system and the quality of the information, individually and/or in concert, affect the use and satisfaction of the user; it also considers that usage and user satisfaction are interdependent. It proposes that usage and user satisfaction affect the managers' individual behaviour, which, in turn, affects the behaviour of the organisation, i.e. the organisational performance (DeLone & Mclean, 1992).

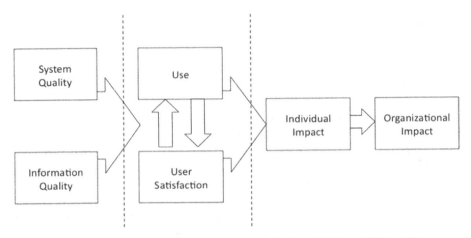

Fig. 1. DeLone & McLean IS Success Model (Delone & McLean, 1992, p.87)

Numerous researchers have stated that the D&M IS success model is incomplete and have suggested more dimensions to be included while others have suggested alternative models (Ballantine and Seddon, 1997). Other researchers have conducted work aiming to validate the model (Rai, Lang and Welker, 2002).

The information system success model proposed by DeLone and McLean (1992) is the one that, so far, has received the greatest amount of attention from researchers, but many of the features proposed in the model are not susceptible of being measured in their entirety. Hence, one should find the ones that best apply to the system in question.

The fact that some features, such as organisational strategy, technology used, tasks performed and the surrounding context of the IS, have not been included has led some authors to criticise the model (Seddon, 1997).

Seddon (1997) introduces four new variables to the model: i) decision makers expectations; ii) organisational and individual impacts; iii) usefulness; and iv) liquid benefits. Seddon, thus, makes the connection between the variables of the model proposed by DeLone and McLean (1992), grouping them into three dimensions – Figure 2 (Seddon, 1997).

DeLone & McLean (2003) agreed with some of the criticisms, and in their review of the 1992 model they replaced some terms and meanings, in line with Seddon's arguments.

The new DeLone & McLean (2003) model (Figure 3) continues to assume the existence of six dimensions, but with some changes: i) beyond the quality of the system and the information, a third dimension of quality is included, which is the quality of the service; ii) instead of considering several dimensions of use, the intention of utilisation is valued, thus representing attitude rather than behaviour; and iii) instead of individual and organisational impact, they point out liquid benefits.

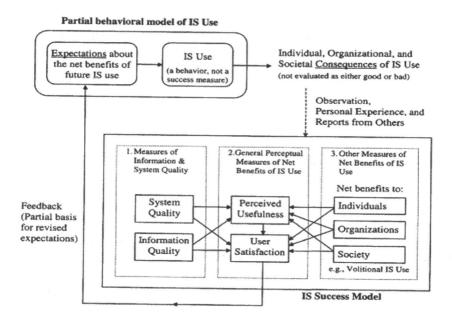

Fig. 2. Respecified model of DeLone and McLean's 1992 Model of Information Systems' Success (Seddon 1997, p. 245)

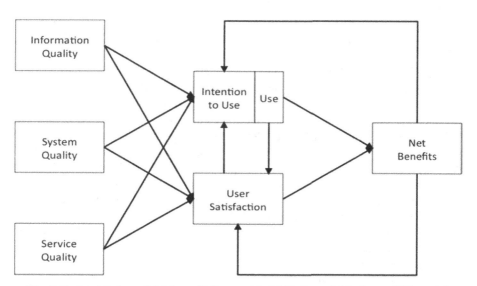

Fig. 3. Updated DeLone & McLean IS Success Model (DeLone & MacLean, 2003, p. 16)

The original model was criticised for not considering the different stakeholders and contexts (Seddon et al., 1999, p. 9), but the authors believe that the model should be adapted to the concrete context (DeLone & McLean, 2003, p. 22), and the focus of the study adjusted. The model can equally be used by Microsoft or an individual user (DeLone & McLean, 2003, p. 22) and the liquid benefits should be defined according to the stakeholders.

3   The Research

The consulting company McKinsey has recently confirmed in a study that over a third of companies are using or are planning to use technology such as wikis and blogs. "Companies are using more Web 2.0 tools and technologies than they were last year. Those that are satisfied with their use of these tools are starting to see changes throughout the enterprise" (McKinsey, 2008).

A wiki is a website designed to have an ease of use that allows the collection of information in a collaborative and cooperative fashion. The users may create articles, or modify them, even if they were not the original authors. Each article is automatically converted into a page that will be immediately available. The different articles can be grouped by categories, mutually referenced, and researched by the website's search engine.

Users not only consume information, but also promote its expansion. Since all users contribute, it is easy to keep the information up to date. Organisations are increasing the usage of wikis to provide support to their employees in terms of knowledge management (Majchrzak, Wagner and Yates, 2006).

3.1   Analysis Unit

This study sets out to test the Delone & Mclean model of 2003, through the implementation of a Web 2.0 tool (wiki), where the stakeholders will be the users of the system. Hence, a set of measures was selected (Figure 4) to serve as the foundation to the questionnaire concerning the study. These measures were adapted from the work of Delone and Mclean (2004) who used the model to evaluate a system based on Internet and user-centered (e-commerce), in many ways similar to a WIKI. This adjustment was carried out to the questionnaire (Table 1). "The Delone & Mclean model has also been found to be a useful framework for organizing IS success measurements. The model has been widely used by IS researchers for understanding and measuring the dimensions of IS success." (Peter et al., 2008).

The wiki, the target of this study, has been in use for six months now; its purpose is not to replace another tool or application, but only to allow communication at the core of the team to take place in a more expeditious and efficient way. Tools like email and network file sharing continue to be used.

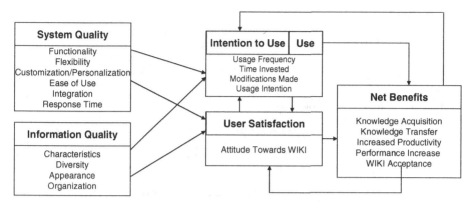

Fig. 4. Model to be used in the study

The DeLone & McLean (2003) success model was adapted to information's systems; its Service Quality dimension was removed, since this application was for companies' internal users, they won't criticise, it is not essential, and the support of this application is in no way different from the others used in the same unit of work.

As a way of potentiating its use, the use of the wiki was compulsory only in some of the tasks, such as in holiday scheduling, training requests and FAQs registration (support area).

3.2   Data Collection

The method chosen for data collection was the questionnaire, for its speed, simplicity and assurance of anonymity. Once the model was defined, the measures to be studied were elaborated in diverse questions (see Table 1) which were posed to 20 individuals of the team, representing around 90 per cent of that same team. All the 20 team members fully completed the questionnaires. The inquiry was conducted anonymously, with no identification element, which facilitated the collection of responses. Around half of the individuals are male and their ages are between 25 and 40 years. The remaining 50 per cent are female and from 30 to 40 years old, but the demographic data hasn't been collected.

A 6-point Likert scale was used which ranged between 'totally disagree' and 'totally agree'.

3.3   Questionnaire

Based on the defined metrics (Figure 4), a questionnaire has been designed to be used in data collection (Table 1).

The several identifiable validation relationships in the proposed model (Figure 4), on which the study will focus, can be summarised as hypotheses (Table 2), that the analysis of the data will try to support.

Table 1. Studied variables

Dimension	Variable	Question
System Quality	SQ1	The wiki is user-friendly
	SQ2	The publication of documents/new content in the wiki is easy
	SQ3	The wiki is stable
	SQ4	The wiki response time is acceptable
Information Quality	IQ1	The documents/pages are presented in a correct form (doc, xls, ppt) in the browser
	IQ2	The information and knowledge available in the wiki are accessible when necessary
	IQ3	The information and knowledge available in the wiki are important and help me at my work
	IQ4	The wiki makes contextual information available in order for one to understand what is being accessed, by whom it was published, and when, so that more data/information can be obtained if necessary
	IQ5	The wiki has a research directory with links
System Usage	SU1	I use the wiki as a support to find information and knowledge
	SU2	I use the wiki to register information and knowledge
	SU3	I use the wiki to communicate information and knowledge with colleagues
Usage Intention	UI1	How many documents have you created in the last month in the wiki?
	UI2	How many documents (not created by you) have you modified in the wiki?
	UI3	How frequently do you use/access the wiki per day?
	UI4	I intend to use the wiki more in the future
Benefits	B1	The wiki helps me to acquire new knowledge
	B2	The wiki helps me to manage and register the knowledge I need
	B3	The wiki allows me to accomplish tasks in a more efficient way and with increased productivity
	B4	My performance at work is better due to the use of the wiki
	B5	Generally speaking the wiki is a success
	B6	I would recommend to workers in other fields that they should use a wiki in the same moulds
User Satisfaction	US1	The wiki responds to my current needs for information and knowledge.
	US2	I am pleased with the efficiency of the WIKI
	US3	Globally I am satisfied with the WIKI

Table 2. Hypotheses to be validated

H1	There is a strong correlation between user satisfaction and the liquid benefits
H2	There is a strong correlation between the quality of the information and user satisfaction
H3	There is a strong correlation between the quality of the system and user satisfaction
H4	There is a strong correlation between the quality of the information and usage
H5	There is a strong correlation between the quality of the system and the usage
H6	There is a strong correlation between system usage and its liquid benefits
H7	There is a strong correlation between user satisfaction and the usage of the system

To test the hypotheses of relationships between the variables, a technique known as structural equation modelling (SEM) was used. According to Hair Jr. et al. (2005, p. 468-9), this is a "multivariate technique which combines multiple regression aspects (examining dependency relationships) and factorial analysis (representing not measured concepts – factors – with multiple variables) to estimate a series of relations of dependency simultaneously inter-related". The Partial least squares regression

(PLS) statistical method has been adopted, since it can be used with very small samples – from 10 samples (Chin, 1998).

The PLS analysis is performed essentially in two phases: one to assess the validity of the data (samples) and the model and the other to determine the relations between the latent variables and between them and the indicators. To draw the model, the SmartPLS 2.0 M3 software was used, which allows the drawing of models and the extraction of reports. Figure 5 shows the results of the modelling.

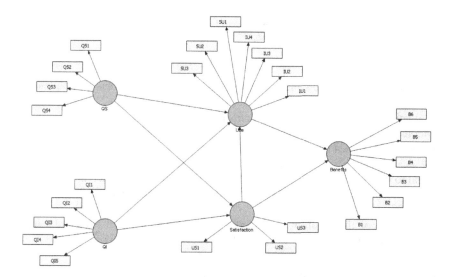

Fig. 5. Model structured using SmartPLS 2.0 M3

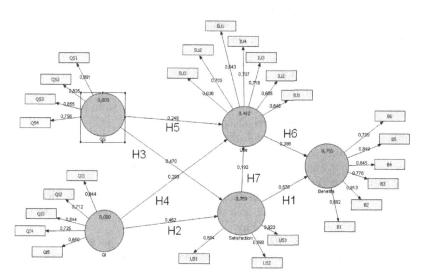

Fig. 6. Result of the application of the PLS calculation to the model

Each circle corresponds to a latent variable and each square corresponds to one of the manifested indicators.

The data from the questionnaire, saved in a text file (csv format), were imported to SmartPLS to allow the import of the variables that can be seen in the squares.

Application of the PLS algorithm to the drawn model plus the scenario path produced the results that can be seen in Figure 6.

4   Data Analysis

The data analysis was done in two phases, and comprised the following validations:

Phase 1:
In this stage the quality of the data and the model was evaluated by:

- the correlations between the indicators and the latent variables, which must be over 0.5 (Hair et al., 1987).
- evaluation of the correlation of each of the indicators with its latent variables, which must be over 0.7, according to Hair Jr. et al. (2005): indicators with values lower than 0.7 must be removed
- the analysis of the validity of each latent variable: the index must be higher or equal to 0.7, as with the Cronbach de Alpha, the function of which is to evaluate if the indicator is properly correlated with the latent variable (Chin, 1998; Hair Jr. et al., 2005)
- verification of the medium explained variance (MEV), which should be higher than 50% (0.5) (Fornell and Larcker, 1981; Hair Jr. et al., 2005).

Phase 2:
In this step the validation of the structural model consisted in:

- verifying the R^2 values, whose meaning is the percentage of the variance of a latent variable which is explained by other latent variables
- testing the hypothesis that the coefficients of the regression are equal to 0 via a Student t test. For a level of significance of 0.05 the t value is approximately 1.96.

In phase 1, and according to the values of Table 3, the correlation between the indicators and the latent variables is superior to 0.5 for all the indicators, which allows one to conclude that the indicators/measures found to calculate each latent variable were understood by the respondents in the same way as they were perceived by the enquirer, making the proposed model acceptable.

According to the values in Table 4, the AVE value is confirmed to be above 0.5, and the indicators Composite Reliability and Cronbachs Alpha higher than 0.7. These indicators allow one to conclude that the questions posed were understood in the same way by all participants (Fornell & Larcker, 1981).

Once phase 1 was finished, with the questionnaire and the verification of the validity of the model used, phase 2 was initiated with the analysis of the results in order to verify the several formulated hypotheses.

The first analysis was the R^2 verification, which allows the assessment of the percentage of the latent variable which is explained by its indicators. It was verified that 75.52% of the latent variable Benefits is explained, and 75.90% of Satisfaction, which is very good. Around three quarters of the explanation is demonstrated by the

Table 3. Pearson correlations between the several variables (highlighted in grey are the relationships between indicators and latent variables)

	Cross Loadings				
	Benefits	QI	QS	Satisfaction	Use
B1	0,6923	0,6736	0,5136	0,6259	0,5105
B2	0,9132	0,4740	0,5368	0,7401	0,6886
B3	0,7779	0,4033	0,1843	0,5270	0,5097
B4	0,8455	0,4279	0,4734	0,5403	0,7453
B5	0,8493	0,5582	0,6316	0,7375	0,5571
B6	0,7993	0,6248	0,6759	0,7727	0,6278
IU1	0,5234	0,2100	0,2438	0,2715	0,6462
IU2	0,5542	0,3048	0,4704	0,4411	0,6055
IU3	0,4504	0,3920	0,3468	0,3183	0,7178
IU4	0,6126	0,6028	0,4531	0,4965	0,7073
QI1	0,1385	0,6444	0,4936	0,4110	0,1407
QI2	0,3882	0,7123	0,6884	0,6283	0,3589
QI3	0,6902	0,8443	0,4952	0,6818	0,6468
QI4	0,7009	0,7253	0,6018	0,6892	0,6010
QI5	0,0496	0,6495	0,4004	0,3742	0,2976
QS1	0,7071	0,6455	0,8909	0,8752	0,5278
QS2	0,6648	0,7180	0,8245	0,6803	0,6130
QS3	0,3215	0,4797	0,8545	0,5875	0,3301
QS4	0,3060	0,6171	0,7584	0,5049	0,5721
US1	0,6244	0,6565	0,5535	0,8036	0,3029
US2	0,7193	0,6684	0,7862	0,8981	0,6688
US3	0,7869	0,8085	0,7743	0,9232	0,6345
SU1	0,4013	0,4695	0,3806	0,3710	0,6428
SU2	0,4931	0,5147	0,5663	0,5814	0,7054
SU3	0,4167	0,3870	0,3823	0,3935	0,6381

Table 4. Standard indicators in PLS analysis

Variables	AVE	Composite Reliability	R Square	Cronbachs Alpha	Communality	Redundancy
Benefits	0,6655	0,9222	0,7552	0,8979	0,6655	0,3955
QI	0,5167	0,8411		0,7777	0,5167	
QS	0,6948	0,9007		0,8540	0,6948	
Satisfaction	0,7682	0,9083	0,7590	0,8493	0,7682	0,4133
Use	0,4454	0,8485	0,4622	0,7919	0,4454	0,1241

model. For the latent variable Use, only 46.22% is explained by the selected indicators, not reaching the 50% value considered the desirable margin to determine a strong correlation.

The second analysis was done through the analysis of the t values (see Table 5), via the bootstrapping analysis.

Table 5. Bootstrapping Analysis (t-test)

	Original Sample (O)	Sample Mean (M)	Standard Deviation (STDEV)	Standard Error (STERR)	T Statistics (O/STERR)
H1:Satisfaction-> Benefits	0,5698	0,5608	0,0737	0,0737	7,7297
H2:QI-> Satisfaction	0,4621	0,4732	0,0633	0,0633	7,3026
H3:QS -> Satisfaction	0,4696	0,4624	0,0727	0,0727	6,4629
H4:QI -> Use	0,2929	0,3341	0,1844	0,1844	1,5886
H5:QS -> Use	0,2481	0,2318	0,1372	0,1372	1,8090
H6:Use -> Benefits	0,3882	0,3974	0,0669	0,0669	5,7982
H7:Satisfaction -> Use	0,1919	0,1724	0,1670	0,1670	1,1489

According to Chin (1998), the standard deviation and the t value allows the measuring of the significance of the path coefficient, being that only values over 1.96 are significant.

For the data analysis we used mean and the standard deviation and variance (see Table 6). There is a high dispersion in the "USE" dimension that has the lowest average of all.

Some people use the system and have little intention of using it (3,29), although they recognize quality in the system (4,88), in the information provided (4,61) and satisfaction when using it (4,25).

The benefits to the organization, are in the opinion of users, relevant (4,29) and reflected in daily work with improvements in knowledge management and efficiency of their work (4,11).

Table 6. Descriptive statistics (Based on a 1-6 Likert scale)

	QS	QI	USE	Benefits-Individual	Benefits-Org	Usatisf
Average	4,88	4,61	3,29	4,11	4,29	4,25
Stand. Error	0,91	0,86	**1,44**	**1,22**	1,10	0,89
Variance	0,82	0,75	**2,06**	**1,48**	1,21	0,80

5   Results Discussion

After analyzing the data presented in the previous section we can see that the hypotheses H1, H2, H3 and H6 were confirmed, having a t-value higher than 1.96. The remaining hypotheses H4, H5 and H7 were not confirmed by the study.

But, according to Petter et al. (2008), which analysed 180 studies, the model relations Quality Information->Use (H4), Quality System->Use (H5) were not confirmed in most studies. However, the relationship User-Satisfaction->Use (H7) was considered strong in most studies which used the Delone & McLean model. The explanation may lie in the low usage of the current system. The fact that the wiki was not compulsory for the generality of the tasks might justify the low usage.

The model has proved its validity and suitability for the measurement of web 2.0 tools, and the model explained an amount exceeding 75% the results obtained. The dimension that most contributes to the success and impact on net benefits was the user satisfaction is also in line with other studies in the literature cited in Petter et al (2008) work.

6   Conclusion

This paper approaches a study in which the DeLone & McLean (2003) success model is applied to the implementation of a wiki. The objectives of studying the model and confirming some of the relations proposed by DeLone & McLean (2003) were accomplished, even though the results of the test did not support the correlations between quality of information/quality of the system and use/intention to use the system, and between user satisfaction and use/intention of use.

Since this study focused on a tool in recent usage that was not compulsory, it would be interesting to conduct a new study after one year of utilisation, in the sense that the user satisfaction index relative to the system as a whole is reasonable. This satisfaction was proved to be influenced by the dimensions of quality of information and quality of the system, which opens good perspectives to a relevant success of the tool.

In the future, an extension of this work could be used for data collection using qualitative methods, for example through interviews with open questions and semi-open questions that allow users to express their views and gather other relevant information.

This work contributes to alert organizations to the need to measure properly the success of their systems, which continue to require substantial resources without the expected return. A simple tool (wiki) can and should see its implementation evaluated at an individual level, like in this study, and also at an organizational level.

Acknowledgements. The authors want to acknowledge the ADVANCE research centre from ISEG – Technical University of Lisbon – strategic project reference: PEst-OE/EGE/UI4027/2011 – Information Systems and Operations track.

References

Chin, W.: Issues and Opinions on Structural Equation Modeling. MIS Quarterly 22(1), 7–16 (1998)

DeLone, W.H., McLean, E.R.: Information systems success: The quest for the dependent variable. Information Systems Research 3(1), 60–95 (1992)

DeLone, W.H., McLean, E.R.: The DeLone and McLean model of information systems success: A ten-year update. Journal of Management Information Systems 19, 9–30 (2003)

DeLone, W.H., McLean, E.R.: Measuring e-Commerce Success: Applying the DeLone & McLean Information Systems Success Model. International Journal of Electronic Commerce 9(1), 31–47 (2004)

Du, H.S., Wagner, C.: Weblog success: Exploring the role of technology. International Journal of Human-Computer Studies 64(9), 789–798 (2006)

Fornell, C., Larcker, D.: Evaluating structural equation models with unobservable variables and measurement error. Journal of Marketing Research 18, 39–50 (1981)

Gide, E.: A study for establishing an E-commerce Business Satisfaction model to measure e-commerce success in SMEs. International Journal of Electronic Customer Relationship Management 1(3) (2007)

Lin, H., Fan, W., Wallace, L., Zhang, Z.: An Empirical Study of Web-Based Knowledge Community Success. In: 40th Annual International Conference on System Sciences, Hawaii, January 3-6 (2007)

Livari, J.: An Empirical Test of the DeLone-McLean Model of Information System Success. The Database for Advances in Information Systems 36(2), 8–27 (2005)

Majchrzak, A., Wagner, C., Yates, D.: Corporate wiki users: results of a survey. In: International Symposium on Wikis, Odense, Denmark, August 22-25, pp. 99–104 (2006)

McKinsey: The next step in open innovation (2008),
`http://www.mckinsey.com/clientservice/bto/pointofview/pdf/the`
`_next_step_innovation.pdf` (accessed October 28, 2011)

Petter, S., DeLone, W., McLean, E.: Measuring information systems success: models, dimensions, measures, and interrelationships. European Journal of Information Systems, 17 (2008)

Pinkerton, W.J.: Project management: achieving project bottom-line success. McGraw-Hill, New York (2003)

Rai, A., Lang, S., Welker, R.: Assessing the Validity of IS Success Models: An Empirical Test and Theoretical Analysis. Information Systems Research 13(1), 50–69 (2002)

Roldán, J.L., Leal, A.: A Validation Test of an Adaptation of the DeLone and McLean Model in the Spanish EIS Field. In: Cano, J.J. (ed.) Critical Reflections on Information Systems: A Systemic Approach. Idea Group Publishing, Hershey (2003)

Seddon, P.B.: A respecification and extension of the DeLone and McLean model of IS success. Information Systems Research 8(3), 240–253 (1997)

Seddon, P.B., Staple, S., Patnayakuni, R., Bowtell, M.: Dimensions of Information Systems Success. Communications of the Association for Information Systems 2(20), 1–39 (1999)

Wu, J.-H., Wang, Y.-M.: Measuring KMS success - A respecification of the De Lone and McLean model. Information & Management 43, 728–739 (2006)

Self-care Portal as a Trigger
for a Work Process Change: A Case from Finland

Kaisu Juntunen and Raija Halonen

Department of Information Processing Science, University of Oulu, P.O.Box 3000, FI-90014
University of Oulu, Finland
{kaisu.juntunen,raija.halonen}@oulu.fi

Abstract. While the innovations of the public health service make promises of better health and quality of life, individual citizens have also become conscious of possibilities of the electronic health care. However, in spite of the wishes and promises the mere technology itself is not enough. Analysed and open information about the possible advantages and drawbacks of the new technology is needed before appropriate technology investment choices could be done. A variety of Health Information Systems (HIS) applications have been described in different references. For the time being, there have been only few if any reviews of a research-based state-of-the-art on the study of HIS based timesaving changes in work processes.

Our paper presents a case study evaluating the effects and quality of an electric appointment and message channel portal (SCP) in Finland. The study shows how the web service improves the throughput of incoming patients and creates new work roles and know-how demands in the organisation. The empirical research material was collected by interviewing and observing both patients and employees in a public health centre. An important finding was that to get full benefit from the implemented appointment and message channel portal, it was advisable to modify the process even if it was not in target in the first place.

Based on future scenarios, the amount of adulthood sicknesses is increasing and need for self-care is evolving. Any instrumental tool in supporting self-care is significant in future. The implemented electric appointment and message channel portal decreased the patients' need to pay visits to health care personnel but more importantly, it both decreased the waiting time in the process and untied time allocations for other patients to use. To support and intensify other service chains, this interactive system can be duplicated for intended and emergent project outcomes.

Keywords: ICT productivity, User empowerment, Patient portal, Appointment and message channel portal, Health processes, Health technology, Delivering health care services, Process improvement, Self-care.

1   Introduction

It is well known that information technology (IT) -enabled systems tend to be complex because of different individual preferences, organisation issues, work system

H. Rahman et al. (Eds.): MCIS 2012, LNBIP 129, pp. 225–240, 2012.

design and technology (King and Lyytinen, 2006). Related to that, Elie-Dit-Cosaque and Straub (2010) expressed their concern about the "the black box" of the information system (IS) usage. As a cure, they recommend additional research on how individuals use and adapt to particular IT systems and IT disruption. One of the primary components in codification of knowledge is the collection of information on the existing situation of the organisation. For this reason, it is crucial to conduct process modelling in cooperation with the personnel (Mumford, 2000). Especially in health care, effectiveness and generalisability are of particular importance because health information technologies are tools that support the delivery of care (Chaudhry et al., 2006). Health care is a critical social and economic component of modern economies in which IS and technologies are expected to play a role in cost-effective delivery of health care services (Chiasson and Davidson, 2004) due to the dual influence on simultaneous increased ageing and decreased health care personnel (Demiris, 2012).

Still, the health care industry has been criticised for being slow in effectively exploiting IT and lagging behind other industries when the delivery of these technologies is perceived to be inappropriate or inadequate for the medical staff (Cho et al., 2008; Suomi, 2001; Spil and Stegwee, 2001; Wickramasinghe, 2000). In the present situation IS, pertaining to the use and impact of technology, can act as an important contributor in society and organisations (Avison and Elliot, 2006; Baskerville and Myers, 2002). It can also serve as a reference discipline in the field of new product development (Nambisan, 2003). According to Ashurst, Doherty, and Peppard, (2008), the return that organisations derive from investments in IS and technology continues to disappoint. Peppard et al. (2007), drawing on over 10 years of research, state that only when IT enables people do things differently, benefits arise. According Porter and Teisberg (2006), the problem is a competition in health care which takes place on discrete interventions rather than the full cycle of care where value is determined. They claim that value can only be measured over the care cycle, not for an individual procedure, service, office visit, or test.

Improvements in the health status of communities through the effective public health and electronic health care infrastructure are increasingly tied to the Internet (O'Carroll et al., 2003). Individuals, care providers, and public health agencies all hope to benefit of the new information systems, use of electronic methods for disease surveillance, and reformation of outmoded processes. However, as O'Carroll et al. (2003) stated, realising the benefits will be neither easy nor inexpensive. Marchibroda (2008) suggests that personal health records may be well suited to patients with chronic diseases who are encouraged to be active in self-care, and full access to electronic records could facilitate engagement with their providers and improve quality and safety.

Taken together all these factors provide the motivation for this research. As a consequence, we present a case study evaluating the implementation of an electric self-care portal (SCP) channel in the new Technology Health Centre (THC) in Finland, focusing on one type of process, namely the type 2 diabetes (t2d) patient nursing process. The empirical research material was collected by interviewing 15 persons that consisted of physicians, diabetes nurses, nurses, patients, project managers and one service manager.

The purpose of our study was to increase knowledge exchange between contextually sensitive health care and IS field and answer the research question: "What are the effects of implementing the innovative self-care portal in the health care context?" The main contribution of this paper was to show the benefits that arose when a patient's care process and a work process of the diabetes nurse transformed into digital. With the help of IT, the use of information was optimised and used when it had the largest effect and value to the user. In addition to catching up a goal of decreasing the number of patient calls and visits by 50%, the study showed how the implementation of a SCP may act as a trigger for further changes in a care process. Next, we show that what we found out and observed regarding HIS goes beyond what the literature leads us to expect, thereby providing us the opportunity to contribute the current body of knowledge.

2   Literature Review

A lot has happened since 1960's when a data system was implemented to monitor aspects of health care delivery in Vermont. The research results beyond 50 years witness that informed choices in the public guidance of the health care sector require knowledge of the relation between medical care systems and the population being served. Wennberg's and Gittelson's (1973) study concludes that population-based HISs as providers of information are an important step in the development of rational public policy for health. In their prognosis for the year 2013 Haux et al. (2002) presented a goal to be a patient-centred recording and use of medical data for cooperative care. They also aspired after relevant patient data that is accessible by all health care professionals, especially physicians and nurses, according to their respective authorisations. Mäenpää et al. (2009) verified that the concept of integrated electronic health record and patient-centred shared health care has been recommended for more than 30 years.

However, to benefit from developed technology properly, a suitable environment is needed. A flexible and adaptive organisation that through its structure and processes supports decision making makes it easier to implement new systems and changes in processes (Greenhalgh et al., 2004). On the other hand Markus (2004) introduces technochange as a way to use IT to drive improvements when seeking for organisational change and improvements. Haux (2006) notes how modern information processing methodology and information and communication technology has strongly influenced societies, including their health care. Haux continues that HISs have to be developed and explored to enhance opportunities for global access to health services and medical knowledge. He also predicts that new computing resources will allow people to consider new types of information systems for health care, including new kinds of health monitoring and also new opportunities for the analysis of biomedical and health data.

Even if the most important contacts in health care will be kept face-to-face (Åkesson et al., 2007), the relationship between physicians and patients is changing. Ball and Lillis (2001) argue that patients as health care users are searching for convenience in the form of more sophisticated health care services offered through the Internet. They want to control of their own health by utilising online health information, and they want to have several choices for every service and product they require. Ball and Lillis add that health services offered through the Internet transform greatly the relationship between physicians and patients that implicitly are called consumers. Further, the change eventually necessitates that both the service providers and service consumers educate themselves (Berg, 2004). Ball and Lillis (2001) highlight that the Internet facilitates crucial components for health care delivery such as consumer education, disease management, clinical decision support, physician/consumer communication, and administrative efficiencies.

In addition, especially public sector as service providers tend to support self-care as the burden of health care is getting ever heavier (Jordan and Osborne, 2007). In their study on chronic disease self-management education programs in Australia Jordan and Osborne (2007) claim that engagement of health care professionals is critical for successful application of self-management education programs. They also note funding problem in case of arrangements between federal and state governments that does not support the multidisciplinary approach needed for chronic disease care. Among chronic diseases, type 2 diabetes is a worldwide concern (Beran and Yudkin, 2006) and the number of people with type 2 diabetes worldwide was estimated at 171 million in 2000 and it is predicted to rise to 366 million in 2030 (Wild et al., 2004, cited in Beran and Yudkin, 2006).

HIS can be defined as an application of IT in health care that builds on a wide range of disciplines including medicine, computer science, management science, statistics and biomedical engineering (Anderson, 1997). Chiasson and Davidson (2004) point out that healthcare represents a markedly different social and technical context compared with many of the industries where IS research is conducted, and IS theory developed. Acknowledging this complexity, Chiasson and Davidson define HIS research as a multidisciplinary body of knowledge related to the design, development, implementation, and use of information-intensive technologies in health care settings. Furthermore, HIS portals allow patients to both communicate with health care professionals and access personal medical information (Marchibroda, 2008).

In the next paragraphs we briefly highlight the state-of-the-art on HIS by classifying some themes according to their relevance for our study.

Acceptance

Klein (2007) explored patient-physician portal acceptance and emphasised the importance to understand and balance both patient and health care provider user requirements. Patients must experience some level of usefulness for expectations of future use to stay as users. Klein also noted how patients in specialised care tend to look for their personal medical information through the patient-physician portal while patients in primary care are interested in utilising communications functions in the portal.

Empowerment
In their summary of literature Åkesson et al. (2007) reported that the patients felt more confident and empowered, their knowledge increased, and their health status improved due to the ICT resources. Their conclusion was that ICT can also improve the nurse–patient relationship and augment well-being for consumers. In addition, Kahn et al. (2009) define a personal health record (PHR) as a tool to use in sharing health information, increasing health understanding, and helping transform patients into better-educated consumers of health care. One example of existing PHRs is MyHealtheVet that allows patients to interact with their health teams, schedule appointments, view for example laboratory tests and renew referrals (Demiris, 2012).

Adopting
Sulaiman and Wickramasinghe (2010) provided a technology assimilation model for hospitals in implementing or adopting HIS. In their model, Sulaiman and Wickramasinghe point out the interrelationships between the assimilation stages and contributing concepts that consist of technology, environment and organisational context. They pay special attention to the gaps between the initiation, adoption and routinisation of the HIS. Mantzana et al. (2007) believe that especially in the health care sector the adoption of ISs is critical in case they are related to human lives. Distinguishing individuals from groups of human and organisational actors is significant as some actors seem to have the power to hold back the adoption or even lead to system's failure.

Quality, efficiency, and costs
Chaudhry et al. (2006) systematically reviewed evidence indexed in MEDLINE (1995 to January 2004) on the effect of health information technology (HIT) on quality, efficiency, and costs of health care. The major effect of HIT on quality of care was its role in increasing adherence to guideline- or protocol-based care. Decision support, usually in the form of computerised reminders, was a component of all adherence studies. Although Chaudry's et al. (2006) studies from 4 benchmark institutions have demonstrated the efficacy of HIT for improving quality and efficiency, the effectiveness of these technologies in the practice settings remains less clear. According to Chaudhry et al. (2006), more information is needed regarding the organisational change, workflow redesign, human factors, and project management issues involved with realising benefits from HIT. Likewise, Maas et al. (2008) describe in their paper benefits and cost consequences of computer based timely access to specialised health care information. A before–after activity analysis regarding 20 diabetic patients' clinical appointments was performed in a Health Centre in Finland. Access to up-to-date diagnostic information reduced redundant clinical re-appointments, repeated tests, and mail orders for missing data. This system brought along several benefits regarding work flow, patient care, and disease management. Even if changes in service process can influence the quality and efficiency of customer processes, the benefit caused by ICT produces only temporal competitive advantage and therefore continuous innovation development is compulsory (Martikainen et al., 2012).

Education and support

According to Torkzadeh et al. (2011), system use in itself does not lead to outcomes; however, increased cognition and understanding of the task at hand would result in improved outcomes. Despite its importance, the relationship between technology and work practices has received only minor attention so far. In their study Torkzadeh et al. emphasise the role of technology as an enabler for job learning and enlargement of work tasks. In addition, Kaufman's (2010) clinical studies and reviews show how IT can help to improve patients' outcomes with diabetes through enhanced education and support. Increasing sophistication of diabetes treatment protocols and diabetes-related devices offers remarkable new opportunities for clinicians and patients. According Kaufman (2010), with online tools clinicians can provide robust and affordable just-in-time support to large numbers of patients, who want to improve and control their diabetes outcomes through enhanced self-management of their lifestyle and behaviour.

In all, ICT in health care has been studied from several viewpoints during the past decades. Despite that, the published evidence of ICT implementations based on the quality and timesaving changes in work processes in the health care sector has remained humble.

3   Research Approach

Our literature review followed Kitchenham's (2004) study selection criteria and analyses focused on databases of information processing science, medical science, nursing science, industrial engineering and management, and work sciences.

The empirical research material was collected as a part of a national project and the study was carried out in a state-of-the-art health care centre. The collection of empirical material in our study was guided by the formal interpretive methodology (e.g. Klein and Myers, 1999). Such an approach can be useful, when researchers are attempting to develop a holistic interpretation of the case study by considering and reconsidering how to connect the missing parts. We carried out over twenty open and semi-structured interviews with personnel at different organisation hierarchical levels. Interviews were conducted in great depth and their length lasted from 1.5 to 2 hours. Extensive notes were taken during each interview and the interview notes then written up as soon after the interview as possible, often on the same day as the interview. All interviews were recorded and the transcribed interview material was subjected to a qualitative content analysis (see Mayring, 2000).

First we characterised the activities and the possible bottlenecks that occurred within the diabetes health care process (see Martikainen, 2007). The goal of our workflow presentation was to make the relationships between people, procedures, information, tasks, and management explicit (see Ciborra, 2006).

In addition to the interviews, statistical data for the 3VPM (Martikainen, 2007; Martikainen and Halonen, 2011) was gathered, for instance from the amount of calls, number of visitors, as well as queuing and reception times.

4   The Study

The mission of the new THC was to be an expert environment where, in addition to the active use of self-care services, companies, citizens and professionals of the public service sector could utilise new technologies in their basic work. In this sense, the THC differed from a common Health Centre where patients came to get treatment or medical examinations. The most central and special characteristic of the THC was to support the cooperation and interaction in developing the quality of the product-service concept of welfare technology. The implementation period of the SCP was from April 2007 to November 2009. Our study continued to December 2010.

The main goals of the SPC were:

- Development of Self-Care Services with new product modules
- Product implementation and user testing on selected professional and patient groups
- To induce work practices complying with Self-Care approach and process-oriented working methods
- Related to preventive work and chronic illnesses, shift the focus of operational culture from organisation-oriented approach to patient-oriented one
- Citizen engagement and empowerment by helping him/her to use available tools and methods to guide and support self-care to enhance client-activity
- National networking and co-operation, also actively affect formation of legislation.

One of the objectives to meet the goals of the SCP was to reduce patients' phone appointments and visits in the health centre by 50%. In this study we show how this goal was reached and how the solution is duplicable in the other services, too. By evaluating the impact of the SCP on patient flow in a diabetes type 2 care process the projects' results were analysed using the criteria of compliance with the expected scope, time frame, and the quality of service (see Martikainen, 2007).

During the years 2008 – 2010, four physicians, four diabetes nurses, two nurses, one service manager, two patients and two project managers were interviewed. One of the patients used the services of the SCP, while the other made contact the traditional way, either by going to the health centre or by telephone. In addition to the interviews, statistical data was gathered, for instance from the amount of calls, number of visitors, as well as queuing and reception times. Through the interviews, we discovered some of the practical reasons why employees and patients were or were not able to use the new service portal or if they were unwilling to use the new service portal. The examples below depict concrete situations in everyday life.

It appeared that Nurse was not satisfied with the technical issues of the new system:

> *"Patients criticised that services of the portal are used with the help of bank codes. Should an underage child have his own bank codes so that his parents can establish his identity?" (Nurse)*

> *"It is frustrating and slow to do the double registration in the cut and paste – style... [a deep sigh]...when the systems do not discuss among themselves"*
> *(Nurse)*

Technical issues concerned Diabetes Nurse, as well:

> *"To answer the patient questions via the portal takes sometimes more time than if I just called them"... (Diabetes Nurse)*

The interviewees noted also issues regarding face-to-face contacts and their importance in the interaction and health care process between patients and health care personnel:

> *"I am afraid that our relationship changes to being less open and stays distant". (Nurse)*

> *"I have noticed that persons are more likely to come to the reception, if I will give them an appointment time, than if they should reserve the time themselves". (Diabetes Nurse)*

> *"Personally, I want to see my patients face-to-face and estimate comprehensively their state, mood and ways of life..." (Physician)*

> *"How can I answer carefully enough to this virtual patient without seeing him...what are my legal responsibilities if I give a wrong instruction?" (Physician)*

On the other hand, the following comments by patients showed that the new system was well received and anticipated:

> *"Once I was on the road and felt really sick. I tried to call for hours to my health centre, but could not get through. At that point I hoped that I had been a user of the mobile Self-Care portal..." (40-year-old male Patient)*

> *"The new communicational channel facilitated me, when I began my insulin care. I could enter my measurement results and the amount of insulin into my electronic folder and change messages with my db nurse." (50- year-old female Patient)*

From the project management approach, the conception of the success appeared more complicated:

> *"Change leadership, attitudes, slowness of progress and demands of flexible and user friendly system have been the most problematic issues..." (Project Manager)*

> *"Professionals do not 'swallow it [new system] whole'; introduction has to be given by managers. We did arrange the comprehensive training package, but it should have been done more by way of their work processes." (Project Manager)*

> *"The best change agent is the colleague, who talks the same language and knows all the tricks." Service Manager*

"It is also a question of reliability. With the help of mobile devices at home, the information transfers automatically, you can not tamper it...". (Project Manager)

"Sometimes people suspect that the message via a net advisor is not as reliable as the one given in phone, but that is not true. Of course you can ask complementary questions and listen to the tone of the discussion and voice, but yet you can get misunderstood...". (Project Manager)

Diabetes Nurse highlighted the possibilities the SCP might bring to health care especially in regarding diabetes and the self-care attitude that is essential in type 2 diabetes:

"In Finland, it is difficult to say, the probability to get t2d is bigger due to excessive fatness of the elderly people. This is a big problem also among schoolchildren. Our one main goal is to try to change their food habits with the assistance of the net." (Diabetes Nurse)

"On the other hand, it is actually good that we do not do everything, but also a patient has to participate in his/her own care. The more conscious they [clients] get of their own state of health, and the issues that correlate with it, the more motivated they become." (Diabetes Nurse)

All of these examples, partly technical, social and legal, depict different kinds of situations, needs, motivations and emotions. They were located in a time and space specific to that particular context. Physicians wanted to make sure that there is a mutual understanding between themselves as physicians and the patient and that there is no "knowledge gap". Equally there were times when a patient might expressly need help without face-to-face contact or might be satisfied with the time saved and might pick a more suitable contact time later. It appeared that most of the technical problems were due to incompatible systems.

4.1   The Current Diabetic Process

Dependent on the case at hand, the process included a contact between the patient and a diabetes nurse or a physician. The contact was to be initiated with the use of a phone or by visiting the health centre. The most common reason for a patient to contact the health centre was to reserve a time with the physician, seek medical advice for an illness, to get a new prescription or to receive laboratory results. In our case, there were approximately 250 known diabetic patients aged 18-90 years in the area of study with estimated 15 new incoming diabetic patients per year.

In the legacy process (Figure 1), the new incoming diabetes patient made the first appointment (30-60 min) with the Diabetes Nurse (DN) and had the necessary laboratory tests done. The Diabetes Nurse examined the situation and status and ushered the patient to a First Stage Information Group. In 6 months the patient got the access into the group (a). In case the patient did not want to participate in the group (b), additional visits (30-60 min) to the Diabetes Nurse were scheduled with intervals of 3 weeks. A referral was made for an eye scan.

The following two appointments with the Diabetes Nurse (60 min) were also in intervals of 3 weeks. After 3-6 months from the initial physician's appointment, the patient was to undergo another set of laboratory tests. The results from the tests were informed to the patient by the physician by telephone (10 min). The follow-up control, if everything had been in order, was the half-yearly control (60 min) conducted by the Diabetes Nurse. The patient had to fetch blood sugar strips from the centralised care instrument distribution point after the Diabetes Nurse had made a referral. The Diabetes Nurse will make internal referrals also with the nourishment therapist and the physical education group and advised the patient to contact a private chiropodist by telephone. The patient visited the eye scan and received the results after about half a year, on the basis of which an extension care plan was made. In an acute case, the patient was directed to the physician's reception at the hospital.

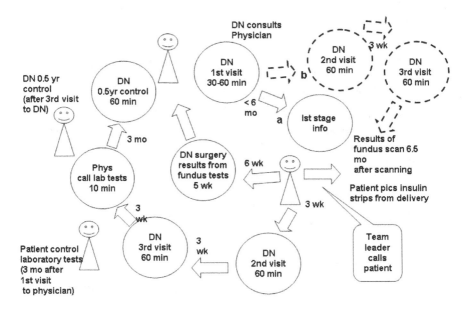

Fig. 1. The current care cycle of the New Diabetic Patient

4.2   The Proposed Diabetic Process

The first appointment is with the Diabetes Nurse (30 min) and time for laboratory tests is allocated by the patient (see Figure 2). During this visit, the patient is briefly told about the Self-Care portal and how to use it. For example, the Diabetes Nurse can advise the patient in the use of the program and computer. The digital referral to the eye scan will be made immediately in connection with the first visit. Before the patient's next arrival at the Diabetes Nurse's reception, the patient has measured in advance certain values (e.g. weight, blood pressure and stomach circumference) and sent them digitally to the personal folder.

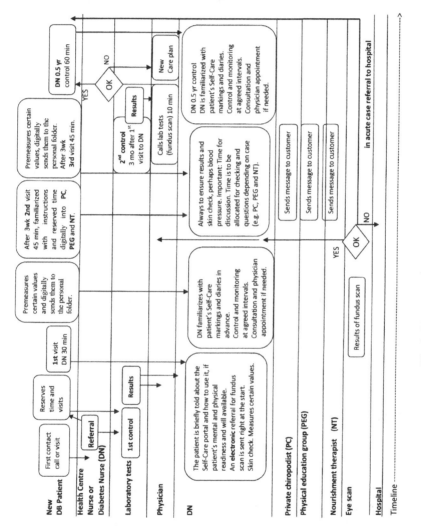

Fig. 2. The proposed diabetic process

The patient has also become acquainted with the instructions. The Diabetes Nurse makes sure that the patient has acted correctly and performs a skin inspection and may also measure blood pressure. The Diabetes Nurse reserves a physician appointment if needed. Furthermore, the Diabetes Nurse has become acquainted beforehand with the patient's own notations in the personal digital food diary and a physical exercise diary through the portal. It is important to allocate enough time for the Diabetes Nurse to read through those diaries and for discussion with the patient.

4.3   Summary of the Improvements

With the help of the SCP it was possible to increase the effectiveness of the db care process significantly. Next we close our proposal to change the t2d care process:

- Surgeries and appointments will be reserved as a self-service
- A referral for fundus will be automated and reserved already in the first surgery
- A patient will find information about his/her illness and the guidance of care before his/her surgery
- A patient transmits information (e.g. exercise group, nourishment adviser, foot carer) through the web
- A patient prepares for a surgery by doing measures at home (e.g. blood pressure, weight and stomach circumference)
- Individual risk tests can be made beforehand anonymously and save the measures in the system to be used in health care if desired.

The before mentioned changes are expected to be realisable in regard of software in use. In addition, the system is duplicable and applicable for other health care sectors as well. For example, student health evaluation, mental status or sleeping disorders are proper fields to adopt the SCP.

5   Discussion and Conclusions

There has been an expectation from government and the public for a reorganisation of the health care sector with the utilisation of the IT network. Globally, the social welfare and public health service sectors will be facing significant challenges in the 21st century. The ageing of the population increases the need for services, while simultaneously having to deal with a reduction of those of working age among the population (Demiris, 2012). The electronic SCP offers many new possibilities over traditional health care service, yet requires concurrent additional changes of work processes, and attitudes. These additional requirements, however, seem to be at odds with the nature of health care work depicted before. According Berg (2004), this may be true because especially in cases of long-term chronic disease, the actual care plan "takes shape through the many ad hoc decisions and improvised interventions of the patient and his or her caregivers". Still, he sees redistribution and reorganising tasks and standardising of care paths the only way to manage the still increasing demand of care.

As our example showed, an information system for both health care professionals and patients is accompanied by social transformations. These transformation processes yield changes in workflows, professional hierarchies and empowerment of patients. Sharing the view with Åkesson et al. (2007) on the importance of the face-to-face contacts in health care, the tools of health informatics and ICT can be seen as a means to answer the evolution of our age pyramid and lack of the health carers in future.

As our interviewees revealed, the SCP was not perceived too positively despite the increase in the effectiveness of the diabetes care process. The portal allowed patients to act more independently; and it changed the work process towards patient-centred as predicted by Haux et al. (2002) as described by the female user: *"... I could enter my measurement results and the amount of insulin into my electronic folder ..."*

Despite the problems the health personnel experienced with the SCP, some constructive comments were also given. Especially type 2 diabetes is expected to expand by millions of patients in future (Beran & Yudkin, 2006) and the Diabetes Nurses pointed out the use of the Internet as a communication and information channel: *" ... the more conscious they [patients] get of their own state of health ... the more motivated they become ..."*

The most central special characteristic of the THC was to support the co-operation and interaction in developing the quality of the product-service concept of welfare technology. In the work process changes, suggested in this study, it had been supposed that the ISs and different applications in use are integrated and perform well. However, at the time of the study, the SCP was in its maintenance state and, regardless of the portal model, the working was semi-automatic and there were still some integration problems. It is also notable that ICT investments do not increase productivity if the work processes remain unchanged (see Greenhalgh et al., 2004). This was realised in our case because the SCP improved the throughput of incoming db patients and the service process had to be changed to cope with the increased incoming flow. This finding led us to seek for more productive tasks and changes in processes even if they were not in focus in the first place. In other words, new work roles and training were needed to ensure that the new work practices would be suited for an organisation culture and context in question (see also Torkzadeh et al., 2011). One could also interpret that the implementation the SCP produced technochange (see Markus, 2004) and brought innovative ideas to improve the t2d care process.

ICT investments do not increase productivity if the work processes remain unchanged. The "invention" of SCP makes it possible for a complex health service organisation to handle an increasing number of clients without the need for constant face-to-face contact. But, as in our case, when the SCP improves the throughput of incoming db patients, the service process has to be changed to cope with the increased incoming flow (see Martikainen, 2007). Furthermore, new work roles and training are needed so that the new work practices would be suited for an organisation culture, context and resources in question.

Same technologies that empower IT's expertise in welfare service producer, have also an impact on patients. Patients, as in our case, can use self-care support tools for a variety of health information activities, e.g. psychosocial support groups as well as a diet diary and physical exercise. Therefore, based on our research results, we list increased self-esteem of the patients, improved health care relationships between patients and health care personnel, and increased information security as qualitative influences caused by ICT.

There is a strong belief expressed by policy makers that the future of the European health system will be modular with its units comprised of the home, basic care, hospitals near, acute hospitals, rehabilitation and living (Haux et al., 2002; Jordan and Osborne, 2007; Kaufman, 2010). At the moment of our study, in Finland problems in the authenticated access to patient data were legislative in nature, related to protecting personal privacy and patient safety. In our case, the authenticating was tied with bank codes and it caused annoyance among the users: *"... Should an underage child have his own bank codes ..."*

In the future, it is expected that patient privacy enhancing technologies will solve most of these problems. When the use of the SCP would spread, telephone traffic could be considered to decrease. At the same time the self-care and choice possibilities of the inhabitants of the municipality would increase; and the work structure of the health care sector personnel would change. In the digitised service production, the ways to meet the patient change, new choke points would emerge while old ones would disappear. Will this model have the desired preventive effect will demand further examination when the service has been established.

A further major topic for future research is how care practices will change in the future. In addition, standards and an open attitude towards technology are needed in the health care sector. Does a digital epicrisis correspond to the patient's physical meeting, or is semantic interoperability sufficient and covering the needs of every user, not to mention the patient's expectations and demands in regard to virtual care? These services will now centre on use of the Internet, but also other online channels, such as television over cable and satellite networks. In any case, we believe that the ICT supported patient process, the distance controlled measures and the well informed patient will give new opportunities for the distribution of the public health service.

Acknowledgments. City of Oulu for funding (Kaisu Juntunen) and eKat project with Project Chief Anne Sormunen (nee Niska), Responsible Chief Keijo Koski, Project Manager Minna Angeria, and all those personnel who contributed our study are warmly acknowledged.

References

Anderson, J.G.: Clearing the way for physicians' use of clinical information systems. Communications of the ACM 40(8), 83–90 (1997)

Ashurst, C., Doherty, N.F., Peppard, J.: Improving the impact of IT development projects: the benefits realization capability model. European Journal of Information Systems 17, 352–370 (2008)

Avison, D., Elliot, S.: Scoping the Discipline of Information Systems. In: King, J.L., Lyytinen, K. (eds.) Information Systems The State of the Field. John Wiley & Sons, Ltd., England (2006)

Ball, M.J., Lillis, J.: E-health: transforming the physician/patient relationship. International Journal of Medical Informatics 61, 1–10 (2001)

Baskerville, R.L., Myers, M.D.: Information systems as a reference discipline. MIS Quarterly 26(1), 1–14 (2002)

Beran, D., Yudkin, J.S.: Diabetes care in sub-Saharan Africa. Lancet 368, 1689–1695 (2006)

Berg, M.: Health Information Management, Integrating information technology in health care work. Routledge, London (2004)

Chaudhry, B., Wang, J., Wu, S., Maglione, M., Mojica, W., Roth, E., Morton, S.C., Shekelle, P.G.: Systematic review: impact of health information technology on quality, efficiency, and costs of medical care. Annals of Internal Medicine 144, 742–752 (2006)

Chiasson, M.W., Davidson, E.: Pushing the contextual envelope: developing and diffusing IS theory for health information systems research. Information and Organization 14, 155–188 (2004)

Ciborra, C.: The mind or the heart? it depends on the (definition of) situation. Journal of Information Technology 21, 129–139 (2006)

Cho, S., Mathiassen, L., Nilsson, A.: Contextual dynamics during health information systems implementation: an event-based actor-network approach. European Journal of Information Systems 17, 614–630 (2008)

Demiris, G.: New era for the consumer health informatics research agenda. Health Systems, 1–4 (2012), doi: 10.1057/hs.2012.7

Elie-Dit-Cosaque, C.M., Straub, D.W.: Opening the black box of system usage: user adaptation to disruptive IT. European Journal of Information Systems 19, 1–19 (2010)

Greenhalgh, T., Robert, G., Macfarlane, F., Bate, P., Kyriakidou, O.: Diffusion of Innovations in Service Organizations: Systematic Review and Recommendations. The Milbank Quarterly 82(4), 581–629 (2004)

Haux, R.: Health information systems — past, present, future. International Journal of Medical Informatics 75, 268–281 (2006)

Haux, R., Ammenwerth, E., Herzog, W.C., Knaup, P.: Health care in the information society. A prognosis for the year 2013. International Journal of Medical Informatics 66, 3–21 (2002)

Jordan, J.E., Osborne, R.H.: Chronic disease self-management education programs: challenges ahead. Medical Journal of Australia 186, 84–87 (2007)

Kahn, J.S., Aulakh, V., Bosworth, A.: What it takes: characteristics of the ideal personal health record. Health Affairs 28(2), 369–376 (2009)

Kaufman, N.: Internet and information technology use in treatment of diabetes. The International Journal of Clinical Practice 64, 41–46 (2010)

King, J.L., Lyytinen, K. (eds.): Information Systems the State of the Field. Wiley Series in Information Systems. John Wiley & Sons Ltd., Chichester (2006)

Kitchenham, B.A.: Procedures for performing systematic reviews. Technical Report TR/SE-0401, Keele University and NICTA Technical Report 0400011T (2004)

Klein, R.: An empirical examination of patient-physician portal acceptance. European Journal of Information Systems 16, 751–760 (2007)

Klein, H.K., Myers, M.D.: A Set of Principles for Conducting and Evaluating Interpretive Field Studies in Information Systems. MIS Quarterly 23(1), 67–94 (1999)

Maas, M.C., Asikainen, P., Mäenpää, T., Wanne, O., Suominen, T.: Usefulness of a regional health care information system in primary care. A case study. Computer Methods and Programs in Biomedicine 91, 175–181 (2008)

Mantzana, V., Themistocleous, M., Irani, Z., Morabito, V.: Identifying health care actors involved in the adoption of information systems. European Journal of Information Systems 16, 91–102 (2007)

Marchibroda, J.M.: The impact of health information technology on collaborative chronic care management. Journal of Managed Care Pharmacy 14(2), 3–11 (2008)

Markus, M.L.: Technochange management: using IT to drive organizational change. Journal of Information Technology 19, 4–20 (2004)

Martikainen, O.: Productivity improvements enabled by ICT based process transformations. In: 3rd Balkan Conference in Informatics, BCI 2007, Sofia, September 27-29, pp. 1–8 (2007)

Martikainen, O., Halonen, R.: Model for the Benefit Analysis of ICT. In: AMCIS 2011 Proceedings - All Submissions (2011), http://aisel.aisnet.org/amcis2011_submissions/19

Martikainen, O., Kulvik, M., Naumov, V.: E-Services and Productivity. Information Technologies and Control, 10 pages (2012) ISSN 1312-2622

Mayring, P.: Qualitative Content Analysis. Forum: Qualitative Social Research. Theories, Methods, Applications 1(2) (2000), http://www.qualitative-research.net/fqs-texte/2-00/2-00mayring-e.html

Mumford, E.A.: Socio-technical approach to systems design. Requirements Engineering 5, 125–133 (2000)

Mäenpää, T., Suominen, T., Asikainen, P., Maas, M., Rostila, I.: The outcomes of regional health care information systems in health care: A review of the research literature. International Journal of Medical Informatics 78(11), 757–771 (2009)

Nambisan, S.: Information systems as a reference discipline for new product development. MIS Quarterly 27(1), 1–18 (2003)

O'Carroll, P.W., Yasnoff, W.A., Ward, M.E., Ripp, L.H., Martin, E.L. (eds.): Public Health Informatics and Information Systems. Springer, USA (2003)

Peppard, J., Ward, J., Daniel, E.: Managing the realization of business benefits from IT investments. MIS Quarterly Executive 6(1), 1–11 (2007)

Porter, M.E., Teisberg, E.O.: Redefining Health Care: Creating Value-Based Competition on Results. Harvard Business School Press, Boston (2006)

Spil, T.A.M., Stegwee, R.A. (eds.): Strategies for Health Care Information Systems. Idea Group Publishing (2001)

Sulaiman, H., Wickramasinghe, N.: Critical issues in assimilation of healthcare information systems. In: PACIS 2010 Proceedings, Paper 176 (2010)

Suomi, R.: Streamlining Operations in Health care with ICT. In: Stegwee, R., Spil, T.A.M. (eds.) Strategies for Health Care Information Systems, pp. 31–44. Idea Group Publishing (2001)

Torkzadeh, C., Chang, J.C.-J., Hardin, A.M.: Usage and impact of technology enabled job learning. European Journal of Information Systems 20, 69–86 (2011)

Wennberg, J., Gittelsohn, A.: Small area variations in health care delivery. Science 182, 1102–1108 (1973)

Wickramasinghe, N.: IS/IT as a tool to achieve goal alignment. International Journal of Healthcare Technology and Management 2(1), 163–180 (2000)

Åkesson, K.M., Saveman, B.-I., Nilsson, G.: Health care consumers' experiences of information communication technology – A summary of literature. International Journal of Medical Informatics 76, 633–645 (2007)

Seeking Information in Social Media:
The Case of the Healthcare Sector

Katerina Fraidaki, Katerina Pramatari, and George Doukidis

Department of Management Science and Technology,
Athens University of Economics and Business,
47a Evelpidon and 33 Lefkados str, Athens, 113 62, Greece
{fraidaki,k.pramatari,gjd}@aueb.gr

Abstract. Information acquisition is one of the most important steps of consumer behaviour. Scholars have designed models which show the factors that affect the procedure of information acquisition, paying specific attention on personality traits and types of information sources. The main objective of this paper is to study the impact of information acquisition in social media on patients' behaviour. In order to achieve this goal, we design a typology of social media and study the impact of information acquisition in each different type on decisions such as the choice of a doctor or the online purchase of medical products/services. Our results are based on a questionnaire-based survey with responses from 1047 Internet users.

Keywords: Social media, information value, propensity to seek information, health.

1   Introduction

Since 1998, McLeod and other scholars have studied the influence of information acquisition through the Internet. Cline (2001) focused her research on the healthcare sector, discussing the way that patients seek information in the Internet. She declares that the most difficult procedure for patients is the evaluation of the information; for this reason they try to seek information in web sites with high *credibility*. Furthermore, she mentions that "patients access online health information in three primary ways: searching directly for health information, participating in support groups and consulting with health professionals". Patients search information in the Internet, in order to minimize the perceived risk they feel when they should take a decision (Cotten, 2004). Nowadays, apart from medical web sites, patients frequently use social media as a source of information. Surveys show that 79% of Internet users seek information about health issues in social media. The terms "social media" can be considered as the hyper-category of different sources with user generated content, such as social networking sites, blogs and reviews. A gap in the literature exists in the way that the information acquisition, in different types of social media, affects patients' decisions.

H. Rahman et al. (Eds.): MCIS 2012, LNBIP 129, pp. 241–253, 2012.
© Springer-Verlag Berlin Heidelberg 2012

In order to study this gap, we should go back to the IS literature and look for the meaning of information in the user's decision process, as well as the importance of the source from which the user receives the information. The role of *information* has received widespread attention both in the IS and in the Marketing fields (Boze, 1987; Zeithaml, 1981, Murray, 1991). A main outcome is that information acquisition reduces the user's perceived risk about his final decision. The process of information acquisition may differ, depending on the type of the need that the user wants to fulfill (Murray, 1991), the type of the product/ service the user wants to buy (Guiltiman,1999), the information source type (Assael, 1984), demographic socioeconomic factors and cognitive/personality traits (Schaninger, 2001). Studying particularly the personality traits, Schaninger declares that six personal characteristics influence information searching/ acquisition: tolerance for ambiguity, rigidity, cognitive style, need for cognitive clarity, self-esteem and trait anxiety. Gefen (2002) and Ridings (2001) recognize one more personal characteristic *a person's information seeking attitude*.

Furthermore, recognizing the importance that the source type plays in the procedure of information acquisition, many scholars have designed typologies, based on criteria such as the distribution channel (offline, online), users' needs, the role of information in the users' decision process (Assael, 1984), characteristics of people who share the information in offline environment (Andreasen, 1968) and in online environment (Senecal, 2004). Social media consist part of the online environment. Using the formal definitions of the different types of social media and taking into consideration the axes that have already been used in the literature by scholars, we may design a typology of social media, which may help us recognize the influence of the different types of social media on the users' decision process.

The main objective of this paper is to study the impact of information acquisition in different types of social media on patients' final decision, when the decision is relevant with health issues.

2   Background and Research Model

Information has been characterised as "*..the basic component of users' decision process*" (Gefen, 2000). In the consumer buying cycle "gathering information" is the second step in the process and the one that helps the user makes the final decision (Churchill, 1993; Berthon et al, 1996). In order to study the user's behaviour in this specific step, researchers have designed models that show the factors that influence *information search/ acquisition*. Two of the models that are frequently met in the literature are Assael's and Vogt's. Assael (1994) recognized three categories of factors that influence information acquisition: the user's trait (involvement in information search), information role (functional, hedonic, innovation, aesthetic, sign) and information source type (social, personal, marketing, editorial). Vogt (1998) in his model declares that the variables which affect the procedure of information acquisition are: user characteristics (demographics, personality, lifestyle, and motivations), environmental characteristics (social, cultural, situation) and marketing characteristics (product, price, place, promotion). Schaninger (2001) tries to collect all the factors, which appear in the literature and influence the information acquisition process. In his paper, he mentions the existence of three hyper-categories of factors: demographics characteristics (e.g. age, family lifecycle, education, income, and social ideas), cognitive personality traits (tolerance to ambiguity, rigidity, cognitive style and need for cognitive clarity, self-esteem and trait anxiety) and product characteristics. The author focuses his research on personality traits, trying to emphasize the importance of their role in the information acquisition process. Some years later, Ridings and Gefen (2002) add one more personal characteristic; the former call it *desire to get information* and the latter a *person's information seeking attitude*. This characteristic refers to the propensity that a person has to look for information. In order to emphasize that this is a personality, we will call it *propensity to seek information*. As a construct, it has not been validated yet in the online environment. Kulviwat (2004) declares that personal characteristics positively affect seeking information in the online environment. Nowadays, social media consist an integral part of the online environment. They are defined as communities in which members interact and influence each other (Preece, 1999). Thus, using Kulviwat's model, we may declare that the propensity to seek information (as a personality trait) positively affects seeking information in social media.

H1: *The propensity to seek information positively affects the information acquisition in social media*

The term "social media" refers to the hyper-category of different sourcea with user generated content, such as social networking sites, blogs and reviews. Taking into consideration the formal definitions of these different types of social media, and underlying their basic characteristics (which refer to the expertise of the person who provides the information), we may create a typology which is along the same lines as the one suggested by Senecal's (2004). Senecal (2004) categorized the online sources into personal sources providing personalized information, personal sources providing non-personalized information, impersonal sources providing personalized information and impersonal sources providing non-personalized information; his typology is based on the characteristics of people who give the information and on the type of information that a user receives. Based on this categorization, we define:

Social Networking Sites (e.g. facebook) are "web-based services that allow individuals to (1) construct a public or semi-public profile within a bounded system, (2) articulate a list of their other users within whom they share a connection, and (3) view and traverse their list of connections and those made by others within the system" (Boyd et al, 2008).

Blogs are defined as "...frequently updated websites containing dated entries arranged in reverse chronological order" (Walker, 2005). Kurtz's (2002) study reveals that that bloggers are considered by consumers as independent experts in a specific area

The third type of online social media is called *online reviews*, which are defined as "...consumer reviews, which serve two different roles: they provide information about product and services; and they serve as recommendations" (Park et al, 2007).

Their influence comes from the fact that they are written by people who have already the experience of a specific product/service. (Bickart et al, 2001).

Using this typology, we may declare that the type of social media moderates the influence of propensity to seek information on information acquisition in social media. Thus, the hypothesis H1 can be reformed as:

H1a: *The propensity to seek information positively affects the information acquisition in social networking sites*

H1b: *The propensity to seek information positively affects the information acquisition in blogs*

H1c: *The propensity to seek information positively affects the information acquisition in reviews*

Bian (2009) declares that information acquisition is one of the factors that influence the user's behaviour; the other factors are the knowledge of the product/service that the user wants to buy, the brand image of the product, the product involvement. In our case information acquisition affects the patient's final decision. In our analysis the patient's final decision refers to the online purchase of a medical product/service and to the choice of a doctor. Thus, based on Bian (2009) we formulate the following hypotheses:

H21: *The information acquisition in social media positively affects the online purchase of a medical product/service.*

H22: *The information acquisition in social media positively affects the choice of doctor*

At this point the question arises whether information acquisition in the different types of social media has the same impact on the user's final decision. Brown's (2007) declares that the value of information that a user receives depends on the source from which (s)he collects the information and designs a framework in order to evaluate the information value from different types of sources. The main characteristics of his framework are the strength of the tie between the user and the source ("...the closeness of the relationship between information seeker and source; basic elements are source reciprocity and emotional closeness"), the homophily ("...it explains group composition in terms of similarity of members characteristics; basic elements of homophily are shared group interests and shared mindset") and source credibility ("a source should be considered as more credible when it (1) processes greater expertise and (2) is less prone to bias; its basic element is source trustworthiness"). Brown proves that these three characteristics are connected in the following way: source credibility is positively affected by source tie strength, source homophily and source usage. Based on this framework, we try to recognize the information value that the user gets from the different types of social media. In table 7 (in the Appendix), we present the synthesis from the literature review referring to the information value of different types of social media. The results of this synthesis show that the value of information a user gets from social networking sites is low or neutral, and, on the other hand, the value of information that a user gets form blogs and reviews is high. Following Brown's concept, source credibility is the factor with the highest impact on the assessment of information value. Thus, in our model we declare that source credibility moderates the impact of information acquisition both on the online purchase of a medical product/service and on the choice of a doctor. The hypothesis H2 is thus formulated as following:

H21a: *The information acquisition in social networking sites positively affects the online purchase of a medical product/service*
H21b: *The information acquisition in blogs positively affects the online purchase of a medical product/service*
H21c: *The information acquisition in product/service review sites positively affects the online purchase of a medical product/service*
H22a: *The information acquisition in social networking sites positively affects the patient to find a doctor*
H22b: *The information acquisition in blogs positively affects the patient to find a doctor*
H22c: *The information acquisition in product/ service review sites positively affects the patient to find a doctor*

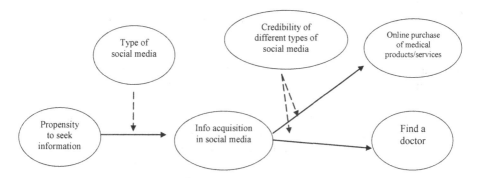

Fig. 1. Conceptual Model

3   Research Methodology

In order to test the above hypotheses, a survey approach was followed, targeted to Internet users. The survey was conducted in Greece and the data were collected from July to September 2011, using an online questionnaire. In the beginning of the questionnaire respondents should answer some general questions about the use of Internet and social media. Furthermore, we gave them a scenario in which they should take a decision in order to find a doctor or to buy online a medical product or service. In this scenario, based on the definitions of different types of social media, we defined blogs as pages which belong to doctors and reviews as pages where people who had an experience from the same health problem, or have used the product/service before, quote their opinion. A banner linking to the online questionnaire was placed in popular web sites and in social media. In addition, direct e-mails were sent to about 400 Internet users, inviting them to participate to the survey. In total, 1.047 valid questionnaires were collected.

The basic constructs of our questionnaire were: *propensity to seek information, information acquisition* and in order to measure the *actual behaviour* we asked the frequency that they find a doctor through the Internet and their agreement/disagreement of buying online medical products/services. Finally, in order to measure *the information value of different types of social media*, we chose to use as a construct the *source credibility/trustworthiness* (Brown, 2007) (see Appendix).

In relation to the construct '*propensity to seek information*', previous scholars who have studied the same construct have used actual data, based on measures such as the time and money that a user consumes in order to find information and the amount of data that (s)he collects in order to make a decision. Thus, based on Churchill's methodology we made the scale development of the construct *propensity to seek information*. Starting with the literature review, we collected all the measures that until now have been used in order to study the construct. In addition, we conducted 5 focus groups using a semi-structured questionnaire. In order to choose the participants of the focus groups we used a questionnaire based on Matthing and Parasuaramant's (2006) typology of users. We collected 70 responses from which we chose 59 people. During the procedure of focus groups we gave two different scenarios: the former was about a decision regarding their vacation, and the latter about a decision regarding their job. Having collected data from both, literature review and focus groups, we made a list with all the possible items that could be part of the construct. In order to measure the reliability and validity of the construct we conducted a survey, using an offline questionnaire. We collected 1.090 responses, and we analysed the data with the use of SPSS. The loadings of factor analysis, as well as the Cronbach's Alpha of the items (0,843) helped us ensure the validity of the construct. The last step of the procedure was the verification of the construct, using it in the real environment of a survey (study of the influence of the construct on other variables). For this purpose, we conducted a survey targeted to Internet users, using an online questionnaire. The questionnaire was answered by 1.171 internet users who have made online purchases, at least once until now. Our construct was placed in Kulwivat's model (2004). The items of the construct are presented in the Appendix.

4   Results

4.1   Descriptive Results

As we may notice in the diagrams, 63% of Internet users, use blogs (20% very often), 63% use Review pages (30% very often) and only 50% of Internet users use social networking sites (23% very often) (for general issues). On the other side, in the question "Do you search for information in social media when you have a health issue?", 56% of Internet users declare that they use blogs, 39% use reviews pages and 10% use social networking sites. Furthermore, 71% of Internet users declare that they use Internet in order find information about a health issue, 84% use Internet in order to find a doctor or a hospital and 57% use Internet in order to purchase online a medical product/service.

Table 1. General use of Social Media   **Table 2.** Use of Social Media for medical issues

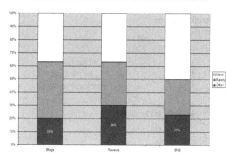   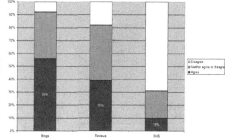

Table 3. Age   **Table 4.** I use Internet in order to....

Age	
18-25	14%
26-40	48%
41-55	31%
>56	7%

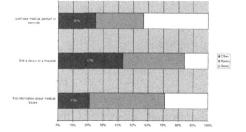

4.2   Model Results

The analysis of data was held using the statistical software SPSS. We examined the hypotheses using regression analysis. As we may notice, all the coefficients are significant (sig.<0,05) (apart from the coefficient of hypothesis H1a, in which the significance level is 0,066, H21a, in which the significance level is 0,08 and H22a in which the significant level is 0,09).

Table 5. Statistical analysis of the hypothesises

Hypothesises	B	R^2	Sig.
H1	0,234	0,043	**0,000**
H1a	0,78	0,005	0,066
H1b	0,159	0,031	**0,000**
H1c	0,187	0,037	**0,000**
H2	0,331	0,082	**0,001**
H21a	0,338	0,075	0,08
H21b	0,158	0,011	**0,006**
H21c	0,262	0,035	**0,000**
H22a	0,354	0,083	0,09
H22b	0,142	0,009	**0,014**
H22c	0,189	0,018	**0,000**

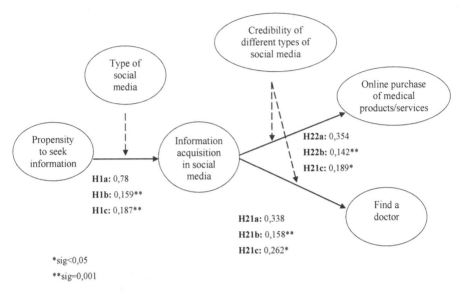

Fig. 2. Research Model

The important element of the analysis is that the hypotheses that were not confirmed are those referring to the social networking sites. In the literature review analysis, we showed that the information value that the user takes from social networking sites is either neutral or low. Our survey was focused on health-issues; a sector with special characteristics. It has further been characterised as a sector with high perceived risk (Cotten et al, 2004). In this case, patients want to receive information from sources with high credibility. Blogs, which are defined as pages in which we may find information by experts and reviews, which are defined as pages in which we may find information by people who have the same problem, are characterised as sources with higher credibility than social networking pages.

5   Discussion- Implications

The basic contribution of our research is to study the way that the different types of social media may affect a patient's final decision. In order to achieve this goal the first step was to create a typology of social media, along the same lines as the one proposed by Senecal (2004), who designed a typology for online information sources, based on two axes: the person who provides the information and the level of personalisation of the information. Then, the impact of information acquisition in each different type of social media on a patient's final decision has been examined. A patient's final decision referred to either the purchase of a medical product/ service online or the choice of a doctor.

The analysis of results has shown that information acquisition in blogs and reviews positively affects the final decision; on the other hand, information acquisition in social networking sites has no significant effect on the final decision. This fact can be explained by Brown's (2007) framework; he declares that the information value that the patient receives depends on the source which (s)he will get the information from. In order to explain if the information value is high or not, in his framework the author uses three axes: tie strength, homophily and source credibility (paying specific attention on source credibility). Thus, a very important part of our study has been to find the information value of the three different types of social media.

The present study has both academic and managerial implications. In terms of academic implications, the typology of social media may help scholars compare their results in different types of social media. Furthermore, it has been empirically shown that the information value may differ in the different types of social media. On the practical side, the percent of Internet users who seek information online about health issues is increasing (71%). Our research has shown that almost 60% of Onternet users seek information in blogs; almost 40% of Internet users seek information in reviews and only 10% in social networking sites. It means that both doctors and companies alike which are active in the healthcare sector (private hospital, pharmaceuticals companies etc.) should choose blogs and review pages in order to communicate with their customers.

6   Further Research- Limitations

Taking into consideration this study we may find new concepts for further research:

- First of all, our research was focused on the healthcare sector, in relation to two specific patient decisions: finding a doctor and online purchase of medical products/services. Our model could further consider the importance of the reason why the patient wants to make the medical decision; for example, if that refers to a serious health problem or not. Moreover, it would be very helpful to study the difference that may appear in the results taking into consideration the frequency with which patients visit the different types of social media.

- Furthermore, the same model could be applied in a different sector, where the decision has lower perceived risk for the user

- Finally, the limitation of our research is that in order to measure the information value we used only one of the three axes of Brown's model, the source credibility. Future research could measure the information value using all the three axes of Brown's model and study the impact of tie strength and source homophily on source credibility.

Appendix

Table 6. Items and constructs of the questionnaire

Items	Construct	Scale
When I have a medical problem....	Seek information in social media	5 point likert scale 1= Completely disagree....5=Completely agree
...I seek information in social media		
...I visit links that my "friends" in facebook have posted		
...I seek information in social networking sites (e.g facebook)		
...I seek information in blogs that belong to specialized doctors		
...I seek information in web pages where people who had the same problem with me write their opinion		
I'm prepared to spend as much time as required to find information on a subject	Propensity to seek information	5 point likert scale 1=never....5=always
I'm prepared to spend as much money as required to find information on a subject		
I believe that the more the information at hand the easier it is for someone to make a decision on a subject		
I make an appointment with a doctor that I found through the Internet	Online Purchase	5 point likert scale 1=never....5=always
I purchase medical products/ services online		5 point likert scale 1= Completely disagree....5=Completely agree
Generally, I trust what I read in social networking sites (e.g facebook)	(information value) Source credibility	5 point likert scale 1= Completely disagree....5=Completely agree
Generally, I trust what I read in blogs		
Generally, I trust what I read in reviews		

Table 7. Information of value of different social media sources

		SNS	Blogs	Reviews
Tie strength	SM reciprocity	• "…latent ties between the connections (actors)" (Haythrnthwaite, 2005)	• "Personal network ties between specific media outlets and bloggers/readers" (Thomas et al, 2004)	• "…particularly influential, with strong ties between members, because they are written from a consumer's perspective, and, thus, provide an opportunity of indirect experience" (Bickart et al, 2001)
	Emotional closeness			
Homophily	Shared group interests	• "…diversity of minds and interests" (Boyd, 2008)	• "bloggers…(and)…users, are people with shared interests" (McAfee, 2006)	• "…provide personal information about a specific topic" (Park et al, 2007)
	Shared mindsets	• "…(possibility of) existence of groups with shared interests " (ibid)	• "…main goal is the facilitation of collaboration" (Mack, 2007) • "Blogs are created around specific topics to facilitate exchange of opinions" (McAfee, 2006)	
Source credibility	SM trustworthiness	• "…lack trust and usage goals may affect what people willing to share…(and)…to belie)" (Drwyer et al, 2007	• "Bloggers of late have served as independent experts" (Kurtz, 2002) • "Users find blogs more credible because they are independent rather than controllers by corporate interests" (Thomas et al, 2004)	• "…the recommendation source "other consumers"/reviews is perceived as more trustworthy than "human experts" and Recommender systems" (Senecal et al, 2004)
	Actor's expertise	"basic characteristic: community, not experts" (ibid)		
Information Value		Low-neutral	high	high

Table 8. Items of the construct "propensity to seek information"

	Component 1	Component 2
When I want to make an urgent decision, I always look for information	0,891	
When I have enough time I look for information about general topics	0,781	
When I have to take an important decision, I always look for information	0,763	
I could spend as time is needed in order to find information about an important topic	0,691	
I could spend as time is needed in order to find information about a general topic	0,700	
I could spend as money is needed in order to find information about an important topic	0,729	
I could spend as money is needed in order to find information about a general topic	0,731	
I think that the more information a person has, the better decision (s)he can take	0,787	
A person should collect information of all aspects of a topic before (s)he takes a decision	0,620	
I feel anxious when I have to make a decision		0,234
I feel anxious when I have to make an important decision		0,345

References

Bernhardt, J.M., et al.: Perceived barriers to Internet-based health communication on human genetics. Journal of Health Communication 7(4), 325–340 (2002)

Brown, J., Broderick, A.J., Lee, N.: Word of mouth communication within online communities: Conceptualizing the online social network. Journal of Interactive Marketing 21(3), 2–20 (2007)

Brown, J.J., Reingen, P.H.: Social ties and word-of-mouth referral behavior. Journal of Consumer Research, 350–362 (1987)

Bruseberg, A., McDonagh-Philp, D.: Focus groups to support the industrial/product designer: a review based on current literature and designers' feedback. Applied Ergonomics 33(1), 27–38 (2002)

Cline, R.J.W., Haynes, K.M.: Consumer health information seeking on the Internet: the state of the art. Health Education Research 16(6), 671 (2001)

Cotten, S.R., Gupta, S.S.: Characteristics of online and offline health information seekers and factors that discriminate between them. Social Science & Medicine 59(9), 1795–1806 (2004)

Dwyer, C., Hiltz, S.R., Passerini, K.: Trust and privacy concern within social networking sites: A comparison of Facebook and MySpace. Americas The 123 (2007)

Ellison, N.B., et al.: Social network sites: Definition, history, and scholarship. Journal of Computer-Mediated Communication 13(1), 210–230 (2007)

Eysenbach, G., et al.: Empirical studies assessing the quality of health information for consumers on the World Wide Web. JAMA: The Journal of the American Medical Association 287(20), 2691 (2002)

Gretzel, U., Yoo, K.H.: Use and impact of online travel reviews. In: Information and Communication Technologies in Tourism 2008, pp. 35–46 (2008)

Herring, S.C., et al.: Bridging the gap: A genre analysis of weblogs. In: Proceedings of the 37th Annual Hawaii International Conference on System Sciences, 11 p. (2004)

Impicciatore, P., et al.: Reliability of health information for the public on the World Wide Web: systematic survey of advice on managing fever in children at home. BMJ 314(7098), 1875 (1997)

Johnson, T.J., Kaye, B.K.: Wag the blog: How reliance on traditional media and the Internet influence credibility perceptions of weblogs among blog users. Journalism and Mass Communication Quarterly 81, 622–642 (2004)

Lai, L.S., Turban, E.: Groups formation and operations in the Web 2.0 environment and social networks. Group Decision and Negotiation 17(5), 387–402 (2008)

Locander, W.B., Hermann, P.W.: The effect of self-confidence and anxiety on information seeking in consumer risk reduction. Journal of Marketing Research, 268–274 (1979)

Mack, R.W., Blose, J.E., Pan, B.: Believe it or not: Credibility of blogs in tourism. Journal of Vacation Marketing 14(2), 133–144 (2008)

Matthing, J., et al.: Developing successful technology-based services: the issue of identifying and involving innovative users. Journal of Services Marketing 20(5), 288–297 (2006)

McLeod, S.D.: The quality of medical information on the Internet: A new public health concern. Archives of Ophthalmology 116(12), 1663 (1998)

Mooradian, T.A., Swan, K.S.: Personality-and-culture: The case of national extraversion and word-of-mouth. Journal of Business Research 59(6), 778–785 (2006)

Murray, K.B.: A test of services marketing theory: consumer information acquisition activities. The Journal of Marketing, 10–25 (1991)

Punj, G.N., Staelin, R.: A model of consumer information search behavior for new automobiles. Journal of Consumer Research, 366–380 (1983)

Schaninger, C.M., Sciglimpaglia, D.: The influence of cognitive personality traits and demographics on consumer information acquisition. Journal of Consumer Research, 208–216 (1981)

Senecal, S., Nantel, J.: The influence of online product recommendations on consumers' online choices. Journal of Retailing 80(2), 159–169 (2004)

Trammell, K.D., Keshelashvili, A.: Examining the new influencers: A self-presentation study of A-list blogs. Journalism and Mass Communication Quarterly 82(4), 968 (2005)

Tufekci, Z.: Can you see me now? Audience and disclosure regulation in online social network sites. Bulletin of Science, Technology & Society 28(1), 20–36 (2008)

Users' Commitment in Information System Implementation:
The Role of Technological Frames

Irene Cardoso[1] and Mário Caldeira[2]

[1] ISEG, Technical University of Lisbon
Rua José Carlos Ary dos Santos, B, 8200-049 Albufeira, Portugal
`irene_cardoso@yahoo.com`
[2] ISEG, Technical University of Lisbon
Rua do Quelhas, n.º 6, 1700-781 Lisboa
`caldeira@iseg.utl.pt`

Abstract. Many attempts at implementing Healthcare Information Technology (HIT) have failed. Studies have pointed to the importance of commitment from all levels during implementation as well as organizational commitment as being central to achieving the desired IT benefits. A case study analysis of two public Portuguese hospitals is undertaken, focusing on stakeholder commitment to the IS/IT implementation. An understanding is sought of the commitment, perceptions, assumptions and knowledge that health professionals hold regarding IT adoption. A qualitative and interpretative approach is used employing semi-structured interviews and document analysis. Technological Frames of Reference (TFR) and The Three Component Model of Organizational Commitment provided a theoretical grounding for analyzing the data collected. Three TFR relevant to the development of commitment and benefit achievement were identified: Control, Liability and Protection.

Keywords: HIT (Healthcare Information Technology), Commitment, Technological Frames of Reference (TFR).

1 Introduction

The healthcare industry is concerned with efficiency and cost saving. Technology adoption has been perceived as a way to improve organizational performance and quality of patient care [1]. High costs, low quality, medical errors, inefficiency, and poor management are often mentioned as major problems, within most healthcare systems [2].

Despite high expectations for the value added by IT in healthcare, in many cases attempts at Healthcare Information Technology (HIT) implementation have failed [3], [4]. A number of studies have advocated the need to attain greater commitment from all levels throughout implementation, while other studies have demonstrated that organizational commitment could be an important issue for realizing IT benefits in organizations [5],[6].

H. Rahman et al. (Eds.): MCIS 2012, LNBIP 129, pp. 254–266, 2012.

Given the critical role that stakeholder commitment has for IT implementation, the research was as such based on multiple case studies in two public Portuguese hospitals. The research questions were developed while acknowledging existing known problems with HIT implementation as well as the extensive literature on organizational commitment and technological frames:

— What is the role of user technological frames in the development of commitment towards an HIT project?
— How does the significance attributed to an HIT by health professionals influence their commitment to a project and the achievement of expected benefits?

A qualitative, interpretative, case-based research strategy was implemented based on semi-structured interviews and document analysis. The technological frames theory of Orlikowski and Gash [7], [8] was used as a theoretical lens to analyze the data, along with commitment theories of Meyer and Allen [9], [10] and their subsequent developments.

2   Theoretical Background

2.1   Organizational Commitment

Empirical research has demonstrated that relationships between the various elements of organizational commitment and the results/work behaviors are potentially relevant to business performance [11], [5].

According to Jensen and Aanestad, [12] 'the introduction of new technology requires conscious work in securing acceptance, as well as commitment among users' [12, p.675]. In addition, Meyer and Herscovitch argue that employees with strong affective commitment are willing to do anything to ensure the success of an initiative for change [11].

Meyer and Allen [9], [10] describe organizational commitment as a psychological state, that characterizes the relationship between the employee and the company. According to these authors, the organizational commitment includes, simultaneously, in variable degrees, the three components or dimensions of organizational commitment which reflect the intensity of the psychological connection that binds the employee with the company: 1) the affective commitment, 2) the continuance commitment and 3) the normative commitment [9], [10].

The affective commitment refers to the employee's emotional attachment, identification and involvement with the organization. The continuance commitment implies the recognition by the employee of the costs associated with leaving the organization. The normative commitment refers to the employee's sense of moral obligation to continue in the organization.

The three component model of commitment of Meyer and Allen [9], [10] has been broadly used [13] and has received extensive empirical evaluations to date [14], [15].

According to Meyer and Allen [10], the antecedents of organizational commitment can be grouped into two categories: the 'close' and 'distant' causes. The first are those that seem to have a direct influence on any component of organizational commitment.

The second exercise their influence on commitment through their impact on close causes.

The close antecedents comprise: a) The characteristics of work and work experiences (e.g. the scope of work, the degree of autonomy, skills and techniques applied and organizational support); b) The level of conflict and role ambiguity experienced by employees; and c) The type of psychological contract (agreement between the employee and the company). The distant causes of organizational commitment include the organizational characteristics, the employee's personal characteristics, environmental conditions and the strategies and practices of human resources [10].

This research bases its definition of commitment on that stated by Meyer and Herscovitch [11]. These authors define commitment as 'a force that binds an individual to a course of action of relevance to one or more targets' (p.301). These targets can be an entity (e.g., an organization), an abstract concept or the intended outcome of a course of action (e.g. attainment of specific goals) [11]. In this research we considered the implementation project of a HIT in the two organizations as an intended outcome of a course of action.

When analyzing the concepts of resistance to change and commitment, Coetsee [16] considers commitment as acceptance of change, and resistance as the opposite, or in other words, rejection of change. These concepts are related to each other in the sense that they represent polarity – two poles of a continuum [16]. According to Coetsee, [16] commitment represents the final phase of acceptance of change.

In line with the definitions of commitment given by Meyer and Herscovitch [11] and Coetsee [16] and considering the scope of this work, the concept of commitment to an IS project implementation is seen as an acceptance of that project, and an enhanced affinity, identification and engagement with the achievement of the expected benefits from it.

2.2   Benefits

A business benefit can be defined as an advantage for a particular stakeholder or group of stakeholders seek to obtain value from the investment [17]. The real benefits are not inherent to IT, but result from the changes in the organizational processes enabled by it [4], [18].

From the literature review, perceived benefits of an information system refer to: (a) the anticipated advantages that the application can provide to the organization [19], (b) the positive impact of IT implementation [20] and, (c) the characteristic that most influences adoption [21].

Most of the benefits induced by the use information technology in health care fall under one of the following categories: quality of care [3]; effect on efficiency [3]; and cost reductions [22].

2.3   The Theory of Technological Frames

Orlikowski and Gash [7], [8] drawing on research in organizational change, developed a theoretical approach centered on Technological Frames of Reference

(TFR). Their framework is based on the principle that 'people act on the basis of their interpretations of the world' [7, p.1].

When people interact with technology, they make sense of it and, in this process of making sense, they develop particular 'assumptions, expectations, and knowledge of the technology' that 'shape subsequent actions towards it' [8, p.175, 178].

Orlikowski and Gash found a set of themes (presented in the Table 1), which were structured in core domains of the participants' technological frames [8].

Table 1. Core domains of the participants' technological frames

Core Domains of TFR	Definition
Nature of Technology	Reflects the technology used. Also includes the comprehension of its capabilities and functionality.
Technology Strategy	Reflects people's views of why it was introduced: an understanding of the motivation or vision behind the adoption decision
Technology in Use	How the technology is used to change working practices on a day-to-day basis: actual changes to conditions and the consequences of its use.

Orlikowski and Gash [7], [8] identified three distinct social groups (managers, technologists and users) which are involved in technological use or change within organizations. These groups have distinct technological frames representing that group's particular experience, interaction, and understanding of the information technology. The TFR framework has been cited in a variety of published work (e.g., [23], [24], [25]).

3   Methodology

Following an interpretivist view of the world, a qualitative and interpretive case-study strategy was adopted, using multiple case studies. This research strategy is appropriate when the investigator is faced with a reality that is complex, subjective and socially constructed [28].Case study research is a strategy that allows a grasp of the different aspects of the complex social reality that surrounds the organizations [26], [27].

3.1   Research Design

Figure 1 provides an overview of how the research was conducted. In the first part of the research a comprehensive literature review was conducted to help define the bounds of the research topic and the research questions, as well as to develop the interview guidelines. In a second phase, hospitals were selected with the third phase comprising the fieldwork. The fourth phase involved the processing and analysis of data from the cases and the production of the written report. Finally, the fifth phase relates to cross-case analysis of findings and the subsequent generation of theory and production of rich insights.

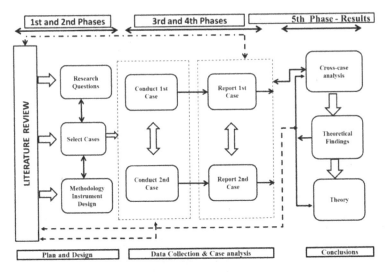

Fig. 1. Research Design

3.2   Data Collection

The field work was carried out in both organizations between 2007 and 2011. Data collection was based mainly on semi-structured interviews, as suggested by Walsham [28] and Yin [27]. To obtain an appropriate degree of internal validity, rigor, richness and depth, other sources of evidence were used. Document analysis related to the implementation process and field notes resulting from direct observation, meetings[1] and informal talks were also subject to analysis and interpretation.

The range of interviewees (64 for organization A and 65 for organization B) included: managers, implementers – both of the supplier firm and from the organization – and, users from each sector where the system was implemented (emergency rooms, out-patient department, surgery and in-patient services). Table 2 shows the number of interviews within each group.

A qualitative approach was used to analyze the data [29], [30], where a form of content analysis was employed. This technique seeks to extract meaning and insight from the words used and patterns found in the texts [30]. In this way, an open approach was taken towards analysis of all transcript data, with the aim of finding the most interesting themes relevant to the research questions. Meaning was attributed to the data, and efforts were made to ensure that the coding process preserved existing relationships in the data [29]. The data was organized into themes and categories suggested by the data rather than being imposed a priori.

The coding process was carried out using the NVivo application, specific software for qualitative research, allowing the collection, organization and analysis of non-numeric data.

---

[1] Meetings between organizational members and IS Provider to discuss the implementation process.

Table 2. Interviews Realized

Hospital A	N°	Hospital B	N°
Implementation team		**Implementation team**	
Project managers	1	Project managers	2
Monitoring Team (MT)	2	Monitoring Team (MT)	2
Managers		**Managers**	
Board Members	3	Board Members	3
IS Manager	2	IS Manager	1
Service Directors	3	Service Directors	6
			1
Nurse Managers	3	Nurse Managers	2
Users		**Users**	
	2		1
Nurses	7	Nurses	9
Assistants	8	Assistants	8
	1		1
Physicians	5	Physicians	2
Total	**64**	**Total**	**65**

4   The Case Studies

The software application installed in the hospitals studied, here designated as the Paper Free Software Solution (PFSS), is a HIT that incorporates characteristics of both an EMR (Electronic Medical Record) and Decision Support Systems (DSS). As a DSS this software supports decision making in medical, administrative and management levels. The PFSS facilitates the registration, consultation and analysis of information produced in the clinical care process of patients in all hospital clinical services.

4.1   Case 1

Hospital A is a large hospital with capacity for 332 beds. Its clinical activity operates through functional services and units, grouped in several areas (departments): Surgical, Medical, Maternal/Paediatric, Physical therapy, Mental health, Emergency and Complementary Methods of Diagnosis and Therapy (CMDT).

On the 31st of December 2010, the hospital employed 1458 people. During 2010, 191262 outpatients were observed, 13637 surgical operations took place, 76014 emergencies episodes occurred, and more than 13000 patients were admitted.

The implementation of the PFSS suite was part of the management strategy for the hospital. The main goal included the expectation 'that processes become automated, contributing to the improvement of medical records and developing the connexion of all structures in order to optimize everything', in the words of the Clinical Director.

The PFSS was implemented gradually and in several stages, starting at the end of February 2007 with the emergency service and gradually extending to other areas (out-patient, in-patient and surgery room departments). As of July 2011 (date of the last visit to Hospital A) the process was not fully completed.

The nursing and assistant's groups exhibited a greater acceptance of the IS. Out of the three professional groups, doctors showed most difficulty in complying with and using the system.

4.2   Case 2

Hospital B is a medium-sized hospital with a capacity of 182 beds. In June 2011, Hospital B employed a total of 589 workers. Clinical activities are grouped into various departments: Surgery, Medicine, Pediatrics Physiotherapy and Convalescence, Emergency and CMDT. During 2010, the activities performed included: 4281 medical consultations, 1533 surgeries, 62050 emergency processes and 6728 patient admissions.

The objectives for the PFSS were: the attainment of reliable clinical information through a unique electronic record that would enhance patient care; the attainment of management and output indicators; an understanding in real-time of the processes being executed on the ground; and, the automation of all the records related to patient care provision, allowing greater process flexibility.

The implementation process of the PFSS was executed in phases and the adoption of the software for the whole hospital was only carried out after the Emergency Service (ER) had completed three or four years of successful implementation. After installing the PFSS in the ER in May 2003, the IS was extended to the Operating Rooms in December 2006, and subsequently to the In-patient area, running through until 2010.

The level of use proved to be very variable between the medical specialties and type of clinical activity (Out-patient, In-patient, Operating Room and ER), as well as between professional groups. Whereas the nurses and the operational assistants were almost 100% committed to IS in all areas, the doctors as a group presented considerably different levels of compliance, including active resistance (e.g. refusal to use the system).

5   Research Findings

Similar patterns were found in the two case studies; here discussion is limited to the set of findings resulting from cross-case analysis. An analysis of the data allowed the identification of common patterns in the two cases. The information collected was attributable to several themes: Organizational Context, Technological Frames, Commitment, and Usage, which in turn encompass categories and sub-categories. The themes that are most directly relevant to this analysis are Technological Frames, Commitment and Usage.

5.1   Technological Frames

The qualitative approach facilitated the capture and analysis of the different assumptions and interpretations (TFR) that the professionals of the two hospitals hold towards the PFSS and their actions relating to it. A set of themes was found in the two research sites, subsequently grouped in order to form the following *core domains* as presented in Table 3.

These domains are interdependent. In addition, relations between them and the other themes (commitment, usage, benefits and organizational context) were discovered in the data.

This paper presents only the analysis of one TFR category found in the data, that of system significance. Therefore we are primarily concerned with the various meanings that the users attribute to IS/IT, and how they interpret the real ends behind the adoption of IS. The relationships between these interpretations and commitment, use and perceived benefits were also analyzed.

Table 3. The main core domains of participants' technological frames

Core Domains of TFR	Definition
Implementation	Refers to all knowledge, expectations, experiences, interpretations, and understanding that professionals have regarding the implementation of the IS project (e.g. objectives, process and evaluation).
Technology-in- use	Refers to the understanding that people have of how technology is used in their day- to-day activities. It also includes the perception of its attributes, capabilities (IS perceptions) and its meaning (system significance).
System Impact	Refers to the positive and negative perceptions relating to the consequences of the system. It includes the perceived benefits and 'disbenefits' accruing from system adoption (e.g., weakened patient relationship, increase in workload)

System Significance. The System Significance category is included in the Technology-in–use domain. From a user's perspective, the information system has a subjective, inexplicit role with the real reasons for implementing the software system being hidden. The PFSS is assigned a meaning, a connotation that goes beyond what is stated in the formal objectives.

As regards the significance given to the system (implicit meanings) in the two hospitals, three types of technology interpretation (TFR) have been identified which impact user's commitment as well as the manner in which they use the software:

(i) *Control*: the intention to control the activities of professionals;
(ii) *Liability*: an instrument that makes activities visible and susceptible to being used against them in case of complaints or medical error; and
(iii) *Protection*: a way to register and protect actions.

Through the *Control* frame, the fear of being controlled, or that the use of the software can bring future adverse consequences, prevents the use of the system whenever possible or, at least, promotes a minimal introduction of information; this runs contrary to the *Protection* frame. Therefore, the perception of *Control* or *Liability* associated with the system reduces the likelihood of achieving the benefits.

These two frames are more notable for the medical group, especially those professionals that take a position against the system or of little commitment to it.

The *Protection* frame reflects an opposite view to the other two frames, with it normally being valued by the proponents of IS. This frame is associated with perceptions of increased legibility, security and accountability of information. According to the professional users that share this frame, the IS helps legitimize and distinguish those workers that work best. It is clear that the IS will only show such things when it is correctly used. The *Protection* frame is valued by only a limited number of doctors, being more characteristic of the professional groups of nurses and operational assistants.

Table 4 shows the three meanings (TFR) that health professionals attributed to the significance of the IS, as well as some of the participant's comments.

Table 4. Participants' technological frames relating to System Significance

System Significance	Evidence
Control	'This is to control us, it'll be simply used to see how many x-rays, how many tests we ask for, and to tell us that we cannot ask for so many – you will be controlled on the time you spend with patients'(Physician 1, Case1). 'I think the PFSS was created as a management system, because of all the information pertaining to when the patient was admitted, the time you took, the tests you asked for – so, all of this is controlled'(Physician 4, Case2)
Liability	'The application has a curious thing, which is the acceptance of responsibility. If we take on responsibility for the patient (...) it makes us more responsible and more careful' (Nurse 4, Case 1). 'That IT system (…) it could violate some constitutional rights, in particular those that assure liberty rights' (Physician 3, Case2)
Protection	'It is a good system (…) there is nobody that can go and cross out the things that a person writes (...). And it is our defense later.' (Nurse 6, Case2) 'For starters, it came to our defense. Defense in the sense that it gives transparency to the situation. (...) It is a safeguard against our work' (Assistant 2, Case 1). 'The nurses were always regarded as [PFSS] allies, (...) because their work has become more visible and they became more protected' (Technologist, Case1).

While the perception that professionals have that the IS system provides a protective mechanism for their job (*Protection*) seems to be a great enabler of commitment and a strong incentive to the appropriate use of the system, therefore contributing to the rapid achievement of benefits, the other two frames (*Control* and *Liability*) act to reduce commitment.

Perceived Benefits. This TFR category is included in the System Impact domain and represents the positive perceptions of the consequences of the system. The benefits most valued by users of the three professional groups that seem to impact their commitment to the project implementation were: increased safety, reliability and accessibility to information. Other benefits were also referred to by many users, as well as by administrators, including: decision support, patient benefits, activity support, and attendance improvement.

5.2   Project Commitment

This category represents the level of commitment that professionals of both Hospitals have towards the PFSS system, and the changes that are associated with it. It includes all comments that were in favor of the IS and its usefulness, somehow revealing its acceptance and a willingness to use it, as the following excerpts show:

'I think that (...) as regards the IS, people have to evolve with the passage of time. We are at a point when, we should update ourselves and to move on with the times' (Assistant 3, Case2)

'I was always a supporter and user of the information system' (Physician 2, Case2)

'It does not make sense that we are against information systems. I am ready for this change' (Nurse 21, Case1)

The level of commitment to the project is variable between the medical services, between medical specialties and between different professional groups. The nursing and assistants groups exhibited a greater acceptance of the IS and a recognition of its importance to the profession, while doctors showed most difficulty in complying with and using the system.

Antecedents of Commitment. In relation to the antecedents of commitment that revealed an influence on System Significance and Use, Autonomy and Authority and Social Representation can be highlighted, both included in participants 'work experiences.

The antecedent Autonomy and Authority was found to influence the commitment to the project, corroborating Wallace [31], particularly because it represents one the most structural dimensions of professional work and is related to the right that the professionals have to control their own work tasks and the work of their colleagues. Since the use of IS highlights the work done by professionals, makes them liable for their clinical decisions, and exposes their skills, the professionals relate to the IS as a control mechanism, reducing commitment, promoting a boycott, or partial use of system and thus, decreasing the benefits.

Social Representation was identified in some professional groups as an important antecedent of commitment to a project. Here, it reflects the way that some professionals (e.g. nurses) have traditionally been seen, in comparison to other groups of dominant professionals (e.g. doctors). It seems to exercise a significant degree of influence over the commitment of the former group to the implementation project, because the visibility supplied by the system promotes the profession, making its role in hospital organization and society clearer.

5.3   Usage and Commitment

In this research, the level of IS/IT usage emerged as a relevant category and a critical point in the context of HIT implementation in the two cases. Analyzed as a direct or indirect consequence of commitment to a project, it can be seen as having a relevant role in benefit achievement. The two professional groups with the highest weighting in terms of computer application usage (doctors and nurses), stressed the importance of a correct usage of HIT in achieving the desired benefits. The correct use is associated with the full and adequate usage of IS.

The perception of benefits related to the use of the system is itself a great stimulus to commitment to the project that in turn acts to increase the correct usage of system. Therefore the perceived benefits and a Correct Use act reinforcing each other, by the influence of commitment, constituting a virtuous cycle of interaction (Project Commitment – System Use – Perceived Benefits), represented in Figure 2.

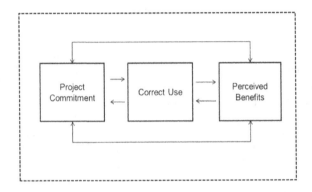

Fig. 2. Virtuous Cycle of Commitment and Perceived Benefits

6   Conclusions

Throughout participants' perspectives it was effectively found that the commitment that stakeholders have towards to the project implementation and IS influences benefits achievement (here described as Perceived Benefits), particularly through the way the users utilize the IS.

Evidence has been provided that the System Significance attributed to HIT by users (Control, Liability and Protection) exert impact on Commitment and Usage as well as on Perceived Benefits, either directly or indirectly by influencing or being influenced by some antecedents of commitment, as with Autonomy and Authority (e.g. Control and Liability) and Social Representation (e.g. Protection).

Considering that this implementation project constitutes a learning process, some ideas resulting from the statements of users and implementers as well as from research findings can be presented:

- An understanding of users' technological frames should be a key factor in managing the adoption of IS and will be decisive in understanding how they interact with the antecedents of commitment to enable changes and improve the use of IS to produce benefits.

- The perception that professionals have that the IS provides a protective mechanism for their job seems to be a great enabler of commitment and a strong incentive to an appropriate use of the system, therefore contributing to the rapid achievement of benefits. Thus, any measure to be taken by management to foster the development of that frame (e.g. protection) or any other frame with positive influence on commitment, either through communication strategies or through a comprehensive disclosure from the outset of the objectives and benefits of the system will help increase commitment to the project and its use.

Previous personal experiences of the author should be acknowledged as a limitation of this work, whereby it is essential to clarify that the phenomenological approach means that this study is not free of bias. Statistical generalization is not an objective of interpretative research. Thus, these research findings may be valuable to other settings and organizations as interpretations of phenomena but are not wholly predictive for future situations.

A research project to validate the comparability of the results found in this work between private and public organizations could provide significant further insights in the area.

References

1. Hillestad, R., Bigelow, J., Bower, A., Girosi, F., Meili, R., Scoville, R., Taylor, R.: Can Electronic Medical Record Systems Transform Healthcare? Potential Health Benefits, Savings, and Costs. Health Affairs 24(5), 1103–1117 (2005)
2. Leapfrog Group: The Leapfrog Group Hospital Quality and Safety Survey What's New in the 2006 Survey (2006), https://leapfrog.medstat.com/pdf/final.pdf
3. Lapoint, L., Rivard, S.: A Multilevel Model of Resistance to Information Technology Implementation. MIS Quarterly 29(3), 461–491 (2006)
4. Dhillon, G.: Gaining Benefits from IS/IT Implementation: Interpretations from Case Studies. International Journal of Information Management 25(6), 502–515 (2005)
5. Shum, P., Bove, L., Auh, S.: Employees' Affective Commitment to Change. The Key to Successful CRM Implementation. European Journal of Marketing 42(11/12), 1346–1371 (2008)
6. Swailes, S.: Commitment to Change: Profiles of Commitment and In-role Performance. Personnel Review 33(2), 187–204 (2004)
7. Orlikowski, W., Gash, D.C.: Changing Frames: Understanding Technological Changes in Organizations, Working Paper, 236. Massachusetts Institute of Technology, Cambridge (1991)
8. Orlikowski, W.J., Gash, D.C.: Technological Frames: Making Sense of Information Technology in Organizations. ACM Transactions on Information Systems 12(2), 174–207 (1994)
9. Meyer, J.P., Allen, N.J.: A Three-component Conceptualization of Organizational Commitment. Human Resource Management Review 1(1), 61–89 (1991)
10. Meyer, J.P., Allen, N.J.: Commitment in the Workplace: Theory, Research, and Application. Sage Publications, Thousand Oaks (1997)
11. Meyer, J.P., Herscovitch, L.: Commitment in the Workplace: Toward a General Model. Human Resource Management Review 11(3), 299–326 (2001)
12. Jensen, T.B., Aanestad, M.: Hospitality and Hostility in Hospitals: a Case Study of an EPR Adoption Among Surgeons. European Journal of Information Systems 16(6), 672–680 (2007)

13. Swiggard, S.B.: Generations and Employee Commitment: An Exploration of the Impact of Changes in Technology, Home and Family Structure, and Employer-employee Relationships. A Dissertation Presented in Partial Fulfillment of the Requirements for the Degree Doctor of Philosophy, Capella University (January 2011)
14. Bryant, S., Moshavi, D., Nguyen, T.: A Field Study on Organizational Commitment, Professional Commitment and Peer Mentoring. Database for Advances in Information Systems 38(2), 61–74 (2007)
15. Valéau, P., Mignonac, K., Vandenberghe, C., Gatignon, A.L.: A Study of the Relationships Between Volunteers' Commitments to Organizations and Beneficiaries and Turnover Intentions. Canadian Journal of Behavioural Science (April 16, 2012)
16. Coetsee, L.: From Resistance to Commitment. Public Administration Quarterly 23(2), 204–222 (1999)
17. Ward, J., Daniel, E.: Benefits Management: Delivering Value from IS and Investments. John Wiley &Sons Ltd., Chichester (2006)
18. Peppard, J., Ward, J., Daniel, E.: Managing the Realization of Business Benefits from IT investments. MIS Quarterly Executive 6(1), 1–10 (2007)
19. Chwelos, P., Benbasat, I., Dexter, A.: Research Report: Empirical Test of an EDI Adoption Model. Information System Research 12(3), 304–321 (2001)
20. Casedesus, M., Karapetrovic, S.: The erosion of ISO 9000 benefits: a temporal study. International Journal of Quality and Reliability Management 22(2), 120–136 (2005)
21. Mehrtens, J., Cragg, P., Mills, A.: A Model of Internet adoption by SME's. Information and Management 39(3), 165–176 (2001)
22. Caldeira, M., Quaresma, R., Quintela, H., Serrano, A.: Avaliação de Benefícios com a Implementação de um Sistema de Informação Paper-free no Hospital do Espírito Santo. CAPSI – 10ª Conferência da Associação Portuguesa de Sistemas de Informação (2010)
23. Mengesha, N.: The Role of Technological Frames of Key Groups in Open Source Software Implementation in a Developing Country Context. The Electronic Journal on Information Systems in Developing Countries 43(1), 1–19 (2010)
24. Walker, S., Creanor, L.: Towards an Ontology of Networked Learning. In: Hodgson, V., Jones, C., de Laat, M., McConnell, D., Ryberg, T., Sloep, P. (eds.) 8th International Conference on Networked Learning 2012, Maastricht, Netherlands, April 02-04 (2012)
25. Aguilar-Zambrano, J.J., Gardoni, M.: An Information System to Support Problems Definition Based on Technological Frames and Organizational Routines. International Journal of Manufacturing Technology and Management 22(3), 219–232 (2012)
26. Caldeira, M., Romão, M.: Estratégias de Investigação em Sistemas de Informação Organizacionais: A Utilização de Métodos Qualitativos. Estudos de Gestão – Portuguese Journal of Management Studies 7(1), 77–97 (2002)
27. Yin, R.K.: Case Study Research, Design and Methods, 3rd edn. Sage Publications, Inc., Thousand Oaks (2003)
28. Walsham, G.: Doing Interpretive Research. European Journal of Information Systems 15(3), 320–330 (2006)
29. Miles, M.B., Huberman, A.M.: Qualitative Data Analysis: An Expanded Sourcebook, 2nd edn. Sage Publications, Thousand Oaks (1994)
30. Denzin, N.K., Lincoln, Y.S.: The Discipline and Practice of Qualitative Research. In: Denzin, N., Lincoln, Y.S. (eds.) The Sage Handbook of Qualitative Research, 4th edn., pp. 1–32. Sage Publications, Inc., Thousand Oaks (2011)
31. Wallace, J.E.: Organizational and Professional commitment in Professional and Nonprofessional Organizations. Administrative Science Quarterly 40(2), 228–255 (1995)

Author Index